LUXURY AND AUSTERITY

HISTORICAL STUDIES

The Irish Committee of Historical Sciences inaugurated a series of biennial conferences of historians in July 1953. Since then the 'Irish Conference of Historians' has circulated among the Irish universities and university colleges and the papers read since 1955 have been published as *Historical Studies*. Since 1975 the conferences have been devoted to a single theme, the full list being as follows:

T. D. Williams (ed.) *Historical Studies I* (London: Bowes & Bowes 1958)

M. Roberts (ed.) *Historical Studies II* (London: Bowes & Bowes 1959)

J. Hogan (ed.) *Historical Studies III* (London: Bowes & Bowes 1961)

G. A. Hayes-McCoy (ed.) *Historical Studies IV* (London: Bowes & Bowes 1963)

J. L. McCracken (ed.) *Historical Studies V* (London: Bowes & Bowes 1965)

T. W. Moody (ed.) *Historical Studies VI* (London: Routledge & Kegan Paul 1968)

T. D. Williams (ed.) *Historical Studies VIII* (Dublin: Gill & Macmillan 1971)

J. G. Barry (ed.) *Historical Studies IX* (Belfast: Blackstaff Press 1974)

G. A. Hayes-McCoy (ed.) *Historical Studies X* (Dublin: ICHS 1976)

T. W. Moody (ed.) *Nationality and the pursuit of national independence: Historical Studies XI* (Belfast: Appletree Press 1978)

A. C. Hepburn (ed.) *Minorities in history: Historical Studies XII* (London: Edward Arnold 1978)

D. W. Harkness and M O'Dowd (ed.) *The town in Ireland: Historical Studies XIII* (Belfast: Appletree Press 1981)

J. I. McGuire and A. Cosgrove (ed.) *Parliament and community: Historical Studies XIV* (Belfast: Appletree Press 1981)

P. J. Corish (ed.) *Radicals, rebels and establishments: Historical Studies XV* (Belfast: Appletree Press 1985)

Tom Dunne (ed.) *The writer as witness: literature as historical evidence: Historical Studies XVI* (Cork: Cork University Press 1987)

Ciaran Brady (ed.) *Ideology and the historians: Historical Studies XVII* (Dublin: The Lilliput Press 1991)

T.G. Fraser and Keith Jeffery (ed.) *Men, women and war: Historical Studies XVIII* (Dublin: The Lilliput Press 1993)

Mary O'Dowd and Sabine Wichert (ed.) *Chattel, servant or citizen. Women's status in church, state and society: Historical Studies XIX* (Belfast: Institute of Irish Studies, 1995)

Judith Devlin and Ronan Fanning (ed.) *Religion and rebellion: Historical Studies XX* (Dublin: University College Dublin Press, 1997)

LUXURY AND AUSTERITY

edited by JACQUELINE HILL
and COLM LENNON

Historical Studies XXI

Papers read before the 23rd Irish Conference of Historians,
held at St Patrick's College, Maynooth, 16–18 May 1997

University College Dublin Press
Preas Choláiste Ollscoile Bhaile Átha Cliath

First published 1999 by University College Dublin Press,
Newman House, St Stephen's Green, Dublin 2, Ireland

ISBN 1 900621 22 3

Cataloguing in Publication data available from the British Library

Index by Helen Litton
Typeset in Ireland in 11/12.5 Garamond by Elaine Shiels, Bantry, Co. Cork
Printed in England by Redwood Books, Trowbridge

Contents

List of Illustrations

The plates are between pp. 114 and 115

Plate

Abbreviations

The bibliographical abbreviations used in this volume are those listed in the revised 'Rules for contributors' in *Irish Historical Studies,* supp. 1 (1968), with the following additions:

B.L.   British Library

B.N.L.   *Belfast News Letter*

Com   David Hume, 'Of commerce' (1752), in David Hume, *Essays, moral, political and literary,* ed. Eugene F. Miller (Indianapolis, 1987)

E.E.T.S.   *Early English Text Society*

F.J.   *Freeman's Journal*

N.A.   National Archives, Dublin

N.L.W.   National Library of Wales

Poor inquiry *Poor inquiry (Ireland). First report from his majesty's commissioners for inquiring into the condition of the poorer classes in Ireland, with appendix (A) and supplement.* H.C. 1835 (369), xxxii, pt. 1, 1

RA   David Hume, 'Of refinement of arts' (1752), in David Hume, *Essays moral, political and literary,* ed. Eugene F. Miller (Indianapolis, 1987)

R.C.B.   Representative Church Body Library, Dublin

R.S.C.G.   Religious Sisters of Charity Generalate, Dublin

Introduction

When the twenty-third biennial Irish Conference of Historians (16–18 May 1997) was at the planning stage, the recent onset of high and sustained levels of economic growth in Ireland – the 'Celtic tiger' phenomenon – suggested the possibility of 'luxury and austerity' as an appropriate theme. The setting of St Patrick's College, Maynooth (the host institution – now NUI Maynooth), with its vivid contrasts between the austere classicism of the early buildings and the more elaborate gothicism of Pugin's Victorian architecture, also seemed in keeping. Once the theme had been suggested, the organisers (now the editors) were struck by how many of the profession were researching areas that fell within its broad scope. And when following the conference the contributors were invited to submit drafts for publication, the editors were very happy with the response. Almost all the papers came in.

The result is a collection of papers that is unusually tightly focused, and breaks new ground in opening up a subject that has received little systematic attention. The volume begins with a valuable overview from Christopher Berry, whose background in the history of ideas enables him to set out a clear context for the changing meanings and implications of the idea of luxury. Professor Berry argues that since classical times luxury has changed from being opposed categorically to 'austerity' to being opposed contingently to 'necessity'. One highly significant result of this shift has been the virtual disappearance of the moral overtones in discourse concerning luxury: the subject has become a much more neutral one. The paper locates the shift in the eighteenth century, and discusses by way of illustration the essays of David Hume. Although not an innovator, Hume encapsulated the change in question by coupling luxury with virtue rather than, in the tradition of the austere moralists, contrasting them. He provided a positive case for the beneficial effects of luxury and criticised the moralised alternative. From the second half of the eighteenth century onwards the argument for luxury was effectively 'won', so that by the late twentieth century 'luxury' could be used unselfconsciously to promote consumption.

There follow twelve more papers that examine the theme of luxury and austerity in concrete historical circumstances, for the most part in the Irish context, but including some studies of England. Chronologically the first is Colmán Etchingham's study of the idea of monastic austerity in the early Irish church. Here it becomes apparent that classical definitions of luxury were already subtly changing under the influence of Christianity. Like the Roman moralists, the church fathers tended to equate luxury with excessive desire and self-gratification, but characteristically for them vices also became sins. Concentrating on the seventh to ninth centuries, Dr Etchingham's paper focuses on the way in which the concept and vocabulary of monastic austerity were used in a remarkably extended manner, and on the importance of the practice of penance. A regime of penitential austerity was deemed to be a prerequisite for the redemption of a laity widely regarded by many churchmen as living in persistent sinfulness. The paper suggests that only those who submitted to a quasi-monastic lifestyle were to be accounted among the truly Christian elite.

In his own contribution, joint editor Colm Lennon examines the nature of charitable provision for the poor and sick on the part of individuals and corporations in the towns of sixteenth-century Ireland. This was, of course, an age in which Christian values still dominated civil society, and the duty of charitable relief of the poor was one that Christian moralists upheld: in the Catholic tradition such 'good works' were held to have redeeming value. The paper traces the transition from essentially monastic welfare to broadly secular initiatives, but contends that there were many continuities in that transition. Down to the 1640s the development of a more centralised system of poor relief was hampered by the exaggerated corporatism of the older boroughs, which were protective of traditional confraternal models of charity, including religious guilds, chantries, and colleges.

Felicity Heal's paper takes a somewhat broader look at the ethics of generosity, discussing the themes of almsgiving and charity, forms of giving that affirmed communal solidarity, mutuality and friendship. As the Reformation took hold in England during the sixteenth century the function of almsgiving altered, and it ceased to have redemptive value. Rather, it was claimed, God would reward generosity in this life; it might also arouse admiration and praise. Among the elites, reciprocity and mutuality were the subject of self-conscious reflection, indicated by the growing popularity of Seneca's *De beneficiis*. And royal largesse and patronage were of major concern to those around the monarch.

The lifestyle of the Irish Protestant elite in the seventeenth and eighteenth centuries is the subject of two thoughtful papers, which question the received wisdom that the propertied classes were abnormally extravagant, lacked any sense of social responsibility, and were economically unproductive. Toby Barnard examines some practices of hospitality and charity among the elite, contending that prodigality was not exceptional by British and continental standards. It arose naturally from the social, political, and cultural obligations of the propertied. Moreover, communal schemes of philanthropy – fostering agricultural and commercial improvement through the Dublin Society, establishing hospitals and the charter schools – revealed some sense of responsibility for the less well-off. To a striking extent, the elite remained preoccupied with public display and with public space, so that privacy featured little, even in the planning of towns and domestic houses. Leslie Clarkson takes up the theme of the eating and drinking habits of the upper classes. In a richly detailed and often humorous account, he attempts the ambitious task of quantifying the amount, variety, and cost of food and drink and compares them with English figures. Pointing out that one person's expenditure is another person's income, he tentatively concludes that such expenditure in Ireland may have given employment to a workforce, in towns and villages, of some 168,000 people.

The enlightenment thinkers of the eighteenth century for whom luxury signified not corruption or sinfulness but progress of the arts and sciences noted that a striving after novelty was a universal human trait. Issues of fashion and emulation come into Brenda Collins's discussion of the transformation of the Irish linen industry from a country-wide, country-based activity to a more specialised one, which by the early 1800s was concentrated in the north-east of the country. Adverting to the modern market stress on the role of the consumer as a driving-force behind economic change, the author considers the influence on the industry of changing tastes and innovations in design, and the shifting balance between the public and private spheres. The role of women as the arbiters of fashion in dress and household linens is considered, as is the development of retail shops and the creation of an alluring environment for the sale of goods.

A change of tone enters with three papers that take up different aspects of the great famine of the 1840s. Laurence Geary considers an important, though neglected, aspect of the life of the poor in pre-famine Ireland: begging. He argues that in Ireland, where (unlike England) there was no legal entitlement to poor relief, begging enjoyed a recognised place in society, and was highly structured. 'Professional' beggars frequented fairs and markets; they often feigned deformity to excite compassion. 'Occasional' beggars might turn to mendicancy for any number of reasons, but in the countryside the notorious 'meal months', when the previous year's crop of potatoes had run out and the new crop was not yet ready, sent large numbers of people begging, especially women and children.

This paper examines the impact of the new poor law of 1838 (which introduced the workhouse system) and considers why it failed to eradicate begging; the famine itself, which cut a swathe through the class most likely to beg, was far more effective in that respect.

Tim O'Neill looks at the role of private relief in Ireland during the famine years, and sets it in a wider nineteenth-century context. His paper examines the major emergency relief committees, domestic and foreign, and considers the reasons why private charity, which was relatively generous in response to earlier crop failures such as that of 1822, was less forthcoming in the 1840s. Estimates are presented of the extent of private charity, and the role of landlords, churches and other agencies is considered. David Miller explores the reaction of Irish Presbyterians to the famine, pointing out that there were Presbyterians among those who starved, and that the response of the Presbyterian church was a complex one. Some regarded the famine as divine punishment, but others saw it as a providential opportunity for missionary work among Irish Catholics. By comparing such missionary efforts in mid-nineteenth century Connemara with Protestant missionary activity in twentieth-century South America, Professor Miller is able to suggest why the former achieved relatively little success. He also argues that the famine hastened the transformation of Irish Presbyterianism from a communal religion to a class-based one.

John Gilmartin's paper turns to a very different aspect of nineteenth-century Irish life: the wealthy Catholic gentry families who played a vital role as patrons of the church. In particular, light is shed on the role of the Redington family of Kilcornan, Clarinbridge, County Galway in bringing the Sisters of Charity to the locality and furnishing the convent chapel with precious works of art. The family's role as patrons is set in the context of its links with the English and Roman aristocracy; the works of art themselves are examined in some detail, and a case made out for Pugin's influence on the chapel's interior. Belief in the efficacy of such 'good works' (which resulted in valuable endowments for the Catholic church) had remained constant, but in the nineteenth century it became possible to display such treasures in a public way that had been impossible in the penal era.

Asa Briggs's paper on 'poverty and plenty' formed the plenary address at the conference, returning to ideological aspects of the conference theme. As noted above, by Victorian times luxury was being coupled not with 'austerity' as in the pre-enlightenment age, but with 'necessity'. Lord Briggs's exhaustive knowledge of the era enables him to flesh out the Victorian debate – which also extended to Ireland – about luxury and necessity. Alexis de Tocqueville drew attention in the 1830s to the paradox that England was the richest country in the world, yet had one-sixth of the population living on 'public charity'. The very fact that the standard of living in England was higher than elsewhere facilitated the extension of pauperism, because the range of 'necessities' became so large.

In the final contribution to this volume, Caitriona Clear examines the popular view of the 'austerity' of the lives of 'women of the house' from the 1920s to the 1950s, and questions how far this view is valid, and how far the result of the idealisation of the 'mother' in twentieth-century Ireland. Working from answers to requests for information from the public, the author argues that while life was undoubtedly hard there is evidence of a growing cult of appearance from the 1940s on, and that by then women were insisting on certain comforts, especially for themselves and for the home. With reference to studies of other modern cultures, it is suggested that women made emotional capital from representing them-selves as the supreme altruists within the family: austerity conveyed a certain moral authority.

J.H., C.L.
NUI Maynooth, February 1999

Acknowledgements

The conference organisers are grateful for financial and other assistance to Dr W.J. Smyth, President, NUI Maynooth, and also to Professor R.V. Comerford of the Department of Modern History, NUI Maynooth. For subsidies towards publication we are indebted to Cork University Press, to Gill & Macmillan, to NUI Maynooth and to the National University of Ireland, as well as to the Irish Committee of Historical Sciences, under whose aegis the conference was held. For advice on jacket design we are grateful to Dr E.J. McParland of Trinity College, Dublin, and for their invaluable help with administration and publicity to Bridget McCormack and Ann Matthews. Our colleagues in the department helped in ways too numerous to mention, and the Conference Centre, St Patrick's College, Maynooth, made everyone's stay on the campus a comfortable one. For permission to reproduce illustrations in their care we are grateful to the Board of Trinity College, Dublin, to the British Library, the National Gallery of Ireland, and to the Trustees of the National Library of Ireland. Finally, we wish to record our thanks to Barbara Mennell of University College Dublin Press, whose calm efficiency has been so important in bringing this volume to publication.

1 Austerity, necessity and luxury

Christopher J. Berry

Some ideas are systematically ambiguous such that trying to grasp them is akin to keeping hold of soap in the shower. One way to try to get a grip is to identify the effective antonym. Hence the systematic ambiguity of 'reason' can often be lessened by seeking out whether it is to be contrasted with instinct or sentiment or experience or folly. Similarly, 'nature' can be more easily pinned down by noting if its appropriate counterpart is the perverse or the rare or the artificial or the miraculous. Without ever approaching the salience and slipperiness of reason and nature, 'luxury' too is an elusive idea.

It is indicative of this elusiveness that, historically speaking, its effective meaning has not remained constant. To read, for example, Livy's account of the policies of Cato the Censor alongside the advertisements in any contemporary magazine is to run the risk of developing schizoid tendencies. A possible prophylactic against that potential pathology is to identify the conceptual context in which the word itself appears. It is in making such identifications that locating antonyms or juxtapositions is useful. Coco Chanel apparently said the opposite of luxury was vulgarity[1] and the theme of this conference is captured by another juxtaposition – luxury and austerity. For my part I wish to explore what that theme involves and I do so by investigating it alongside another contrast – luxury and necessity. My suggestion (I hesitate to use the word 'argument') is that the historically elusive meaning and significance of 'luxury' can be informatively illuminated by observing how it has changed from being effectively opposed categorically to austerity to being opposed contingently to necessity.

As an initial scene-setter I wish to state schematically and abstractly what, when set against 'luxury', the difference between austerity and necessity can be seen to involve. I have no wish in what follows to act as some sort of lexical legislator but, that said, austerity when paired with luxury belongs in a moralised vocabulary. It is a virtue which, along with its cognates like 'frugality' and 'poverty', refers to the estimable practice of temperance and continence. To be austere is to be in control of oneself and thus of one's actions; it is to know the true and proper value of things and be in a position of forswearing temptations, that is, things of illusory value. One consequence of situating austerity in this vocabulary or discourse is that it is not synonymous with 'necessity'. To be austere out of necessity has no place in *this* discourse because where there is no choice there cannot be a virtuous practice. And since, in this moralised discourse, luxury is conceptually tied (as a counterpart) to austerity then just as the indigent cannot be austere nor can they be luxurious. This has the important further consequence that the subjects of moral criticism are not the necessitous poor but either corrupt aristocrats (like Catiline who was lambasted by Sallust) or the upwardly mobile (who were the focus of the sumptuary laws of early modern Europe).

Of course, in line with everything which has been said thus far, 'austerity' can be understood contrastively in a non-moral context. Indeed, perhaps its commonest contemporary usage is in an economic sense as when, for example, in 1996, President Chirac is reported to have introduced an 'austerity' programme (tax increases and the like) in order to attempt to meet the conditions for European monetary union. Here the contrasted meaning is synonymous with the distinction between a deflationary and an inflationary or expansionist economic policy.

While allowing for the flexibility of linguistic usage, the distinction between austerity and necessity is what is central to my story. These terms should not be conflated. Apart from its technical usage in logic and other specialised vocabularies, 'necessity' also has everyday uses which distinguish it from the moralised context of austerity – eggs are necessary for an omelette. More germane is that while the eggs are necessary that does not compromise the presence of ham or mushrooms or onions or all three. That is to say that just because X is necessary does not make Y though less necessary without value. Y can partake, we might say, of 'superfluous value'. Two points of relevance are raised by this notion. First, from the moralised perspective of austerity, 'superfluous value' is an oxymoron. Second, from the perspective of necessity the only issue that would arise is that of priority. There can be room for censure if Y is put ahead of X – buying caviar ahead of eggs. But this censure is not mandatory. It is not necessarily the case that putting the superfluous ahead of the necessary is always wrong.

The upshot of these initial schematic remarks is that when luxury is juxtaposed to austerity it is a vice, when it is juxtaposed to necessity it can be innocent, it can, as the source of pleasure, even be 'good', and if it is criticised it is so by proxy, as the manifestation of folly. Historically the former juxtaposition has given way to the latter. Allowing that to be the case, any answer as to why that should have been so would involve rounding up all the usual suspects implicated in the 'making of the modern age'. I am going to take that as given and instead wish to focus on a particular emblematic example of the displacement of the moralised vocabulary that housed austerity/luxury by the more neutral vocabulary of necessity/luxury. But before turning to my exemplar I have a few more abstract observations to make.

These pertain to the interaction between the notions of 'desire' and 'need'.[2] Perhaps the crucial fact about needs is their non-privileged status. Whether or not you need something is not definitively answered by your beliefs about that something. Usefully this point can be brought out by means of a contrast with wanting or desiring. Hence (I simplify) you need a heart bypass without wanting surgery and, conversely, you desire another slice of cake without needing it to ensure your daily intake of calories. It is the latter of these examples that throws most light on the current issue. A simple rephrasing will illustrate why. From the moralised perspective of austerity, taking that extra slice is a luxurious indulgence, a deleterious lack of resolve that panders to desire and betrays a defect in character. From the perspective of the necessary, though that slice is superfluous yet to indulge myself is a treat, I get positive pleasure from its consumption.

The shift between these two perspectives is the shift from a view that sees meeting needs as part of some value-laden purposive order with definite limits, such that desire can be understood as transgressing those limits, to the view that desires far from transgressing some pre-determined or naturally fixed boundary are, rather, the definitive element in human motivation and are thus to be accepted for what they are – the motors and determiners of human values. The reference here to 'transgression' invokes the attendant idea of police or discipline. The virtue of austerity is expressed by the individual who, in the light of a rational apprehension of the natural order, self-disciplines desires so that luxurious indulgence is forsworn. I have in mind here the Stoic sage who will drink but not get drunk or the Patristic prohibition of sex with, or by, a pregnant woman. This virtue is expressed socially by policing these desires in the light of the objectively valid constituents of the 'good life' or 'good and politic order'. I have in mind here sumptuary laws (the phrase 'good and politic order' comes from the preamble to the English act of apparel of 1553[3]) or the proscription of ecclesiastical luxury by Cistercians among many others. However, once desires are seen as the bearers of values then any individual self-discipline is a matter of calculation – the desire for the slice of cake against the desire to fit into that new dress. In other words, I have in mind here any utilitarian. The social counterpart is a matter of manipulating the motivational levers so that some socially beneficial outcome is achieved. I have in mind here the rationale for inequality as an incentive so that production can be increased to the overall benefit, or that the infliction of pain in a punishment regime should be used economically to deter and not be inflicted retributively for its own sake.

This I realise is all very abstract and what I want to do in the remainder of this paper is to make it more concrete by means of an exemplification. My exemplar is Hume's essay 'Of refinement of arts', which on its initial publication in 1752 was entitled 'Of luxury'.[4] I stress the instrumentalism here. I am using this essay (drawing also on some other contemporary writings of both Hume and others) to illuminate this shift in the valuation of desire and thus the shift from luxury/austerity to luxury/necessity. The justification for this exploitation of Hume's essay is that a relatively unforced reading can shed the promised light. It is able to do that because, aside from Hume's acuity as a thinker, the essay stands historically at a key point. On the one hand, it is sufficiently distant from the initial assault on austerity whether, as undertaken by Montaigne,[5] on it as the hallmark of a virtuous individual or, as undertaken by theorists of trade like Barbon,[6] on it as the touchstone of a virtuous political society. It is also removed from the immediate flak generated by that assault's most notorious exponent, Mandeville.[7] Hume, in other words, is less an innovator than a brilliant encapsulator of the shift – hence his putative status as an exemplar. On the other hand, to the same effect, after Hume (which is not to say *because* of Hume) the shift has largely been completed. Of course, there are no sharp edges in these matters. There were always moralists about like Proudhon in the mid-nineteenth century who defended the austere virtue of honest poverty[8] and in the twentieth century some attacks on consumerism can be interpreted in the same light. But as I shall conclude these are unable to turn the clock back.

One indication of Hume's historically sensitive situation is his own self-consciousness. He opens this essay by stating that 'luxury' is a word of 'uncertain signification' (*RA*, 268). He knows full well the position of those 'severe moralists' (as he calls them – Sallust is named as an example) that 'luxury' is a vice and he also knows that Mandeville has attacked this line and that more soberly it had been taken up by contemporaries like Melon. Against this backcloth Hume gives his own definition: luxury is 'great refinement in the gratification of senses' (ibid.). Any thought that this is intended to be read censoriously as an endorsement of the moralists is displaced by his generalising remark that 'ages of refinement' are 'both the happiest and most virtuous' (*RA*, 269). In a clear break from the moralist tradition, therefore, Hume is coupling luxury/refinement with happiness/ virtue, *not* opposing them.

If people are now 'happier', in what does this happiness consist? Hume identifies three components – repose, pleasure and action (*RA*, 269–70). Of these the last is crucial. The first is merely derivative, only valued as a break from action. The second is integrally connected with action because 'being occupied' is itself enjoyable. It is the twist that Hume gives to 'action' that is crucial. The focus is not the Ciceronic *negotium*, with its preoccupation with public or political affairs (the *rei publicae*), but the private endeavour of industry. Where industry abounds then individuals will be not only opulent but happy as its members 'reap the benefit of . . . commodities so far as they gratify the senses and appetite' (*Com*, 263). If we ask what motivates them, Hume answers 'avarice and industry, art and luxury' (ibid.). The fact that 'avarice' was uniformly condemned by the austere moralists signals the switch in evaluations that has occurred. We can pursue what was involved in that switch by picking up on Hume's further remark that humans are roused to activity or industry by a 'desire of a more splendid way of life than what their ancestors enjoyed' (*Com*, 264).

It is the use of 'desire' here that is significant because it testifies to the presence of the premises of 'modern' psychology. According to Aristotle humans aim at or 'desire' *eudaimonia*, which is a 'perfect and self-sufficient end'.[9] Those who attain *eudaimonia* are living life as it should be led; it is a complete life and, as such, one without 'desire'. In this very precise sense 'desire' is limited. Perhaps the clearest, and in our context telling, example of this general line of thought is when the 'end' of food is identified as assuaging hunger (and fuelling the body) so that, it follows, to desire food when not hungry is to manifest 'imperfection'. And to care about the quality of the food is also beside the point, as Seneca said Nature demands the belly be filled not flattered.[10]

The modern view rejects this teleological perspective and also rejects thereby both the possibility of a desire-less state and the idea that desires can be limited to some fixed end. As Hobbes pointed out, the only way to be 'free' of desire is to be dead. Motion, or 'uneasiness of the mind' as Locke had defined 'desire',[11] is the correct description of how the world (including mankind) *is*. Humans move toward what they imagine pleases them and away from what they imagine will occasion pain. For Aristotle mutability was characteristic of normative imperfection and this set up the basic classical/Christian distinction between, on the one hand, the tranquil/ ascetic life, devoted to the contemplation of the immutable First Cause or the eternal perfection of God, and, on the other, the mundane life which is unceasingly at the beck and call of the demands of bodily desires.

It is in this pre-modern context that the virtue of austerity is perfectly at home. This virtue is an expression of the 'natural life' – a life *kata phusin* or *secundum naturam*. There is a proper, 'natural' limit to meeting the body's requirements because the fulfilment of these requirements is itself naturally limited. Cicero declares it to be self-evident that nature's requirements are few and inexpensive.[12] The 'natural life' is the 'simple life'. Those who live simply will not be poor because poverty is only experienced by those who have exceeded nature's bounds, that is, by those who desire more. It was held to be the definitive characteristic of desires that focus on the body (that focus on what Hume called 'a more splendid way of life' where the senses are gratified) that they are boundless. It is a criterion of the 'unnatural' that it has no terminus.[13] Once the natural limit is passed then there is no resting place and, viewed from that perspective, life will always appear too short. Those who see matters in this light will (to quote Seneca again) become 'soft through a life of luxury' and accordingly afraid of death.[14] Such fear is unmanly and it is here that we can discern the long-running association between luxury and softness and effeminacy. As Cicero put it in the *Offices*, a frugal life of temperance, sobriety and austerity is worthy or *honestum* while, in contrast, a life of *luxuria et delicate ac molliter* is corrupt or *turpe*.[15]

Here is a clear case of my first moralised juxtaposition – luxury/ austerity. On this understanding luxury was a corruption. On an individual level men who live a life of luxury become effeminate. That is to say they become 'soft', unable to endure hardship and to act courageously in the definitively (even etymologically) masculine fashion.[16] To live luxuriously is to devote oneself to the pleasures of self-indulgence and avarice. Such a life has social consequences. A society where luxury is established will devote itself to private ends since men will be unwilling to act (fight) for the public good. This society, it follows, will be militarily weak – a nation of cowards will easily succumb.

It was further assumed that pre-eminent among those who served their private interest were traders or merchants. Compared to a general or a statesman, that is, one who dedicated his life to the public good, a merchant lived a less fulfilling, less humanly worthwhile life. This disparagement, present in Aristotle for example,[17] was sharpened once commerce began to spread. Over and beyond that commerce was suspect because of the uncertainty or risk that lies at its core – there is no guarantee that you will be able to sell your goods. And since the system rests on nothing more tangible than belief, opinion and expectation then it seemed clearly too insubstantial to support a social order.[18] These jeremiads were fuelled by the spectacular financial collapses of the late seventeenth and early eighteenth century (the Darien scheme, the South Sea bubble). These worries were given a focus by the presence of a contrasting model in the person of the independent landowner or country gentleman. This individual enjoys stability and certainty. In sharp and deliberate contrast to the fluidity of a money economy, the giddy whirl of fashion and the evanescence of 'profit', the landowner with his commitment to a fixed 'place' is able to practise the virtues of loyalty, responsibility and steadfastness. These are suitably 'masculine' traits[19] and they can be contrasted to the proverbial unreliability of women – not for nothing is it their 'prerogative to change their mind', truly '*la donna e mobile*'. Given its link with effeminacy, luxury now resurrects itself.

The only way a luxurious, soft nation could meet its military commitments or needs was by hiring others to play that role. To make that feasible the nation had to have the wherewithal. Hence arose the important association between luxury, wealth (commerce) and mercenary armies. For civic humanists or classical republicans, like Algernon Sidney, for whom poverty is 'the mother and nurse of . . . virtue',[20] this was a negative association so that commerce too became tarred with the anti-luxury brush. This meant that to defend commerce required a deflection or subversion of the traditional case against luxury.

This is where we can now return to Hume's essay, 'Of refinement of arts', and its contemporary companion, 'Of commerce'. Hume in his defence of luxury rebuts the moralised case. One strategy in this rebuttal was to accept the connexion between commerce and softness but to construe this positively.[21] He does this by developing a contrast between the civilised or refined on the one hand and the barbarous or rude on the other. He declares that it is 'peculiar' to 'polished or . . . luxurious ages' that 'industry, knowledge and humanity are linked together by an indissoluble chain' (*RA*, 271). It is a mark of the growth in 'humanity' that it has, in part, expressed itself in the 'tempers' of men being 'softened' and one manifestation of this softening of manners is that wars are less cruel and the aftermath more humane (*RA*, 274). Here is a basic rescheduling of virtues. There is a shift from an emphasis on martial virtues, like courage and glory, to a stress upon the 'gentle' virtues of humanity, industry and justice.[22] In this context Adam Smith neatly contrasts the exercise of the prime Stoic virtue of self-command between civilised and earlier eras. In the case of the latter, self-command is more a matter of repression for, like a coiled spring that leaps unpredictably and uncontrollably once the tension is released, so the actions of the 'uncivilised' when they lose their self-command are 'furious and violent' and their recriminations 'always sanguinary and dreadful'.[23] On the other hand, in commercial societies, alongside the promotion of such values as probity and punctuality,[24] it is 'the gentler exertions' of self-command such as decency, modesty and moderation that prevail.[25]

Despite this Hume denies that this softening has enervated 'the martial spirit'. The supposed causal link between luxury and military weakness is undermined by the cases of France and England, that is, of the two most powerful *and* most polished and commercial societies (*RA*, 275). Since a state's 'power' hinges on its military capacity it means that Hume is contending that a commercial society is potent not impotent, is virile not effeminate. His contention has both a positive and a negative aspect. Negatively he holds that the population of a non-trading society will be indolent and its soldiers will lack knowledge, skill and industry. These deficiencies make them fit only for sudden confrontations, because regular attack or defence is beyond them (*RA*, 260). Positively, a civilised nation, precisely because it is industrious and knowledgeable, will be an effective military power. The root cause is that a nation's power increases in proportion as it increases labour employed 'beyond mere necessaries'. The effect of this cause is that the nation possesses a storehouse of labour (*RA*, 272; *Com*, 262). This store can be drawn on to meet military need. In a civilised nation an army is raised by imposing a tax, this reduces consumption of unnecessary luxury goods thus releasing manufacturers of such goods for military service (*Com*, 261).

There is an implicit running critique here of Sparta – the paradigm of a regime founded on hard, austere virtues.[26] Sparta, however, is unworthy of emulation because its much vaunted virtue and military prowess rested on slavery and slavery, if nothing else, is 'disadvantageous' to 'happiness'.[27] It was precisely the growth of commerce and luxury that had eroded slavery and personal dependency more generally.[28] Commerce had brought with it not only civilisation but also the rule of law. Civilised monarchies can truly be said to possess now what was formerly the prerogative of republics alone, namely, that 'that they are the government of laws not of men'.[29] Luxury, as an ally of commerce, thus not only undercuts the case for republics but also inhibits absolutism since, when it is diffused among the population, it diminishes the force and ambition of the sovereign (*Com*, 257).

There is a deeper dimension to Hume's analysis. This is revealed in his comment that the sort of society presupposed by the critics of luxury is contrary to the 'natural bent of the mind' (*Com*, 263). Here Hume refers explicitly to Sparta. Spartan policy goes against the grain of human nature because its devotion to the 'public good' is too difficult to sustain. Hume supposes that if a 'city' today became a 'fortified camp', such that its inhabitants had both a 'martial genius' and 'passion for the public good', then, indeed, all 'arts and luxury' could be banished (*Com*, 262–3). But this supposition is unrealistic. The touchstone of realism is human nature. The requisite devotion to the public good is 'too disinterested' to have an effective purchase on human behaviour. While Hume had argued that, on the basis of 'common experience', the 'kind affections' overbalance the selfish, yet it is true that 'in the original frame of our mind, our strongest attention is confin'd to ourselves'.[30] Two noteworthy consequences follow. First, civic virtue is too fragile a base on which to erect a system of government and second, relatedly, this means that in the normal run of things governments must govern men by those passions that most effectively animate them.

It is accordingly sensible, and in practice greatly preferable, to conduct public affairs from the solid foundation of natural human inclinations rather than anything that might have transpired in Sparta. To govern men along Spartan lines would require a 'miraculous transformation of mankind' (*RA,* 280). Government, however, is not in the business of miracles; it must deal with the world as it is and men as they are. All it can do is channel the passions so that their effects minimise social disharmony. What underpins this is Hume's modern epistemology. In contrast to the classical framework, where the proper response to unruly passions was the cultivation and application of reason, Hume regards reason as inert.[31] Accordingly, the 'magistrate' can 'very often' only cure one vice by encouraging another, where the latter's effects are less damaging. It makes no sense to criticise the magistrate for not imposing in line with 'classical' principles some objective, rational doctrine of the 'good life'. Instead the appropriate judgment is: does this policy promote the material well-being of those individuals subject to it? Understood in this way then luxury can be justly cultivated because it is superior to sloth. Moreover, by defending luxury in this way Hume is still able to allow that it can be 'vicious' as well as innocent. Yet even then it might still be better to accept it than attempt vainly to eradicate it (*RA,* 279–80).

What we find in Hume, therefore, is a decoupling of luxury from its role as the negative counterpart to the virtue of austerity. In his hands luxury can be viewed positively because of its beneficial social effects. In fact his idea of 'vicious luxury' itself intimates the 'shift' I am here exploring. Luxury comes to be criticised on economic rather than moral grounds. The contemporary argument of the Physiocrats was that luxury was 'sterile', that is, was expenditure devoted to unproductive rather than productive ends?[32] Of course, the evolution of ideas is not smooth, and 'luxury' as the prerogative of the 'idle rich' continued (and perhaps continues) to be criticised, though even here it is Hume's bugbear of 'sloth' rather than luxury itself that is the real target. Rather more symptomatic is that once luxury was detached from a moralistic context, and 'economics' developed as a discipline, 'luxury' came to attain a technical, neutral meaning as high income elasticity of demand.

The shift away from moralism that Hume's account exemplifies means that luxury can be understood as the opposite of necessity. A life of necessity now signifies not the austere life of poverty but an impoverished one, a life of misery. There is nothing ennobling or redemptive about this poverty. As Smith put it in the Introduction to the *Wealth of nations,* those who are 'miserably poor' are 'frequently reduced or, at least, think themselves reduced, to the necessity sometimes of directly destroying and sometimes abandoning their infants, their old people and those afflicted with lingering diseases, to perish with hunger or to be devoured by wild beasts'.[33] In stark contrast for Smith 'opulence and freedom' were the 'two greatest blessings men can possess'.[34]

Once luxury is seen in this light then its development into the twentieth century's lexicon of 'ad speak' can be understood. 'Luxury' can without hesitation be tacked on to almost any article of merchandise from pizzas to handbags, from a fountain pen to a dressing gown and done so presumably to make it more desirable and thus more likely to be bought. Of course no one *needs* a pair of embroidered slippers for, as Epictetus said of this example, the purpose of footwear is protection and its decora-tiveness is superfluous.[35] But in the modern world there is no such thing as superfluous value. Embroidered slippers are more pleasing than plain ones and where's the harm in that pleasure? Moreover, think of all the extra industry generated and employment created by the desire to have those exquisitely produced slippers and think, too, of the economic benefits that will flow from my desire next year to own an even more fashionable and luxurious pair.

The dynamism of desire in this way fuels the engine of modern economies. One way of depicting this dynamism is to chart the seemingly never-ceasing transformation of luxuries into necessities. This transformation demonstrates that whereas luxury and austerity existed as categorical oppo-sites, luxury is only contingently contrasted with necessity; they are terminal points on a single scale or continuum. This difference between categorical and contingent opposition is not without more general significance. The rampant consumerism implicit in this luxury-to-necessity dynamic is not without its contemporary critics and my final remarks link up this critique with the one generated by the classical perspective of austerity.

From that perspective these 'necessities' are misdescribed; they are rather the manifestation of corruption. The basic reason why is because, as noted earlier, the mutable is the imperfect. Any alteration to Epictetus's functional slipper is unwarranted. There is seemingly no place for change or innovation. One of the striking things about the critique from austerity is that very often in practice it served to underwrite a hierarchical status quo. Sumptuary legislation bears this out. The overwhelming concern there was to preserve the pecking-order, to attempt through display to maintain 'distance',[36] and thus to confine the incidence of a good and prevent its diffusion. Luxury, 'new' wealth, always threatened to overturn this. Those in the lower ranks of these societies may well have wanted some of those privileged goods but that 'wanting' was a mark of their unworthiness, since they desired them for their own personal use; opulence was definitely not a 'blessing'. The decline of sumptuary laws is a marker not necessarily of greater economic equality but of what Werner Sombart called *Versachlichung*, the wish to enjoy the tangible reality of magnificent clothes and comfortable homes.[37] And that itself signals the recognition that the desire on the part of the have-nots for those goods currently possessed by the 'haves' is legitimate or, at least, is functional; indeed is part of human nature, realistically, that is, materialistically understood.

One consequence of rejecting the normative superiority of the eternally immutable was the acceptance of the worth of the mundanely mutable. Life, self-preservation, from being for the Stoics a 'thing indifferent' or for civic moralists being sacrificeable *pro bono publico* became valued for its own sake. Politically this means that desires are to be accommodated not proscribed. It is the particular desires of individuals that determine what they judge subjectively to be worthwhile and not, as with Aristotle, that something is objectively worthwhile and therefore individuals desire it. The sovereign's interest lies not in the specific content of the desires only in the likelihood of their peaceful co-existence; not in the choice of music but the volume at which it is played, not in the religious ritual performed but in its confinement to those who have chosen to practise it, not in the nature of the business enterprised but in its conformity to general rules and so on. This is the view that comes to be called liberalism. In effect, liberalism valorises the mundane.

Central to the critique of liberalism is the critique of the legitimation of infinite desires, 'possessive individualism', in C. B. Macpherson's well-known phrase,[38] that modern capitalist/consumerist societies are held to imply. Not least among the problems that any genuinely socialist society, or any radical 'green' proposal, faces is how to square, on the one hand, the recognition of the value of individual desire with, on the other, the critique of a society based on the satisfaction of desire. The classical critique of luxury in the name of austerity did the latter, but the former precludes (electorally at least) the viability of any appeal to that virtue. The consequence, one might speculate, is that any contemporary criticism of luxury has seemingly to be levelled not at any intrinsic defect but on its status as a symptomatic mis-ordering of priorities, of the less necessary being promoted ahead of the more necessary. That symptomatic or token role is a far cry from the moralist indictment. This illustrates that the linkages between luxury and austerity and between luxury and necessity reflect two very different conceptual packages that have successively manifested themselves historically. Or such at least I have tried to suggest.

NOTES

1 As quoted by Hans Magnus Enzensburger, 'Reminizenzen an der Überfluss' in *Der Spiegel*, 51 (1996), p. 116

2 I have developed this at some length in my *The idea of luxury: a conceptual and historical investigation* (Cambridge, 1994). See especially chs 1, 7, 8. I draw on some of this discussion in what follows.

3 As quoted in N. B. Harte, 'State control of dress and social change in pre-industrial England' in D.C. Coleman and A. H. John (ed.), *Trade, government and economy in pre-industrial England* (London, 1976), pp 132–65, p. 139.

4 References to this essay will be inserted in parenthesis. The text used is *Essays: moral, political and literary* (1779), ed. Eugene F. Miller (Indianapolis, 1987). Another reference from this text inserted is: *Com* ('Of commerce', 1752).

5 Cf. *Essays* (1580–) especially 'Of cruelty' with its critique of virtue (including austerity) understood as the perfectionist requirement to conquer, and thus be dependent upon, contrary impulses.

6 Cf. *A discourse of trade* (1690).

7 Cf. *The fable of the bees* (1732).

8 Cf. *Selected writings*, ed. Stewart Edwards (London, 1970), p. 259.

9 *Nicomachean ethics*, ed. John Burnet (London, 1900), 1097b. Admittedly 'desire' in Aristotle covers a range of terms. In this passage it is *hairetos* – this can be distinguished from *orexis* and *epithumia*. While the latter was the term most clearly and commonly used in the context of 'bodily appetites/desires' the teleological framework is constant.

10 *Epistulae morales ad Lucilium* (London, 1932), no. 119.

11 *Essay concerning human understanding* [1690], bk. 2, ch. 21, sect. 31.

12 *Tusculanarum disputationum* (London, 1927), 5.35.

13 Cf. Seneca, *Epistulae*, no. 16.

14 Cf. Seneca, *Epistulae*, no. 78.

15 *De officiis* (London, 1913), i, 30.

16 It is not mere coincidence that in both Greek and Latin the words for 'man' (*aner/andra* and *vir*) have the same root as those for 'courage' (*andreia* and *virtus*).

17 Cf. *Politics* (London, 1927), 1257a–1258a.

18 I have elaborated upon this in my *Social theory of the Scottish enlightenment* (Edinburgh,1997), ch. 6. I draw on this discussion in what follows.

19 Cf. Edmund Burke, '. . . the great and masculine virtues, constancy, gravity, magnanimity, fortitude, fidelity and firmness': 'Speech on American taxation' (1774) in *Works* (London, 1889), v. I, p. 427.

20 Algernon Sidney, *Discourses concerning government* [1698], ed. Thomas G. West (Indianapolis, 1990) ch. 2, sect. 25, p. 254.

21 Albert O. Hirschman, *The passions and the interests* (Princeton, 1977), p. 64, calls it the doctrine of 'the *doux* commerce' and sees Montesquieu as its most influential exponent (see *De l'esprit des lois* [1748], bk. 20, chs 1 and 2). William Robertson neatly summarises what the positive case argued: 'commerce tends to wear off those prejudices which maintain distinction and animosity between nations. It softens and polishes the manners of men. It unites them by one of the strongest of all ties, the desire of supplying their mutual wants. It disposes them to peace . . .' (*A view of the progress of society in Europe* [1769], ed. Dugald Stewart in *Works* (in one volume) (Edinburgh, 1840), p. 333).

22 Referring to sixteenth-century Scotland, Hume remarks that when 'arms' prevail over 'laws' then 'courage preferably to equity or justice was the virtue most valued and respected' (*History of England* [1786 ed.], London, 1894) 3 vols, ii, p. 81. Cf. 'among

all uncultivated nations, who have not as yet had full experience of the advantages attending beneficence, justice, and the social virtues, courage is the predominant excellence' in *Enquiry concerning the principles of morals* [1751], ed. L. A. Selby-Bigge and P. H. Nidditch (Oxford, 1975), p. 255.

23 *The theory of moral sentiments* (6th ed., 1790), ed. A. L. Macfie and D. D. Raphael (Indianapolis, 1982), p. 208.

24 *Lectures on jurisprudence*, ed. R. L. Meek, D. D. Raphael and P. G. Stein (Indianapolis, 1982), p. 539.

25 *Moral sentiments*, p. 242.

26 For a fuller discussion of Hume on Sparta, see my *Idea of luxury*, pp 143–52.

27 'Of the populousness of ancient nations' (1752) in *Essays*, ed. Miller, p. 396.

28 Hume had recounted how this happened in his *History of England* – see, for example, iii, p. 99. Smith developed the story in bk. 3 of the *Wealth of nations*.

29 'Of civil liberty' (1741 – original title 'Of liberty and despotism'), in *Essays,* ed. Miller, p. 94.

30 *A treatise of human nature* (1739–40), ed. L. A. Selby-Bigge (Oxford, 1888), pp 487–8.

31 *Treatise*, p. 458.

32 See Mirabeau's *Table économique* (1760) extracted in R. L. Meek (ed.), *Precursors of Adam Smith* (London, 1973), pp 138ff.

33 *An inquiry into the nature and causes of the wealth of nations* (1776) ed. A. S. Skinner and R. L. Meek (Indianapolis, 1981), p. 10.

34 *Jurisprudence*, p.185. I have explored Smith's argument in 'Adam Smith: commerce, liberty and modernity' in Peter Gilmour (ed.), *The philosophers of the enlightenment*, (Edinburgh, 1989), pp 113–32. Cf. for a nuanced view of Smith, Donald Winch, *Riches and poverty* (Cambridge, 1996), pt 1.

35 Cf. *The encheiridion of Epictetus* (London, 1928), par. 39.

36 Cf. Pierre Bourdieu, 'le pouvoir économique est d'abord un pouvoir de mettre la nécessité économique à distance; c'est pourquoi il s'affirme universellement par le destruction de richesses, le dépense ostentoire, le gaspillage et toutes les formes de luxe gratuit' in *La distinction: critique sociale du jugement* (Paris, 1979), p. 58.

37 Werner Sombart, *Luxus und Capitalismus* (Munich, 1913), p.112. The ostentation of the rich few (*their* magnificence) could be criticised as 'luxury' but that criticism focused on the misdirection of the wealth, that is, it was being used for private aggrandisement rather than public beneficence, which certainly for the Romans was a proper use of riches – see Cicero, *Pro murena* §76, *De officiis*, ii, 22.

38 C. B. Macpherson, *The political theory of possessive individualism* (Oxford, 1962).

2 The idea of monastic austerity in early Ireland

Colmán Etchingham

This contribution is concerned exclusively with the dimension of austerity, and specifically with the significance of monastic austerity in the Irish church of the seventh, eighth and ninth centuries. Irish monasticism, with its reputation for particular devotion to austerity, has attracted much attention among students of early medieval Ireland in the nineteenth and twentieth centuries. An extensive literature notwithstanding, a fresh look at the matter is needed. Ongoing reappraisal of other aspects of the early Irish church holds implications for monastic austerity. Moreover, a review seems an appropriate way to mark the fourteenth centenary year of the death of Columba of Iona. It is intended to concentrate here not so much on the austerities practised by monks as on the broader relevance of the monastic idea in the institutional church as a whole. In particular, I wish to highlight, as a crucial feature of the early Irish church, extension of the concept and vocabulary of monastic austerity to persons not immediately identifiable as true monks. This paper draws in summary on parts of a long promised monograph on early Irish ecclesiastical organisation which, at the time of writing, is at last approaching completion.

As regards the historiography of Irish monasticism, the Irish monk's remarkable ascetic zeal was regularly hailed in an age more pious than our own. Consider, for example, Louis Gougaud, the English translation of whose *Les chrétientés celtiques* was published in 1932. Gougaud confidently proclaimed the single-minded devotion of the Irish monk to the standard observances of obedience, poverty and chastity. Yet doubts about the authenticity of this picture were expressed by a reviewer as early as 1933: 'He seems at times to assume that early Celtic monks were walking in the full light of the counter-reformation'.[1] Comparable anachronism and a generally uncritical approach to his sources also distinguished John Ryan's *Irish monasticism: origins and early development*, published in 1931.[2] Kathleen Hughes's *The church in early Irish society*, which appeared in 1966, adopted a more detached view and became the essential modern study. In particular, Hughes confronted a worldly dimension which she identified in the eighth century and after. Hereditary control of church offices, a preoccupation with lands, tenants and revenues and the involvement of churches in politics and violence, appropriately supplemented the picture of ascetic devotion drawn by Hughes's predecessors. Others, including Tomás Ó Fiaich and most notably Donnchadh Ó Corráin, followed Hughes in stressing the prominence of temporal affairs in the concerns of the church. Wealth, aristocratic connections and political entanglements were, for many (though not all) early Irish churchmen, an acceptable part of ecclesiastical affairs.[3] In a seminal paper published in 1986, Richard Sharpe pointed the way to a further revision,[4] acknowledging his debt to Patrick Corish, whose appreciation of the importance of pastoral care had led him to modify in some respects the received wisdom that the early Irish church was entirely dominated by monasticism.[5] I have discussed the significance of Sharpe's contribution and its historiographical context elsewhere. Some recent writers have ignored Sharpe's critique or misconstrued it as amounting to no more than a further modification of the traditional model. In truth, if it be borne out, Sharpe's hypothesis entirely undermines that model.[6] It will be necessary to summarise the argument.

The predominance of monasticism in the early Irish church was propounded by J.H. Todd in the 1860s,[7] refined by Hughes in the 1960s and accepted by subsequent writers, such as Ó Corráin. It was generally agreed that, in or about the sixth and seventh centuries, bishops became subordinate to abbots and that small early dioceses were absorbed or superseded by large and widely dispersed federations of monasteries.[8] It was further maintained that the change from a diocesan to a monastic system was followed by a second transformation, as monasticism in turn succumbed to worldliness and secularisation.[9] Reaction to change was also postulated at each stage. Thus Hughes detected episcopalist resistance, albeit unsuccessful, to the growing dominance of monasticism and abbatial government in the seventh century.[10] An indigenous reformist response to secularisation was attributed to the *Céli Dé* or Culdees, an ascetic tendency of the eighth and ninth centuries, though it did not achieve and, perhaps, did not attempt, any structural transformation.[11] Much later, in the twelfth century, a reform movement of external inspiration was credited with greater success.[12]

Sharpe's response to all of this was to question the dominance of monasticism, whether pure or degenerate, in accounts of the Irish ecclesiastical system. He challenged the theory of change, reaction and consequent division into rival camps as, in large measure, an arbitrary imposition on evidence which was susceptible to other explanations.[13] In particular, he noted that the evidence for a conventionally organised diocesan church of the missionary period, subsequently overwhelmed by monasticism, is later than the date of its supposed displacement.[14] Instead of the theory of successive changes, he postulated diversity and continuity. Sharpe suggested that, at all times for which we have reliable contemporary evidence, from the seventh century onwards, the church seems to combine monastic and clerical dimensions and the administration of temporalities in various permutations within a single, eclectic system.[15] He observed 'the distinction of two systems is the work of modern historians: the Irish church knew only one'.[16] Sharpe's contribution is an innovative but by no means fully worked out critique of the received wisdom, accompanied only by the barest and most tentative outline of an alternative interpretation. It is not without its apparent inconsistencies and obscurities, which may partly explain its limited impact.

In three recent papers I have sought to show that several vital elements, closely examined, confirm the broad thrust of Sharpe's insight. I detail the importance and the limitations of pastoral care, the continuing, crucial role of bishops throughout the first millennium and the persistence of territorially defined spheres of ecclesiastical jurisdiction during the same period.[17] It does not seem that pastoral ministry, episcopal authority or diocesan jurisdiction were at any point in the first millennium supplanted or subsumed by monasticism. In these fundamental respects the received wisdom appears not to bear scrutiny. What, then, of monastic austerity, the evidence for which has hitherto been fitted to the traditional model of change and reaction? That model portrayed asceticism firstly as the essence of the earliest monastic phase in the sixth and seventh centuries, secondly as the victim of secularisation in the eighth century and after, and thirdly as the focus of Culdee reform in the later eighth and ninth centuries. If the model of change and reaction can be shown not to account satisfactorily for the evidence regarding pastoral ministration, episcopal authority and spheres of jurisdiction, what is the relationship of monastic austerity to other elements in a revised model?

The picture of an all-consuming monastic fervour, in the earliest post-missionary period of the sixth and earlier seventh centuries, was derived by Ryan and others in large measure from an uncritical acceptance of the literal truth of the saints' Lives. All are of a later date – and many of a much later date – than the period for which they were pressed into service as evidence. Such a flawed methodology has long been discredited.[18] Some genuinely early hagiography, notably Adomnán's late seventh-century Life of his predecessor Columba,[19] is, however, valid evidence for the practice of monasticism in the seventh and eighth centuries. The Irish canon-law collection known as the *Hibernensis*, vernacular law and other prescriptive texts such as the Penitentials also shed vital light on the subject. Vernacular monastic rules and the so-called 'monastery of Tallaght', associated with the *Céli Dé* or Culdees, attest to the practice of monasticism in the later eighth and ninth centuries.

The picture presented by these sources is considered at length in my book and space permits only brief comment here. Four salient points may be mentioned. First, the self-mortificatory heroics celebrated in mostly later hagiography have undoubtedly influenced greatly the traditional picture of Irish monasticism. Yet the impression created by the earlier sources, especially the prescriptive or descriptive texts, is that regimes of greater and lesser severity coexisted and that the norm was not exceedingly austere: the guiding principle was moderation. This is largely true even of the 'Tallaght' memoir, which might be expected to reflect the most extreme asceticism.[20] Second, although labour features prominently in many hagiographical anecdotes of the monastic routine, other texts, especially of the prescriptive variety, give little attention to it and some suggest the existence of a purely contemplative elite who did not stoop to labour: for example, the vernacular law-tract *Bretha Nemed Toísech* evidently distinguishes as separate groups within the community those devoted to contemplation and labour.[21] As to the third point, the traditional belief in the thoroughly monastic character of early Irish ecclesiastical life was accompanied by a conviction that the eremitic or anchoritic solitary was the essence of Irish monasticism. One may instance the remarks of Ryan that 'Irish monks, too, regarded the solitary as more perfect than the cenobite' and 'the desert was the goal held out to every monk' and again 'though the body of Irish monasticism was predominantly cenobitical, the spirit which animated it was everywhere anachoretical'.[22] While the anchorite was indeed often highly regarded, being accorded the same status as a bishop,[23] this must be set against the suspicion with which free-lance holy men were sometimes viewed. The *Hibernensis* accords precedence to communal monasticism, which is preferred to anchoritism. Even the 'monastery of Tallaght' depicts rigorous conventual monasticism and deprecates the ascetic excesses of anchorites.[24] Fourthly, the evidence as a whole does not seem to bespeak dramatic changes during this period, with an original ascetic zeal diluted in the eighth century by worldly degeneracy, followed by a drive for ascetic revival in the later eighth and ninth centuries. Rather, the appearance is of a large measure of continuity, with austerity and the temptations of luxury juxtaposed at all times.

The quality of monastic life in the seventh century must be judged not only by Adomnán's idealised picture but also, for example, by the offences which the Penitentials indicate might be committed by monks. In addition to lesser infringements of the rule, there are provisions for monks who defame, assault, or steal from their brethren, who commit homicide, who become so drunk that they vomit the host or are unable to sing the psalms, who are guilty of immodesty when bathing, or of a remarkable range of sins of the flesh involving heterosexual, homosexual and bestial practices, which are treated in unparalleled detail – detail which, indeed, is so graphically illustrative of the sexual offences possible in an early Irish monastery that successive editors of the Old Irish version declined to translate it into English.[25] It would be a mistake, no doubt, to conclude that these reflect the behavioural norm among monks of the seventh century and earlier, just as it would be, conversely, to rely exclusively on Adomnán's more elevating picture. By the same token, the 'monastery of Tallaght' and the vernacular monastic rules show the continuation of rigorous monasticism during the eighth century, when the received wisdom is that worldly degeneracy prevailed. These sources also attest to the persistence beyond the eighth century of true monasticism (*pace* Sharpe[26]) which, moreover, while critical of the more worldly element, continued to come to terms with it,[27] as doubtless it had always done.

Having endeavoured briefly to sketch where I see monasticism, in the ordinary sense of the term, in a revised picture of the church as a whole, I now come to focus on the issue raised at the outset and consideration of which will occupy the remainder of the paper. This is the extended or figurative application of monastic ideas and language. Returning to Sharpe's critique of the received wisdom, one must emphasise that ecclesiastical organisation and authority in early Ireland had not two aspects, but three. Alongside the pastoral or episcopal and the monastic or abbatial stands the temporal or what Sharpe dubbed the 'coarbial'.[28] This epithet he derived from the Irish *comarbae* 'heir, successor', one of the words for a church-ruler which is, as Sharpe put it, 'neutral in its ecclesiastical significance'.[29] Such a church-ruler was not necessarily either in major clerical orders or a monastic abbot in any sense familiar to us. He was, in essence, an ecclesiastical lord. The apparent singularity of early Irish ecclesiastical administration, from a modern perspective, lies not in the prevalence of monastic abbacy over diocesan episcopacy, but in the fact that government of temporalities is sometimes overtly acknowledged as a separate, third strand of ecclesiastical authority.[30] This third element was recognised by scholars before Sharpe, but they tended to stigmatise it as merely a degenerate by-product of a process of change affecting the second element – that is, monastic abbacy. As Sharpe put it, 'where church-historians have pointed to secularisation, usually regarding it as an abuse, it has generally meant the separation of the abbatial and the coarbial functions'.[31]

Yet the emergence of the church ruler who was neither a cleric, nor a true monastic abbot, is not simply the pragmatic outcome of a postulated degeneration of monasticism during and after the eighth century, against which the supposed zealotry of the *Céli Dé* has been portrayed as a reaction. The hypothesis of degenerative 'secularisation' assumes that ecclesiastical lordship was a secondary development of this period.[32] But was it? In fact, it would seem that, already by the early eighth century, the administration of temporalities, the 'coarbial' function, was established as a distinct institutional concept on a par with those of abbot and bishop. The evidence is that of Hiberno-Latin and vernacular law, hagiography and annals, which reflect the seventh and earlier eighth centuries.[33] Vernacular law, indeed, conveniently summarised by Liam Breatnach, ignores the regular abbot in distinguishing three groups among leading churchmen: those in clerical orders (*gráda ecalsa*), headed by the bishop, ecclesiastical scholars (*gráda ecnai*) and *gráda uird ecalsa* 'officers of the church', headed by the *airchinnech* 'principal, head, ruler'.[34] It is not at all clear when the 'coarbial' function as an Irish solution to the problem of ecclesiastical temporalities was devised, but it is misleading to represent it as a late falling away from earlier monastic ideals. It had certainly developed by the seventh century. Sharpe's remarks that 'the distinction of the third function, that of the coarb, depends on the increasing scale of the church's temporalities' and that 'secularization of ecclesiastical office . . . is a phenomenon of the eighth and ninth centuries' are among several unwarranted concessions to the traditional model which perhaps confuse and dilute his message (elsewhere, by contrast, he refers to Armagh's 'coarb' in the seventh century).[35]

The issue is complicated, however, by the fact that there is also an evident blurring of distinctions between 'coarbs', on the one hand, and bishops and especially monastic abbots, on the other. This is treated in detail in my book; it must suffice here to note the substantial overlap of 'coarbial' and abbatial vocabulary. While Latin and vernacular terms for 'abbot' do often refer to a monastic abbacy, equally frequently they are used where the function is, rather, that of 'coarbial' lordship. It may be suggested that this overlap stemmed partly from the fact that the two functions might in practice be separate or performed by one individual. That is to say, many governors of ecclesiastical temporalities also headed truly monastic communities and could be described in the language of either form of authority. Where such governors had no truly monastic role, specifically 'coarbial' terminology was not always adopted, but the vocabulary of abbacy was instead retained.

Moreover, it is well known that *manach*, literally 'monk', often denotes a state of dependence upon the church, its *airchinnech* 'head' or *ap* 'abbot', which vernacular law explicitly likens to being in clientship to a secular lord (*flaith*) and to membership of a kin-group. These *manaig* are depicted in a contractual relationship involving reciprocal legal obligations. I have pointed elsewhere to indications that such ecclesiastical dependants are likely to have been among the chief beneficiaries of a regular pastoral ministry, which they sustained by rendering reciprocal dues such as tithes.[36] In making such payments, *manaig* of this kind also resembled the rent-paying retainers of a secular lord. The church to which they were attached may have been considered the ultimate owner and supplier of the land and livestock with which they farmed. It would seem, too, that some of these *manaig* had wives and that their sons could inherit their property and functions, like their secular counterparts.[37] The frequency with which *manach* is rendered 'church-tenant', 'monastic client', 'ecclesiastical dependant', or the like in scholarly literature since the 1960s stems from wide recognition of some of these points. It is less generally appreciated that *monachus* in Hiberno-Latin canon law and hagiography often bears similar connotations.[38]

That *monachus* and *manach* may designate both a regular monk and a legal, socio-economic and pastoral dependant of the church bespeaks more than terminological imprecision. It bears an implication which has not been sufficiently emphasised. Modern scholars tend to assume that, behind a loose use of the word *manach* in particular, there lay in reality two clearly distinguishable classes of persons, namely, true monks and 'monastic tenants'. In early medieval Ireland, admittedly, a distinction was sometimes drawn, perhaps by advocates of rigorous monasticism. Designations such as 'lay monk', 'lawful/faithful laity' and 'subject' are sometimes used of ecclesiastical dependants identifiable with those elsewhere described simply as *monachus* or *manach*; alternatively, *fírmanaig* 'true monks' could denote monks in the ordinary sense. It is perhaps significant, given the ambiguity of *manach*, that the term is usually eschewed in references to true monks in the 'monastery of Tallaght'.[39] Yet far more of the evidence points to the conclusion that the relationships between monk and abbot, 'monastic tenant' and 'coarb' were often not clearly distinguished, as Thomas Charles-Edwards appreciated.[40] Monastic vocabulary and concepts were thus extended to encompass those who, in terms of the standard monastic vows of obedience, poverty and chastity, were obedient to ecclesiastical rule, but poor only insofar as they were economically dependent on the church and chaste only insofar as they were legitimately – that is monogamously – married. Whether distinctions between such ecclesiastical dependants and monks in the ordinary sense were clear or blurred apparently varied from one church settlement to another and in accordance with the observer's perspective.

The extended application of monastic ideology in early Ireland beyond monks, as ordinarily understood, is further illustrated by the system of penitence. The Penitentials show that a purgative regime of considerable austerity was prescribed for repentant sinners, whether ecclesiastics or laity. Stipulated periods on a diet of bread and water, with abstinence from meat and wine, seem to have been standard, while various sexual offences by lay persons also entailed desisting from intercourse with their spouses.[41] In general, sinners were denied sacramental communion until their penances were complete.[42] Particularly serious sins (especially homicide) incurred penance in exile[43] and those so sentenced were often placed under the supervision of a monastic abbot.[44] The Penitentials apart, other prescriptive texts in both Latin and Irish also treat the abbot as the typical overseer of penitents.[45] It would appear that, although those undergoing prescribed penance were not under vow, there was a connection between the monastic dimension of the early Irish church and its function as a penitentiary.[46]

There was also a remarkable mechanism of the penitential system by which persons other than monks, strictly defined as such, were permanently assimilated to a paramonastic state. In Irish thinking the penitent was seen as a type of martyr. This was an extension of the more widespread early Christian conceit that abandonment of all that is dear to one, in order to undergo the mortifications of monasticism, is a kind of martyrdom. Monasticism was thus cast as 'white martyrdom', to differentiate it from real or 'red' martyrdom. However, Irish texts, notably the so-called Cambrai homily of the seventh century, also distinguish a third type, *glasmartrae*, variously translated as 'green' or 'blue martyrdom'.[47] Some years ago Clare Stancliffe argued that Gougaud was right, as against Ryan, to conclude that *glasmartrae* denotes the discipline of a penitential regime.[48] Furthermore, she interpreted a passage in the *Hibernensis* as evidence that there existed a kind of penitent different from those compelled to purge themselves of specific sins. This was a person who abandoned ordinary secular life and voluntarily sought the status of penitent as a *conuersus* 'convert', living a quasi-monastic life. Stancliffe tentatively suggested that *glasmartrae* refers to this class of person, rather than to the sinner who was allotted a fixed term of penance.[49]

The aptness of her conjecture is borne out by the depiction of penitents in some texts as a distinct and apparently honoured sub-group, sharing in the religious life of the ecclesiastical community. In the seventh-century Book of the Angel, for instance, the three orders who heard the gospel preached on Sunday in the northern church at Armagh comprised virgins, penitents and those serving the church in legitimate matrimony (that is, monogamy).[50] The eighth-century *Bretha Nemed Toísech* refers to the *áes aithrige ascnamo sacarbaic a réir anmcharat* 'penitent folk going to communion at the direction of a confessor'. They are represented as beseeching God's pardon and asking permission to receive the sacrament. Clearly these were not fixed-term penitents debarred in principle from communion.

Bretha Nemed Toísech, indeed, numbers them among the 'good qualifi-
cations ennobling a church'.[51] The tract on the mass in the Stowe missal,
also of the Old Irish period, depicts the *áes aithrige* 'penitent folk',
together with others, including clergy and those in legitimate matrimony,
as recipients of the eucharist.[52]

   The indications are that these penitents had renounced the world for a
quasi-monastic existence, in the manner of a *conuersus* 'convert'. Their
penitential regime was, therefore, intended to be perfective, rather than
purgative of specific sins. *Conuersus* occurs occasionally in the Latin
Penitentials to describe a layman who converts from his evil ways, specifically fornication, bloodshed and bearing arms, but in these instances a
fixed-term penance, followed by a return to lawful married life, is
indicated.[53] Yet fixed-term penance and permanent conversion from the
ways of the world need not be mutually exclusive, but might be stages on
a path to redemption. A reference to the *athláech* – which translates
literally as 'ex-layman' – in the Old Irish legal tract *Míadslechta* sheds light
on the matter:

Atáit trí haithlaích i neclais .i. athláech ara tabair anmcara a thest 7 [ad-chosnaí]
sacarbuic, bís a fíráentaidh eclasa cin comus coise ná láime . . . Athláech ara tabuir
[anmchara] a test, nád nascnai sacarbuic cadacht . . . athláech aile dobeir crích fria
tola, 7 dotáet co cléirchiu iniu, ná tabair anmcara a teist.

There are three ex-laymen in the church .i.e. an ex-layman for whom a confessor
gives testimony and who goes to communion, who is in true ecclesiastical union,
without capacity of foot or hand . . . an ex-layman for whom a confessor gives
testimony, who does not go to communion yet . . . another ex-layman who
abandons his desires and enters the church today, for whom a confessor does not
[yet] give testimony.[54]

Here we seem to have a three-stage progression, described in reverse order.
The first is the point of conversion, at which worldly desires are
renounced. The second is that at which a confessor gives testimony,
although the penitent is still excluded from the sacrament, presumably
because he must first purge himself of sin by penance, his commitment
being verified by the confessor. In the case of the 'ex-layman' who
progresses to the third stage and is admitted to communion, the confessor's testimony doubtless verifies completion of the purgative penance,
after which the 'ex-layman' enters a state which calls to mind the permanent
penitence identified by Stancliffe.[55] The 'ex-layman' is then 'in true
ecclesiastical union, without capacity of foot or hand', a formulation with
specific connotations of monastic fellowship and obedience.[56] The assumption underlying this eighth-century text, then, is that renunciation of
worldly desires necessarily involved a process of purgation before one

could be admitted to full Christian communion. A corollary is that the 'ex-layman' in his former state, unconverted and unpurged, was deemed unfit to receive the eucharist.[57]

Disapproval of the former lifestyle of an 'ex-layman' is outspoken in the Old Irish Penitential Commutations, which provide for penances of reduced duration but increased intensity. With reference to commutations proper to 'ex-laymen' and 'ex-laywomen', this text observes *húare nád mbí coimdich laíech nó laíches duná bé cuit oc marbad duíni* 'for there is hardly a layman or laywoman who has no part in slaying people'.[58] In the monastery of Tallaght, 'a layman' (*laoch*) is said to have lived 'under a confessor's direction' (*fo anmchairdes*) and 'in lawful wedlock' (*hillanamnas dligid*), but was killed by his enemies. As a consequence, 'all the lay folk' (*omnes plebilis*) [*sic*] questioned the worth of his reformed life. One of his sons and his wife were then instructed by his confessor to perform vicarious penance on the deceased's behalf for seven years, only after which were they admitted to communion. The spirit of the dead man then appeared to announce his deliverance from hell.[59] Evidently this *láech* at his death was a penitent but unexpurgated sinner, not as yet admitted to communion. He is, nevertheless, depicted as more 'Christian' than the rest of the laity, who doubted the benefits of such a conversion.

Sharpe demonstrated that vernacular *láech* and its Latin progenitor *laicus*[60] denote not only 'layman', but also 'warrior' and 'brigand' and deduced that it developed the meaning 'pagan'.[61] Kim McCone argued that organised brigandage involved bands of mostly young men, led by the aristocracy, in homicide, plunder and sexual promiscuity. Their flouting of Christian precepts and association with notorious reprobates, including practitioners of non-Christian ritual, rendered many churchmen implacably hostile. Yet brigandage was certainly an integral part of early Irish social fabric, to which attitudes were fundamentally ambivalent. It was tolerated as a means of enforcing legal sanctions on behalf of settled members of the community, especially beyond borders. Its practitioners, in McCone's view, could be expected to abandon brigandage when they came into their landed inheritances.[62] Both Sharpe and, in particular, McCone recognised the fine line separating brigandage from martial activity deemed legitimate.[63] One might expect that line to have been drawn rather subjectively, even by churchmen, depending on the identity of the perpetrators and victims of such activity. This is exemplified by the distinctly mixed press accorded the well-known and colourful career of the mid-ninth-century Munster king, Feidlimid mac Crimthainn. Shrill condemnation of his depredations and pleasure at his death were expressed by the chronicler of Clonmacnoise, which he persecuted. Yet against this, the favourable Armagh annalist offers a respectful obituary,

terming him a 'scribe and anchorite', designations particularly associated
with those contemporary proponents of rigorous monasticism, the *Céli
Dé*. Some have suggested that Feidlimid's raids on the old-established
church-settlements of the midlands combined political expediency with a
genuine puritan zeal.[64]

The verdicts on Feidlimid mac Crimthainn illustrate the potential for
ambivalence in practice about behaviour which was liable to be condemned
in principle as unacceptable in a true Christian. This ties in with that
blurring of distinctions, highlighted by McCone, between legitimate
martial activity and brigandage. McCone also identified brigandage with
the survival of organised paganism, however, and Sharpe in particular felt
that disparaging references to *laicus /láech* stigmatise an altogether distinct,
pagan element in society. He rejected any notion that the laity in general
might be thought by some to be beyond the Christian pale, for 'under
such circumstances, a pastoral mission to the laity would have been
virtually impossible'.[65]

This seems to me to beg the question on both counts. On the first, I
argue in detail in my book that *laicus /láech* does not bear the meaning
'pagan', that brigandage was treated simply as gravely sinful behaviour and
that the association with pagan survival is not a strong one. Limitations of
space preclude outlining the argument here, but one point is that redemption from a lifestyle of martial prowess and concupiscence required not a
profession of Christian faith and baptism, but repentance. The Old Irish
Apgitir Chrábaid 'Alphabet of Piety' provides a suggestive example which
must suffice: *maic bethad* 'sons of life' are characterised by *credbud inda tol*
'erosion of the desires', whereas *pecthaig* 'sinners' are distinguished by the
fact *nád fácbat a tola* 'that they do not abandon their desires' and are *cen
aithrigi* 'without repentance'; the *cetharda fo-[f]era fiannas do duiniu* 'four
(evils) that brigandage causes to a person' are then listed.[66] The association
of ideas suggests brigandage is viewed as deeply sinful rather than pagan.
On the second count, I have maintained elsewhere[67] that there is no reason
to assume a regular ministry to the laity as a whole. Admittedly, piety is
occasionally attributed to the general populace and the principle that all
benefit from the pastoral mission of the church is sometimes stated.[68]
There must be a suspicion that this is somewhat aspirational. It must surely
be measured against intimations that, notwithstanding the willingness of
some churchmen to tolerate polygamy,[69] this and the plunder and bloodshed practised by many of the laity were more commonly thought to constitute a persistently sinful existence which, while not exactly pagan, was
not truly Christian either. A distinction was evidently felt to exist between
the unredeemed *laicus* of this kind and the person who had elected to
become what was occasionally termed a *laicus fidelis* 'faithful layman'.[70]

Sharpe did not consider the possibility that early medieval Irish society at large was beset by a chronic tension. On the one hand, the Christian church was the only coherent, respectable, endowed religious system. On the other, the extent of devotion among the laity seems to have been limited and there were intrinsic features of society which carried anti-Christian resonances for many churchmen. The legal text on the three sub-types of 'ex-layman' implies that repentance, abandonment of worldly desires and purging of guilt were prerequisites for admission to the truly Christian elite. This source, together with others I have cited, suggest that one might then live in a state of quasi-monastic permanent penitence. Alternatively, the repentant sinner, after completion of a fixed penance, might dwell in lawful matrimony as a devout layman. Those serving the church in lawful matrimony are mentioned alongside the permanent penitents, as we have seen, and were also bound by penitential restrictions. The Old Irish Penitential expands on regulations derived from its Hiberno-Latin exemplars to the effect that *áes lánamnais dligthig* 'lawfully wedded folk' must normally abstain from meat and marital intercourse for forty days before receiving communion.[71]

While penitence has long been recognised as characteristic of the early Irish church, the process by which it contributed to the practice of austerity therein has not been properly appreciated. Penitential purgation offered the sinful laity renunciation of the world as the gateway to true Christian living, in a quasi-monasticism or paramonasticism of one kind or another, involving an ongoing regime of austerity. The phenomenon parallels and overlaps with the extension of explicitly monastic vocabulary to encompass adherents of the church who do not seem to conform to conventional definitions of 'monk'. The corollary is that some churchmen envisaged an elective Christian elite from which the rest of the population was distinguished in principle. That monasticism was everything in the early Irish church is, indeed, a long-standing misapprehension. It has been imagined that it was all-pervading at official level, but this involves a failure to appreciate the true position of bishops and clergy on the one hand and ecclesiastical lords and administrators on the other. The wider influence of monastic austerity in the early Irish church was, it appears, rather different from that which has been supposed. It lay in the tendency to conceive of the lifestyle appropriate to the flock or people – or, at any rate, that segment regarded as truly Christian – in terms of the vocabulary and concepts of monasticism and the practice of penitential austerity.

NOTES

1 E.W. Watson in *E.H.R.*, xlviii (1933), p. 687.

2 See *I.H.S.*, xxviii (1993), pp 442–3.

3 Tomás Ó Fiaich, 'The church of Armagh under lay control' in *Seanchas Ardmhacha*, v (1969), pp 75–127; Donnchadh Ó Corráin, 'Dál Cais: church and dynasty' in *Ériu*, xxiv (1973), pp 52–63; idem, 'Nationality and kingship in pre-Norman Ireland' in *Hist. Studies*, xi (Belfast, 1978), pp 1–35: 14–19; idem, 'The early Irish churches: some aspects of organisation' in Ó Corráin (ed.), *Irish antiquity: essays and studies presented to Professor M. J. O'Kelly* (Cork, 1981), pp 327–41; Charles Doherty, 'Exchange and trade in early medieval Ireland' in *R.S.A.I. Jn.*, cx (1980), pp 67–89; idem, 'Hagiography as a source for Irish economic history' in *Peritia*, i (1982), pp 300–28; idem ,'The monastic town in medieval Ireland' in H. B. Clarke and Anngret Simms (ed.), *The comparative history of urban origins in non-Roman Europe* (Oxford, 1985), pp 45–75; Donnchadh Ó Corráin, Liam Breatnach and Aidan Breen, 'The laws of the Irish' in *Peritia*, iii (1984), pp 382–438.

4 Richard Sharpe, 'Some problems concerning the organization of the church in early medieval Ireland' in *Peritia*, iii (1984), pp 230–70; see also idem, 'Churches and communities in early medieval Ireland: towards a pastoral model' in John Blair and Richard Sharpe (ed.), *Pastoral care before the parish* (Leicester, 1992), pp 81–109; Abigail Firey, 'Cross-examining the witness: recent research in Celtic monastic history' in *Monastic Studies*, xiv (1983), pp 31–49: 35.

5 P. J. Corish,'The pastoral mission in the early Irish church' in *Léachtaí Cholm Cille*, ii (1971), pp 14–25; idem, *Ir. Catholicism*, i, 3 (Dublin, 1972), especially pp 32–40, 44–9; see Sharpe, 'Some problems', p. 252.

6 Colmán Etchingham, 'The implications of *paruchia*' in *Ériu*, xliv (1993), pp 139–62: 139–40; idem, 'Bishops in the early Irish church: a reassessment' in *Studia Hib.*, xxviii (1994), pp 35–62: 36–8; idem, 'Early medieval Irish history' in Kim McCone and Katharine Simms (ed.), *Progress in medieval Irish studies* (Maynooth, 1996), pp 123–53: 138–40, 151–2; Sharpe, 'Pastoral model', p. 100.

7 J. H. Todd, *St Patrick, apostle of Ireland* (Dublin, 1864), pp 1–189, especially 87–149.

8 K. Hughes, *The church in early Irish society* (London, 1966), pp 57–90.

9 Ibid., pp 134–72.

10 Ibid., pp 103–33.

11 Ibid., pp 173–226.

12 Ibid., pp 253–74.

13 Sharpe, 'Some problems', pp 247–51.

14 Ibid., p. 239.

15 Ibid., pp 261–70.

16 Ibid., p. 263.

17 Colmán Etchingham, 'The early Irish church: some observations on pastoral care and dues' in *Ériu*, xlii (1991), pp 99–118; idem, '*Paruchia*'; idem, 'Bishops'.

18 Famously by D. A. Binchy, 'Patrick and his biographers, ancient and modern' in *Studia Hib.*, ii (1962), pp 7–173.

19 A. O. and M. O. Anderson (ed.), *Adomnan's Life of Columba* (London, 1961; revised ed. M. O. Anderson, Oxford, 1991).

20 E. J. Gwynn and W. J. Purton, 'The monastery of Tallaght' in *R.I.A. Proc.*, xxix, section C (1911), pp 116–79: 141 § 34, 146–7 § 52, 151–2 § 63, 155–6 § 68, 158–60 §§ 76, 77, 161 § 80.

21 Liam Breatnach, 'The first third of *Bretha Nemed Toísech*' in *Ériu*, xl (1989), p. 8 § 3; see, on hermits and anchorites, Hermann Wasserschleben, *Die irische Kanonensammlung* (Leipzig, 1885), pp 147–9 § 3.

22 Ryan, *Monasticism*, pp 260, 408.
23 E.g. Ludwig Bieler (ed.), *The Irish Penitentials* (Dublin, 1963), pp 162 § 29, 174 § 11; Binchy, '*Bretha Crólige*' in *Ériu*, xii (1934–8), pp 1–77: 6–7 § 4, 10–13 § 12.
24 Wasserschleben, *Kanonensammlung*, pp 144 § 10, 148–9 § 3, 152 §§ 15, 16; Gwynn and Purton, 'Monastery of Tallaght', pp 159–60 § 77.
25 Bieler, *Penitentials*, passim; E. J. Gwynn (ed.) 'An Irish Penitential', *Ériu*, vii (1914), pp 121–95 (retranslated by Binchy in Bieler, *Penitentials*, pp 258–77).
26 'Pastoral model', p. 102.
27 e.g. Gwynn and Purton, 'Monastery of Tallaght', pp 128 § 4, 148 § 57, 159–60 § 77.
28 'Some problems', pp 263–70.
29 Ibid., p. 264; others are Latin *princeps* 'principal, head, ruler' (vernacular *airchinnech*) and *heres* (= *comarbae*).
30 Ibid., p. 266.
31 Ibid., p. 265.
32 See e.g. Gougaud, *Christianity*, pp 390–8; Hughes, *Ch. in early Ir. soc.*, pp 134–42, 157–72.
33 Evidence discussed fully in my book is noticed briefly in Etchingham, 'Bishops', pp 40–1, 44; idem, '*Paruchia*', pp 143–8; Hughes recognised this concept of temporalities existed in the seventh century (*Ch. in early Ir. soc.*, pp 138–42, 158–60), but relied on the much richer annalistic record of the eighth and ninth centuries for her thesis that 'secularisation' only then became full-blown; arguments from the silence of the annals are potentially deceptive, however: for a comparable case, see Etchingham, *Viking raids on Irish church settlements in the ninth century: a reconsideration of the annals* (Maynooth, 1996).
34 Breatnach (ed.), *Uraicecht na Ríar* (Dublin, 1987), pp 84–7.
35 'Some problems', pp 264, 266.
36 Etchingham, 'Pastoral care', passim.
37 See my book and, briefly 'Pastoral care', pp 104 ff, and 'Bishops', p. 40; Thomas Charles-Edwards, 'The church and settlement' in Próinséas Ní Chatháin and Michael Richter (ed.), *Irland und Europa: die Kirche im Frühmittelalter* (Stuttgart, 1984), pp 167–75; Hughes, *Ch. in early Ir. soc.*, pp 136–41.
38 It was appreciated by Hughes, *Ch. in early Ir. soc.*, pp 139–41.
39 Etchingham, 'Pastoral care', pp 105, 111; idem, '*Paruchia*', p. 145; Binchy (ed.), *Corpus Iuris Hibernici* (6 vols., Dublin, 1978), p. 918.12–17; Gwynn, 'An Irish Penitential', pp 150–1 § 15 (= Binchy in Bieler, *Penitentials*, p. 261); Whitley Stokes (ed.), *Félire Óengusso Céli Dé* (2nd ed. London, 1905), p. 4.11–12 (= *Bk Leinster*, iii, p. 621.19046).
40 'Church and settlement', p. 171.
41 Bieler, *Penitentials*, passim.
42 Ibid., pp 76 § 6; 78 §§ 14, 15; 80 § 21; 82 § 27; 86 § 35; 92 § 53; 98 § 2; 100 §§ 6, 11; 102–6 §§ 13, 15, 18, 19, 20, 25; 114 § 2; 118 §§ 14, 15; 122 § 12; 126 § 3; 192 § 22; 226 § 6.2; Gwynn, 'An Irish Penitential', pp 140 § 4 (= Binchy in Bieler, *Penitentials*, p. 263); Anderson and Anderson, *Adomnán*, pp 422–3; Wasserschleben, *Kanonensammlung*, p. 200 § 12; Gwynn and Purton, 'Monastery of Tallaght', pp 148 § 56, 153–4 § 66; Binchy, 'The Old Irish table of penitential commutations' in *Ériu*, xix (1962), pp 47–72: 56, 58 § 6 (= Binchy in Bieler, *Penitentials*, p. 278 § 6).
43 Bieler, *Penitentials*, pp 78 §§ 12, 13; 82 § 24; 98 §§ 1, 2; 102 § 13; 104 § 20; 114 §§ 7, 17; 118–20 §§ 5, 6; 228 § 3.4.
44 Ibid., pp 80–2 § 23; 112 § 12; 114 § 5; 214 § 4.1.
45 E.g. Wasserschleben, *Kanonensammlung*, pp 30 § 3; 198–9 § 8; J.G. O'Keeffe, 'The Rule of Patrick' in *Ériu*, i (1904), pp 216–24: § 4; Binchy, *Corpus*, pp 2.2–24, 523.5–8.

46   Clare Stancliffe, 'Red, white and blue martyrdom' in Dorothy Whitelock, Rosamund McKitterick and David Dumville (ed.), *Ireland in early medieval Europe* (Cambridge, 1982), pp 21–46: 41–2.

47   Gougaud, 'Les conceptions du martyre chez les Irlandais' in *Revue Bénédictine*, xxiv (1907), pp 360–73.

48   Stancliffe, 'Martyrdom'; at p. 23 she follows Stokes and John Strachan (ed.), *Thesaurus Palaeohibernicus*, ii (Cambridge, 1903; reprinted Dublin, 1975, 1987), p. 247.39, where they leave untranslated *céste sáithu* 'who suffer tribulations'.

49   Stancliffe, 'Martyrdom', pp 42–4; Wasserschleben, *Kanonensammlung*, p. 183 § 12.

50   Bieler (ed.), *The Patrician texts in the Book of Armagh* (Dublin, 1979), p. 186 § 15.

51   Breatnach, '*Bretha Nemed Toísech*', pp 8–9 § 3, 10–11 § 6.

52   Stokes and Strachan, *Thesaurus*, ii, pp 252–5: 255 § 18; compare the Middle Irish *Fís Adamnáin*, Ernst Windisch (ed.), 'Die Vision des Adamnán' in *Irische Texte*, i (Leipzig, 1880), pp 165–96: 185 § 23.

53   Bieler, *Penitentials*, pp 86 § 35; 116 § 22; 220 § 4.

54   Binchy, *Corpus*, p. 589.7–13 (length-marks and translation supplied); see Fergus Kelly, *A guide to early Irish law* (Dublin, 1988), p. 267; Breatnach, 'Varia II' in *Ériu*, xlv (1994), p. 197.

55   See *teist for anmannuib ala n-aile* 'testimony for the souls of others' in Vernam Hull (ed.), '*Apgitir Chrábaid*: the Alphabet of Piety' in *Celtica*, viii (1968), pp 44–89: 68–9 § 18.

56   Compare *óentu na mbráithre* 'community of the brethren' and *eclais óentad* 'communal church' (Gwynn, 'An Irish Penitential', pp 154 § 6; 156 § 10; 158 § 20; 168 § 14; 172 § 3) and *co comét cos ocus lám* 'with restraint of feet and hands', used of a monastic regime, in Kuno Meyer (ed.), '*Incipit Regula Mucuta Raithni*' in *Archiv für celtische Lexicographie*, iii (1905–7), pp 312–21: p. 320 § 99 (= 'Mac Eclaise', 'The Rule of St Carthage' in *I.E.R.*, xxvii (1910), pp 495–517: 508–9 § 13).

57   For *aithrige* 'penitence' characterising an 'ex-layman', see the *epscop aithrige* 'penitent bishop' (Binchy, *Corpus*, p. 588.39), beside the *grandevus laicus* 'elderly layman', who enters the church and advances to episcopal rank, (Wasserschleben, *Kanonensammlung*, p. 8 § 11).

58   Binchy, 'Penitential commutations', p. 60 § 8 (length-marks added) (= Binchy in Bieler, *Penitentials*, p. 279 § 8).

59   Gwynn and Purton, 'Monastery of Tallaght', pp 163–4 § 86.

60   Damian Mc Manus, 'A chronology of the Latin loan-words in Early Irish' in *Ériu*, xxxiv (1983), p. 50.

61   Sharpe, 'Hiberno-Latin *laicus*, Irish *láech* and the Devil's men' in *Ériu*, xxx (1979), pp 75–92.

62   McCone, '*Aided Cheltchair maic Uthechair*: hounds, heroes and hospitallers in early Irish myth and story' in *Ériu*, xxxv (1984), pp 1–30; idem, 'Dán agus Talann' in *Léachtaí Cholm Cille*, xvi (1986), pp 9–53: 42–53; idem, 'Werewolves, cyclopes *díberga* and *fianna*: juvenile delinquency in early Ireland' in *Cambridge Medieval Celtic Studies*, xii (1986), pp 1–22; idem, *Pagan past and christian present in early Irish literature* (Maynooth, 1990), pp 203–32.

63   E.g. Sharpe, '*Laicus, láech*', p. 87; McCone, '*Aided Cheltchair*', pp 14–17; idem, 'Werewolves', pp 6–12.

64   See F. J. Byrne, *Irish kings and high-kings* (London, 1973), pp 211–13, 220–9; Hughes, *Ch. in early Ir. soc.*, pp 182, 192–3, 200, 212; Ó Corráin, *Ireland before the Normans* (Dublin, 1972), pp 97–9; Peter O'Dwyer, *Céli Dé: spiritual reform in Ireland, 750–900* (2nd ed. , Dublin, 1981), pp 40–3, 47–9.

65   Sharpe, 'Hiberno-Latin *laicus*', p. 78; McCone, *Pagan past*, pp 226–7; 'Dán agus talann', p. 48.

66 Hull, '*Apgitir Chrábaid*', pp 72–3 §§ 22–5.
67 'Pastoral care', passim.
68 Ibid., pp 104, 116–18.
69 See Kelly, *Early Irish law*, pp 70–1.
70 Bieler, *Penitentials*, pp 190–2 § 18; 214 § 2.4 (compare p. 230 § 6.3: *cohabitatorem vel cohabitatricem fidem habentem* 'a male or female spouse having the faith'); W.W. Heist (ed.), *Vitae Sanctorum Hiberniae* (Brussels, 1965), p. 219 § 31 (compare p. 206 § 26); Cogitosus mentions *populi fideles masculini generis . . . et faeminarum fidelium congregatio* 'faithful people of the masculine kind . . . and the congregation of faithful women' (*Acta SS* February 1, p. 141 § 37); see references to the legitimately married (e.g. above, note 52 and *Cáin Adamnáin*, pp 24–5 § 34).
71 Gwynn, 'An Irish Penitential', pp 150–3 § 36; compare Ó Corráin, Breatnach and Breen, 'Laws of the Irish', pp 404–5; Etchingham, 'Pastoral care', p. 105.

3 Concepts of generosity in early modern England

Felicity Heal

'The nature and condition of man,' wrote Sir Thomas Elyot in *The book named the governor*, 'wherein he is less than God Almighty, and excelling notwithstanding all other creatures on earth, is called humanity; which is a general name to those virtues in whom seemeth to be a mutual concord and love in the nature of man. And although there be many of the said virtues, yet be there three principal by whom humanity is chiefly compact: benevolence, beneficence, and liberality, which maketh up the said principal virtue called benignity or gentleness.' Benevolence was that quality of love or charity that men possessed towards one another: put into specific action the sentiment transmuted into beneficence and became, as Elyot puts it 'the deed (vulgarly named a good turn) [that] may be called a benefit'. When some substantive entity, be it money or other material good, became involved in the benefit, then liberality was the proper language to describe the behaviour of the giver. The three interconnected virtues were clearly hierarchialised. While benevolence was wholly disinterested, representing the nearest that man might attain to the qualities of God, who is 'all goodness, all charity, all love', liberality, involving the transmission of material rewards, 'may transgress the bonds of virtue, either in excessive rewards, or expenses, or else employing treasure, promotion or other substance on persons unworthy, or on things inconvenient, and of small importance'.[1]

Elyot's summary of the virtue of generosity was intellectually fashionable, in that it employed classical sources with true Renaissance zeal, but its essential content would have represented no surprise to the early Tudor nobility and gentry whom he intended as his principal audience. The words of scripture, interpreted by the Fathers, especially Chrysostom and Ambrose, enjoined charity to all men. Benevolence should be shown with no immediate thought of reward, though God had promised that the generous would be recompensed both in this world – 'cast thy bread upon the waters' – and the next – 'lay up treasure in heaven'. On liberality those perdurable guides to European ethical behaviour, Aristotle's *Nichomachean ethics* and Cicero's *De amicitiis* and *De officiis,* underpinned most late medieval writing about the cardinal and social virtues. Liberality should be the judicious use of wealth for the benefit of others, with the principle of the mean always in mind.[2] Thus Peter Idley, basing his fifteenth-century advice on a thirteenth-century tract of Albertanus of Brescia, told his son:

> Off thy mete and drynke be free algate;
> Daparte with such as thou haste
> With good wille erly and late,

but . . .

> In mesure to spende, thus y meane,
> Eche man after his astate;

Liberality, like benevolence, might reap a divine reward: however, it was more explicitly linked to the expectation of reciprocity from men. Hugh Rhodes, in the fifteenth-century *Book of nurture*, advised his householders to:

> Retayne a stranger after his
> estate and degree;
> Another tyme may happen he
> may doe as much for thee.

We will find that throughout the sixteenth and early seventeenth centuries these sentiments provided the intellectual bedrock for thinking upon giving to others.[3]

In this paper I wish to pursue both the development of these basic concepts and the relationship between cultural practice and its articulation. More explicitly, I wish to ask what ideas of giving are conveyed in social action, and how those actions are judged by contemporaries. What daily practices did men associate with Elyot's category headings of benevolence, beneficence and liberality? I would suggest that charity and almsgiving, neighbourly support, gift-giving, and hospitality were the most obvious, but that there were also the political virtues of bounty and patronage, socially specific, in that they were the prerogative of the crown, or at least of those who by virtue of birth and wealth were 'generous'. Almsgiving and charity, offered by individuals to needy neighbours and strangers, seem to approximate most closely to a disinterested pattern of giving. This shades almost imperceptibly into a second category that is difficult to label with precision, but which involves mutuality, friendship, and collective support, exchange articulated by the language of giving and reciprocity. Thirdly, there is the field of patronage and largesse, which in this century of the growing power of the state means above all the exercise of royal bounty. 'For a King not to be bountiful were a fault', said the earl of Salisbury in 1610. This royal bounty, like the lesser versions exercised by nobles and by gentlemen in their localities, was a form of restricted exchange, in which honour, as well as material reward, was the outcome of asymmetrical generosity.[4]

Alms, a recent debate in *Past and Present* has reminded us, are 'gifts to God', that is to say we do not expect our charitable endeavours to be rewarded with any immediate or direct form of reciprocation. Indeed some anthropologists argue that the essential feature of such gifts is that they must be consumed in such a way that they cannot be recycled to the material advantage of the individuals who have given. They may benefit others – the needy, the church – but the only advantage they bestow on the donor is the indirect one of divine approbation. The bodily care of the poor, said Chrysostom, was analogous to the bodily care of Christ, and should therefore be a logical emanation of faith, virtuous in and for itself. But scripture promised that divine reward would follow approbation which should encourage those too weak to act so disinterestedly to 'think of the prizes' of giving instead. His summary of those prizes was repeated in sermons down the ages:

[the prayers] of the poor will go up to God Himself, and will make thy present life sweet, and put away thy sins, and thou shalt gain glory from God and honour from men.[5]

In the late middle ages the general belief that the prayers of the poor would intercede for the benefactor acquired specificity as the doctrine of purgatory assumed a central place in Catholic belief. The noble householder who established almsmen under his roof, was committed to ensuring their prayers for his soul as was the townsman who paid lavishly for funeral doles. Care for the salvation that the prayers of the poor could aid by no means excluded other arguments for generosity, but they gave a clear focus to giving, and sharpened that sense of the putting away of sins of which Chrysostom had spoken. 'It delivereth a man from death', said Fitzherbert in his *Book of husbandry*, 'it joineth a man with angels and severeth him from the devil'.[6]

As the Protestant challenge to the theology of works began (very slowly) to seep into English consciousness in the later sixteenth century even this particular representation of reciprocity in almsgiving had to be abandoned. Giving no longer contributed to salvation: it offered the opportunity to display the fruits of faith. Yet the rich Protestant literature on charity continued to acknowledge the importance of some notion of exchange if men were to be persuaded to act generously. Robert Crowley assured his readers that 'though the beggars be wicked thou shalt have thy reward'. William Vaughan, writing in 1600, urged men to accept that by giving alms they were giving their substance to Christ 'who in the day of judgment will redeliver the same unto you with a glorious interest'.[7] Such long-term investment strategy needed to be supplemented, the moralists recognised, by a more direct appeal to men's material hopes. God, out of his own unknowable goodness, would also reward beneficence in this world. 'Forsake not strangers,' urged Edward Topsell in 1607, 'for the Lord loveth them and goeth with them'. They could therefore provide 'uncovenanted' blessings, and not necessarily only in the world to come for, asked Robert Allen, 'who knoweth how great blessing God will grant at their holy suit and supplication?'[8] The topos of bread cast upon the waters, and of the earthly blessings that were sealed to those who gave without constraint to the poor, was appropriated with unreserved enthusiasm by godly divines and became part of the assurance to the saints. To question God's care in this matter, said Richard Allestree, was to risk blasphemy, for did not the scriptures promise that 'the liberal soul shall be made fat'? The powerful chorus of pleas to be generous, especially in the late sixteenth century is indicative of the scale of the problem of poverty. Its emphasis on reward also shows how difficult it was to construct a convincingly altruistic theory, and how close even zealous Calvinists often had to tread to the forbidden territory of merit-works divinely rewarded.[9]

Appeal to Chrysostom's theory of reputation, and to the earthly honour arising from almsdeeds, would seem more culturally convincing than resort to abstract images of divine reciprocity. The theatres of generosity – the household, the church, the guild to take obvious examples – could offer the opportunity to affirm status through largesse. The pre-Reformation funeral, in which one important element of extravagance was the dole offered to all comers, was a process which both secured appropriate prayers and enhanced the reputation of the deceased and his family. It was not unusual to find bequests like that of Thomas Brete of Balcombe in Sussex from 1554, specifying funeral generosity 'for mine honour'.[10] When there was a social expectation of largesse, loss of face would ensue if proper generosity to the poor was not displayed. One of the amended clauses of the 1536 poor law, for example, secured the rights of nobles and gentlemen to continue to give alms at their doors, and another ensured that ordinary parishioners could give local alms as had been customary. In both cases reputation was at stake. When Protestant reformers began to advocate communal forms of giving via a poor box, as a means both of displacing the theology of works and securing proper support for the needy, they met with little enthusiasm. Martin Bucer, who had operated such a system in Strasbourg, praised its rationality, as did Peter Martyr in his *Loci communes*: their English counterparts were less vocal. They saw that growing centralisation and compulsion in the distribution of poor relief would too easily liberate men from the social imperative to be seen to be generous.

Robert Allen, quoting Martyr, approved public relief but insisted that it could 'not take away and suppress mens private benevolence, as they shall see good upon their own godly and private considerations'.[11]

Reformers wrestled with the problem of the role of the individual in giving to the poor. On the one hand they feared that care of the poor could simply be the excuse for lavish housekeeping and insisted that giving must eschew ostentation and vainglory which exchanges the 'vain blast of mens breath for those substantial and eternal joys of heaven'. On the other, it was of the essence of the proper practice of almsgiving that individuals should be engaged, undertaking the corporal works of mercy in person, having the honour of being almoner 'under the most high and Mightie Monarch of heaven and earth'.[12] In this way men could show their own thankfulness for the gifts that had been bestowed upon them. Moreover a precise categorisation of need could be established, and giving could proceed seasonably and with due care. The practice of charity in early modern England, as we are well aware, seems to have been more concerned with the differentiation between types of the needy than with any universal openness. A marked growth in the objective problem of impoverishment, combined with a perceived threat to social order, legitimated discrimination between the deserving and undeserving, between the neighbour and stranger. Arguments that giving should mainly be confined to cases of known need, and that the sturdy beggar should be rejected, seem logical enough in these circumstances. What is less often noted is that contemporaries seem partially aware of the pacifying effects of asymmetrical giving. The deserving poor, whose needs could be judged, were almost by definition the local indigent. Their obligation was to feel endlessly grateful to those who protected them – 'the poor mans mouth commendeth' the rich – and to acknowledge debt. That debt, Henry Crosse suggested, is binding upon the poor 'for a good mind doth always commemorate a good turn'.[13] Those not wholly impotent might be drawn more directly into the web of reciprocity to keep them in the paths of righteousness. The preacher of William Lord Russell's funeral sermon in 1614 described vividly how he sometimes gave the worthy poor money intended to be a gift, but called a loan 'in policie to make them continue their labour and to be good-husbands'. This binding and acknowledgment in theory created the environment in which the threat posed by the dispossessed could be neutralised as well as the possessioners morally legitimised. Masterless men, the outsiders of Elizabethan England, could not readily be bound into this nexus.[14]

Everyday generosity in English communities must have involved casual alms to the truly indigent, but was more closely bound up with the doing of good turns to those neighbours and kin who could in the fullness of time return the favour. These 'gifts to man' would normally be differentiated by anthropologists from 'pure' almsgiving precisely because they were actually, or potentially, more symmetrical and embodied a system of exchange which was fully understood to bring practical, as well as symbolic, good, to donor and recipient. In practice, the distinction between alms and mutual aid is often hard to draw, as Judith Bennett has shown in her work on rural conviviality. There is much practical and proverbial advice on being good to neighbours – through entertainment, giving when asked and returning favours – that is clearly in the latter category. But economic difficulties of a general or particular kind could easily blur the distinction between the need for neighbourliness and for charity.[15] Help-ales – those events where ale was brewed for the benefit of one individual – are a tricky case in point: they were directed at members of the community, and their success in persuading men to pay more than the commercial cost of a drinking was presumably dependent on a sense of neighbourly identity. A Tamworth balladeer who held an ale was 'among all my neighbours . . . well beloved'. They therefore did him a good turn, yet it is not clear whether they envisaged a reciprocation, or felt him bound beyond the debt of gratitude. Bishop Piers, describing the practice of ales to Archbishop Laud, said that the help-ales were to assist honest men 'decayed in [their] estate'. The same observation might be made about the bride-ales which were one of the most common occasions for giving in English rural society: they were above all a test of the generosity of the bidden guests. The aldermen of Kendal, seeking to discipline the population in the 1570s, complained that these were not just the opportunity for neighbourly mirth, but 'most chiefly for the taking of money'.[16] The issue of immediate reciprocation seems far less significant here than a broad understanding of the nature of good social behaviour. The point is well illustrated by a form of bride-ale that involved asymmetrical relationships. The Norfolk gentry were in the late sixteenth century in the habit of asking one another for money when a servant married. The pattern was made explicit in a later letter from Martin Stuteville to Framlingham Gawdy, seeking to fund-raise for local church repairs instead. 'It hath been a manner amongst us (still used) to make marriage dinners and to invite our friends in favour of our well deserving servants'. There is neighbourly reciprocity, but between the gentry the giving process is essentially charitable.[17]

It seems likely that contemporaries were less concerned with the precise form of reciprocity which would be the response to their generosity, than in the network of relationships that giving defined. The broad notion of charity as mutual care and amity, which was expressed through religious ritual and charitable giving, was ideally also displayed in communal feasting and exchange. Such activities defined both the included and the excluded. Just as the help-ale, or bride-ale, identified neighbourliness through prestations, so individuals were cast out of the circle of identity by a denial of exchange. The most dramatic example of denial occurs in witchcraft cases, in which refusal of a gift is at the basis of so many accusations. Charges of witchcraft, like positive gestures of neighbourliness, often exist on a continuum between almsgiving and mutual help. It was common to denounce a cursing neighbour to whom you had denied alms of milk, bread or wool.[18] But the accusation of Mistress Walter, who supposedly bewitched a neighbour's sheep after being denied access to a sheep-shearing dinner, suggests friendship turned sour. And when Bennet Lane accused Agnes Heard of *maleficium* in 1579, her testimony revealed a pattern of gifts exchanged and denied, of mutuality subverted rather than of almsgiving.[19] In more positive contexts, gifts and tokens were a major means by which individuals might be enmeshed in a web of identity and obligation. The process of courtship was strewn with such offerings – usually by the man to the woman – creating the need to respond, if not directly to reciprocate like for like, and also generating ambiguities about intention and commitment that kept many an ecclesiastical court busy. This often began, as Diana O'Hara has shown, with small gestures designed to keep contact alive, symbolising friendship, and then escalated to more significant material gifts – coin and rings, which were thought to have some binding efficacy.[20]

In a more directly material way, the lines between gift-giving and generosity on the one hand, and loan and commercial transaction on the other, were often blurred in early modern society by the language of credit. Money loaned, but with no clear interest or date of repayment, could be defined as a gift reflecting the credit both of the donor and the recipient. Loans, in this sense, were seen as expressions of charitable beneficence, for, to quote Tusser,

> . . . lending to neighbour, in time of his need,
> wins love of thy neighbour and credit does breed.[21]

The exchange of benefits could be idealised as the fructifying sentiment in local relationships, binding neighbours to one another and constructing the bonds of an 'artificial' kinship. 'Gifts of one friend and neighbour to another,' says Robert Allen, '[show] they are kindly affected the one to the other and . . . [strive] to overcome the other with kindness and benefits: according to the common saying which goeth concerning such: there is no love left between them. . . .'. In this competition there were no winners and losers, provided that all had striven to display generosity. The most specific evidence for this type of behaviour comes from William Harrison's descriptions of the entertainment that prosperous householders gave at weddings and other rites of passage, and from John Stow's famous image of

Londoners competing to welcome passers-by at their doors at midsummer. It is worth emphasising, however, that writers usually comment on the atypicality of such displays. These are moments of 'potlatch' giving, clearly demarcated from everyday social exchange and, in Stow's view at least, part of a vanishing world of customary largesse.[22]

Traditionalists lamented the loss of mutuality in late sixteenth-century society. Yet among the intellectual and political elite there was a growing concern with the proper exchange of benefits. The conduct of political and social relationships now seemed to demand a moral self-awareness that had previously been regarded as the prerogative of only a small number of the professionally learned. This became the Senecan moment. The moralist's *De beneficiis* had been known to a number of the early humanists: it informs, for example, the Elyot comments from which this paper started. Only as it became available in translation in the 1570s, however, did it emerge as the principal guide to the ethics of giving. Seneca demanded of his readers a thoroughly reflective understanding of benefits given and received. He also spoke with particular force to a culture analogous to his own Roman one, in which many believed that customary norms of beneficence had been subverted by competitiveness, envy and ambition.[23]

Beneficence, as defined by the classical moralists, was essentially a 'public' virtue, associated with distributive justice. Men might show generosity to one another within the 'private' bonds of friendship, and if the object was, for example, to alleviate the suffering of a friend, then privacy should characterise the transaction. But since proper giving and grateful receiving were intended to fructify social exchange, it was axiomatic that others should normally know of these processes and be able to test the true intent of both parties by their gestures. It is interesting that, for Seneca at least, the art of receiving benefits was a greater test of ethical quality than that of giving: in many ways *De beneficiis* is a text about the vice of ingratitude rather than the virtue of generosity. The giver has the initial freedom of spirit to set in motion the circulation of benefits: the recipient is doubly bound to 'testify by speech' to his gratitude, and to reciprocate 'by external gifts as the comprobation and satisfaction of . . . expectations'.[24] As Marcel Mauss observed in his classic study of gift-exchange, in these circumstances, 'face is lost forever if a worthy exchange is not made'.[25]

There are many ways in which we might seek to test the importance of Seneca in late Tudor society. The ethical tracts of the period drew heavily upon him, often as an unacknowledged source – Robinson, Vaughan, Crosse and Cooper all inserted large blocks of *De beneficiis* into their writings. Advices from fathers to sons, a genre of growing popularity, turned to a reading of Seneca for the proper calculus of giving: 'keep one great man thy friend', William Cecil advised his son, 'but trouble him not for trifles. Compliment him often with many yet small gifts and of little charge'.[26] Nowhere, however, is his importance more obvious than in the theatre. Shakespeare found the Senecan understanding of gift-giving rich in possibility. Both *Timon of Athens* and *The merchant of Venice* can be read as representations of Seneca in action. Timon offers a very direct warning of the kind that reverberates through both classical and sixteenth-century sources that liberality and prodigality must not be confused. The latter actually breeds ingratitude through its failure to understand the proper nature of giving: Timon, for example, refuses to receive any recompense from the friend he has delivered from captivity because:

> I gave it freely ever, and theres none
> Can truly say he gives if he receives [Act 1: sc. 2: ll. 9–10]

And ingratitude is what Timon reaps in his prodigal descent, for, as his faithful steward Flavius remarks: 'the bounty that makes gods, does still mar men' [Act 4: sc.2: l.41]. But Timon has a greatness of spirit which ameliorates the vice of prodigality, a form of openness that is not reciprocated by any of his beneficiaries except Flavius. It may be that, as Wallace has suggested, we should read Timon as a critique of Senecan ethics, because the inability of the Athenians to transcend ingratitude (the worst of vices) shows that generosity and good turns were 'not a glue that could be trusted to keep society stuck together'.[27] Yet the more optimistic tone of *The merchant of Venice* might lead us to the opposite conclusion. Both Bassanio and Antonio have to hazard much for and with their gifts – Portia's casket, you may recall, is labelled:

> Who chooseth me must give and hazard all he hath [Act 2: sc. 9: l. 20]

and Antonio has to learn a willingness to depend on others as well as giving. But the economy of the gift, of material generosity and of its spiritual reward is here confidently contrasted to the destructive force of Shylock's usurious contract.[28]

To turn to Shakespeare is in some measure to look at the perdurable issues of gratitude and ingratitude, generosity and avarice that make Seneca's investigations of benefits pertinent in any culture. There are two more specific contemporary anxieties which *De beneficiis* addressed that help to explain its popularity in late Elizabethan and early Stuart England. The first was the problem of separating liberality from prodigality, an old Aristotelian conundrum, in which the perspective of the observer played the dominant role in establishing legitimate behaviour. This was no new dilemma, but it acquired a distinctive intensity in a period when old social patterns were believed to be under threat. I have written elsewhere of the much-proclaimed death of hospitality, a death most loudly lamented in the decades around the turn of the sixteenth century. There were superabundant contemporary explanations for hospitality's demise: the growth of London, the rise in prices, excessive expenditure on clothing and houses and that staple pair of vices, avarice and pride. Unifying the particular analyses was a sense that the obligatory largesse of the noble and gentleman, the prestations that they were compelled in honour to make to all comers, no longer had binding cultural force. The picture of a gentleman 'with his hands open, to signify that liberality was the honour of a gentleman and that to give was always heroical' was an image feared to be in terminal decline.[29] Paradoxically, though, one of the chief enemies of true hospitality was believed to be prodigality which 'kills many with surfeits, whiles as many starve at their gates with famine', according to William Cornwallis. 'Prodigality considers neither time, nor person, nor humanity; but humour will and vainglory', said the duchess of Newcastle a generation later. Aristotle had taught that temperance was as significant in giving as in other forms of moral conduct, and Seneca added to this detailed advice on the exactness of the virtue of liberality. Liberality is the virtue of gratefully bestowing gifts upon others and 'consisteth not in that which is done or given, but in the mind of him that either giveth or doeth the pleasure'.[30] Hence it exercised a restraint upon lavishness in hospitality while guiding its true adherents in proper openness to the needy, the deserving and true friends and kin.

Such sentiments seem to have had a powerful attraction at a time when competitive prodigality was a feature of court behaviour, and when a growing elite had to adapt itself to environments such as London. Seneca's view of gift-giving offered incorporative generosity without the economic strain of old-style largesse, and justified prudential calculation as a moral good. It must just be said that, of course, these confident definitions, which became the commonplace coin of Jacobean ethical debate, proved disconcertingly flexible as a set of ethical standards. As Robert Burton commented in *The anatomy of melancholy*, liberality is 'many times mistaken' so that 'under the name of Bounty and Hospitality, is shrouded Riot and Prodigality'. Classical writers and their heirs were well aware of the rhetorical technique of reascription, designating virtue as vice, and contemporaries used this with zest when debating proper social behaviour. No wonder that when Hobbes finally took an axe to the classicised pronouncements of his countrymen he reserved particular scorn for the relativism of these ideas: we find 'scarce two men agreeing, what is to be called good, and what evil, what Liberality, what Prodigality, what Valour, what Temerity'.[31]

The second concern was more directly associated with politics, the networks of patronage that sustained political exchange and the proper behaviour of the monarchy. Public generosity was in no sense the prerogative of the crown, yet it was around the monarch that competition for patronage was focused and anxieties about bounty and reward were most sharply displayed. All the adult monarchs from Henry VIII to Charles I were intensely aware of the equation between largesse and loyalty, of the need to be able to display a generosity in giving to subjects that would be reciprocated above all in service. James I, who predictably said more about this than other monarchs, told Prince Henry in *Basilikon Doron* that he must 'use true liberality in rewarding the good and bestowing frankly for your honor and weal'.[32] Offices were the principal coin of this cycle of exchange, though there were a range of other concessions within the royal gift, most notably monopolies and patents, the source of bitter controversy at the end of Elizabeth's reign, and honours, which played much the same role under James. These substantive and substantial rewards had to be offered and received in a spirit of gift-giving and 'spontaneous' generosity that preserved for all parties the appearance of freedom and the good reputation. These qualities are displayed in minor key in the regular exchanges of new year gifts at the court. These exchanges were routinised, a fact reflected in the careful record-keeping of the wardrobe on which we can base a systematic analysis, and were clearly prestations, in that both sides – monarch and courtiers – were constrained to give. The crown normally gave plate, standing cups and the like, carefully graded by status and sometimes by favour – the earls of Leicester and Essex did well in this process, and there was a marvellous occasion in 1542 when Anne of Cleves only received some glass pots and flagons in return for her crimson cloth. On their side the courtiers had to offer gifts of appropriate value; bishops and others less intimately involved with the court could often resolve this simply by offering gold, but were expected to calculate the precise gestural effect of their offering. Only favourites, for example, seem to have risked offering personal images or emblematic texts to Elizabeth. Most interesting for our purposes, however, is the context of these exchanges rather than their value: they were, at least in the Elizabethan period, given in a collective court ceremony, in which the effects of generosity could presumably be weighed by all parties.[33]

The essential expectations were that reward would circulate in an appropriate manner in return for the assurance of service, love and loyalty, usually supported by some material token of adherence. The dedications of books are one obvious source to look to for the expression of these identities: Natalie Davies, in a foretaste of her larger work on gifts and exchange, has looked at books as public gifts. Authors apparently give freely the best of their modest substance, 'no common present' as Erasmus says, to display their good minds towards the noble or royal recipient.[34]

Thus Thomas Paynell, dedicating a series of scriptural extracts to Princess Mary in 1550, commented: 'esteem the content of my book and gift, that is the word of God . . . esteem my faithful and true heart unto your grace, and not my simple and slender gift'.[35] But this prestation, like any other, is intended to bind to a response, sometimes made explicit as in Davies's lovely example of the commentary on the privileges of Lyon, sent to the governor begging him to protect them as the representative of the king 'who has made the gift of these privileges to us'. This last example comes near to making the reciprocal element in the anticipated exchange too overt. The crucial patterns in most patron-client exchanges of the period as I have said were that the appearance of freedom had to be maintained for the patron, and that while deference and token gestures of loyalty flowed upwards, it was expected that substantial benefits would flow in the opposite direction.[36]

This brings us to the heart of the anxieties expressed or hinted at by the 'Senecan' generation. Princes, and indeed other great men, had to exercise particular discretion in their giving: they must of course reward the virtuous, avoiding 'buffoons and flatterers' and give seasonably to the worthy. But they also had to avoid, in Cornwallis's words, leaving suitors 'empty or gorged'. Men are 'won with what they feel and delighted with what they hear, so are the chief tools of this trade [princely control] Liberality and Rhetoric, these must serve one another's tune, amplifying gifts and the actions performed for their commodities with Eloquence'.[37] Under the aging queen it was an absence of generosity that most troubled the commentators: even the rhetoric of giving seemed to have frozen in the cold years of the 1590s. Under James both the language and substance of benefits appeared appropriate – largesse indeed flowed – but it transpired often did so in return for cash, or bribes, rather than merely for those gestures and affirmations of future service that had been the common coin of earlier exchanges. Sir John Holles, in a famous passage writing to the duke of Lennox, commented 'these latter years have given me experience that money prevails beyond all obligations of merit or nature', great men 'choose neither kindred nor virtue . . . but profit only, who having their turn served will repay such ladders with the like coin'.[38] Corruption, like generosity, was in the eye of the beholder, and both Elizabeth and James were in practice struggling with a system where the inadequate resources at the command of the monarch could not hope to satisfy the demands of all those who, in Senecan terms, defined themselves as worthy of receiving benefits. When Buckingham effectively inverted the pyramid of royal bounty and transformed the gestural politics of exchange into a cash nexus he unleashed a political reaction that contributed significantly to the breakdown of relationships between king and subjects in the 1620s.[39]

So were English conventions of generosity in crisis in the decades surrounding the end of the sixteenth century? Evidence, of a kind, can be found to support the claim that they were. Not only was there a perceived disjunction between expectations of public beneficence and the reality of politics, but much contemporary angst about the decay of hospitality which had some basis in the changing habits of the elite and the growth of the London season. Moreover, the fears for the decline of charity and of individual beneficence at all levels of the society were grounded in an awareness of the growing problem of poverty, and of the complexity, but ultimate inadequacy, of the state's response. A consequence of these changes was an increasing cynicism about the possibility of applying of classical and Christian ethical precepts to daily behaviour. Here the vogue for Tacitean readings of history, for Machiavelli and for the art of statecraft ironically combined with the gloomier reaches of Calvinist thought to produce pessimistic attitudes that were profoundly at odds with those of the earlier sixteenth century.[40] The representation of crisis has its attractions, if only because it appears to synthesise the inherently fissiparous tendencies of social and political change. In the end, however, it must be resisted, precisely because of the social and cultural diversity of the patterns of behaviour that can be comprehended under Sir Thomas Elyot's definitions from which we began. Generosity comprehended gifts to God and gifts to men, charity to the poor and the exchanges of friendship, the status theatre of hospitality by the great, and the forms of giving that supposedly bound together client and patron, king and subjects. Its study raises many important issues, most notably the degree to which general exchange in early modern English culture was gift based. Adapting Seneca: 'amongst the many and manifold errors of such as do rashly and inconsiderately lead their lives, there is nothing for the most part . . . more hurtful than that'[41] we do not understand the giving and receiving of benefits.

NOTES

1 Sir Thomas Elyot, *The book named the governor*, ed. S. E. Lehmberg (London, 1962), pp 120–1.
2 St John Chrysostom, *Homilies on St John*, 2 vols (Library of the Christian Fathers, Oxford, 1848), ii, pp 517–9, 678–83; N. de Romestin (ed.), *Some of the principal works of St Ambrose* (*The Nicene and post-Nicene Fathers*, vol. x , New York, 1976), pp 59 ff; Susan Brigden, 'Religion and social obligation in early sixteenth-century London', *Past and Present*, ciii (1984), pp 67–112; Fritz Caspari, *Humanism and the social order in Tudor England* (Chicago, 1954); W. L. Ustick, 'Changing ideals of aristocratic character in seventeenth-century England', *Modern Philology*, xxx (1932),

pp 147–62; Quentin Skinner, *Reason and rhetoric in the philosophy of Thomas Hobbes* (Cambridge, 1996), pp 10–11, 149–65.

3　C. D'Evelyn (ed.), *Peter Idley's instructions to his son* (London, 1935), p. 84. Hugh Rhodes, 'The boke of nurture' in *The babees book*, ed. F. J. Furnivall (*E.E.T.S.*, xxxii, London, 1868), p.102. For a later expression of similar views see Thomas Tusser, *Five hundred pointes of good husbandrie*, ed. W. Payne and S. J. Heritage (London, 1878), pp 19, 67, and advice literature for the gentry, such as Richard Brathwaite, *The English gentleman* (London, 1630).

4　An important theoretical statement of this approach is Pierre Bourdieu, *The outline of a theory of practice* (Cambridge, 1977), pp 4–6, 13–15. I am grateful to Ilana Krausman Ben-Amos for discussions on reciprocity and exchange in early modern England. She has been kind enough to show me an unpublished paper: 'Gifts and favours: informal support in early modern England'. Salisbury is quoted in L. L. Peck, '"For a King not to be bountiful were a fault": perspectives on court patronage in early Stuart England' in *Journal of British Studies*, xxv (1986), p. 36.

5　Maria Moisa, 'Conviviality and charity in early modern England' in *Past and Present*, cliv (1997), pp 231–4; C. A. Gregory, 'Gifts to men and gifts to God: gift-exchange and capital accumulation in contemporary Papua', *Man*, xv (1980), pp 626–53; Chrysostom, *St John*, ii, pp 678, 681.

6　Felicity Heal, *Hospitality in early modern England* (Oxford, 1990), pp 16–20, 68–70. Anthony Fitzherbert, *The book of husbandry* (London, 1523), f. 86.

7　J. W. Cowper (ed.), *The select works of Robert Crowley* (*E.E.T.S.*, extra ser. xv, London, 1872), p.14; William Vaughan, *The golden grove* (London, 1600), sig. I i.

8　Edward Topsell, *The house-holder or perfect man* (London, 1610), p. 172; Robert Allen, *A treatise of Christian benevolence* (London, 1600), p. 88.

9　Richard Allestree, 'The whole duty of man' in *Works* (Oxford, 1684), p. 139.

10　On funeral practice see Clare Gittings, *Death, burial and the individual in early modern England* (London, 1984), pp 24–38; David Cressy, *Birth, marriage and death: ritual, religion and the life-cycle in Tudor and Stuart England* (Oxford, 1997), pp 443–55; W. J. Godfrey (ed.), *Sussex wills* (*Sussex Record Society* xli, 1935), p. 66.

11　27 Hen.VIII, c.25. G.R.Elton, *Reform and renewal: Thomas Cromwell and the common weal* (Cambridge, 1973), pp 122–5; Martin Bucer, *A treatise how . . . christian menss almose ought to be distributed* (?, 1557), p. 11; Peter Martyr Vermigli, *The common places*, Eng. trans. (London, 1583), p.520; Allen, *Christian benevolence*, p. 37.

12　Allestree, 'Whole duty', p. 139; John Downame, *The plea of the poore or a treatise of beneficence* (London, 1616), p. 232.

13　On generosity to the poor both as a form of legitimation of possession and a guarantor of social control see Bourdieu, *Outline*, pp 194–5; Henry Crosse, *Vertues commonwealth* (London, 1602), sig. K.

14　William Walker, *A funeral sermon for William Lord Russell* (London, 1614), p. 48. See the argument of Thomas Harman that a proper understanding of the tricks of vagrants would encourage housekeepers to give to the local poor 'for the amendment of the commonwealth', *A caveat or warening for common cursitors*, ed. E.Viles and F. J. Furnivall (*E.E.T.S.*, extra ser. ix, London, 1869), p.21. A.L.Beier, *Masterless men: the vagrancy problem in England, 1560–1640* (London, 1985).

15　There is a rich literature on the significance of reciprocated giving. For a good collection of recent work see A. E. Komter, *The gift: an interdisciplinary perspective* (Amsterdam, 1996). The classic statements are Marcel Mauss, *The gift: the form and reason for exchange in archaic societies* (London, 1950); Marshall Sahlins, *Stone age economics* (London, 1978); Judith Bennett, 'Conviviality and charity in medieval and early modern England', *Past and Present*, cxxxiiii (1992), pp 19–41; see also her reply to Moisa in *Past and Present*, cliiii (1997), pp 235–42.

16 *Calendar of State Papers Domestic, 1633–4*, pp 275–6; R.S. Ferguson (ed.), *A boke off recorde . . . within the town of Kirkbiekendall* (*Cumberland and Westmorland Antiquarian and Archaeological Society*, extra ser. vii, 1892), p. 86.

17 On bride-ales see Heal, *Hospitality*, pp 369–71; *Historical Manuscripts Commission Gawdy MSS*, pp 27, 32, 35, 80, 116.

18 K. V. Thomas, *Religion and the decline of magic* (London, 1971), pp 660–80; Alan Macfarlane, *Witchcraft in Tudor and early Stuart England* (London, 1970). For a recent analysis of a similar kind see Robin Briggs, *Witches and neighbours: the social and cultural context of European witchcraft* (London, 1996), esp. pp 144–6.

19 Heal, *Hospitality*, pp 357–8; Diane Purkiss, *The witch in history* (London, 1996), pp 94–7.

20 Many of these exchanges fit neatly with David Cheal's definition of a gift economy, comprising 'a system of redundant transactions within a moral economy, which makes possible the extended reproduction of social relations': Cheal, *The gift economy* (London, 1988), p.19. Diana O'Hara, 'The language of tokens and the making of marriage' in *Rural History*, iii (1992), pp 1–40.

21 Tusser, *Good husbandrie*, p.22. On credit and community see C. Muldrew, 'Interpreting the market: the ethics of credit and community relations in early modern England' in *Social History*, xviii (1993), pp 163–83.

22 Allen, *Christian benevolence*, p. 13; William Harrison, *The description of England*, ed. F. J. Furnivall, 2 vols (New Shakespeare Soc., 6th ser. 1, 5, London, 1908), i, p. 150; John Stow, *Survey of London*, ed. C. L. Kingsford, 2 vols (Oxford, 1908), i, p. 101.

23 The first partial translation of *De beneficiis* was made in 1569 by Nicholas Haward, *The line of liberalitie* (London, 1569). This was followed by Arthur Golding's full translation of 1578, *The woorke of the excellent philosopher Lucius Anneus Seneca concerning benefyting* (London, 1578) intriguingly subtitled 'the doing, receiving and requiting of good turns', and then by Thomas Lodge's very popular translation in *The workes of Lucius Anneus Seneca both morrall and natural* (London, 1614). L. L. Peck, 'Benefits, brokers and beneficiaries: the culture of exchange in seventeenth-century England' in B. Y. Kunze and D. D. Brautigan (eds), *Court, country and culture* (Rochester, N.Y., 1992), pp 111–13; J. H. M. Salmon, 'Stoicism and Roman example: Seneca and Tacitus in Jacobean England' in *Journal of the History of Ideas*, i (1989), pp 199–25.

24 The quotation is from Richard Robinson, *The vineyarde of vertue* (London, 1579), p. 30, one of a number of contemporary moral tracts dependent above all on the Senecan model.

25 Mauss, *The gift*, p. 41.

26 Apart from Robinson, other examples are Vaughan, *Golden grove;* Crosse, *Vertues commonwealth;* and Thomas Cooper, *The art of giving* (London, 1615). William Cecil's 'Precepts' to his son Robert, printed in Francis Peck (ed.), *Desiderata curiosa* (London, 1732), p. 66.

27 L.A.Montrose, 'Gifts and reasons: the contexts of Peele's *Araygnment of Paris*' in *Journal of Literary History*, xlvii (1980), pp 433–61. J. M. Wallace, '*Timon of Athens* and the three Graces: Shakespeare's Senecan study' in *Modern Philology*, lxxxiii (1986), p. 362.

28 Lewis Hyde, *The gift: imagination and the erotic life of property* (New York, 1979); R.A.Sharp, 'Gift exchange and the economies of spirit in *Merchant of Venice*' in *Modern Philology*, lxxxiii (1986), pp 260–85.

29 Heal, *Hospitality*, pp 91–140. Allestree 'Whole duty', p.139. Crosse, *Vertues commonwealth*, sig. K.

30 Sir William Cornwallis, *Discourses upon Seneca the tragedian* (London, 1601), sig. D4. Margaret Cavendish, duchess of Newcastle, *This world's olio* (2nd ed. London, 1671), p. 74. Lodge trans. p. 7.

31 Robert Burton, *The anatomy of melancholy*, ed. T. C. Faulkner et al. (Oxford, 1989), pp 97–8; Skinner, *Reason and rhetoric*, pp 172–80; Thomas Hobbes, *The elements of law natural and political*, ed. Ferdinand Tonnies (London, 1969), p. 23.

32 James I, 'Basilikon doron' in *The political works of James I*, ed. C. H. McIlwain (New York, 1965), p. 52.

33 Wallace MacCaffrey, 'Place and patronage in Elizabethan politics' in S. T. Bindoff et al. (ed.), *Elizabethan government and society* (London, 1961), pp 95–126; Peck, 'Court patronage', pp 33–9. The gifts of the Elizabethan period are printed in J. G. Nicholls, *The progresses of Queen Elizabeth*, 3 vols (London, 1823). *Letters and papers foreign and domestic of the reign of Henry VIII*, xvi, 1489.

34 N. Z. Davies, 'Beyond the market: books as gifts in sixteenth-century France' in *Transactions of the Royal Historical Society*, 5th ser. xxxiii (1983), pp 69–88.

35 Thomas Paynell, *The piththy and moost notable sayinges of al scripture* (London, 1550), dedication.

36 Davies, 'Books as gifts', p. 79. S.N. Eisenstadt and Louis Roniger, 'Patron-client relations as a model of structuring social exchange', *Comparative Studies in Society and History*, xxii (1980), pp 42–77.

37 Sir William Cornwallis, *Essays* (London, 1600), sig. Rvi.

38 *H.M.C. Portland MSS* (London, 1923), ix, p.140.

39 Peck, 'Court patronage', pp 51–9.

40 Peter Burke, 'Tacitism' in J. A. Dorey (ed.) , *Tacitus* (London, 1969), pp 149–71. Margo Todd, 'Seneca and the Protestant mind: the influence of Stoicism on Puritan ethics', *Archiv fur Reformationsgeschichte*, lxxiv (1983), pp 182–99.

41 Lodge trans. p. 1.

4 *Dives* and Lazarus in sixteenth-century Ireland

Colm Lennon

As a sixteenth-century embodiment of *dives* or the rich man in the gospel parable, Patrick Sarsfield, who was mayor of Dublin in 1551, deviated from type. Unlike his scriptural counterpart, Sarsfield kept 'so great porte' in his mayoral year, according to a near-contemporary chronicler, 'as his hospitalitie to his fame and renowne reasteth as yet in fresh memorie'. Refusing to count the cost of his 'three barnes well stored and thwackt with corne' or 'twentie tonnes of Claret wine, white wine, Sacke, Maulmesey and Muscadel' consumed by visitors, this generous householder (who stood comparison with Chaucer's franklin) 'was fully resolved that his worshippe and reputation coulde not be more distayned than by currish entertainment of any guest'. When upbraided by friends for his 'lavishing expenses', he chided them: 'Who so commeth to my table, and hath no neede of my meate, I knowe he commeth for the goodwill he beareth me, and therefore I am beholding to thanke him for his good companie: if he resorte for neede, how may I bestow my goodes better then in releeving the poore?'[1]

There was no shortage of such objects of pity in Dublin or elsewhere in sixteenth-century Ireland. Perhaps the best-known description of victims of austerity is Spenser's characterisation of the survivors of warfare and famine in Munster in the 1580s:

They were brought to such wretchedness as that any stony heart would have rued the same. Out of every corner of the woods and glens they came creeping forth upon their hands, for their legs would not bear them. They looked anatomies of death; they spake like ghosts crying out of their graves. They did eat of the dead carrions, . . . and if they found a plot of watercresses or shamrocks there they flocked as to a feast for the time. . .[2]

Within the counterpointing of the two types, *dives* and lazarus, lies the area of investigation of this paper. At the interface between the affluence of the urban patricians and county aristocracy and the dire neediness of the sick and poor was manifested the range of charitable responses and actions, aimed at bridging the 'deep pit' of the parable between rich and poor. Contemporary writers differed in their views of the philanthropy of the age. Richard Stanihurst, a native of Dublin, extolled the beneficence of his fellow-citizens thus:

What should I here speake of their charitable almoyse, dayly and hourely extended to the needie? The poore prisoners of the Newgate and the Castle, with three or foure hospitalles, are chiefly, if not onely, releeved by the citizens. Furthermore there are so many other extraordinarie beggers, that dayly swarme there, so charitably succoured as that they make the whole citie in effect theyr hospitall.[3]

Edmund Campion, an English guest at Stanihurst's home, contrasted the altruism of the past with the niggardliness of his time: 'With such plenty were our fathers blessed, that cheerfully gave of their true winnings to needfull purposes, whereas our time that gaineth excessively, and whineth at every farthing to be spent on the poore, is yet oppressed with scarcity and beggery'.[4] The two commentators – friends and co-working scholars – had different purposes in these separate passages: Stanihurst was vaunting the merits of his native place, while Campion's criticism was general, reflecting another concern of humanist scholarship, the reform of the ills of the common weal. Both writers were in agreement, however, about the scale of mendicancy and neediness.

   This paper explores the variety of charitable responses and institutions which were employed to cope with the problems of deprivation, poverty and illness in urban Ireland in the 'long' sixteenth century, down to the 1640s. In the context of recent historiography of charity and poor relief in the early modern period, I would like to sketch in the background of welfare in late medieval Ireland, taking account of increasing municipal involvement in hospitals and other institutions, and the development of a more discriminating attitude towards almsgiving and begging in the pre-Reformation period. Within the framework of state legislation for the alleviation of poverty and the regulation of vagrancy during the century from 1542 to 1641 were set the various municipal initiatives, institutional, administrative and disciplinary, directed at the poor. The meshing of older monastic types of hospitality and alms-giving with new agencies ensured that there were substantial continuities in the period of mid-Tudor religious and socio-political reform. More innovative forms of social control of the able-bodied poor were attempted in the later part of the period but some of these fitted less well into the milieu of the older boroughs in Ireland. As in other European countries, competition between public and private charitable ventures was evident, and also in the Irish urban context tensions between religious reformers and traditionalists may have retarded institutional advances. It may be shown that the construction of an

integrated poor law regime in early modern Ireland around the nucleus of
urban schemes and policies was delayed principally because of the obsessive
corporatism of the boroughs which was protective of confraternal models
of charity, including religious guilds, chantries and colleges.

The problem of widespread poverty and disease was not of course
unique to Ireland. All over Europe authorities and individuals were
striving to cope as the medieval institutions of welfare for the deprived
came under severe pressure from increased numbers of poor and sick
people.[5] Against the backdrop of new concepts of charity and poor relief,
stimulated by the intense debates among humanists and reformers, state
and municipal control was being asserted over older, mostly religious-run
hospitals through legislation and official regulation.[6] Moves to centralise
and professionalise welfare services were afoot even before the reformers
propounded their principles. In fact both Protestant and Counter-
Reformation theorists were at one in their broad approach to the question
of poverty, while differing over details.[7] Most were committed to
discriminating between the deserving and the undeserving poor, as
reflected in the laws and institutions which were established throughout
the continent and England.[8] Similar strategies were adopted in relation to
vagrancy in most European countries. The role of piety in informing new
systems may have been subsidiary to secular concerns in many communities, although a strand of religious-based welfare, based on confraternities
and new religious orders, was retained.[9] As has been shown, the real competition in terms of poor relief systems in the early modern period was not
that between Catholic and Protestant welfare but the contention between
more centralised welfare regimes and private, decentralised forms of charity.[10]

Although there were agencies for the relief of the poor and diseased in
rural Ireland in the sixteenth century, the provision of welfare centred
largely on the towns.[11] Even the larger boroughs such as Dublin, Drogheda,
Waterford, Kilkenny, Cork, Limerick and Galway were comparatively
small in terms of population, and the city councils constantly complained
of corporate poverty. Importunacy to the crown for the alleviation of civic
indebtedness and for the expansion of privileges dominated borough-state
relations down to the seventeenth century.[12] While the cities, especially
Dublin, aspired to the grandeur and sophistication of their counterpart-
boroughs in England, straitened resources and very tight budgets had a
constricting effect on civic pageantry and hospitality. Few of the large
urban centres had extensive vicinities from which municipal rents could
be drawn to support charitable or other ventures.[13] The income of some
of the private corporations including monastic houses exceeded that of the
municipal treasuries. Yet in all of the cities mentioned and in towns of
lesser rank there were coteries of wealthy merchant families, often

intermarried with the gentry of the surrounding countryside, whose wealth outshone that of the municipal corporations of which they were members. The benevolence of the state towards the boroughs benefited these patrician families through the enhancement of trading opportunities and the enlargement of corporate privileges. As well as contributing to the running of the boroughs in office-holding and management roles, they also played a significant part in the provision of charity, both in their public and private capacities.[14]

A multiplicity of charitable institutions in late medieval Ireland – hospitals, almshouses, fraternities, chantries and hospices – reflected the responses of individuals and communities to manifestations of austerity. Gwynn and Hadcock list over 200 hospitals and hospices among the medieval religious houses of Ireland,[15] and there are just over 100 leper hospitals included in Gerard Lee's annotated list for the four Irish provinces.[16] While the majority of these may have been small and short-lived, a significant number continued to function down to the time of the Reformation, mostly under ecclesiastical control. Some monasteries had maintained hospitable functions in the narrower sense during the later middle ages: in Waterford, for example, the Benedictine order was associated with the founding of the hospital of St John the Evangelist.[17]

Notable among the orders specifically dedicated to the running of hospitals as their primary purpose were the Fratres Cruciferi (or Crutched Friars), a hospitaller community (which included sisters as well as brothers) who ran at least a dozen hospitals for the poor and sick in the late middle ages in Leinster and Munster. The most important of these were at Ardee, Drogheda, Dundalk, Dublin and Limerick.[18] St John's hospital outside the New Gate at Dublin was the largest in the country, providing 155 beds for sick and poor people at the time of its greatest flourishing in the fourteenth century.[19] Perhaps closely associated with the Cruciferi was the hospitaller order of St Thomas of Acre which had substantial foundations at Carrick-on-Suir and Kilkenny.[20] The great military hospitaller order St John of Jerusalem with its Irish headquarters at Kilmainham did not have an outstanding role in the dispensation of poor relief, concentrating mainly on the reception and maintenance of pensioners who had served the order, the community or the state.[21]

The Knights had some involvement with the sick through the appointment of a leper-house of St Laurence at Chapelizod, County Dublin. The incidence of leprosaria or lazar-houses throughout the country in the late middle ages attests the virulence of the disease of leprosy and its associated infections in Ireland. Maudlin or Magdalene houses, deriving their dedication from St Mary Magdalene, believed to be the sister of St Lazarus, stood outside the walls of many Irish towns in the late middle ages, as did houses dedicated to St Stephen and St Laurence, the martyrs.[22] While it has been speculated that there may have been a dedicated order called the Hospitallers of St Lazarus of Jerusalem at work in medieval Ireland, most of the lazar-houses in medieval Ireland seem to have been run by independently functioning communities or corporations, headed by a prior or guardian and comprising men and women, among whom were incorporated the lepers.[23] The greatest of the leprosaria were those of St Mary Magdalene at Kilkenny, St Stephen at Cork, Waterford and Dublin, and St Laurence at Limerick and Drogheda.[24] By the sixteenth century the term 'hospital' may have been applied generically to these institutions, and the records testify to the continuing communal concern for the seclusion of lepers in specially appointed premises, at a remove from towns.

While the role of the religious orders in sustaining the system of charitable relief may have been in decline in the early sixteenth century, there is evidence for increased lay involvement in the relief of distress. In the larger towns the ruling magistracies had staked a claim to participation in the running of the hospitals well before the Reformation. The lazar-houses of St Stephen in Dublin and Waterford, for example, were headed by *custodes* or guardians who were nominated by the mayor and corporations of those boroughs.[25] The funding of St Stephen's, Dublin, had been integrated into the round of civic hospitality through the custom of the mayor and aldermen 'keeping their drinking' on St Stephen's day and distributing alms collected from the citizens to the lepers.[26] In Drogheda, the mayor, sheriffs, aldermen and commons had the right to appoint and remove the warden and the infirm in the poor-hospitals of St Mary de Urso and St Laurence the martyr, both in the charge of the Fratres Cruciferi. In 1502 a dispute between the corporation and the archbishop of Armagh about jurisdiction over these institutions was referred to Rome.[27] Reciprocating privileges between orders proferring hospitality and welfare and the borough authorities consolidated the pre-Reformation connection: in Limerick the prior of the hospital of St Mary, St Edward and the Holy Ghost had first voice in the election of a new mayor.[28]

Much charitable beneficence of laity and clergy in the late medieval period was tied very closely to the obitual system of guilds and chantries. These foundations provided for the spiritual well-being of the benefactors and their families, not just by the appointment of clergy to say mass in perpetuity for their souls' salvation but also by the facilitating of good works towards the needy. The part played by confraternities in the provision of assistance for the poor and sick is not as well documented as it is elsewhere but there is little doubt that these religious guilds, founded primarily for the spiritual welfare of pious benefactors and their families, had social and charitable functions. St Sythe's guild, in St Michan's parish,

Dublin, maintained a number of charity houses down to the seventeenth century.[29] The well-endowed associations under the patronage of St Anne in both Dublin and Drogheda had between them over a dozen chaplains whose duties included not only celebrating mass on the anniversaries of deceased members, but also the carrying out of the wishes of testators in respect of good works for the health of their souls.[30] Chantries, established by pious individuals rather than corporations, could also incorporate charitable social functions in chaplains' duties. The dean of Waterford, John Collyn, 'motus misericordia et pietate', provided in 1478 for a twelve-bedded God's house for men to be founded as part of his chantry of St Saviour, beside the cathedral of Holy Trinity.[31] In 1496 Dean John Aleyn of St Patrick's cathedral, Dublin, provided for an almshouse in St Kevin's Street for twelve almsmen, each to receive £5 per annum.[32]

The charity of individual wealthy people, whether clerics or lay, and whether conveyed through the establishment of a chantry with provision for an almshouse or by endowment of existing institutions, is a feature of the period.[33] The great benefactors of institutions in the twelfth and thirteenth centuries such as Ailred the Palmer, Elena Mocton and Simon Minor had their counterparts at the turn of the fifteenth century in the forms of Deans Collyn and Allen, Thomas Browne who bequeathed property to maintain the refection of the poor of St John's, Newgate, and Mayor Stephen Lynch who founded a hospital in High Street, Galway, for the relief of the poor in 1505.[34] Motivated by 'misericordia et pietas', they believed that they were promoting the health of their souls and the souls of the faithful departed. While all the bequests and grants were predicated upon belief in purgatory and the efficacy of good works, the terms were not undiscriminating. Dean Collyn imposed a strict moral code upon his 'goddesmen': those who committed violence, fornication, spouse-breach and theft were ruled out as recipients of his charity in Waterford.[35] In the case of a hospital beside All Hallows in Dublin, which was revived in 1473, the beneficiaries of lodgings and victuals were to be 'the necessitous, whether poor or pilgrims, who had travelled to the shrine of St James in Compostella'.[36] The almsmen of Dean Allen were most discriminatingly chosen of all: not just poor, they should be 'faithful Catholics of good repute, honest conversation and of the English nation, especially of the nation of the Aleyns, Barretts, Beggs, Hills, Dillons and Rodiers, living in the dioceses of Meath and Dublin'.[37]

The framework of state provision for the poor and needy was constructed by the acts of the Irish parliament in 1542, 1635 and 1640.[38] This legislation replicated English poor law measures, without specific reference to Irish conditions. The basic distinction was drawn between the deserving and undeserving poor, the former being allowed to beg and to receive indoor and outdoor relief, and the latter being liable to physical punishment such as whipping and forced return to their birthplaces. The later two acts attempted to provide for statutory parish relief and oversight, and the confinement of vagrants in county houses of correction. Within this framework, powers were devolved upon local justices and officials to act in the matter of the impotent and sturdy poor. The weakness of the state's administrative machinery for most of the period made the governors dependent on the initiatives of local authorities such as town corporations for the implementation of the laws. From the Elizabethan period onwards, the provincial presidents and provost marshals were instrumental in controlling masterless people but proposals such as that of Rowland White in 1569 for the construction of twelve hospitals for the poor throughout the country came to nothing.[39] One small instance of state initiative is the revamping of the almshouse associated with St Patrick's cathedral, founded by Dean Allen. When St Patrick's was suppressed as a cathedral in 1547 and reduced in status to a parish church, the letters patent for the surrender by the dean and chapter stipulated that a hospital should be erected in the precincts for twelve poor men 'who have done the state some service, and who by hurt or wounds have been incapacitated from labour'.[40] The maintenance cost of five marks yearly per person was to be borne by the crown, but this burden reverted to the church authorities when the cathedral was restored under Queen Mary in 1554.[41]

The role of the municipalities in mediating the thrust of state legislation in respect of poverty and neediness was crucial. As has been established, the corporations had asserted a role in relation to hospitals in the late medieval period, and after 1540 they attempted to fill the vacuum left in terms of poor relief by the dissolution of the monasteries. The response of civic corporations was multi-faceted, encompassing forms of indoor and outdoor relief, inspection, and control, but the salient feature was institutional continuity and adaptation, often with state support. Existing hospitals were transferred to municipal charge or absorbed more firmly within their jurisdiction. In Dublin, St John's, Newgate, passed from the control of the Crutched Friars to that of the corporation by 1561, through the agency of a surgeon, Edmund Redman, who had taken a lease of the institution in 1538.[42] Thereafter St John's was the focus of communal philanthropy and the asylum for the neediest cases with a claim on municipal charity. The lazar-house of St Stephen also survived the upheavals of the mid-century, despite the dissolution of the order which ran the institution. The civic corporation continued to appoint the *custos*, who was now typically a layman.[43] In Waterford and Cork the lazar-hospitals of St Stephen survived the dissolutions to become centres of municipal care. In both cases the fact that the city corporations already participated in the running of the institutions resulted in efficient transfers to secular control. By 1600 the hospital of St Stephen in Waterford was functioning as a refuge for the 'poor sick or vagrant poor' of the city.[44] Its counterpart in Cork developed a governing body comprising priests, prominent laypeople and corporation appointees.[45] The Crutched Friars' hospitals for the poor and sick in Limerick and Drogheda, which were already subject to corporation rights of inspection and visitation, were transformed into civic hospitals. In Limerick the citizens successfully appealed for the preservation of the house of St Mary, St Edward and the Holy Cross through the agency of the prominent Sexton family which acquired some of the property, and the house remained in being as a hospice.[46] A similar situation obtained in Drogheda where the houses of St Mary de Urso and the hospital of St Laurence survived the dissolution in 1540 and continued to operate under the management of the mayor and corporation.[47]

Besides the continuation of older institutions as hospitals under civic control, there were major new foundations which owed their origins to both public and private initiative. The Shee almhouse, established by Sir Richard Shee in Kilkenny in 1582, was one of a number of such private foundations in the late sixteenth and early seventeenth century, but it is of interest here because of its being incorporated as the hospital of Jesus Christ, Kilkenny, with ordinances for the regulation of the master, brethren, sisters and chaplain.[48] In Galway the foundation of the hospital of St Brigid may also have been at the initiative of an individual citizen, Thomas Lynch Fitzstephen, in 1542.[49] The Waterford hospital of the Holy Ghost, founded in 1545–6, was one of the most important of such institutions in the country. Set up on the site of the former Franciscan friary, a leading citizen, Henry Walsh, obtained a charter from Henry VIII, establishing (in terms very similar to those of a chantry) a community of master, brethren and sisters and poor with a common seal, with three or four priests to celebrate divine service in the hospital, to be elected and nominated with the consent of the mayor, bailiffs and four city councillors. Sixty people of both sexes were to be accommodated from among the poor sick or vagrant poor. The recipients of the charity were to pray for the soul of the king, the souls of his progenitors, and for Patrick Walsh and Catherine Sherlock, Henry Walsh's father and wife respectively. The founding charter was confirmed in 1582 by Queen Elizabeth and the hospital of the Holy Ghost continued to care for the needy, and principally poor widows, throughout the early modern period.[50]

Firmer civic regulation of hospitals was only part of a more co-ordinated response of magistracies to the problems of poverty and sickness from the mid-Tudor period onwards. While empowered by the poor law of 1542 to act against the increasing incidence of vagrancy, the city councillors needed little prompting to take measures to preserve civic order. They were aware of their own growing power vis-à-vis the state and the need for their enhanced ascendancy to be matched by more professionalism in their administrations. Most of the evidence for such an approach in the sixteenth century is drawn from the municipal records of Dublin but all the indications are that civic rulers elsewhere were similarly minded. In 1549 five senior aldermen of the corporation of Dublin were appointed by the civic assembly to survey the 'sick houses' within the franchises for the admitting and ordering of 'all poor men'.[51] Conciliar inspection and supervision were thereafter prominent features of the city's management of poverty. Two aldermen were delegated to order and have oversight of all the poor in 1563.[52] In 1575 it was decreed by the corporation that none of those who had poorhouses within the city were to admit almspeople without the assent of the mayor and the two overseers of the poor.[53] The order for the 'perusal' of the poor in St John's, Newgate, and other poorhouses in 1580 and 1581 to the mayor and four aldermen enjoined them to place and displace at their discretion the poor born in the English Pale as they thought fit and to exclude the employable and fit for labour.[54] In 1591 it was ordained that only decayed citizens of Dublin were to be admitted to St John's.[55]

Apart from the structures for the oversight of poor and sick relief, municipal financing of welfare measures was innovative. The corporation of Dublin devised a levying system for the maintenance of the poor in St John's, Newgate. One brown loaf from every peck of grain baked and one quart of ale of every peck of malt brewed within the city franchises were to be set aside for the Newgate poor. Aldermen were to be mulcted two shillings per quarter with proportionate taxes falling on other ranks and grades within the civic body, down to four pence from every unmarried huckster.[56] In addition to the levy for the poor of St John's, every house-holder was expected to pay four pence per annum to the belman or beadle of beggars who was employed by the corporation to rid the city of vagrants and swine, and who normally qualified for a place in St John's poorhouse himself.[57] The ward was the municipal unit used for gathering the city tax for the poorhouse of St John, but the parish was the focus for casual almsgiving, perhaps for the non-institutionalised poor and sick. Besides the taxing of enfranchised citizens, a system of alms-gathering within the city parishes was approved, two honest men in every parish being deputed to collect contributions on Sundays and holydays.[58] In Galway each burgess was required to send a maid-servant to collect alms every sabbath day for the support of the hospital of St Brigid founded in 1542.[59] In Youghal, a man and woman from the almshouse in the town were required to tour the town every Sunday with a bell to gather the charity of the inhabitants.[60] The overlapping of ward and parish jurisdictions may have rendered the exacting of taxes and extracting of alms difficult and the legislation of the 1630s for a scheme of organised, parish-based administration and financing of poor relief was an attempt to impose order on local experiences.

Besides the institutionalised recipients of municipal and private charity, the other group of impotent poor who came under the supervision of the civic magistrates were the licensed beggars. Under the terms of the 1542 act for vagabonds, aged, poor and impotent persons were to be enrolled by justices, mayors and bailiffs and licensed to beg within their native wards.[61] In implementing this policy of segregation and licensing the corporations took unto themselves greater powers of control. In Dublin it was decreed by the city council in 1559 that no beggar was to beg out of his or her ward: if found outside, the offender was to be consigned to the stocks for twenty-four hours.[62] Apparently the badging of licensed beggars was attempted in some places. There are a number of references in the treasurers' accounts of Dublin to beggars' tokens, the first as early as 1548 and a later one of 1608 to a number of pewter badges being purchased by the city.[63] In both Galway and Kilkenny in the seventeenth century, tokens or badges were in use to distinguish the worthy mendicant from the foreign beggar.[64]

Apart from the beadles or masters of beggars of the towns, the front-line of defence for urban communities against the unwanted migrant were the porters or gatekeepers. Civic authorities stepped up security measures during the nine years war when the problem of refugeeism became acute. In Kilkenny porters were charged in 1601 with intercepting foreign poor and bringing them before the magistrates who would have them whipped and banished from the town.[65] The selection process was part of the exercise of tighter municipal control towards the end of the sixteenth century, particularly in time of war and infection. But the tradition of a discriminatory attitude to foreigners, especially Gaelic migrants, had a long history in the towns as attested in bye-laws in the late fifteenth and earlier sixteenth centuries. In Dublin, Galway and Waterford, for example, orders expelling Irish vagabonds and excluding Gaelic Irish as citizens and apprentices were passed repeatedly.[66] It was a small step from this discriminatory mode of administration to the dichotomous rhetoric of sixteenth-century poor law legislators. Indeed the conjunction of Gaelic and vagabond was often made explicit: 'all suspicious persons, mere Irish, the poor and the aged' were banished from Galway in 1579, relief in the poorhouses of Dublin was to be confined to those who were born in the 'English Pale' by direction of the city council in 1580 and in 1600 the warders of city gates were to detain any suspicious Irishmen and examine

them as to 'the causes of their tarrying within the city'.[67] The urgency and
alarm with which magistracies reacted to periodic crises is manifested in
the rhetoric of the ordinances formulated by town councils, especially
from the late sixteenth century onwards. 'Stout beggars', rogues and 'idle
vagabonds' were coupled with 'naked hasards', 'shameless slaves', 'thieves
and cutpurses', 'badd livers and idell persons'.[68] Foreign families settling in
the suburbs of Dublin were regarded as responsible for 'many disorders
and wicked acts', and 'sturdy beggars, young and old' represented the 'great
danger' of 'breeding infections and other contagious diseases'.[69]

The house of correction and bridewell, based on the London model, in
which the sturdy poor would be punished and set on work, were first
mooted in Ireland at the end of the sixteenth century. In 1602 Sir George
Cary proposed a building for the 'poor, sick and maimed soldiers or other
poor folks or a free school or college or else a place for punishing offenders'
like the bridewell in London.[70] Perhaps because of its ill-defined aims,
Cary's hospital failed to fulfil any of those functions, and became the
residence of Sir Arthur Chichester, the lord deputy, and later the site of
the parliament house.[71] A bridewell was in fact built in close proximity to
the hospital in 1604–5 at the proposition of Dr Lucas Challiner, fellow of
Trinity College, Mr John King, James Ware and Alderman James Carroll.
The purpose was to reform the able poor through setting them on work
on stocks of materials (wool, hemp, flax, iron), and to turn a profit. In 1609,
however, the city corporation withdrew its permission to make the building
a bridewell and allowed it to be put to other uses.[72] Later attempts to
establish a house of correction in Dublin were marginally more successful,
St John's house steeple being converted to such a purpose in 1630.[73] Most
success in the establishment of such houses for the reformation of the
poor and the disciplining of the recalcitrant was achieved in the south of
the country in towns such as Bandon, Bandonbridge and Mallow, where
under the auspices of New English proprietors such as the earl of Cork in
the 1630s some ventures prospered.[74] In Ulster houses of correction were
established at Derry and Armagh.[75] Belatedly the central government
established a legislative framework within which such projects could be
organised with at least one house of correction in each county. This proposal
in 1635 which was to be supported by the revenues from a county levy or
rate was delayed at the request of prominent parliamentarians for a space
of five years.[76] The impression is gained that the disciplinarian type of
institutions had a very slow beginning in Ireland and that many local
authorities were less than fully committed to their establishment.

While the institutionalisation of the vagrant poor may have been
approached half-heartedly by the older boroughs in the early seventeenth
century, there were signs of a more punitive regime on the part of the

magistracies in other ways. Obviously the advent of plague necessitated stringent security measures such as the confinement of victims in specially appointed pest-houses such as All Hallows in 1575 and St George's Lane in 1604, both in Dublin.[77] Regulations for the whipping of strange beggars seem to have been enforced in Kilkenny at the turn of the century.[78] In Dublin in the later Tudor and early Stuart periods, there was much buying of instruments of public punishment and humiliation, such as stocks, gibbets, pillories, irons and ducking-stools.[79] During the wars of the Elizabethan period and later, the office of provost marshal was used for the punishment and execution of idle and masterless people, and the maintenance of that authority in peacetime conditions, though controversial, was countenanced throughout the country.[80] In 1634 the failure of various initiatives in respect of the multitudes of beggars and other sorts of disorderly persons in or near the city prompted the proposal that a marshal be established in office with ten 'able and well qualified men armed' to range ' in all places in the city and three miles from the city' to chase vagrants.[81] This was an admission that local officers such as beadles of beggars were not proving to be effectual. Perhaps the ultimate solution to the problem of the vagrant was banishment overseas. The assisted passage of disbanded soldiers and idle swordsmen to the continent there to fight in the Elizabethan armies in the Netherlands or in the armies of other powers was undertaken by the state from the mid-1580s onwards.[82] Banishment of civilians to the New World was legislated for in England at the beginning of the seventeenth century and was proclaimed for Ireland in 1625.[83]

An organised and centralised poor law regime failed to emerge in Ireland in the period prior to 1640, though a multiplicity of local schemes was initiated for the deserving and undeserving poor. As has been pointed out by Dr Patrick Fitzgerald, the legislation imported into Ireland merely replicated the English laws without adapting itself to local conditions.[84] The context within which the new system was supposed to operate was one of socio-political disturbance for most of the period and the institutionalised poverty of the principal authorities – state, church and municipal governments – precluded significant investment in the schemes. And while there was evidence of the application of new modes of thought concerning the relief of the poor, the multiplicity of categories of the poverty-stricken caused a lack of focus in relief ventures. Charity still tended to be bestowed in a catch-all way, despite the efforts to separate out the needy elements, as demonstrated in the confusion over the designation of Cary's hospital.[85] Some signs of sectarianism may be noted as entering into the dispensation of charity before 1640 but rivalry between proponents of the opposing confessions was more a symptom than a cause of lack of effective relief structures. A high proportion of the backers of schemes for new-style hospitals and houses of correction in Dublin and elsewhere were either older-established or newly-settled Protestants, but little or no element of religious distinction can be traced in the intended selection procedures for inmates. In the Munster plantation centres and those of the Ulster plantation most proponents of confinement centres would have been Protestant, but in times of deep distress such as harvest crises, for example, relief seems to have forthcoming for all, whether Gaelic or English, Catholic or Protestant.[86] Some new foundations such as Anne St Lawrence's endowment of £200 for the maintenance of six poor widows in Dublin in 1637 specified religious criteria: they were to be selected from those who 'go to church'.[87] And in Clonmel in 1623, what was described as a Roman Catholic almshouse was operating, possibly that referred to as having been established by James White Fitzrobert with a bequest of £40 from his estate.[88] Other religion-specific instances occurred in the channelling of outdoor relief through Church of Ireland parishes such as St John's, St Bride's and St Werburgh's in Dublin, the disbursal of recusancy fines to relieve the Protestant poor and the mooting by the Catholic bishop, David Rothe, of the erection of a new hospital in the city.[89]

A more fundamental rift with implications for the provision of charitable services for the unprivileged opened between civic magistrates and state and ecclesiastical authorities. In the initial responses of the municipalities to the problem of poverty after the closure of the monasteries the ward was the chosen unit for organisation of relief.[90] By the 1620s and 1630s the parish was emerging as an alternative focus for the dispensation of charity but due to friction between the municipalities and the church, lines of administrative demarcation between parish and ward were not clearly drawn.[91] Allied to this problem was that of funding: should alms be raised through voluntary charity in the wards or parishes, or through a levy imposed by the city or the churchwardens of the parishes (in the name of the established church)? Also the system of collection and the means whereby money should be raised (by voluntary or compulsory giving) were not clearly agreed. The events surrounding the passage of poor legislation through the Irish parliament in the 1630s and early 1640s attest these tensions. The original bill presented to parliament in 1635 replicated that passed by the English parliament in 1610.[92] It provided for at least one house of correction in each county to be funded by the proceeds of a county rate. The bill was passed but the operation of the law was to be delayed for five years, because of reservations of some members over the capacity of counties to pay. In 1640 a bill proposing the parish system of poor relief, enshrining the role of churchwardens, having passed through parliament, seems never to have been persevered with. It is likely that at least a substantial part of the opposition to both of these measures emanated from borough representatives who resented the over-riding of the powers of their magistrates in relation to the raising of local taxation and the organisation of internal schemes outside the competence of the corporations.[93]

The protectiveness of the municipalities in respect of corporate rights extended to the older institutions of charitable relief. A residual element of monasticism was left in being after the dissolution of the lazar-houses. As they were constituted at their foundation as corporations with masters, sisters and brethren, their dissolution could not abolish the community of lepers who were incorporated within the orders. Thus the mayors and civic corporations in the boroughs continued to nominate the *custodes* (who were normally lay people) but the leper communities seem to have been left to manage their own affairs.[94] The legal crux concerning the standing and possessions of St Stephen's leper-house, Dublin, embroiled the city corporation in litigation with the state.[95] In the mid-1590s, Launcelot Money, *custos* of St Stephen's, had, by his authority on the seal of the hospital and with the backing of the mayor and commonalty of Dublin, leased the lands at Ballinlower (or Leopardstown) to Alderman William Gough.[96] The lease was disputed by Sir Jacques Wingfield, a crown official, who claimed to have a title to the property from the state. The case of Alderman Gough was upheld, the lease under the seal being held to be valid.[97] The nub of the proceedings was the question of the succession of authority from the *custos*, brethren and sisters of the late medieval period. Did the guardian and lepers comprise the legal pro-prietorship or did the crown become possessor of the house and estates after the dissolution of the community? The court case was a prelude to the questioning of the warrant of a number of surviving late medieval institutions in the municipalities in the early Jacobean period, but in general the pre-Reformation corporate institutions overcame the challenge by pleading the protection of their charters.[98]

Aspects of older communal institutions and traditional obitual impulses blended with the 'new philanthropy' of the humanistic, reforming era in the founding of private almshouses between 1540 and 1640. Some emanated as hospitals with joint municipal patronage from the phase of monastic dissolutions, their establishment or renovation owing much to zeal of individuals or merchant patrician families such as the Sextons in Limerick, the Walshes in Waterford, and the Lynches in Galway.[99] The most common unit was the poorhouse for from two or three to twelve poor, sick or indigent men and women, some for both, such as the Shee almshouse in Kilkenny, or some favouring widows such as William Lattin's in Naas or Anne St Lawrence's in Dublin.[100] At least five individual aldermen-gentlemen founded houses for the poor in the period between

1580 and 1610 in Dublin, and similar establishments were set up by rich townspeople in Clonmel, New Ross and Dundalk, the average annual value of endowments being about £90.[101] The three large poorhouses of Stephen Skiddy in Cork, William Lattin in Naas and Sir Richard Shee in Kilkenny, all founded within a decade or so of one another, targeted the beneficiaries carefully, and two had foundation stones upon which were engraved the charitable rationale. Skiddy aspired to relieving ten of 'the poorest, honestest people aged forty at least', Lattin to helping poor women, Shee to benefiting 'six poor unmarried men, of honest behaviour and conversation, able to read and write, at least thirty, unmarried, blind, lame, impotent or diseased, and if unable to labour, aged at least fifty, who were to hear divine service according to the laws and statutes of the realm'.[102] Lattin's almshouse had a foundation stone inscribed with the words of Proverbs: 'Wealth maketh many friends but the poor is separated from his neighbour', while the Shee stone had inscribed on it: 'Alms free from death, purge sin and lead the way to pity and eternal life'.[103] In the community of this almshouse there were incorporated the master, brothers and sisters and an assistant chaplain.

Foundation of Almshouses in Ireland, 1537–1637

Date	Place	Founder(s)	Type/Terms
1537	Limerick	E. & S. Sexton	Hospital
1542	Galway	T. Lynch Fitzstephen	St Brigid's
1544	Dundalk	James Brandon	House for old, sick, poor
1545	Waterford	Henry Walshe	Hospital of Holy Ghost
1556	Galway	Michael Lynch	3 houses for poor and needy
c. 1580	Balgriffin	John Bathe	House for 4 poor people[104]
c. 1580	Dublin	Richard Rounsell[105]	
1582	Kilkenny	Sir Richard Shee	6 poor unmarried men, 6 poor widows
1584	Cork	Stephen Skiddy	10 of poorest people
1590	Naas	William Lattin Anne Luttrell	Support of poor women
1602	Dublin	Philip Conran	Hospital[106]
1604	Dublin	John Morphy[107]	
1608	Kilkenny	Stephen Luker[108]	
1609	Dublin	Nicholas Ball	Poorhouse for 2 or 3 people[109]
1600s	New Ross	Thomas Gregory	
1618	Youghal	Richard Boyle[110]	
1624	Clonmel	James White Fitzrobert	Poorhouse/hospital
1637	Dublin	Anne St Lawrence	6 poor church-going widows

The evidence suggests that the patriciates of the older towns at least favoured a system of poor relief which drew upon traditional charitable springs of *pro anima* bequests and donations. They insisted, however, on a more focused and discriminating targeting of recipients of charity and also on situating relief measures in a more ordered system of social control. Moreover they were uncomfortable with the new corrective institutions for the disciplining of vagrants. The magistracies' attitude derived principally from their self-confidence in their ability to provide stable government for the common good of the citizenry, accentuated by their resilient defence of civic liberties in the face of threats of intrusion from the central government and its agents. By extension, the religious guilds and chantries which had continued in existence despite the Reformation, some exercising charitable functions, and all having land and property for disbursement among the members and their chosen beneficiaries, were upheld in defiance of *quo warranto* proceedings and commissions of enquiry.[111] In Galway the college of St Nicholas was the centre for a broadly conservative, recusant organisation or 'shadow corporation'.[112] In Waterford, Cork and Kilkenny, old-established municipal families clustered around the accumulated gains of ecclesiastical lands of cathedrals, guilds and confraternities, defending their holding against prospective challengers. Within this milieu, the hospitals and almshouses were seen as municipal institutions, controlled and inspected by the corporations.

The city corporations presided over a series of initiatives in their attempts to cope with the rising tide of mendicancy down to 1640, sometimes employing older institutions which survived in a state of increasing decrepitude and depending upon the work of individual benefactors. When Richard Stanihurst described the whole of Dublin as a 'hospital' for the reception of the needy, he was echoing the dictum of Erasmus: 'what is the city if not a great monastery?'[113] Even though the monastic institutions of welfare were dissolved, many aspects of the system of dispensing aid through the religious orders persisted, and in some cases quasi-monastic entities survived legally. Above all, however, the cities derived their sense of purpose and surety in the helping of the weak from the concept of the civic communities as extended brotherhoods and sisterhoods, bonded in mutual support, the patricians ruling with 'fatherly care', preserving order and harmony within and protecting from the disorderly without the walls.

62 *Luxury and austerity*

NOTES

1 The portrait of Alderman Patrick Sarsfield is to be found in Richard Stanihurst, 'The description of Ireland' in *Holinshed's Irish chronicle*, ed. Liam Miller and Eileen Power (Dublin, 1979), pp 400–2.
2 Edmund Spenser, *A view of the state of Ireland*, ed. Andrew Hadfield and Willy Maley (Oxford, 1997), pp 101–2.
3 Stanihurst, 'Description' in *Holinshed's Irish chronicle*, p. 42.
4 Edmund Campion, *Two bokes of the histories of Ireland*, ed. A. F. Vossen (Assen, 1963), p. 114.
5 For a very useful survey of the scale of the problem of and the range of responses to poverty, see Robert Jütte, *Poverty and deviance in early modern Europe* (Cambridge, 1994).
6 See, for example, Brian Pullan, *Rich and poor in Renaissance Venice* (Oxford, 1971), pp 287–336.
7 Jütte, *Poverty and deviance*, pp 128–31.
8 Cf. ibid., pp 105–25; for the English poor law regime, see Paul Slack, *Poverty and policy in Tudor and Stuart England* (London, 1988).
9 See, for example, Christopher Black, *Italian confraternities in the sixteenth century* (Cambridge, 1989); Pullan, *Rich and poor in Renaissance Venice*, pp 216–39.
10 Jütte, *Poverty and deviance*, chapter seven.
11 For a valuable overview of the institutions of hospitality, see Michael Maher, 'Hospitality in the Irish tradition' in *Milltown Studies*, xl (1997), pp 87–118; see also Katharine Simms, 'Guesting and feasting in Gaelic Ireland' in *R.S.A.I. Jn.*, cviii (1978), pp 67–100.
12 See Gearóid Mac Niocaill, 'Socio-economic problems of the late medieval Irish town' in David Harkness and Mary O'Dowd (ed.), *The town in Ireland: Hist. studies, xiii* (Belfast, 1981), pp 7–22; Colm Lennon, *The lords of Dublin in the age of Reformation* (Dublin, 1989), pp 32–7.
13 Peter Gale, *An inquiry into the ancient corporate system of Ireland* (London, 1834), pp 66–71.
14 On the contribution of the Dublin patriciate, see Colm Lennon, *The lords of Dublin in the age of Reformation*, pp 64–91.
15 Aubrey Gwynn and R.N. Hadcock (ed.), *Medieval religious houses, Ireland* (Dublin, 1988), pp 344–57.
16 Gerard Lee, *Leper hospitals in medieval Ireland* (Dublin, 1996).
17 R.H. Ryland, *The history, topography and antiquities of the county and city of Waterford* (London, 1824), p. 122; Gearóid MacNiocaill (ed.), 'The register of St Saviour's, Waterford' in *Anal. Hib.*, xxiii (1966), pp 153–5, 205–6.
18 Gwynn and Hadcock (ed.), *Medieval religious houses*, pp 208–16.
19 Charles MacNeill, 'Hospital of St John without the Newgate, Dublin' in Howard Clarke (ed.), *Medieval Dublin: the living city* (Dublin, 1990), pp 77–82.
20 Gwynn and Hadcock (ed.), *Medieval religious houses*, p. 343.
21 C.L Falkiner, 'The hospital of St John of Jerusalem in Ireland' in *R.I.A. Proc.*, xxvi, sect. C, (1906–7), pp 275–317; Charles MacNeill, 'The hospitallers at Kilmainham and their guests' in *R.S.A.I. Jn.*, liv (1924), pp 20–1, 29–30.
22 Lee, *Leper houses in medieval Ireland*, pp 15–19.
23 Ibid., pp 65–7; Gwynn and Hadcock (ed.), *Medieval religious houses*, pp 344–5.
24 Lee, *Leper houses in medieval Ireland*, pp 32–4, 39, 42–5, 46–8, 52–3, 53–4; Myles Ronan, 'Lazar houses of St Laurence and St Stephen in medieval Dublin' in John Ryan (ed.), *Essays and studies presented to Professor Eoin MacNeill on the occasion of his seventieth birthday* (Dublin, 1940), pp 480–9.

25 Ronan, 'Lazar houses' p. 487; Lee, *Leper houses in medieval Ireland*, p. 43; 'Inquisition into the lazar house of Waterford', 1650s (B. L., Add. MS 9750).

26 Ronan, 'Lazar houses' pp 485–7; Stanihurst, 'Description' in *Holinshed's Irish chronicle*, p. 45.

27 *Calendar of entries in the papal registers relating to Great Britain and Ireland. Papal letters, vol. xvii, pt 1: Alexander VI (1492–1503): Lateran registers, pt 2: 1495–1503*, ed. Anne P. Fuller (Dublin: Irish Manuscripts Commission, 1994), pp 591–2.

28 Ibid, pp 491–2.

29 'Christ Church cathedral muniments' (R.C.B. Library, C.6.1.26.12, fol. 5).

30 Henry Berry, 'History of the religious gild of St Anne, taken from its records in the Haliday collection, R.I.A.' in *R.I.A. Proc.*, section C (1904–5), pp 21–38; John D'Alton, *The history of Drogheda with its environs* (2 vols, Dublin, 1844), i, pp 12, 16,17, 21.

31 MacNiocaill (ed.), 'The register of St Saviour's, Waterford', pp 214–15.

32 Gwynn and Hadcock (ed.), *Medieval religious houses*, p. 350.

33 See, for example, Margaret Murphy, 'The high cost of dying: an analysis of *pro anima* bequests in medieval Dublin' in W. J. Sheils and Diana Wood (ed.), *The church and wealth: studies in church history, xxiv* (Oxford, 1987), pp 111–22.

34 Ronan, 'Lazar houses' pp 485–7; Colm Lennon and James Murray (ed.), *The Dublin franchise roll, 1468–1512* (Dublin, 1988), p. 70; Hardiman, *Galway*, p. 77.

35 MacNiocaill (ed.), 'The register of St Saviour's, Waterford', pp 214–15.

36 'Notes towards a history of Dublin, compiled by William Monck Mason', p. 230 (Dublin, Gilbert Library [hereafter DGL], MS 62).

37 W. Monck Mason, *The history and antiquities of the collegiate and cathedral church of St Patrick near Dublin* (Dublin, 1820), app xii, pp xiv–xv; for a fascinating discussion of the mentality of Dean Allen, see James Murray, 'The Tudor diocese of Dublin: episcopal government, ecclesiastical politics and the enforcement of the reformation, c. 1534–1590' (Unpublished PhD thesis, University of Dublin, 1997), pp 64–72.

38 For the text of the statutes, see *Stat. Ire.*, 33 Hen. VIII, c. 15; 10&11 Charles I, c. 4; for a comprehensive analysis of responses to poverty, see Patrick Fitzgerald, 'Poverty and vagrancy in early modern Ireland' (Unpublished PhD thesis, Queen's University, Belfast, 1994).

39 'Rowland White's "Discors touching Ireland", c. 1569', ed. Nicholas Canny, in *I.H.S.*, xx, p. 462.

40 *Cal. pat. rolls, Ire., Hen. VIII–Eliz.*, p. 152.

41 Ibid., p. 524.

42 Brendan Bradshaw, *The dissolution of the religious orders in the reign of Henry VIII* (Cambridge, 1974), pp 220–1; *Anc. rec. Dub.*, ii, pp 16–17.

43 Ronan, 'Lazar houses', pp 480–9; *Anc. rec. Dub.*, ii, p. 145; *Holinshed's Irish Chronicle, 1577*, p. 45.

44 'Inquisition into the lazar house of Waterford' (B. L., Add. MS 9750).

45 Lee, *Leper houses in medieval Ireland*, pp 32–4; Denis O'Sullivan, 'Monastic establishments of medieval Cork' in *Journal of the Cork Historical and Archaeological Society*, xlviii (1948), pp 13–15.

46 Bradshaw, *The dissolution of the religious orders in the reign of Henry VIII*, pp 148–9.

47 John D'Alton, *History of Drogheda*, i, p. 118.

48 James Robertson, 'Shee's almshouse, Kilkenny' in *R.S.A.I. Jn.*, series v, vol. ii (1892), pp 435–6; iii (1893), pp 81, 249.

49 Hardiman, *Galway*, p. 81; M.D. O'Sullivan, *Old Galway: the history of a Norman colony in Ireland* (Cambridge, 1942), p. 426.

50 Richard Lahert, 'Some charitable institutions of old Waterford' in *Decies*, xxviii (1985), pp 43–4.

51 *Anc. rec. Dub.*, i, p. 421.
52 Ibid., ii, pp 28–9.
53 Ibid., ii, p. 97.
54 Ibid., ii, p. 143.
55 Ibid., ii, p. 238.
56 Ibid., ii, pp 16–17.
57 Ibid., ii, pp 142, 232.
58 Ibid., ii, pp 28–9; cf. ibid., iii. p. 251.
59 Hardiman, *Galway*, p. 81; O'Sullivan, *Old Galway*, p. 426.
60 Fitzgerald, 'Poverty and vagrancy', pp 28, 35–7.
61 *Stat. Ire.*, 33 Hen. VIII, c. 15.
62 *Anc. rec. Dub.*, ii, p. 479.
63 'Account-book of Dublin, 1540–1613' , p. 40 (D[ublin] C[ity] A[rchive], MS MR/35).
64 Fitzgerald, 'Poverty and vagrancy', pp 44, 62; O'Sullivan, *Old Galway*, p. 429; see also,
     W.A. Seaby, 'Ulster beggars' badges' in *Ulster Journal of Archaeology*, xxxiii (1970),
     pp 95–7.
65 Fitzgerald, 'Poverty and vagrancy', pp 45–6.
66 See, for example, O'Sullivan, *Old Galway*, pp 53, 59; *Anc. rec. Dub.*, i, pp 272, 280–1,
     286–7, 298; William O'Sullivan, *The economic history of Cork* (Cork, 1937) pp 53–4;
     James Lydon, 'The city of Waterford in the late middle ages' in *Decies*, xii (1979),
     pp 5–15.
67 O'Sullivan, *Old Galway*, p. 108; *Anc. rec. Dub.*, ii, p. 143; DCA, MS MR/17, 'Friday
     book', 1569–1611, f. 58r.
68 Fitzgerald, 'Poverty and vagrancy', pp 65, 92; *Anc. rec. Dub.*, iii, pp 47, 99.
69 *Anc. rec. Dub.*, iii pp 99, 117.
70 *Anc. rec. Dub.*, ii, pp 390–2.
71 Ibid., iii, pp 62–3.
72 Ibid., ii, pp 420, 498; iii, pp 62–3.
73 Ibid., iii, pp 220–1, 225.
74 Fitzgerald, 'Poverty and vagrancy', pp 136–9.
75 Ibid., pp 139–41.
76 *Stat. Ire.*, 10&11 Chas. I, c. 4; Fitzgerald, 'Poverty and vagrancy', pp 124–7.
77 *Anc. rec. Dub.*, ii, pp 103–4, 536–7.
78 Fitzgerald, 'Poverty and vagrancy', p. 52.
79 'Account-book of Dublin, 1540–1613', pp 22, 40, 59, 70, 72, 73, 89, 95, 100, 102,
     106, 110 (DCA, MS MR/35).
80 Fitzgerald, 'Poverty and vagrancy', pp 90–7.
81 Ibid., p. 152.
82 Gráinne Henry, *The Irish military community in Spanish Flanders, 1586–1621*
     (Dublin, 1992); see also, Mary Ann Lyons, 'Franco-Irish relations in the sixteenth
     century' (Unpublished PhD thesis, NUI, Maynooth, 1997), pp 321–79; Fitzgerald,
     'Poverty and vagrancy', pp 170–229.
83 Fitzgerald, 'Poverty and vagrancy', p. 143.
84 Ibid., p. 57.
85 *Anc. rec. Dub.*, ii, pp 390–2.
86 Fitzgerald, 'Poverty and vagrancy', pp 63–4.
87 *Anc. rec. Dub.*, iii, pp 346–7.
88 William Burke, *History of Clonmel* (Waterford, 1907), pp 45–6, 58.
89 Fitzgerald, 'Poverty and vagrancy', p. 123; *H.M.C., rep. iv*, app., (1874), p. 568.
90 *Anc. rec. Dub.*, ii, pp 28–9.
91 Fitzgerald, 'Poverty and vagrancy', p. 61.
92 *Stat. Ire.*, 10 & 11 Chas. I, c. 4.; Fitzgerald, 'Poverty and vagrancy', pp 57, 58,127.

93 For the text of the proposed bill, see Gale, *An inquiry into the ancient corporate system of Ireland*, pp 185, clxxix–cxcv.
94 *Anc. rec. Dub.*, i, pp 399, 439; ii, p. 145.
95 Ronan, 'Lazar houses', pp 480–9.
96 *Anc. rec. Dub.*, ii, p. 308.
97 Ronan, 'Lazar houses', pp 448–9.
98 R.I.A., MS 12 E 1, pp 149–51, 275–9.
99 'Sexton's notebook', p. 44 (N.L.I., MS 16085); 'Sexton papers', p. 61 (B.L., Add. MS 19865); Lahert, 'Some charitable institutions', pp 43–5; O'Sullivan, *Old Galway*, p. 426.
100 Robertson 'Shee's almshouse'; Walter Fitzgerald, 'Lattin almshouse at Morristown' in *Kildare Arch. Soc. Jn.*, i (1891–5), p. 38; ii (1896–9), p. 270; *Anc. rec. Dub.*, iii, pp 346–7.
101 *Anc. rec. Dub.*, ii, p. 120; ibid., iii, pp 346–7; Lennon, *Lords of Dublin*, pp 227, 239 ; Burke, *History of Clonmel*, pp 45–6, 58; Gwynn and Hadcock (ed.), *Medieval religious houses, Ireland*, p. 355; N.L.I., MS D 2434.
102 Smith, *County and city of Cork*, i, p. 382; Robertson 'Shee's almshouse'; Fitzgerald, 'Lattin almshouse at Morristown'.
103 Fitzgerald, 'Lattin almshouse at Morristown'; Robertson 'Shee's almshouse'.
104 Seán Ó Mathúna, *An tAthair William Bathe, C.Í.: ceannródaí sa teangeolaíocht* (Dublin, 1981), p. 25.
105 *Anc. rec. Dub.*, i, p. 193.
106 Ibid., p. 383.
107 Ibid., p. 409.
108 Copy of charter to Stephen Luker, 1608 (Dublin, G.O., MS 87).
109 *Anc. rec. Dub.*, ii, 218.
110 Fitzgerald, 'Poverty and vagrancy', p. 28.
111 Colm Lennon, 'The chantries in the Irish Reformation: the case of St Anne's guild, Dublin, 1550–1630' in R.V. Comerford, Mary Cullen, J. R. Hill and Colm Lennon (ed.), *Religion, conflict and coexistence: essays presented to Monsignor Patrick J. Corish* (Dublin, 1990), pp 6–25.
112 Martin Coen, *The wardenship of Galway* (Galway, 1984).
113 Stanihurst, 'Description' in *Holinshed's Irish Chronicle*, p. 42.

5 Public and private uses of wealth in Ireland, *c.* 1660–1760

Toby Barnard

In 1742 an army officer who had been serving in Ireland for some years reviewed his impressions. He had happily mingled with the Protestant elites of the kingdom. Now he credited them with two distinctive qualities. One was commonly remarked by other contemporaries and visitors: profuse, even excessive hospitality. But the second – philanthropy – is less often noticed.[1] Charity may have been more strongly in evidence in these years because of the famine which had followed 'the Great Frost' of 1740–1. Communal and private schemes addressed the worst symptoms and some of the underlying causes of this catastrophe.[2] These built on initiatives of the early and later 1720s.[3] In that earlier decade, individual, civic and parochial doles had been accompanied by more ambitious and systematised projects. In Dublin, a precocious hospital movement had emerged. It generated an economy of concerts, assemblies and subscriptions, and was most famously the occasion for the first performance in 1742 of Handel's *Messiah*.[4]

At the same time, the dean and chapter of St Patrick's cathedral in Dublin had demonstrated their concern by retrenching corporate entertainment. The money customarily spent on the annual audit dinner was instead distributed directly to the poor.[5] Similarly, the primate set an example by relieving the indigent from his own purse.[6] Even in the crowded capital, older habits of giving, with the prosperous handing their donations directly to the recipients, survived longer than in contemporary Britain.[7] In this personalised and apparently undiscriminating generosity, well-to-do newcomers may have adopted the practices of the Irish Catholics whom they had lately supplanted. Alongside the individual acts there developed collective endeavours. The hospitals, with their associated calendar of music, were one way in which the public-spiritedness of the privileged and propertied could be diverted into entertainments.[8] Concurrently the hitherto diffuse efforts to train up the population to useful labour were drawn together through the royal charter granted in 1733 to the Incorporated Society for Protestant Schools.[9] These activities fitted together into a pattern the template of which has yet to be reconstructed. They tell of philosophies and practices through which the fashionable cults of sociability, conviviality and civic virtue were directed into institutions and public works. It was widely recognised that property carried obligations as well as rights. The former could be discharged pleasurably through these variegated outlets. Such altruism constitutes the less often chronicled obverse of the ostentation and prodigality for which the members of the Protestant ascendancy were so often reproved.

Self-indulgence had been espied in the lavish tables and attire of the new owners of Ireland. As early as the 1680s, the sententious decried the moral as much as the economic damage thereby inflicted. When appeals to self-restraint and patriotism could not curb the excesses, sumptuary laws were proposed.[10] The arguments about luxury which have been analysed by Christopher Berry were imported into eighteenth-century Ireland.[11] The issues aired by Davenant and Mandeville were debated by pamphleteers in Hanoverian Dublin.[12] Controversies which in Britain and Europe were heated enough, in Ireland excited even stronger passions owing to the distinctive confessional and ethnic mixtures there. Throughout the sixteenth and seventeenth centuries outsiders routinely described the Irish as feckless, idle, irrational and primitive. Now these failings were discovered among the recently entrenched Protestant elite. By the eighteenth century, the latter was accused of behaviour which at best deviated worryingly from the norms of polite society in lowland Britain. At worst, Irish Protestants recalled the weaknesses common throughout several centuries, in which immigrants were assimilated with distressing ease to the uncouth ways of the indigenes. Indeed, in a startling reversal of stereotypes, by the mid-eighteenth century, Irish Catholics were being characterised by thrift, industry and restraint. The new Protestant order, in contrast, manifested those failings said hitherto to have been monopolised by the Catholics. The practical consequences of these shortcomings – of sparse resources wasted and of potential unrealised – alarmed many critics. But so too did the ethical damage.[13] There persisted the idea that the Protestants of Ireland had been chosen by God for a special role. Their history veered between rebukes and deliverances. But if, as pessimists warned, the Protestants continued to neglect their larger mission – to improve the land and its inhabitants, and thereby themselves as well – then divine vengeance might again fall on them.[14] The natural disasters which enveloped much of the kingdom in each decade of the eighteenth century were readily interpreted as warnings of the final judgement which only the most strenuous efforts would avert. Accordingly churchmen were to the fore in counselling insouciant and vicious Protestants how best to use their riches.[15]

The worried monotonously stressed profligacy and extravagance. Eye-catching examples abounded, and were tellingly employed by the reformers. Even so, we should not too readily look to these portrayals for their verisimilitude. The partisan accounts compiled by those keen to mend Irish Protestant manners have been much used by later analysts. As a result, patterns of consumption and display in Hanoverian Ireland have been seen as idiosyncratic. Some aspects of this material world are slowly being reconstructed. It is possible, for example, to quantify what was imported, even to trace the first appearance and subsequent spread of consumer novelties such as tobacco and tea.[16] In a few cases, the expenditure of specific households can be recovered. As yet, such studies are in their infancy. It is not clear whether Irish householders were favoured by the low costs of many home-produced staples or hurt by the ruinous expense of foreign claret, gold-lace or well-bred coach-horses, to which the smart became addicted. It was not uncommon for a squire to escape, at least temporarily, from the costly obligations of maintaining open house in the Irish countryside, by retiring to the obscurity of Britain or the continent. For two notables from Queen's County, the Cosbys and Parnells, the amplitude of their hospitable establishments taxed their finances.[17] More typical as a cause of difficulties, nevertheless, were resources too meagre to satisfy even modest needs. An inhabitant of Dublin during the 1740s, in indifferent health and without any official salary, expressed a heartfelt desire: 'I wish I could get out of Dublin from among my acquaintance, &c. and a place I am so well known in and not any way advantageous to me'. What he craved was a retired and cheaper spot, 'where I could live more private and agreeable with my family'.[18] A contemporary who also struggled to eke out a respectable existence in the Irish provinces, and reduced to lodging with one of his own tenants rather than incur the charge of keeping house for himself, cast a jaundiced eye over the antics of carefree neighbours. In particular, he charted the proliferation of clubs in the border country of Cork and Limerick. The most popular, he concluded, was the Dettingen Club, which devoted itself principally to carousing. However, the correspondent was not himself a member, nor of any of the other sociable groups in his locality.[19]

These examples can do little more than sketch in something of the economic and cultural stratification which ran through the Irish Protestant interest. It is unlikely that it will ever be possible to generalise about the patterns of spending among the elites. Certainly, for those whose annual budgets can be retrieved, moderation not excess marked their lives.[20] This should serve to correct both the vivid images and the explanations offered by a succession of influential commentators. From Arthur Young in the 1770s and 1780s, through Lecky a century later, to their more recent disciples, impressionism in the use of evidence has been married to psychological theories which are looking naive.[21] What is postulated is an order of *parvenus*, advanced too speedily to social as well as economic eminence by the revolutions of the seventeenth century, and beset alike by the insecurities of the social climber and the uncouthness of the intruded colonist.[22] The new proprietors lived and disported themselves much as their immediate predecessors had. In the hospitality which they dispensed and the goods with which they surrounded themselves, they responded rationally to the roles into which they had been pushed.[23] Recent work on perceptions of the English in the eighteenth century suggests that the chilliness, restraint and obsessive privacy were viewed by many travellers as odder than the generosity, openness and cultivation which marked the Scots and Irish.[24] Yet, to offer examples of the careful and moderate does no more than substitute a new impressionism for the old. Meticulous accountants eager to itemise the last sixpence handed to a beggar or paid to pass a turnpike were unlikely to descend helter-skelter into bankruptcy.[25]

By the mid-eighteenth century the kind of squire elected to the Dublin parliament probably enjoyed an income around £1,500 p.a. The peers, of whom there were no more than 130 in the middle of the century, like aristocrats everywhere at the apex of their society, might command an annual £3,000.[26] Often, however, the vicissitudes to which any hereditary system was prone seriously reduced this total. Where direct comparisons can be made, Irish peers and gentlemen received less than their social equivalents in lowland Britain, but were closer in revenues to the notables in the uplands and peripheries of Britain and the European monarchies. The numbers of those at the top of the Irish Protestant pyramid were small. The spending power of this group may easily have been surpassed by that of the pseudo-gentry, the shadowy middlemen, the professionals and the town-dwellers. No less than the nobility and gentry, the latter experienced the pressures to dress, to house themselves, to eat and drink, and to entertain differently. Even the *menu peuple* and the depressed were not impervious to these impulses. For the poor, however, whether Catholic or Protestant, public responsibilities were few, other perhaps than to show a seemly gratitude for their doles.

An inevitable haziness envelops efforts to gauge how deeply the use of manufactured goods and consumer fashions penetrated into the provinces and lower social strata of Ireland. With the enormous gulf between the means of the modestly prosperous and the bulk of the labouring and landless populations, much of this new world of material goods lay beyond the reach of the majority. In the 1760s, an inquisitive Sligo landlord Charles O'Hara, calculated that £5 8s 6½d sufficed to maintain a rural labourer and his family for a year.[27] O'Hara, himself a high-spending and thoroughly anglicised socialite, did not explain how he had arrived at his figure. However, as with similar calculations offered by Petty almost a century earlier, he assumed a life stripped down to bare necessities, other than regular smokes of tobacco.[28] Yet, as some of O'Hara's other comments implied, by the 1760s tastes for consumer articles had reached the remote and humble.[29] Fairs, patterns and markets brought within sight, and sometimes within grasp, a beguiling choice of colourful fabrics and accessories. D. E. C. Eversley has suggested that an income of £50 annually marked the threshold at which it was possible to become an active consumer[30] in England. Others have investigated alternative strategies which allowed those below this level to join in consumption.[31] In Ireland, if a comparable hurdle existed, few would have cleared it, and the proliferation of cheap goods, evident in imports, advertisements, inventories and accounts, would be incomprehensible. The stock of three general merchants in the Irish provinces during the 1720s – two at Offaly, the other at Nenagh in County Tipperary – reveals the assortment of articles kept and the numerous customers (more than 200 with each trader). The bulk of those with accounts belonged to the indigenous and Catholic populations. Each of the 200, it appears, spent on average £1 8s on haberdashery, lengths of cloth and groceries. In aggregate these modest customers easily outnumbered and probably outspent the few unequivocal gentlemen and ladies who shopped at the small-town dealers.[32]

The long tentacles of skilfully manipulated demand can be traced through other sources. Late in the eighteenth century, a County Monaghan parson penned some sprightly verses. As he remembered the participants at a local pattern in the 1760s, he emphasised appearances:

> Here Oonagh stands; her pumps, you see, are new;
> Her gown striped linen, and her stockings blue;
> Last week in Glaslough were her buckles bought,
> How bright they shine, tho purchased for a groat! . . .
> Dolly with care her scarlet coat displays
> Lac'd tightly in her mistress's cast off stays,
> While Laughlin struts, and seemingly looks big,
> With coarse black stockings and his one row wig.
> Here Peggy skips, dressed in a yellow gown,
> Which cost at Skernageragh, just a crown.
> New cap and ribbons set her off with grace,
> And add fresh honours to her rosy face;
> While Denis smartly trips along to show
> His sheep-skin breeches, bought some weeks ago.[33]

These lines, despite the hints of disapproval or condescension, attest to a world in which labourers and servants spent on gewgaws and frivolities.

They convey something of the pleasure which was derived from these cheap versions of what their betters wore. Little of their costume was made by the wearers themselves. What in total these poorer sections of the people could spend on dress is unknown; also, how their spending power affected local industries or imports. In the pursuit of fashion, servants may be a special case. They had unusual incentives and opportunities to embrace the new. Furthermore, their employers expected of them decent clothing. They assisted their servants, buying cloth and ready-made articles at fairs; supplying liveries; and advancing cash for gaudy handkerchiefs and aprons.[34] The frequency with which clothing and textiles were stolen or pawned suggested that in Ireland, as throughout western Europe, the second-hand was not spurned.[35]

Patterns were merely one of several occasions when the poor regularly assembled. There emulative display was both expected and gratified. Similarly, but more frequently, more exacting deportment and dress were demanded by the formalised settings, at least in towns, for worship. Ideas of civility and politeness, explicit in the Tridentine programme, were taught by continentally trained priests. Simultaneously, the middle sort of the Protestants, especially when urban, were subjected to more onerous requirements in demeanour. The problem, for the clergymen no less than for the laity, was to steer between an absurd excess and unbecoming frugality. An unlucky curate at St Michan's church in Dublin in the 1720s was ridiculed for his foppishness and sartorial vanity: so much so that his rector tried to be rid of him.[36] For members of the laity the expectations, although not codified, exerted a tyranny. A young woman from Mayo, heedless of the expense as she amused herself in Dublin, soon ran out of money and credit. Pathetic appeals were despatched to her relations in the country to rescue her with borrowed petticoats, aprons and kerchiefs. Unable to equip herself with fitting shoes and dress, she was forced to contract her social circuit until church-going ceased.[37]

Cutting the 'grand figure' obsessed the ambitious within Protestant Ireland. Central to this was appearance. It raised the risk, familiar elsewhere, of imposture. Through public display, the bold could pass for what they were not. But since attire, houses, horses and equipages were so intimately linked with public position, it followed that those excluded from or with no ambition to join in civic affairs would have less need to spend heavily on these goods. In seventeeth-century Ireland, politics, society and economy had been remodelled. As a result Catholics were largely debarred from any recognisably public arena. Indeed, the legal exclusions had been seconded by drives to expel Catholics from the ports, walled towns, coastal districts and best land. These had rarely succeeded. Nevertheless, official discrimination abetted an informal process of physical sorting and zoning. In many boroughs, extra-mural 'Irishtowns' embodied the lot of the Catholics. In the countryside, Catholics had generally retreated into less fertile regions. The most ardent exponents of a Protestant monopoly over power in the kingdom of Ireland welcomed this physical segregation.

If, as these measures threatened, the more affluent districts in Protestant corporations were turned into ghettoes, Catholics were denied both the spaces where and the means through which they might publicly use their wealth. Well into the eighteenth century, tolls and dues, no less than walls and gates, controlled entry into urban markets and fairs.[38] Irish boroughs were also adding smart amenities in order to steal a march on rivals. New spaces were laid out in Cork, Limerick, Kinsale and Waterford, as well as Dublin.[39] Ingress was regulated. Furthermore, a commercialisation of leisure, extending to such demotic events as patterns, fairs, horse-races and plays, set a price on enjoyment. Elaborate mechanisms of tickets, fees, subscriptions and oaths determined access to clubs, voluntary societies, pleasure gardens, assembly rooms and bowling greens. Even those spots of apparently open resort, such as the new promenades and malls, and perhaps particularly the rebuilt churches with their grids of seating, exacted more rigorous standards of dress and conduct.[40]

The entertainments which multiplied in eighteenth-century Irish towns varied the already well-stocked calendar of state and municipal jollifications. These occasions have already been described as 'rites of exclusion', underscoring the separation of Protestants from Catholics.[41] But to the confessional criterion were added others which then determined entry to public pleasures. Most recreations were available to those who could pay. More often it was not a ticket or subscription which had to be purchased, but suitable clothing or the correct manners. These financial barriers were not ones which automatically shut out Catholics. Nevertheless, two reasons ensured that few Catholics participated. Catholics were located disproportionately among the poor. In part this was because they far outnumbered the Protestants. Also, the system of exclusions had cut them off from many of the most remunerative occupations. If money was needed to enter these theatres of delight, then most Catholics simply lacked the wherewithal. But there was, too, the question of attitudes. Some Protestant nonconformists, themselves objects of legal discrimination, deliberately refrained from what they despised as unnecessary ostentation, and so further distanced themselves from communal festivities.[42] By the eighteenth century, many Catholics, whether from preference or necessity, eschewed display. Where they husbanded resources, they calculated politicly that riches were better concealed than advertised in high living. Having to pay over the odds to rent lands and houses which once they had owned, contributing covertly to the upkeep of the religious or to educate their own children, well-to-do Catholics held back from frantic consumerism.[43] Above all, disabled from public life, they escaped the onerous obligations which attended it. Otherwise, it is hard to believe that these modestly successful Catholic merchants and farmers were entirely immune from the tug of fashion and novelty. Their habits are mostly hidden, and likely to stay so, owing to the absence of surviving accounts of their expenditure.

The crepuscular quality which invests the lives of the once dominant Catholic elite accentuates the visibility of much that their Protestant successors did. In the 1720s, the sophisticated proprietor of Castle Durrow, William Flower, on course for a peerage, scarcely needed to be reminded that 'money is always best spent where one makes the best figure'.[44] This calculation justified motley indulgences, since all upheld interest. Interest – of family, estate, locality or Protestant Ireland – encapsulated the concerns of all engaged, no matter how humbly, in running the kingdom.[45] A few examples suffice to demonstrate how far into their homes and families the sense of public responsibilities extended, so explaining what otherwise might have been censured as self-regarding excesses.

William Waring was a landowner in Ulster who had gained from the redistributions of the mid- and later seventeenth century. He moved from the ranks of the gentry into the undoubted social prominence of an esquire. In the 1690s he still maintained – on about £600 p.a. – a sombre gravity which he commended to his sons. William Waring knew that his restraint now looked old-fashioned. Despite his attachment to these older ways, he was not impervious to changing conventions. In order to live up to the position which he had attained he interested himself in such matters as his house, with its furnishings and staff, and even his own attire. He sought a female servant who could cook and serve meat, so freeing his wife to attend to their guests.[46] Earlier in their lives, it seemed, Mrs Waring had overseen preparations in the kitchen. At this time, Waring, like other gentlemen in the neighbourhood, took advantage of the services of an itinerant painter to have his wife, his heir and himself portrayed.[47] Further, he requested of a son in Dublin, cloth, wigs and hats for his own use. These orders at once told of an imperious paterfamilias and of an uncertain voyager lately embarked on the choppy waters of fashion. In 1697 he asked the advice of his eldest son when selecting stuff for a cloak, as to what 'is worn by men of my age'.[48] Next the appropriate lining for the cloak bothered him. Similarly, in ordering a new hat and wig he struggled to explain precisely what he wanted.[49] These preferences could most readily be communicated through comparison with what he had seen kinsfolk and neighbours wearing. But it was sometimes hard to find the words which accurately told of what he desired. Of the periwig, therefore, he wrote, 'I would not have too much hair in it, but a moderate one to come to my face and not to fly back'.[50] These uncertainties in an elderly man who had hitherto moved assuredly in his local society were created by unfamiliar relationships as well as by commodities. William Waring anxiously sought the right formula with which to invite a daughter-in-law and her parents to visit. A first try was sent open to the son to be vetted, with instructions, 'if the letter please you, you may deliver it. If not, let me know how you would have it and it shall be amended'.[51]

In these matters William Waring deferred to the younger generation. In doing so he ceded some of the authority which he exercised over his offspring. His sons flourished in the polite worlds of Ulster, Dublin and London. Their skills had not been acquired effortlessly. It had obliged them to mimic their obvious social superiors: notably the viceregal and ducal house of Ormonde, into the orbit of which they had gravitated. Grander neighbours, like the Brownlows of Lurgan and the Hills at Hillsborough, also supplied models. The elder Waring had been frank in disclosing his uncertainties. He adopted some of the material trappings of social and economic success. Notwithstanding the occasional signs that these habits had had to be learnt, neither he nor his sons were mocked for pretensions or ostentation. Rather they conformed themselves to what was expected of those of similar standing and income. Furthermore, while the younger Waring had picked up some of his ideas of the smart from nearby grandees, the Brownlows and Hills, so far from deriding this imitation, came to rely on his judgement and taste. The younger Waring, reputed a man of discrimination and accomplishment, able to choose what he pleased in the provinces of building, furnishings and dress, advanced himself to a position of superiority among his neighbours.[52]

The example of the Warings tends to confirm the common assumption that the landed were the arbiters of taste. Thanks to their wealth, they bought travel, education, public positions and the accoutrements which went with them. In practice, though, much of the polish which dazzled their contemporaries reflected the continuing links of the family with their mercantile relations in Belfast, Dublin and London. Furthermore, Waring *père* had purchased for his sons the university education and foreign travel which only a minority of the Irish Protestant gentry esteemed.[53] Something of the cultivation of the Warings may be explained by their lingering intimacy with more distant and urban environments and with the professions and trades into which the cadets of the dynasty happily entered. Necessarily the progeny of the Protestant proprietors of Ireland sought their livelihoods away from the land. Professions, office, trades and crafts all beckoned. At best, these openings provided financial security and status. Yet, there existed ambiguities about just where these callings fitted in the social hierarchy. Thus, for their practitioners, appearance, behaviour and habitation might make a crucial difference, ensuring that at least they were accepted as genteel if not truly gentle.[54]

The law afforded one of the most popular, although also a treacherous, route to financial security and social respect. Attorneys were accorded the courtesy style of 'gentlemen'. It was widely known that vast disparities in accomplishment, culture and means separated the ignorant who practised in the borough courts, the drudges in the legal departments in Dublin and a few 'toppers'. One of the last was Charles Cauldwell.[55] Between 1744 and 1746 he corresponded with a colleague in London. As well as writing of professional matters, the Dubliner fussed over having new wigs sent from London. In what might be represented as a characteristic abdication of the provincial to the cosmopolitan, Cauldwell concluded, 'I know you are a man of taste, and therefore say nothing about the fashion, but remember I would have them [the wigs] good as well as handsome'.[56] When, after many delays, the wigs arrived in Dublin, they did not please. Cauldwell expostulated about the inferior quality and declared that they 'wont wear as well as an Irish wig. They have already lost all their curl. He thought any hair good enough for an Irish chap.'[57]

This episode, trivial, even absurd, restates the theme of the provincial lost in, and looking to a metropolitan to lead him through, the maze of fashion. The incident can be read in other ways. Cauldwell was worried lest he be cheated or exploited. In the event he railed against the impostures practised by the London supplier. These experiences paralleled, and may sometimes have strengthened, Irish fury at what was imposed – in government or in taste – by London. Such anger nourished a fitful Irish patriotism. British tyranny must be resisted, whether it be constitutional subjection, economic discrimination or enslavement to imported novelties. In this mood, the smart decreed that the modish should henceforth buy Irish. Thus the public displays of wealth could be read as all too legible indices of patriotism. Those who did not accommodate themselves to these campaigns, as in 1750, might be intimidated and attacked, with shop windows smashed, imported cloth rifled and offending dresses slashed.[58]

Undercurrents of anxiety ran through the efforts of the Warings and Cauldwell to buy the right commodities. Since the correct use of riches did not always come naturally, instructors were needed. Much comment suggested that the resulting relationships fortified the dominance of Dubliners over provincials, town-dwellers over country people, the metropolis over the peripheries, Britons (especially Londoners) over the Irish. The shrieks of exaggerated amusement let out by Lady Theodosia Crosbie as she endured the clumsy efforts of a Limerick vintner and his wife to welcome her in the city told of the conventional belief that the aristocracy, in Ireland as elsewhere, were the proper custodians of refinement.[59]

Equally the panic into which an agent in Youghal was thrown by the impending visit in 1755 of the lord lieutenant revealed how far even a sizeable port could lag behind. This agent confided that he would have to procure from Cork city a cook to prepare the meats, 'for my wife is not able to do it, scarcely to see it done'. He had quickly bespoken silver butter boats from a Cork silversmith to grace the table, but still lacked either a salver or coffee pot.[60] Yet, as has been argued from the case of the Warings, the linked worlds of goods and manners offered chances for the wealthy, the opportunists and the adroit to rise above their inherited stations. Cauldwell, as we have seen, questioned the dictatorship of London. Moreover, he exemplified the tendency of successful Dubliners to fashion material and mental cultures from assorted elements: some local, others imported. It was in these quarters, where occasions for the public display of resources abounded, that innovations were most likely to begin.[61]

The Irish, even when striving to be in the pink of fashion, seldom submitted uncritically to the English. Nor was it only provincials in Ireland who turned to Dubliners to guide them towards the smart. Throughout the 1730s and 1740s a leading Dublin doctor regularly performed commissions for a squire from north Wales. Subsequently, the doctor's widow continued these services, despatching bolts of choice linen to Flintshire. The care lavished on these errands, like the goods themselves, were intended, and understood, as tokens of esteem and friendship. But among the already unequal these forays into the business of consumerism further complicated relationships, and could occasion misunderstandings and offence as well as gratitude and delight.[62]

A final example serves to remind of the complex problems either revealed or created by the multiplicity of goods available to the fortunate. In 1744, as international dangers and the prospect of domestic unrest grew, the militia was revived. The earl of Egmont, in common with his ancestors, prided himself on the zeal of his tenantry on his north County Cork estates. In the recent past they had been organised as a troop, with their own colours and equipment. Now, in 1744 and 1745, Egmont's agent reported difficulties both in mustering the contingent and persuading the men to drill. In some cases the reluctance arose from a lack of money to buy arms. But many troopers also objected to the colour which had been suggested for their uniforms. Red, which Egmont had proposed, was disliked because worn by 'none but gentlemen's servants'. In consequence it was seen as 'a badge of servile dependency'. Not only must it be altered, but also the cut of sleeves and pockets of the garments until they resembled those worn by the troops quartered in nearby Mallow and Charleville.[63] This awareness of fashion, as much as penury, hampered the bid to form the tenantry into an effective force. Only when news arrived that the

Young Pretender had captured Edinburgh did the north Cork Protestants act. Still not all would bow to uniformity. Despite contrary commands, some bought themselves laced hats, 'which will put others not so well able upon doing so too'.[64] Soon all the men were requesting gold-laced hats, 'which they say are worn by every troop in the kingdom'.[65] The agent demurred, and instead bought plain hats with cockades in Cork city. But the regimentals had been modified: to coats of blue cloth lined with red serge.[66]

Unease at being compelled to don garb demeaning to their idea of their own status eclipsed the sense of imminent danger to Protestant Ireland. The Egmonts' tenants may have understood very well how best to extract desirable new clothes from their absentee landlord. The militia also offered them subsidised conviviality. At the height of the emergency, a respectable 129 mustered at Lohort Castle. After the review only the properly attired were treated by their officers; the motley were left to slink away. As the agent, obliged to superintend the occasion, reported, 'the men would expect to be made drunk'.[67] A possible result was that some might tumble down the stone stairs of the castle. In the event, although the merry-making lasted until two in the morning, nothing 'disagreeable' marred the day.[68] Soon enough, as the likelihood of insurrection receded, the troop atrophied into a pretext for sociable assembly. The officers of the corps were now asked for details of their armorial bearings so that they could be painted onto the back of the chairs on which they sat when dining at Lohort.[69] Perhaps with good reason the authorities in Dublin expressed scepticism about what the local militias would do if called upon to fight.

Property-owning, as has been stressed, involved duties towards the rest of society. This was as true for possessors of moveable goods and money as for the landed. One of these obligations had been written into the terms on which newcomers had been granted estates in seventeenth-century Ireland: to keep Protestant tenants in a state of military readiness. The martial origins of the plantations were remembered through the rituals and traditions of Protestant communities. Indeed, this military ethos together with careers in the army and navy shaped many Irish Protestants' lives.[70] However, by the eighteenth century, the soldiery were linked with the traits of excess which outsiders detected throughout Protestant Ireland.[71] The willingness of Irish citizens to assume the titles and trappings of the army, but not always to shoulder the duties, was widely mocked.[72] Landlords, like the Egmonts, continued to spend on the notional defence of the kingdom. For their tenants, arrayed in finery and drilling perfunctorily, military service enabled them to advertise the privileges of citizenship which they monopolised. Yet the riotousness which attended gatherings like those at Lohort was at odds with the attitudes which the Egmonts wished to promote: of politeness, domesticity, intimacy and conjugality.

Unfortunately proprietors such as the Egmonts were now almost habitually absent from Ireland. In time, other leaders for Irish Protestant society emerged: sometimes from the landed, but also within the towns and professions. They espoused the doctrines of moderation and restraint. But, paradoxically, reticence required wealth. Moreover, the wealthy had to be tutored to realise that it was better to mask than to parade riches. In this atmosphere, privacy came to be highly valued.[73] Some in Ireland, particularly those who had travelled widely, subscribed to this fashion. Again, though, it took money to reserve space for specific purposes. For want of it, even activities such as personal devotion, appropriately conducted in solitude, seldom were. This remained true of a longer list of pastimes: reading, writing, sewing, even sleeping.[74]

The gap between an ideal of privacy and a reality in which most actions were seen by others can be illustrated from the design of houses. Two late seventeenth-century commentators on domestic architecture in England agreed that an important innovation had been devices which segregated owners and their families from their menials. Subsidiary or back stairs, coupled with corridors and servants relegated to attics, basements or service wings, accomplished this.[75] In Ireland one who quickly understood the meaning of these novelties was William Waring's son, Samuel. In particular he was impressed by the convenience of giving houses two staircases: the public and the private. Waring glossed the development: 'the public one being as much for ornament and state as use'. In contrast, 'the lesser or private stairs run the height of the whole house, designed only for back lodgings and the servants and children to make use of'.[76] Not only did Waring praise this feature, he adopted it as an essential element in his County Down residence. Also, he copied and devised schemes which incorporated two sets of stairs.[77] His interest in this matter could be regarded as continuing his father's attempts in the 1690s to divide the public from the private activities of the household. Then, by hiring a competent servant, he had hoped to hide from guests the less glamorous domestic chores. Even so, the circumstances of a squirearchical family like the Warings, still in the 1730s worth only £900 p.a., precluded physical arrangements through which the owners could seclude themselves from those who served them. Rooms were too few to be used other than flexibly. A subsidiary flight of stairs was introduced at Waringstown. It allowed the house to be made into two apartments: one for the widow of William Waring; the other for her son and his family. But even in a building of the size and ambition of the Warings' house, rooms could not be dedicated to particular uses or sealed off from servants.[78] The more modest dwellings which housed the bulk of the Irish population stifled any aspiration to, let alone the practice of, privacy.[79]

Since a private life was so difficult to accommodate, most actions, including the conjugal and domestic, were on public view. In England, the wish to keep out intruders has been connected with the decline in aristocratic retinues and the lower standing of those servants who were retained.[80] In Ireland, where wages were low and where many gentry houses doubled as working farms, the decline in the size of establishments may have been less dramatic. Furthermore, there remained functionaries – tutors, chaplains, stewards, and housekeepers – whose backgrounds and duties did not consign them to invisibility. The residences of Irish noblemen and gentlemen contained a constantly changing staff of footmen, maids and grooms. Most also held a nucleus of respected servants who had been there a decade or longer.[81] Even had the physical structure of the interior allowed, which was not often, there was neither wish nor need to banish these retainers from sight. Rather the servants, like the other appurtenances on which money was lavished, were to be seen and admired. Servants, most clearly through their liveries, but also by their stature and demeanour, proclaimed the standing of their employers. Thus, they strutted through the streets before and behind carriages, or were ranged like the plate on the sideboard behind the dinner table.

These displays were public, and houses were generally organised to maximise rather than minimise them. Spending of the kind described here projected and sustained flattering images of the family and individual. A building with its increasingly diversified contents embodied both the physical reality and the abstraction of the dynasty or 'house'. Where privacy was sought and achieved it was usually stage-managed. Accordingly it served to add to the style and sophistication of the actors. As such it was simply another example of disbursing funds to make 'the best figure'.

NOTES

1 Memoir of A. Oughton, pp 37, 46, 87 (National Army Museum, London, MS 8088.36.1).

2 David Dickson, *Arctic Ireland* (Dundonald, 1997).

3 James Kelly, 'Jonathan Swift and the Irish economy in the 1720s' in *Eighteenth-Century Ireland*, vi (1991), pp 7–36.

4 Brian Boydell, *A Dublin musical calendar 1700–1760* (Dublin, 1988), pp 81, 267–9; Brian Boydell, *Rotunda music in eighteenth-century Dublin* (Dublin, 1992).

5 Proctors' account book, 1735–55, St Patrick's cathedral, Dublin, entries for 16 Jan. 1740[1], 26 April 1741 (R[epresentative] C[hurch] B[ody] Library, Dublin, MS C.2.1.10(1&2)).

6 Account book of Abp. H. Boulter, pp 131,135 (T.C.D., MS 6399). Another tribute to Boulter's charitable impulses is in E. O'Leary, 'The O'More family of Balyna in the County Kildare, by James More, circa 1774' in *Journal of the County Kildare Archaeological Society*, ix (1918–21), p. 325.

7 Accounts of Richard Edgeworth, 1720–70 (N.L.I., MSS 1507–36); accounts of Ralph Howard from 1748 (ibid., MS 1725).

8 Something of the movement can be gleaned from: I. Campbell Ross (ed.), *Public virtue, Public love: the early years of the Dublin Lying-in Hospital* (Dublin, 1986); J. B. Lyons, *The quality of Mercer's: the story of Mercer's Hospital, 1734–1991* (Sandycove, 1991); Elizabeth Malcolm, *Swift's Hospital: a history of St Patrick's Hospital Dublin, 1746–1989* (Dublin, 1989).

9 D.W. Hayton, 'Did Protestantism fail in early eighteenth-century Ireland? Charity schools and the enterprise of religious and social reformation, *c.* 1690–1730' in Alan Ford, James McGuire and Kenneth Milne (ed.), *As by law established: the Church of Ireland since the Reformation* (Dublin, 1995), pp 166–86; Kenneth Milne, *The Irish charter schools 1730–1830* (Dublin, 1997).

10 R. Lawrence, *The interest of Ireland in its trade and wealth stated*, 2 vols (Dublin, 1682), i, 22–9.

11 C. J. Berry, *The idea of luxury* (Cambridge, 1994), pp 101–76.

12 P. H. Kelly, '"Industry and virtue versus luxury and corruption": Berkeley, Walpole and the South Sea bubble crisis' in *Eighteenth-Century Ireland*, vii (1992), pp 57–74.

13 T.C. Barnard, 'Integration or separation? Hospitality and display in Protestant Ireland, 1660–1800' in L. W. B. Brockliss and D. S. Eastwood (ed.), *A union of multiple identities: the British Isles, c. 1750–1850* (Manchester, 1997), pp 127–46.

14 Explorations of this ideology include: T.C. Barnard, 'The uses of 23 October 1641 and Irish Protestant celebrations' in *E.H.R.*, cvi (1991), pp 889–920; Barnard, 'Reforming Irish manners: the religious societies in Dublin during the 1690s' in *Historical Journal*, xxxv (1992), pp 805–38; Barnard, 'The Hartlib circle and the cult and culture of improvement in Ireland' in M. Greengrass, M. Leslie and T. Raylor (ed.), *Samuel Hartlib and universal reformation* (Cambridge, 1994), pp 281–97.

15 M. Cox, *A sermon preached at Christ-Church, Dublin, on the 20th day of March, 1747[8]* (Dublin, 1748); R. Davies, *The right use of riches. A sermon preach'd . . . August the 11th 1717* (Dublin, 1717); E. Synge, *Universal beneficence: a sermon preached . . . the nineteenth day of March 1720/1* (Dublin, 1721).

16 T.C. Barnard, 'The political, material and mental culture of the Cork settlers, *c.*1650–1700' in C. G. Buttimer and P. O'Flanagan (ed.), *Cork: history and society* (Dublin, 1993), p. 331; Barnard, 'The world of goods and County Offaly in the early eighteenth century' in Tim P. O'Neill (ed.), *Offaly: history and society* (Dublin, 1998), pp 371–92; L. M. Cullen, *Anglo–Irish trade* (Manchester, 1968).

17 M. Parnell to J. Parnell, 27 Nov. 1759 (Southampton University Library, Congleton MS, MS 64/614); 'An autobiography of Pole Cosby of Stradbally, Queen's County, 1703–37 (?)' in *Journal of the County Kildare Archaeological Society*, v (1906), pp 79–99, 165–84, 253–73, 311–24, 423–36; D.M. Beaumont, 'An Irish gentleman in England: the travels of Pole Cosby, *c.* 1730–35' in *Journal of the British Archaeological Society*, cxlix (1996), pp 37–54.

18 R. Edwards to F. Price, 7 Jan. 1747[8] (N[ational] L[ibrary of] W[ales]. Puleston MSS, MS 3577E).

19 E. Spencer to same, 6 Dec. 1743 (ibid., MS 358OE).

20 Ware household accounts, c. 1740–75 (T.C.D., MS 10528); Edgeworth accounts, 1720–70 (N.L.I., MSS 1507–36); T.C. Barnard, 'The worlds of a Galway squire: Robert French of Monivae (1716–1779)' in Gerard Moran (ed.), *Galway: history and society* (Dublin, 1996), pp 271–96.

21 A. Young, *A tour of Ireland*, 2 vols (Dublin, 1780), ii, appendix, pp 17–25; W. E. H. Lecky, *History of Ireland in the eighteenth century*, new ed., 5 vols (London, 1912), i, 284, 287.

22 Examples which continue the tradition include: N. Canny, *The upstart earl: a study of the social and mental world of Richard Boyle, first earl of Cork, 1566–1643* (Cambridge, 1982); S. Tillyard, *Aristocrats* (London, 1994).

23 The argument of Barnard, 'Integration or separation?'. An attempt in this direction is made in Barnard, 'Land and the limits of loyalty: the second earl of Cork and first earl of Burlington (1612–98)' in T. Barnard and J. Clark (ed.), *Lord Burlington: architecture, art and life* (London, 1995), pp 167–99.

24 P. Langford, 'British politeness and the progress of western manners: an eighteenth-century enigma' in *Transactions of the Royal Historical Society*, 6th series, vii (1997), pp 53–72.

25 For an obsessive accountant, Richard Edgeworth's records between 1720 and 1770 (N.L.I., MSS 1507–36).

26 The basis of these calculations will be explained in Barnard, *The Protestant ascendancy* (forthcoming). On the peerage, see F. G. James, *Lords of the ascendancy: the Irish house of lords and its members, 1600–1800* (Dublin, 1995).

27 Account of Sligo (N.L.I., MS 20397).

28 W. Petty, *The political anatomy of Ireland* (London, 1691), pp 75–82; cf. L. M. Cullen, 'Incomes, social classes and economic growth in Ireland and Scotland, 1600–1900' in T. M. Devine and David Dickson (ed.), *Ireland and Scotland 1600–1850: parallels and contrasts in economic and social development* (Edinburgh, 1983), pp 248–60.

29 Account of Sligo (N.L.I., MS 20397).

30 Quoted in B. Lemire, *Fashion's favourite: the cotton trade and the consumer in Britain, 1660–1800* (Oxford, 1991), p. 62.

31 B. Lemire, 'Peddling fashion: salesmen, manufacturers, tailors and the second-hand clothes trade in England, *c.* 1700–1800' in *Textile History*, 22 (1991) pp 67–80; C. Shammas, *The pre-industrial consumer in England and America* (Oxford, 1990); J. Styles, 'Manufacture, consumption and design in eighteenth-century England' in J. Brewer and R. Porter (ed.), *Consumption and the world of goods* (London and New York, 1993), pp 527–54.

32 Barnard, 'The world of goods and Co. Offaly'.

33 These verses appear in T.C.D., MS 10665, pp 80–1, and J. Anketell, *Poems on several subjects* (Dublin, 1793). Extracts are included in A. Carpenter (ed.), *Verse in English from eighteenth-century Ireland* (Cork, 1998), pp 493–4.

34 Vigors account book, 1711–20 (Carlow County Library, Vigors MSS); accounts of R. Fitzpatrick, 1705–1715 (N.L.I., MS 3000, ff. 23, 75); account book of Lawder of Bunnybeg, 1760s (P. R. O. N. I., D 4123, f. 55).

35 Crown entry books, city and county and Dublin, 1741–52 (National Archives, Dublin).

36 Memorandum book, St Michan's (R.C.B., MS P.276.12.1, pp 82–88).

37 M. Moore to J. Moore, 11 Dec. 1759; same to M. Moore [Dec. 1759] (Brabazon MSS, box I, private collection, London); Barnard, 'Integration or separation?', p. 137.

38 Journal of N. Peacock, 1 March 1743[4], 25 Nov. 1744 (N.L.I., MS 16091); C. Massy, *A collection of resolutions, queries, &c. wrote on the occasion of the present dispute in the city of Limerick* (Limerick, 1769).

39 J. Fitzgerald, *The Cork remembrancer* (Cork, 1783), pp 165, 167, 173, 174, 203; Massy, *Collection of resolutions*, p. 20; Kenneth Milne, 'The corporation of Waterford in the eighteenth century' in William Nolan and T. P. Power (ed.), *Waterford: history and society* (Dublin, 1992), p. 331; M. Mulcahy (ed.), *Calendar of Kinsale documents*, i (Kinsale, 1988), p. 35.

40 Minutes of Hanover Society, Youghal (P.R.O.N.I., D. 2707/C1/1); minutes of Mallow Loyal Irish Protestant club (T.C.D., MS 7105); plan of St Peter's church, Dublin (R.C.B., PS. P.45.6.1, p.66); accounts of Balfour, 18 Feb. 1740[1], 4 March 1741[2]

(N.L.I., MS 9535); accounts of Balfour 18 Feb. 1747[8] (N.L.I., MS 10277); R. Caulfield (ed.), *Council book of the corporation of Youghal* (Guildford, 1878), pp 394, 442, 446.

41   Barnard, 'Uses of 23 October 1641', p. 914.

42   *A narrative of the Christian experiences of George Bewley* (Dublin, 1750), pp 11, 15, 33, 43; *Some account of the life of Joseph Pike of Cork* (London, 1837), pp 59–61, 64–6.

43   L. M. Cullen, 'Catholics under the penal laws' in *Eighteenth-Century Ireland*, i (1986), pp 23–36; Cullen, 'Catholic social classes under the Penal Laws' in T. P. Power and Kevin Whelan (ed.), *Endurance and emergence: Catholics in Ireland in the eighteenth century* (Dublin, 1990), pp 57–84; David Dickson, 'Catholics and trade in eighteenth-century Ireland: an old debate revisited' in ibid., pp. 85–100; Kevin Whelan, 'An underground gentry? Catholic middlemen in eighteenth-century Ireland' in *Eighteenth-Century Ireland*, x (1995), pp 7–68; reprinted in Whelan, *The tree of liberty* (Cork, 1996).

44   Lord Palmerston to W. Flower, 8 Oct. 1728 (N.L.I., MS 11478).

45   A preliminary discussion of this protean concept is in T.C. Barnard, 'The gentrification of eighteenth-century Ireland' in *Eighteenth-Century Ireland*, 12 (1997).

46   W. Waring to Sara Waring, [10 April 1697] (Private collection, County Down); same to Samuel Waring, 14 Nov. 1696 (ibid.).

47   P.R.O.N.I., D 695/69, 76, 78.

48   W. Waring to Samuel Waring, 20 Feb. 1696[7] (Private collection, County Down).

49   P.R.O.N.I., D 695/63.

50   W. Waring to S. Waring, 3 April 1697, 1 May 1697 (Private collection, County Down).

51   Same to same, 3 April 1697 (ibid.).

52   P.R.O.N.I., D 695/69,229; A. Hill to Samuel Waring, 3 Nov. 1703, 26 July 1705, 1 Jan. 1707[8] (Private collection, County Down); same to G. Waring, 25 April 1705, 22 Sep. 1707 (ibid.).

53   P.R.O.N.I., D 695/225,226,227; G.D. Burtchaell and T.U. Sadleir, *Alumni Dublinenses* (Dublin, 1935), pp 859–60, Cf. D. Hannigan, 'The University of Dublin, 1685–1750: a study of matriculation records', unpublished MA dissertation (St Patrick's College, Maynooth, 1995).

54   J. Bayley to G. Dodington, 1 Jan. 1735[6] (Clements MSS, Oldtown, Co. Kildare); J. Ingram to W. Smythe, 6 Dec. 1740 (N.L.I., PC 445); R. Waring to W. Waring, 11 Oct. 1691 (Private collection, County Down).

55   E. Keane, P. B. Phair and T. U. Sadleir (ed.), *King's Inns admission papers 1607–1867* (Dublin, 1982), p. 71. For jaundiced remarks on attorneys' pretensions: G.E. Howard, *A compendious treatise of the rules and practice of the pleas side of the exchequer in Ireland*, 2 vols (Dublin, 1759), i, pp. iii–vii.

56   C. Cauldwell to J. Pickard, 13 June 1745 (Dorset County Record Office, D/BLX/B19).

57   Same to same, 27 May 1746 (ibid., D/BLX/B17).

58   Presentments, Co. Cork, 12 March 1754; Co. Dublin, 12–18 May 1750, 27 July 1752 (National Archives, Dublin, Calendar of presentments); Fitzgerald, *Cork remembrancer*, p. 166.

59   Lady T. Crosbie to Lady Anne Bligh [1746] (P.R.O.N.I., D 2092/1/6), printed in D. Fitzgerald, The Knight of Glin, 'Three eighteenth–century letters from Lady Theodosia Crosbie' in *Journal of the Kerry Archaeological Society*, 17 (1984), pp 76–81.

60   W. Coughlan[?] to W. Conner, 22 May 1755 (Chatsworth House, Derbyshire, Lismore MS 36/138).

61   P. Earle, *The making of the English middle class: business, society and family life in London 1660–1730* (London, 1989); D. Roche, *The people of Paris* (Leamington Spa, 1987); L. Weatherill, *Consumer behaviour and material culture in Britain, 1660–1760* (London, 1988).

62 T. Kingsbury to F. Price, 3 & 17 July 1736, 14 March 1737[8], 24 Feb. 1746[7]; E. Kingsbury to A. Price, 17 Nov. 1753, 22 Dec. 1753, 28 Oct. 1754 (N.L.W., Puleston MSS 3584E).
63 R. Purcell to Lord Perceval, 13 April 1744, 8 May 1744 (B.L., Additional MS 47001B, ff 61ᵛ–2, 64).
64 Same to same, 1 Oct. 1745 (ibid., f. 146).
65 Same to same, 19 Nov. 1745 (ibid., f. 162).
66 Same to same, 15 Oct. 1745, 6 Dec. 1745 (ibid., ff 152, 169).
67 Same to same, 22 Oct. 1745 (ibid., f. 154).
68 Same to same, 22 Oct. 1745 (ibid., f. 154v).
69 Same to same, 28 Sep. 1747 (ibid., Additional MS 47002A, f. 125).
70 T.C. Barnard, 'Settling and unsettling Ireland: the Cromwellian and Williamite revolutions' in Ohlmeyer (ed.), *Ireland from independence to occupation*, pp 280–1.
71 Barnard, 'Integration or separation?', p. 138; Barnard, 'Athlone, 1685; Limerick, 1710: religious riots or charivaris' in *Studia Hibernica*, 27 (1993), pp 61–75; Barnard, *The abduction of a Limerick heiress* (Dublin, 1998), pp 11–12.
72 E. Spencer to F. Price, 29 June 1744 (N.L.W., Puleston MSS, MS 3580E); Barnard, 'Settling and unsettling Ireland', pp 280–1.
73 J. Brewer, '"The most polite age and the most vicious". Attitudes towards culture as a commodity, 1660–1800' in A. Bermingham and J. Brewer (ed.), *The consumption of culture 1600–1800: image, object, text* (London, 1995), pp 341–61; L. E. Klein, 'Politeness for plebes: consumption and social identity in early eighteenth-century England' in ibid., pp 361-82; A. J. La Volpa, 'Conceiving a public: ideas and society in eighteenth-century Europe' in *Journal of Modern History*, 64 (1992), pp 79–116.
74 T.C. Barnard, 'Learning, the learned and literacy in Ireland, *c.* 1660–1760' in T. C. Barnard, Dáibhí Ó Cróinín and Katharine Simms (ed.), *'A miracle of learning': studies in manuscripts and Irish learning* (Aldershot and Brookfield, 1998), pp 214–19.
75 H. Colvin and J. Newman (ed.), *Of building: Roger North's writings on architecture*, (Oxford, 1981), pp 127, 134–5; R. T. Gunther, *The architecture of Sir Roger Pratt* (Oxford, 1928), p 64. See, too: J. Bold, 'Privacy and the plan' in J. Bold and E. Chaney (ed.), *English architecture: public and private* (London and Rio Grande, 1994), pp 107–19; L. A. Pollock, 'Living on the stage of the world. The concept of privacy among the *elite* of early modern England' in A. Wilson (ed.), *Rethinking social history: English society 1570–1920 and its interpretation* (Manchester, 1993), pp 78–91.
76 P.R.O.N.I., D 695/338.
77 Plans and drawings by S. Waring (Private collection, County Down).
78 Scheme for dividing Waringstown House, 1702; inventory of Waringstown House, 12 Oct. 1704 (ibid.).
79 The intimate arrangements of a Dublin tenement, c.1727, are conveyed in the note-book of Stephen Green (P.R.O.N.I., T 898/1). They can be contrasted with D. J. Griffin, 'The building and furnishing of a Dublin townhouse in the eighteenth century' in *Bulletin of the Irish Georgian Society*, xxxviii (1996–7), pp 24–39.
80 M. Girouard, *Life in the English country house* (London and New Haven, 1978), pp 120–51.
81 Accounts of R. French (N.L.I., MSS 4918–19); accounts of Ware household (T.C.D., MS 10528).

6 Hospitality, housekeeping and high living in eighteenth-century Ireland

L.A. Clarkson

(i)

Historians and economists have rarely judged the consumption habits of the upper classes with unqualified approval. 'A great housekeeper', it was remarked in the early seventeenth century, 'is sure of nothinge for his good cheare save a great Turd at his gate'.[1] In 1745, the 4th earl of Chesterfield spluttered his notorious condemnation of the Irish gentry, that has hung like an albatross around their collective necks ever since:

Drinking is a most beastly vice in every country, but it is really a ruinous one in Ireland; nine gentlemen out of every ten are impoverished by the great quantity of claret which, from the mistaken notions of hospitality and dignity, they think it necessary should be drunk in their houses; this expense leaves them no room to improve their estates by proper indulgence upon proper conditions to their tenants, who pay them to the full, and upon the very day, that they may pay their wine-merchants.[2]

In 1776 Adam Smith discussed the economic consequences of gentry consumption in more sober terms. His purpose was to extol the virtues of merchant expenditure over that of the landowner. 'A merchant is accustomed to employ his money chiefly in profitable projects, whereas a mere country gentleman is accustomed to employ it chiefly in expense.' His analysis continued:

In a country that has neither foreign commerce, nor any of the finer manufactures, a great proprietor, having nothing for which he can exchange the greater part of his produce of his lands which is over and above the maintenance of the cultivators, consumes the whole in rustic hospitality at home. If this surplus is sufficient to maintain a hundred or a thousand men, he can make use of it in no other way than by maintaining a hundred or a thousand men. He is at all times, therefore, surrounded with a multitude of retainers and dependants . . .[3]

Smith drew examples from early-modern England and his native Scotland, but not from Ireland. Yet he might well have done so had he been better acquainted with that country, in the process contrasting the stimulating economic benefits of the rapid expansion of Dublin, Cork and the smaller towns during the eighteenth century with the lesser gains arising from bucolic hospitality in the countryside.

There is, nevertheless, an alternative view of the impact of gentry expenditure. Lawrence Stone has argued that the conspicuous consumption of the English aristocracy 'was of critical importance in galvanising into activity the sluggish Tudor economy'.[4] In her Ford Lectures published in 1978, Joan Thirsk provided a magisterial survey of the consumer industries in early modern England that benefited from the demands of the better off.[5] At the end of the seventeenth century, if we are to believe Gregory King, the top six per cent of families in England received about one-quarter of the wealth of that country. They spent perhaps thirty per cent of their income on food. At the bottom of the heap, half the population spent more than it received; the great bulk of it went on basic diet.[6] In Ireland wealth was distributed even more unevenly than in England and the commercial sector was less well developed. In these circumstances it is arguable that during the eighteenth century high living by the gentry yielded disproportionate economic benefits. It is this hypothesis that the present paper explores.

(ii)

Conspicuous consumption can take many forms. Most tangibly there were the building projects – houses and estate villages – that remain visible features of the Irish landscape to this day.[7] It does not stretch categories too far to regard the expenditure on these as capital rather than consumption since successful estate villages promoted commerce, and country houses functioned almost like small industries. More obvious consumption goods were clothes, pictures, furniture and household equipment, travel and travel accoutrements, funeral goods and finery, the study of which is just beginning under the perceptive eye of Dr Barnard.[8] Because of the mundane nature of such articles it is easy to overlook the magnitude of demand. To take a single example, the inventory of the household goods of an elderly Armagh gentlewoman, made at her death in 1797, itemised dozens of pictures, scores of tables, chairs, beds and cupboards, hundreds of books, bottles by the barrowload, china and kitchenware in profusion, sufficient clothing and shoes to adorn a regiment of women, gaming boards and mathematical instruments, fine silverware, and enough miscellaneous lumber to stock a charity shop. As far as one can tell, most of these things were Irish-made. Gentry demand created the market for the fine woollen fabrics manufactured in Dublin and the high-quality rateens, the production of which supported the economy of Carrick-on-Suir for much of the eighteenth century.[9]

This essay has a narrower focus. It concentrates on the eating and drinking that went on in upper-class households during the eighteenth century. Some of this was, indeed, the extravagant bingeing that Chesterfield condemned. Some of it, on the other hand, was essential consumption, for even gentlemen must eat. The greater share, however, was the normal household hospitality expected of a country gentleman. Much of the argument is based on an analysis of thirteen sets of reasonably comprehensive household accounts between 1674 and 1828 – a long eighteenth century.[10] This is a small sample, but it is supplemented by numerous fragmentary accounts, newspapers, notebooks and letters, notably the magnificent series of letters written almost daily during the summer months of 1746–1752 by Bishop Edward Synge from his palace in Elphin to his daughter, Alicia, who kept house for him in Dublin.[11]

The accounts vary in scale. The smallest was a personal book of a member of the Balfour family of Townley Hall near Drogheda, who spent more than £4 on food during five days in 1782. Townley Hall also provides a set of household accounts. The longest running is a set of accounts belonging to the Plunkett family, earls of Fingall, County Meath, stretching over the 1780s and 1790s. Total expenditure exceeded £1,000, although the purchase of groceries seems to be understated. Almost certainly the Fingalls, like many gentry families, kept separate grocery account books. The largest expenditure was over £7,000 in the household of Thomas Conolly, of Castletown, County Kildare, between 1783 and 1787. Two accounts belong to the households of bishops of Down and Connor. Edward Pierce, steward of the absentee Thomas Hacket, kept one in 1674 at the bishop's house in Dromore. The other was the account book for the 1730s of Francis Hutchinson whose residence was in Lisburn.

(iii)

The account books illustrate a common feature of gentry housekeeping, or at least of the upper gentry; much of their consumption needs were supplied from their estates and not by purchases from shopkeepers. Beef, pork, mutton, beer, milk, cream, butter, and flour consumed by the Conollys, for example, came from their own fields, animals and dairies. Gifts from friends, neighbours and relations supplemented what could be obtained from shops and dealers. References to fruit and vegetables, apart from oranges and lemons, are not numerous in any of the account books, perhaps because they were not eaten very often, but more likely because these were grown in orchards and kitchen gardens. In June 1747 Edward Synge wrote to his daughter, 'I take it for granted that now the Fruits are coming in, you'll provide largely for Pyramids to be look'd at'. His Dublin garden produced a surfeit of melons and he told Alicia to give away those she could not use at home: 'One or two at different times to the Arch-Bishop would not be amiss. But send none that are not very good.'[12] Even oranges and lemons might be grown in carefully tended hot houses.

Another difficulty is determining how many people were being fed within a household. Even the small Balfour account itemising the expenditure of £4 in 1782 covered more than one person; £4, after all, was the equivalent of six months wages for an unskilled labourer. The Conolly establishment contained over 100 servants as well as the family. The maids, as well as being fed, received money wages (£8 a year) and were allowed two lb of sugar a month, but they had to buy their own tea.[13] Gentlemen also fed people who were not part of their households. The Conollys purchased oatmeal to give to the poor. More than a century earlier the steward of the outrageously neglectful bishop of Down and Connor regularly bought bread 'for the poor'. It was common practice to feed neighbours and poor people who turned up at the door. Dudley Cosby of Stradbally, Queen's County, was typical. As his son recalled:

From the time my Father came [back] from England [in 1716] he lived very handsomely . . . , he kept a very plentiful house and table, his allowance was twelve beefs a year, 40 mutton, 26 barrels of wheat for bread, 60 barrels of Mault, 2 hogsheads of Wine, Pork, Veal, lambs, Wilde and tame fouls, and all other things in proportion. He continued in this method and never encreased or decreased, when there was the least company, his table was never covered with less than 5 or 6 and very often with more. He used to have variety of wines. The Poor never went away empty from his door . . .[14]

Gentry housekeeping was extremely labour-intensive. Household management was generally the business of a housekeeper working to the commands of the mistress of the house and in the great houses there was a large and ordered hierarchy of retainers. At Carton, home of the duke of Leinster in the 1760s, the steward was responsible for the outdoor servants, including lodge keepers, farmers, a miller, chandler and brewer, carters, wheelwrights, smiths, grooms and stable hands. A housekeeper, a butler, and clerk of the kitchen controlled the indoor servants. There were ladies' maids, upper and lower housemaids, nursery maids, a wet nurse, and a large band of cleaners.[15] Bishop Synge had at least 35 servants at Elphin during the summer months and around 30 at Dublin and Finglas.[16] For a bishop he spent a surprising amount of his own time attending to the minutiae of domestic life. He had strong opinions about the qualities that servants ought to possess, including an ability to cook and clear starch, modesty, meekness, a good figure and competence at arithmetic.[17] Synge was a fusspot and bombarded the long-suffering Alicia with household instructions, many of them concerning the quality of his bread, beer and wines. He must have driven his household staff near demented by his interfering.

Table 1. Spending on food and drink by category (per cent)

Account	Date	Total spent £	Meat, poultry, rabbits %	Bread, cakes, grain %	Dairy, eggs %	Fish %	Fruit, vegetables %	Groceries %	Beer, whiskey %	Wines, spirits %	Misc. %
Hacket	1674	37.7	24.8	52.3	6.6	1.7	1.8	5.4	0	3.4	3.8
Hutchinson	1729–34	992.7	29.8	36.7	10.7	5.1	3.4	4.3	3.3	5.3	1.5
Carew	1738–82	397.1	5.2	18.9	8.9	15.3	3.3	16	3.3	27.9	1.3
Inchiquin	1746	6.2	17.4	6.1	17.3	45.3	1.3	2.8	6	0	3.8
King	1763	32.8	26.9	54	2.3	13.2	0	0.5	0	0	3.1
Townley	1774–7	194	47.3	19.3	5.5	4.9	2.3	13.2	5.9	0	1.4
Balfour	1782	4	51.2	26.7	7.8	6.3	5.5	0.6	0	0	1.9
Aldercron	1785–6	6.4	11.3	5.7	10	0.8	28.1	40.7	2.4	0.6	0.5
Fingall	1781–99	1028	15.6	26.9	2.9	2.8	0.8	2.3	4.6	42.5	1.7
Conolly	1783–7	7130.9	40.8	17.6	11.2	3.1	0.5	12.2	14.3	0	0.4
Drogheda	1812–6	228.7	48.6	9.5	26.6	4.2	9	0.7	0.8	0	0.7
Grattan	1821–4	37.7	54.4	37.9	1.4	0.9	0.3	0.6	2.9	0	1.6
Castletown	1828	77.5	81.6	10.6	3.3	1.4	0.1	1.4	1.1	2.1	0.6
Unweighted average			34.9	24.7	8.8	8.1	4.3	7.8	3.4	6.3	1.7
Coefficient of variation			0.6	0.6	0.8	1.4	1.7	1.4	1.3	2.1	0.6
Weighted average			36.3	20.8	10.3	3.8	1.2	10.1	11.1	5.9	0.8

The broad categories of spending on food in the thirteen households are set out in table 1. Averaging the accounts obscures changes occurring over time and differences between large and small households. The unweighted averages give undue dominance to the large accounts; for this reason both the unweighted and weighted averages are shown. It is reassuring that in the main categories of expenditure – meat, etc., bread, etc., dairy and eggs – the unweighted and weighted averages are similar. Meat, poultry and rabbits accounted for over one-third of all spending on food and drink, bread, cakes and grain for a quarter more, and dairy and eggs for another eight or ten per cent. It is also noticeable that the greatest dispersion around the unweighted mean, measured by the coefficient of variation, was among the items of small expenditure.

Before discussing the separate categories of expenditure it is useful to compare the gastronomical behaviour of Irish gentlemen with that of their social peers in England. This is done in table 2 where the Irish figures in table 1 are rearranged and compared with percentages derived from Gregory King's calculations for 1688.[18]

Table 2. Percentage expenditure on food and drink, England and Ireland

Category	England 1688	Ireland 1674–1828
Meat	15.0	31.0
Fish, poultry, eggs	10.0	14.0[1]
Milk, butter, cheese	13.0	7.0
Fruit, vegetables	9.0	4.0
Salt, oil, spices	6.0	10.0[2]
Beer, ale	16.0	3.0[3]
Wines, spirits	9.0	6.0
Bread, cakes	23.0	25.0[4]

[1] Includes rabbits
[2] Groceries and miscellaneous
[3] Includes whisky.
[4] Includes grain

The comparisons are crude: a single point in time in the late seventeenth century against a range of observations spread over 150 years. Nevertheless, they are not without interest. Expenditure on meat in eighteenth-century Ireland appears to have been double the expenditure in late-seventeenth-century England. King, however, probably underestimated English meat consumption. Household accounts from the fourteenth and fifteenth centuries suggest that anything between a quarter and a half of upper class spending on food went on meat. During the sixteenth and seventeenth

centuries aristocratic appetites for meat were so voracious that one contemporary remarked caustically, 'I think we have stowed more sorts of
flesh in our bellies than Noah's ark received'. Impressionistic evidence
from later centuries suggests that wealthy Englishmen could match their
Irish cousins in meat consumption.[19]

The share of spending on grain-based foods (excluding beer) was about
the same in both countries. This is a coincidence, but it underlines the fact
that eating patterns among the higher social groups in the two kingdoms
had much in common. It is initially surprising to find the proportion of
Irish incomes devoted to groceries higher than that indicated by King.
However, King's estimates were made before commodities such as tea,
sugar, coffee and rice became almost daily items of consumption. Import
data show that *per capita* consumption of groceries in Ireland was
substantially lower than in England during the eighteenth century.

The meats most commonly eaten in Ireland were beef and mutton.
Contrary to the claim of Crotty, the account books indicate that beef was
consumed more often than mutton.[20] In May 1752 Bishop Synge instructed
Alicia to use more mutton and less beef because there were too many sheep
at Finglas where he had a 67 acre farm.[21] The gentry spent surprisingly little
on pork and bacon but a good deal on rabbits, poultry and game. Few
chickens in County Kildare were safe from the carnivorous appetites of the
Conollys. In four years 4,560 chickens ended up on the Conolly dinner
table, in the company of 726 geese and ducks and 444 turkeys. The hapless
birds were bought from local poulterers or butchers. Rabbit warrens were
an established commercial activity on poor sandy soils but many households were supplied with wild rabbits by gamekeepers and hawkers.[22]

Individual families ate meat in prodigious quantities. In 1747 an ecclesiastical party was entertained by Dr Delany, dean of Down, and Mrs Delany.
The guests were Archbishop Stone of Armagh and his sister, and the
bishop of Derry and his wife. They dined on 'fish – beefstakes – soup –
rabbit and onions – Fillet Veal', followed by 'Turkey Pout – salmon grilde –
pickled salmon – quails – little Terrene Peas – Cream – Mushrooms –
Apple Pye – Crab – Leveret – Cheese-cakes'. Mrs Delany thought she was
being economical: 'I give as *little hot meat* as possible, but I think there
could not be less, considering the grandees that are to be here: the invitation
was to "*beef stakes*" which we are famous for'.[23] Another cleric, the Rev. John
Nixon of Killesher, County Fermanagh, held a dinner party in April 1769
for sixteen people. He served a brisket of beef, a roast leg of mutton, cow
heels and mutton broth, as well as vegetables and fish. There was enough
meat over to provide cold beef, with cheese and butter, for supper. In
September Nixon fed a party of six on fowl with celery sauce, a sirloin of
beef, two roast ducks, and ham, as well as vegetables and fruit.[24]

The Delanys and Nixon were entertaining guests; everyday fare may have been more frugal, but not obviously so. Between November 1765 and March 1766 Mr Balfour of Townley Hall bought on average 84 lb of beef a week.[25] The larder books of the Annesley household at Castlewellan, near Newcastle, County Down during the autumn of 1813 recorded weekly stocks of beef well in excess of 200 lb as well as smaller quantities of mutton. Dinner for the Annesleys on Sunday 26 September 1813 included hare soup, sheep's head mince, and roast loin of beef; there was a rump of cold beef on the side table. On Monday there were bacon and beans, boiled and roast chicken, roast mutton, rabbit and teal, with cold roast beef on the side table. Tuesday was a modest day with boiled leg of mutton, 'colcannon', roast goose, rabbit and cold beef. Wednesday, likewise, passed relatively abstemiously with two boiled chickens, a neat's tongue, roast saddle of mutton, roast duck and cold rib of beef. Thursday was greeted carnivorously with bacon and eggs, fricassee of chicken, roast chump of beef, roast chicken and cold chicken. If Friday were a day of abstinence, it was not apparent from the menu that included soup, stewed giblets, roast shoulder of mutton, roast chicken, cold roast beef, and cold chicken. And so the daily round was passed by the consuming of all God's creatures.[26] It is hardly likely that every individual ate every item, but the food was there if desired.

How much meat did individuals eat? According to estimates relating to the 1830s and 1840s, Irishmen ate on average 56 lb of meat a year.[27] If this figure applied also to the eighteenth century, a weekly consumption of one lb a week does not appear excessive. However by the end of the century meat eating was confined to perhaps to one-third of the population. At the beginning of the eighteenth century beef and mutton were out of the reach of many of the poor who, if they ate meat, consumed rabbits, hares, game and the scraggy bits of carcasses.

Turning to bread, cakes and grains, there were large variations in expenditure patterns (see table 3). The term grain covers meal, bran, and malt, as well as unmilled wheat, barley and oats that were fed to animals as well as humans. Contemporaries occasionally commented on the small amount of bread eaten in Ireland. 'Would not a Frenchman give a shrug', asked an anonymous traveller about 1750, 'at finding in every little inn Bordeaux claret and Nantz brandy though in all likelihood not a morsel of Irish bread!'[28] Generally, little money was laid out on flour before 1750.[29] The Balfours bought flour in the 1770s, possibly from the nearby bolting mill at Slane, built in 1768 and the biggest in Ireland. The Conollys, at Celbridge, County Kildare, were supplied with fine flour from Dublin and second rate flour from Naas, which had been one of the centres of English milling techniques from the 1750s.[30]

Table 3. Percentage expenditure on cereals

Account	Spent (£)	Bread	Cake	Flour	Grain
Hacket	16.9	5.7	0.1	1.2	93.0
Hutchinson	364.5	21.5	1.7	0.0	76.8
Carew	75.2	1.1	0.0	0.0	98.0
Inchiquin	0.4	0.0	100.0	0.0	0.0
King	17.7	3.6	0.3	0.0	96.1
Townley	35.7	74.8	4.4	1.5	19.4
Balfour	1.1	55.6	42.9	1.2	0.4
Aldercron	0.4	89.1	7.4	3.4	0.0
Conolly	1256.5	0.0	0.0	0.0	100.0[1]
Fingall	276.4	90.1	5.1	1.5	3.3
Drogheda	21.0	74.8	0.3	0.0	25.1
Grattan	14.2	22.4	0.0	5.4	66.2
Castletown	8.2	90.3	0.0	0.6	9.1
Unweighted average		41.1	12.5	1.1	45.3
Weighted average		18.4	1.1	0.3	80.2

[1] Includes flour.

Large households often did their own baking. The Fingalls were unusual in being large purchasers of bread. During more than two decades they spent almost £250 on 10,000 loaves. Even so, this was hardly a vast quantity, averaging only about 500 loaves a year – say ten a week. Most demand for ready-baked bread came from small and generally poor households lacking the means of baking. Retail bakeries existed in practically every town. There were dozens in Dublin and Cork, regulated by municipal authorities and working under the control of the assize of bread.[31] In a small provincial town, such as Coleraine, there was a single bakery. Armagh, with a population of about 2,000 in 1770, had six bakers, bread men and gingerbread makers, as well as two meal men, and a flour and bread dealer.[32]

Keeping a household in wholesome bread was hard work. The bishop of Elphin was obsessed by the quality of his bread. Some was baked with flour made from wheat grown on his own farm. His steward in Dublin was instructed to get 'a Bagg of right good Flower'. And most important of all, the bishop concluded it was necessary to use the purest barm, the preparation of which required the skills of an analytical chemist. In July 1751 Synge sent two pages of detailed advice to his daughter on the subject. The bread at Elphin, he told her, was superior to the bread in Dublin and he looked forward to his return every autumn without enthusiasm. 'It will mortify me much, to have as indifferent bread this Winter coming, as We had the last. Pray Has your house-keeper no skill of this kind?' The problem with the Dublin bread, he decided, was that the dough was made too wet.[33]

Bread existed in many varieties. 'Housel bread', that is common household bread, featured regularly in the Balfour accounts. In the 1730s, Bishop Hutchinson regularly bought 'fresh rolls' made of wheaten flour and enriched with milk, butter or eggs after the French fashion.[34] Among the Fingall purchases in the 1780s and 1790s were barm bracks. Friends of the Herbert family of Carrick-on-Suir in 1789 gave them 'a huge Barm Brack, thinking it a wonderful fine thing . . . to a set of half famished wretches as they supposed us to be'.[35]

Several household accounts itemise the purchase of biscuits. Originally biscuit was twice-baked bread and was the basis of military rations. By the eighteenth century biscuit had turned sweet and verged into the category of cakes.[36] Gingerbread was another bridge into the cake world.[37] The Fingalls maintained a regular cake account with a local baker who supplied large cakes, small cakes, plum cakes, mixed cakes, cheese cakes, seed cakes, and cakes unspecified. The Fingalls also bought rusks, hard biscuits, naples and seringo biscuits. Fasting cake was purchased during Lent, but for less austere occasions there were lemon sponges, raspberry tarts, apple pies and apple puffs, macaroons and caramel baskets. Such luxuries were often conjured from the kitchens of the gentry. In the summer of 1793 Dorothea Herbert and her friends held a housewarming at their seaside summer cottage:

We set all Hands to work, got our Pastry and Music from Carrick with every Rarity the Season afforded in Meats Fruits or Vegetables – The two Blundens got us all manner of fish and wildfowl – Miss Butlar, Miss Blunden and Fanny manufactord the Whipps Jellies and Creams and I made a Central Arch of Pasteboard and Wild Heath with various other Ornaments and Devices. . .[38]

The discussion has taken us into the territory of sweet and savoury pastries that graced the tables of every gentry family in the land.[39] Although the proportions of incomes devoted to these delicacies were small, the absolute cost of such trifles could be large. The entire 'bread, grain, and cakes' expenditure of the Inchiquin account in 1746 was taken up with apple tarts, a saffron cake and jelly and cakes. A single apple pie purchased by the Balfour family in 1782 cost five shillings; they could have had fifteen to twenty lb of beef for the same money.

A long way behind bread, grain and cakes came spending on dairy produce and eggs. Butter was the most common purchase. It was usually supplied in reusable crocks containing 30 to 60 lb and empty crocks littered the pantries of the gentry, although when butter reached the dining room it sat on silver butter dishes.[40] A great deal of butter was not purchased but was made in the domestic dairies. The condition of the Synge dairies did not please the bishop: '. . . the whole affair of the Dairy, and poultry was left to Jennet [the maid]. She order'd Milk, and butter and bought in Meal and dispens'd it as she pleas'd.' The bishop, though, did sometimes buy butter. In June 1750 he instructed Alicia to 'make such good Terms [with the Butter-Woman] as you could.'[41] Around Dublin the trade in dairy produce was well organised:

The near neighbourhood of the metropolis [Dublin], gives the Countryman an easie opportunity to convey thither the products of his Farm, Wicklow veil, Bacon, and ale, are noted for their goodness, so is their Butter & Cheese, the Effect of their Cleanliness[42]

The frequency with which fresh milk was purchased is remarkable. Bishops Hacket and Hutchinson both had daily deliveries to their house in Dromore and Lisburn, as did the Balfours at Townley Hall. Town dwellers often kept a cow or two. Annaritta Cust had 'at the house in Armagh two milch cows' when she died in 1797. There was a haystack in the yard to provide them with winter feed and milk pans in the pantry.[43]

Cheese was generally an insignificant purchase, although the Conollys bought cheese locally to feed the estate workers. The best cheese came from England; Mrs Delany, for example, obtained fine 'Berkeley' and 'Frogmill' cheeses from friends and relations in Gloucester.[44]

The Fingalls occasionally bought 'iced cream' although at six shillings and sixpence a quarter, it was an expensive luxury. More often, though, ice cream was produced on the great estates. It was made by placing cream in metal pots and burying them in pails of ice. This required an ice house where the ice was made in winter and a place to store the cream.[45]

Gentry expenditure on fish was small. Large estates had their own fish ponds and streams; and consumers of all kinds were supplied in very informal ways. In County Fermanagh in the 1730s, 'it is usual for Innkeepers to ask his Guests how many Trouts he will have for Supper and throwing in his line [into the river] he bring up the defined number in a minute or two.'[46] The bulk of bought fish was herring, cod, ling, hake, whiting, turbot, and trout, and shellfish. Salmon and herrings were consumed in large quantities, together with eels and fresh water fish.

Fish was rarely more than a supplement to meat. In October 1749 Edward Synge looked forward to returning to Dublin and warned his daughter, 'My scheme is to dine with you about four – some Sole, Whiting, or other good Sea Fish will be a treat. But you must have roasted mutton for Lawson, and a couple of roasted Fowl, not rank'.[47] When in 1757

Mrs Delany was a guest at a Dublin dinner party, she was faced by the largest turbot she had ever seen; the creature was nevertheless dwarfed by a huge pig, roast veal and a shoulder of mutton.[48] Fish featured regularly on the daily menus at Townley Hall, Drogheda, and in the Annesley household at Castlewellan in the early nineteenth century, but was always outnumbered by the profusion of meat, poultry, dairy produce, pies and patties.[49]

With the development of horticulture during the seventeenth and eighteenth centuries fruit and vegetables gained an assured place in upper-class diets.[50] Only small fractions of total food spending went on fruit and vegetables, and a good deal of that was used to buy potatoes, an indication of their popularity even among the gentry. Apples, pears and soft fruits dominated purchases of fruit. Every estate of substance cultivated gardens for pleasure and profit. The Delanys had eleven acres on the outskirts of Dublin. In September 1750 Mrs Delany spent a day 'gleaning my autumn fruits – melon, figs, beury pears, grapes, filberts, and walnuts'.[51] Bishop Synge took a keen interest in his gardens and hot house, pestering poor Alicia with instructions about apricots, grapes, melons, nectarines, pears and strawberries.[52] The demands of the gentry generated substantial business for specialist nurserymen. Prominent among these in the mid-eighteenth century was Daniel Bullen who had a four-acre nursery in New Street, Dublin. Bullen grew the first pineapples in Ireland, one of which was eaten by Alicia Synge in July 1747. He kept a variety of fruit, vegetables, herbs and fruit trees that would put a modern nursery to shame.[53]

Unlike most of the items discussed so far, groceries and wines were bought from shops or wholesalers. Newspapers carried regular advertisements for groceries. Within a year of its first publication in 1737, the *Belfast News Letter* displayed an advertisement from Henry Agnew, 'having just opened shop at the four sugar loaves in Belfast . . . sells several sorts of Grocery Goods, either by wholesale or retail as cheap as any in the Place'. In November 1757, James Dobbin of Lisburn advertised a 'great quantity of choise fine groceries, that he will sell at the most reasonable rates, by wholesale or in Parcels'. Tea merchants offered an impressive range of varieties. In the summer of 1800 a Belfast importer received 'direct from London' 211 chests containing Sanchong, fine and common Congou, Twankay, Hyson and Bohea teas.[54]

Retained imports of the four main categories of groceries are shown in figures 1 to 4.[55] Imports of coffee were very low until the end of the eighteenth century, but then there was a large surge of imports that probably has more to do with changing supply conditions than changes on the demand side. Compared to tea, the consumption of coffee was modest.

Figure 1. *Retained coffee imports by cwt (five-year averages)*

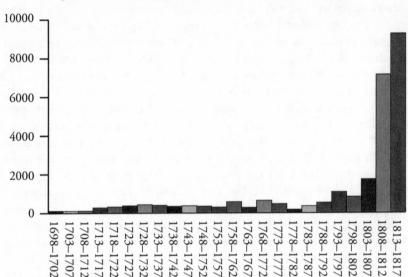

Imports of currants and raisins more or less doubled during the eighteenth century although in an erratic fashion. The greater increase was during the second half of the century. Quantities, however, never exceeded 7,000 cwt.

Figure 2. *Retained currant and raisin imports by cwt (five-year averages)*

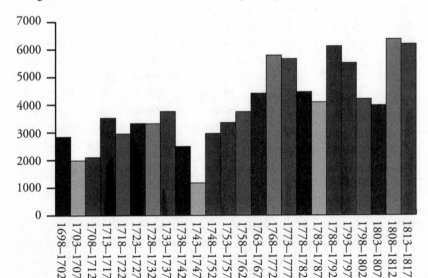

Imports of tea, like those of coffee, were of little consequence before the mid-century. Thereafter they increased five or six fold as the price of tea fell and taste for tea spread. There was some similarity between the trends in tea and sugar imports since the two products were almost in joint demand. In the nineteenth century, by which time the taste for tea had moved well down the social scale, tea was heavily sweetened by sugar.

Figure 3. *Retained tea imports by cwt (five-year averages)*

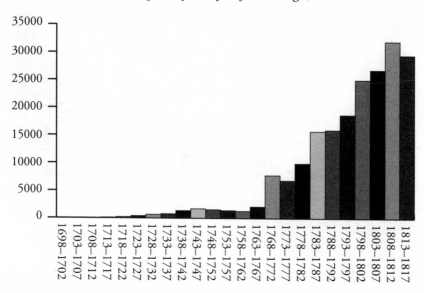

Sugar imports, though, were substantially higher than those of tea. Sugar was used in cooking of many kinds, including whiskey punch, an infusion of whiskey, hot water and sugar.

Figure 4. *Retained sugar imports by cwt (five-year averages)*

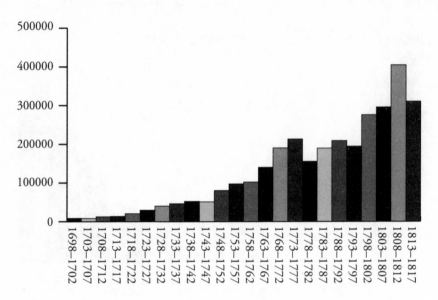

Per capita consumption of all groceries was low by English standards. The consumption of coffee in Ireland during the 1780s, for example, was only one-tenth of the English level, and that of tea and sugar were both about one-third.[56] Consumption was also highly concentrated within a narrow social group. During the 1740s the household of Viscount Gormanston in Dublin bought 168 lb of sugar a year at a time when average household consumption could scarcely have exceeded 20 lb. In the 1780s the Conollys consumed annually nearly 1,900 lb of sugar and 50 lb of tea when the average was 25–30 lb of sugar and 2–3 lb of tea.[57]

Turning to imported wines and spirits, total consumption is best traced through the port books (see figures 5 and 6).[58]

Figure 5. *Retained imports of wine by tuns (five-year averages)*

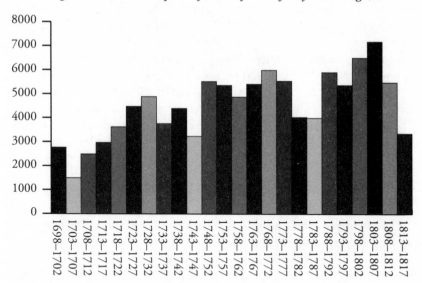

Wine imports doubled in the first half of the eighteenth century but increased little thereafter until the very end of the century. Imports were enough to provide three pints per person per year in 1700, five pints at mid-century, and two and a half pints in 1800. Comparable *per capita* figures for Britain were eight pints, five pints and six pints.[59]

Figure 6. *Retained imports of spirits in gallons (five-year averages)*

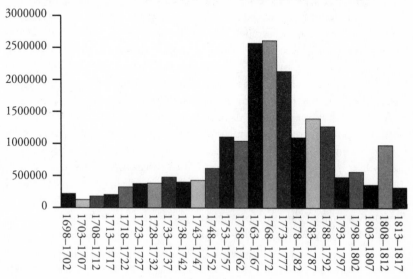

Imports of rum, brandy, whisky and gin behaved in a very erratic fashion. They peaked in the 1770s and then fell back sharply. The legal trade in spirits, particularly of brandy, was sensitive to the level of import duties. *Per capita* consumption of imported spirits in Ireland was less than one pint per year in the early 1700s, three and a half pints at mid-century, five pints around 1770 and less than a pint at the end of the century.[60]

Legal imports are an imprecise measure of the total consumption of alcohol because of smuggling. Nevertheless, they tell a story and broadly support Arthur Young's remark in the 1770s that 'hard drinking is very rare among people of fortune'.[61] This is not to deny that the gentry possessed a well-developed taste for alcohol. For one thing a decline in the volume of imported wines masks a switch to drinks with a higher alcoholic content. More important, some of the space vacated by imports was filled by an increased consumption of English and Irish beer and whiskey.

Trends in beer drinking are difficult to chart. Home brewing was probably never very widespread outside the largest households. There was a decline in the number of small retail brewers as the large-scale porter breweries in Dublin and Cork captured a growing share of the market. Between the 1750s and the 1790s imports of beer from England also increased substantially.[62] The net effect may have been some reduction in *per capita* consumption; but any slack was taken up by whiskey. There are plentiful statistics of the quantities of spirits distilled in Ireland and paying excise duty. These suggest a doubling of *per capita* consumption from half a pint to one pint per year between the 1720s and 1760s. Thereafter there was a great surge in production, both of legal and illicitly distilled spirits. Even confining ourselves to legally produced whiskey, there was an annual *per capita* consumption in excess of six pints at the end of the eighteenth century.[63] The quantities of illicit whiskey consumed can only be guessed at.

Modest though average levels of consumption in the eighteenth century appear to be by modern standards, individual consumption could be high. The Rev. John Nixon, whom we have already met as a prodigious meat eater, had evidently taken the advice of St Timothy to heart. In April 1769 he and sixteen guests drank fourteen bottles of claret and four bottles of port at lunch and four more bottles of claret, two of port and a bottle of whiskey at supper.[64] Some years earlier Sir Edward O'Brien was counselled by a friend to confine himself to three pints of wine instead of 'bumping away all night' with a gallon.[65] But what today might be regarded as excessive drinking was often regarded as a guarantee of good health. In December 1783 William Conyngham received a letter from a friend in Forkhill, County Armagh, sympathising with his recent illness:

occasioned by your being a Disciple of that foolish Dr Cadogan. It is not fit for you and me at our Time of Life to drink Water etc. He was a drunkard. We never were. Sometimes we have exceeded, as who of a good-natured Temper have not often. I beseech you not to drink less than a Bottle of good claret in condition after your Dinner and a Pint of old Port after your Supper.[66]

Finally in this survey of food consumption, there were miscellaneous items that do not fall into any of the obvious categories, such as salt, vinegar and ice. All households bought salt from time to time, usually in small quantities costing a only penny or two; but the Conollys purchased salt by the hundredweight for preserving their meat and butter. Many households bought vinegar that had many culinary and preservative uses. Account books also note occasional purchases of isinglass, a form of gelatine used for preserving eggs and making jellies. The Fingalls occasionally bought ice; presumably they did not own an ice house of their own. There were other items such pickles, mustard and herbs, included here among groceries or vegetables that should perhaps be more properly regarded as preservatives or flavourings. Many accounts include the costs of packaging. The presence of such items do not alter the general picture of the consumption patterns of the upper and middling classes, but they do hint at the details involved in catering for gentry households.

(iv)

We have reached the point at which tentative conclusions may be drawn. What was the impact of upper-class housekeeping, hospitality and high living? Was it, as the seventeenth-century English gentleman with whom we started, an elaborate way of sending 'revenues downe the privy house'?[67] Or was there a fertilising effect that Adam Smith overlooked?

Some political arithmetic may help. According to one recent authority, relying on the estimates of Sir William Petty, the richest 14 per cent of Ireland's population in the 1670s enjoyed incomes nearly four times larger than those of the remaining 86 per cent. In 1791–2 the richest 11 per cent received incomes more than four times greater than the poorest 59 per cent.[68] Professor Cullen has suggested a possible rise in national income from £15 million to £75 million between the 1730s and 1815.[69] These figures imply a total upper class income of around £6 million per annum in the early eighteenth century and £30 million at the end of the century. If we assume that 30 per cent of this went on food and drink, we have sums of £1.8 million and £9 million respectively. Such magnitudes offer food for thought.

One person's expenditure is another person's income. Housekeeping and hospitality generated an enormous demand for food and drink and required a host of acolytes to attend to the wants of the high-livers. The towns and villages of Ireland bustled with brewers, butchers, bakers, millers, cooks, and dealers dedicated to the service of the human stomach. In Armagh in 1770 close to 20 per cent of the demonstrably employed population (28 per cent of the total) processed or dealt in food and drink; and another 12 per cent were domestic servants.[70] Perhaps fewer than half of these processors, dealers and servants – say 15 per cent – catered for the wants of the upper classes. If we apply these proportions nationally, we can generate some tantalising totals. Assuming a national population of around four million in 1770 gives us a work force of 168,000 devoted to feeding the upper classes. In truth the number was probably a good deal higher since the economically active population was greater than occupational listings indicate. It is unnecessary to stress the fragile nature of these calculations and no doubt some bold econometrician will toughen them up. Their calculators, allied to the empirical labour by historians among the documents, may demonstrate that the dining table if not the privy house deserves a respectable place in supporting the economic prosperity of eighteenth-century Ireland, alongside that of the balance sheet and the counting house.

NOTES

1 Quoted in Lawrence Stone, *The crisis of the aristocracy 1558–1641* (Oxford, 1965), p. 562.
2 *The letters of Philip Dormer Stanhope, 4th earl of Chesterfield*, ed. Bonamy Dobrée, 6 vols (London, 1932), iii, p. 945.
3 Adam Smith, *An inquiry into the nature and causes of the wealth of nations* [1776], Everyman ed. (London 1910), i, p. 363.
4 Stone, *The crisis of the aristocracy*, p. 585.
5 Joan Thirsk, *Economic policy and projects: the development of a consumer society in early modern England* (Oxford, 1978).
6 Carole Shammas, *The pre-industrial consumer in England and America* (Oxford, 1990), pp 123–31; Richard Stone, 'Some seventeenth century econometrics: consumers' behaviour' in *Revue Européene des Sciences Sociales*, no. 81 (1988), pp 40–1.
7 L. M. Cullen, *The emergence of modern Ireland 1600–1900* (London, 1981), pp 61–82; L. J. Proudfoot, 'Spatial transformation and social agency: property, society and improvement, *c.* 1700 to *c.* 1900' in B. J. Graham and L. J. Proudfoot (ed.), *An historical geography of Ireland* (London, 1993), pp 219–57.
8 T.C. Barnard, 'Integration or separation? Hospitality and display in Protestant Ireland, 1660–1800' in L. W. B. Brockliss (ed.), *The union of multiple identities* (Manchester, 1997), pp 127–46; 'The world of goods and County Offaly in the early eighteenth century', in T. O'Neill (ed.), *Offaly: history and society* (forthcoming). I am grateful to Dr Barnard for allowing me to read these articles before publication.
9 L. A. Clarkson and E. Margaret Crawford, *Ways to wealth: the Cust family of eighteenth century Armagh* (Belfast, 1985); L. A. Clarkson, 'The Carrick-on-Suir woollen industry in the eighteenth century' in *Irish Economic and Social History*, xvi (1989), pp 22–41.

10 The sources are (1) Account book of Edward Pierce, steward of Thomas Hacket, bishop of Down and Connor, 1674 (P.R.O.N.I., DIO/26/1); (2) Account book of Francis Hutchinson, bishop of Down and Connor, 1729–34 (P.R.O.N.I., DIO/1/22/2); (3) Accounts of Carew family, County Waterford, 1738–82, *Shapland Carew Papers*, ed. A.K. Longfield (Dublin, 1946); (4) Daily account book of Mathew Weekes, steward of earl of Inchiquin, County Clare, 1746 (N.L.I., MS 14477); (5) Weekly purchases of the King household, County Offaly, 1763 (N.L.I., MS 3519); (6) Daily accounts of the Balfour family, Townley Hall, Drogheda, 1774–7 (N.L.I., MS 11909); (7) A five-day account of the food expenditure of a member of the Balfour family, 1782 (N.L.I., MS 10276 (3)); (8) Weekly food purchases of the Aldercron family 1785–6 (N.L.I., MS 3846); (9) Household accounts of the Plunkett family, earls of Fingall, County Meath, 1781–99 (N.L.I., MS 8038 (5–11)); (10) Household accounts of the Conolly family, Castletown, County Kildare, 1783–7 (P.R.O.N.I., Mic. 435); (11) Household accounts of the Balfours of Townley Hall, Drogheda, 1812–6 (N.L.I., MS 11901); (12) Household accounts of the Grattan family, Dublin, 1821–4 (N.L.I., MS 14168); (13) Household accounts of the Conolly familty, Castletown, County Kildare, 1828 (N.L.I., MS 14342). A full discussion of the sources and the methods of analysis will appear in L. A. Clarkson and E. Margaret Crawford, *Food in Ireland 1500–1920: a social history* (Oxford, forthcoming).
11 Marie-Louise Legg (ed.), *The Synge letters: Bishop Edward Synge to his daughter Alicia, Roscommon to Dublin 1746–1752* (Dublin, 1996).
12 Legg, *Letters*, pp 41, 72, 206, 230, 294.
13 Christopher Moore, 'Lady Louisa Conolly: mistress of Castletown 1759–1821' in Jane Fenlon, *et al., New perspectives: studies in art history in honour of Anne O. Crookshank* (Dublin, 1987), pp 134–5.
14 [Pole Cosby], 'Autobiography of Pole Cosby, of Stradbally, Queen's County, 1703–1737' in *Journal of the County Kilkenny Archaeological Society*, v (1906–8), pp 90–1.
15 Stella Tillyard, *Aristocrats: Caroline, Emily, Louisa and Sarah Lennox 1740–1832* (London, 1995), pp 211–14.
16 Legg, *Letters*, pp 521–2.
17 Legg, *Letters*, p. 270.
18 The Gregory King figures come from Stone, 'Some seventeenth century econometrics', p. 38.
19 Christopher Dyer, *Standards of living in the later middle ages* (Cambridge, 1989), p. 59; Stone, *The crisis of the aristocracy*, pp 557–9; J. C. Drummond and Anne Wilbraham, *The Englishman's food: a history of five centuries of English diet* (London, 1959), pp 210–18; John Burnett, *Plenty and want: a social history of diet in England from 1815 to the present day* (London, 1979), pp 80–98.
20 R. D. Crotty, *Irish agricultural production: its volume and structure* (Cork, 1966), p. 17.
21 Legg, *Letters*, pp 41, 402.
22 Graeme Kirkham, 'Economic diversification in a marginal economy: a case study' in Peter Roebuck (ed.), *Plantation to partition: essays in Ulster history in honour of J. L. McCracken* (Belfast, 1981), pp 72–5; Townley Hall Papers (N.L.I., MS 10276 (3)); Walter Harris, *The ancient and present state of the County of Down* (Dublin, 1744), p. 81; A.W. Hutton (ed.), *Arthur Young's tour in Ireland, 1776–9* (London, 1892), vol. I, p. 194; Sir Charles Coote, *Statistical survey of the county of Armagh* (Dublin, 1804), p. 295. Cf. B.A. Holderness, 'Prices, productivity and output' in G. E. Mingay (ed.), *The agrarian history of England and Wales*, vi, *1750–1850* (Cambridge, 1989), pp 147–9.
23 *The autobiography and correspondence of Mary Granville, Mrs Delany*, ed. Lady Llanover, first series (London 1861), vol. ii, p. 468; Angelique Day (ed., *Letters from Georgian Ireland: the correspondence of Mary Delany, 1731–68* (Belfast, 1991), pp 174–6.

24 George Mott, 'Eating and drinking habits in Ireland two hundred years ago' in *Irish Ancestor*, v, no 1 (1973), p. 8.

25 Townley Hall papers (N.L.I., MS 10276 (3)).

26 Annesley estate papers, (P.R.O.N.I., D1854/7/1) (Bill of fare book).

27 Richard Perren, *The meat trade in Britain 1840–1914* (London, 1978), pp 1–3; Holderness, 'Prices, productivity and output', p. 56.

28 Mott, 'Eating and drinking habits in Ireland' p. 8.

29 L. M. Cullen, 'Eighteenth-century flour milling in Ireland' in *Irish Economic and Social History*, iv (1977), pp 9–10.

30 Townley Hall (N.L.I., MS 11909); Conolly household accounts (P.R.O.N.I, Mic. 435); Cullen, 'Eighteenth-century flour milling', pp 10–13.

31 William O'Sullivan, *The economic history of Cork city from the earliest times to the act of union* (Cork, 1937), pp 121, 146–7; John Swift, *History of the Dublin bakers* (Dublin, no date).

32 T. H. Mullin, *Coleraine in Georgian times* (Belfast, 1977), p. 87; L.A. Clarkson, 'An anatomy of an Irish town: the economy of Armagh, 1770' in *Irish Economic and Social History*, v (1978), pp 36, 45.

33 Legg, *Letters*, pp 71, 90, 171–2, 309, 320, 325–7, 331, 338, 350, 382, 489.

34 C. Anne Wilson, *Food and drink in Britain* (Harmondsworth, 1976), pp 230, 337–8.

35 Dorothea Herbert, *Restropections of Dorothea Herbert 1770–1806* (Dublin, 1988), p. 198.

36 For a description of biscuit see Wilson, *Food and drink in Britain*, pp 226, 240.

37 Wilson, *Food and drink in Britain*, pp 223, 237.

38 Herbert, *Restropections*, pp 38, 311.

39 See, for example, the menu books of the Balfours of Townley Hall, Drogheda, 1811–17; and the Annesleys of Castlewellen, 1813–14 (N.L.I., Townley Hall, MS 10247; P.R.O.N.I., Annesley estate papers, D1854/7/1).

40 Clarkson and Crawford, *Ways to wealth*, pp 67, 77, 80; Mina Lenox-Conyngham, *An old Ulster house* (Dundalk, 1956), pp 103, 104.

41 Legg, *Letters*, pp 69, 186.

42 Papers of the Physico-Historical Society of Dublin. Report on County Wicklow, fos. 11–2 (Armagh Public Library, undated, but *circa* 1740).

43 Clarkson and Crawford, *Ways to wealth*, pp 67, 82.

44 Day (ed.), *Letters from Georgian Ireland*, p 176.

45 Wilson, *Food and drink in Britain*, pp 154.

46 Rev. William Henry, *Topographical description* [of County Fermanagh], 1732, fo. 96 (Armagh Public Library, MS G.1.14).

47 Legg, *Letters*, p. 173.

48 Day (ed.), *Letters from Georgian Ireland*, pp 174–7.

49 Menu books of the Balfours of Townley Hall, Drogheda, 1811–17 (N.L.I., Townley Hall MS 10247); menu books of the Annesleys of Castlewellen, 1813–14 (Annesley estate papers, P.R.O.N.I., D1854/7/1).

50 For an important and perceptive survey see T.C. Barnard, 'Gardening, diet and "improvement" in later seventeenth-century Ireland' in *Journal of Garden History*, x no. 1 (1990), pp 71–85.

51 Day (ed.), *Letters from Georgian Ireland*, p. 187.

52 Legg, *Letters*, pp 34, 41, 46, 72, 121, 144, 206, 230, 246, 294, 327, 367, 489.

53 *Essay on the rise and progress of gardening in Ireland*, in Joseph C. Walker, *Historical memoirs of the Irish bards; an historical essay on the dress of the ancient and modern Irish; and a memoir of the armour and weapons of the Irish*, ii (Dublin 1818), pp 17–1. I am grateful to Mr Malcolm Thick of Oxford for this reference, Legg, *Letters*, pp 59, 60, n. (N.L.I., Powerscourt MSS 8367, folder).

54 *Belfast News Letter* (30 March 1738, 24 Nov. 1755, 12 Aug. 1800).

55 P. R.O. (London), Customs 15.
56 Calculated from B.R. Mitchell and W.A. Cole, *Abstract of British historical statistics* (Cambridge, 1971), p. 355.
57 Gormanston MS (N.L.I., 14233); P.R.O.N.I. (mic. 435).
58 P. R.O. (London) (Customs 15).
59 Calculated from E.B. Schumpeter, *English overseas trade statistics 1697–1808* (Oxford, 1960), Tables xvi, xvii.
60 Ibid.
61 Hutton (ed.), *Arthur Young's tours*, ii, p. 152.
62 L. M. Cullen, 'Economic development, 1750–1800', in T. W. Moody and W. E. Vaughan (ed.), *A new history of Ireland*, iv, *Eighteenth-century Ireland, 1691–1800* (Oxford, 1986), p. 183; George O'Brien, *The economic history of Ireland in the eighteenth century* (Dublin and London, 1918), pp 210–12, 279–82; Elizabeth Malcolm, *'Ireland sober, Ireland free': drink and temperance in nineteenth-century Ireland* (Dublin, 1986), p. 22; Patrick Lynch and John Vaizey, *Guiness's brewery in the Irish economy 1759–1876* (Cambridge, 1960), pp 37–84.
63 O'Brien, *Eighteenth century*, pp 212–15; 283–4; E. B. McGuire, *Irish whiskey: a history of distilling, the spirit trade and excise controls in Ireland* (Dublin, 1973), pp 102–42; K.H. Connell, 'Illicit distillation', in K. H. Connell, *Irish peasant society: four historical essays* (Oxford, 1968), pp 26–46.
64 Mott, 'Eating and drinking habits in Ireland', pp 8–9.
65 Quoted in Malcolm, *Drink and temperance*, p. 31.
66 Mina Lenox-Conyngham, *An old Ulster house* (Dundalk, 1946), p. 93.
67 Stone, *Crisis of the aristocracy*, p. 562.
68 David Dickson, *New foundations: Ireland 1660–1800* (Dublin, 1987), pp 97–8.
69 Cullen, 'Economic development, 1750–1800', pp 185–6.
70 Clarkson, 'The economy of Armagh, 1770', pp 27–45.

7 Matters material and luxurious – eighteenth and early nineteenth-century Irish linen consumption

Brenda Collins

Between the early eighteenth and the early nineteenth centuries, the Irish linen industry changed dramatically from being a country-wide and country-based production to an industry twenty times larger, increasingly concentrated in the north-east of Ireland and dominated by the demands of customers in England and abroad as much as by patterns of consumption in Ireland. This paper analyses the patterns of consumption of linen which contributed to such expansion – a framework which modern market philosophers would suggest is the driving force behind economic change and business survival.

Conventionally, an analysis of linen consumption would view it as part of an explanation of the key topic of the origins of the industrial revolution – the push me/pull you debate over the engine of economic growth. Those who probe the timing and place of the take-off into sustained growth have tended to emphasise the significance of this period although until recently they have been inclined to regard it from the viewpoint of production. In 1973, Eric Jones wrote that economic history was conventionally treated as a supply side subject, before he moved on to consider the role of consumer tastes in British industries.[1] It is, of course, the case that industrialisation in the linen industry based on technological innovation led to reduced prices, raised total incomes and expanded the market. Regardless of the rate and extent of technological innovation in any specific industry, the aggregate impact of technological change is not in doubt, for the path of meeting increased demand could ultimately only be advanced by the developments in mechanised dry and then wet spinning and ultimately by power-loom weaving.[2]

However, both historical opinion and contemporary political philosophy have moved on from thinking, as Jones put it, that 'preferences may be learned by some more mysterious process than reading price tags'[3] and there is acknowledgement now that price tags may adjust to preferences as well as the other way around. The publication of *The birth of a consumer society* by McKendrick, Plumb and Brewer set an agenda for addressing the consumer revolution which defined the consumer society as having a far wider significance, characterising changing social orders whose expectations increasingly depended on the smooth expansion of the system of goods.[4] This paper examines the case for seeing the widening of the market for linen goods not solely as an outcome of lower prices and greater volume of production but also as arising from independent changes in consumer demand. Such a viewpoint has an ancestry at least as far back as Adam Smith who wrote that all objects of taste were 'under the dominion of custom and fashion'. Veblen's work on the leisure class in late nineteenth-century America identified the middle ranks of society as providing the basis of the consumer revolution by their attempts to purchase the luxury goods previously restricted to the upper ranks of society.[5] This 'elite emulation' led to the overthrow of 'custom' as the criterion for purchase and its replacement by fashion. However, this mono-causal explanation has been expanded by those historians of the eighteenth century who have provided less simplistic accounts of the role of changing attitudes in contributing to the consumer revolution. Source material such as inventories, diaries and trade cards indicates the extent to which individual decisions played a discriminating part in moulding lifestyles. Attitudes displayed through decisions on appropriateness of place, in terms of social situation, indicate an awareness of active choice. One aspect of these interpretations was the active role of the state, both as government and as monarchy and nobility, directly and indirectly. A second aspect was conformity, not merely to tradition or custom, but also to the symbolism of social solidarity which was provided by shared patterns of acquisition through expenditure. Above all, perhaps, it is the communication or transmission of the ideas that led to the attitudes that informed the behaviour which may be the most startlingly revolutionary aspect of an age when physical journeying was difficult and printed material and the literacy with which to read it not widespread.

A general view of the increased consumption of Irish linen can be derived from the gross estimates of production. These suggest that the volume of Irish linen production probably increased by a factor of 40 between 1700 and 1820. This can be observed in the increase in Irish linen exports. In 1712 Irish linen cloth exports were about 1.4 million yards and yarn exports were about 8000 cwt. By 1752, cloth exports were 10.6 million yards and yarn exports were about 23,000 cwt. Forty years later, in 1792, linen cloth exports had risen to 45.6 million yards while linen yarn exports were 17,000 cwt. Despite the severe international trade disruption of the Napoleonic wars linen cloth exports were recorded at this high level until 1821.[6] By the beginning of the nineteenth century such exports accounted for about half of all Irish linen production

compared with one-quarter in the 1720s. This increased export ori-
entation, mainly to England and through England to the colonies, saw
linen rise from 45 per cent of Irish exports in 1700 to account for 85 per
cent of Irish exports by 1800. It was greatly stimulated by the waiver of
English duty on the importation of Irish linens from the beginning of
the eighteenth century which gave great advantage in price over the
linens imported from Holland, France, Saxony and Silesia.[7] The English
market came to be dominated by Irish and, to a much lesser extent,
Scottish linens. Direct export from Ireland to the colonies was permitted
after 1705, and from the 1740s the bounties that were given in England
for the export of linens to the colonies were extended to cover the direct
shipments. Much of the coarser plain woven Irish linen cloth destined for
England found its way to North America and the West Indian colonies.
Overall, the marketplace of the British Isles was the largest free trade area
in Europe.

At the same time the tremendous increase in linen production was also
taken up by an expanding home market in Ireland. Irish population probably doubled between 1706 and 1791. More people lived in towns where
new ideas and attitudes were as contagious as the diseases of the time.
While Cork's population rose from 17,595 in 1706 to 57,033 in 1796,
Dublin increased from 62,000 in 1706 to 182,000 in 1798, becoming easily
the second city in size in the British Isles. After the seventeenth-century
tumults of military and political subjugation, the eighteenth century was a
time of civilisation through industriousness and through aspirations to
identification with contemporaries in Britain, Europe and North America.[8]
The domination of Dublin as a centre of commerce was reinforced by the
'court', the parliamentary and social round stimulated by Dublin Castle.
The extent of spending power by the influential can be gauged by the
lavish expenditure of those peers with Dublin addresses who participated
in this social round and by the 300 members of parliament who are
estimated to have spent an average £1400 each year in the city.[9]

Not only was linen in a growth market, home and abroad, but its
products and uses were wide. In modern parlance, its markets were highly
segmented. Production included damask and diaper for table linen and
towels, coarse plain linens for shirting for 'common people', chequered
and striped woven linens and printed linens for everyday household and
personal use, fine plain cambrics for dresses, shirts and accessories such as
ruffles and kerchiefs, unbleached, bleached and dyed fabrics, yarn and
thread. Each of these areas of sale or custom had distinct 'customer
profiles' which were addressed by producers and merchants, most of
whom traded in more than one linen product.

The eighteenth century world of influence was a small place as is evident in the social movement and communication of ideas between London and Dublin, and other European capitals such as Paris and Vienna. Within Ireland, there were two social groups whose patronage and influence on the development of the linen industry was vital. The most readily identifiable is the Board of Trustees of the Linen and Hempen Manufactures of Ireland, also known as the Irish Linen Board, founded in 1711 with the aim of developing the industry throughout the island and dissolved in 1828.[10] The trustees were drawn from those in political office, the aristocracy and members of the Irish parliament, as well as county representatives. At the local level in the northeast of Ireland, the county representatives who were active included Matthew Ford of Downpatrick, Michael Ward, Bangor, Lord Conway, whose estate included Lisburn, William Brownlow, M.P. for County Armagh, and Samuel Waring, M.P. for Hillsborough. Such men exerted efforts to promote the development of the industry in their home districts. However, to encourage stable production at a local level it was necessary to provide a means of sale. Even before the Linen Board was established, Arthur Brownlow of Lurgan, father of William, had not only founded the Lurgan linen market but also acted as exemplar in buying all the webs of linen cloth brought to market by the weavers.[11]

The Board's encouragement of production was often explicitly couched in terms of awareness of the customer market. In 1724, for example, the Board responded to a request by the duke of Chandos to encourage Irish imitation of Silesian damasks so that the Irish could compete successfully in the English market.[12] The Board also displayed an awareness of the need to keep abreast of rival production techniques in Europe. In 1728–9 it responded to James Bradshaw who submitted a sleying table for the Board's approval, which set out the specifications in terms of yarn fineness and reed calibration for ranges of weights of diaper cloth, by requesting him to travel to Holland, expenses paid, to ascertain the comparable Dutch methods. By 1750 annual bounties were paid to stimulate damask linen production, specifically in continental methods such as 'after the manner of the Hambro damask'.[13] The designation 'Hambro' was applied to linens originating in Saxony, Silesia and Central Europe, which passed through the port of Hamburg on their way to England.

Less than a generation after the creation of the Irish Linen Board, the Dublin Society was established in 1731 to foster agriculture, manufacture and the arts, including the decorative arts.[14] Its membership was much wider than that of the Board. The Society acknowledged the importance of design skills for manufacture by establishing three drawing schools (of architecture, figure and ornament) in the middle of the century, a timing which paralleled the creation of similar institutions in Paris, Vienna,

Mainz and Edinburgh.[15] The school of ornament had two main functions, firstly, to take up and spread the ideas of the European enlightenment in practical instruction, and secondly, to encourage Anglo-Irish patriotism for Irish economic development. One of the Society's earliest preoccupations in the 1740s and 1750s was the improvement of standards of pattern drawing for industrial purposes on damask and printed linens, delft ware and silks. Premiums for annual competitions were given and specific petitions for funding technical innovations were granted.[16] Art historians have emphasised the extent to which French models, treatises and pattern books were used in the schools, particularly the use of stylised natural forms and repeat patterns, and that the 'real advance in the everyday quality of workmanship in the second half of the eighteenth century in Ireland is largely due to these schools . . . because . . . most of the craftsmen trained in the same school under the same masters'.[17] The influence of the school of ornament may well have been more pervasive than that of the Linen Board. Apart from the lord lieutenant, who acted as president of the Society, its membership was unrestricted by titular position and within three years of its foundation stood at 267. Unlike the Linen Board, the committee members of the Dublin Society were not representatives of political office. Membership of both societies was common within the higher circles of Dublin society.

The highest and most valuable type of patronage was that of royalty. Where royalty led, the courts and nobility followed. This has been ably demonstrated by Neil McKendrick's study of the impact of the 'legislators of taste'[18] in advancing Josiah Wedgwood's pottery in the late eighteenth century. Wedgwood realised the importance of design and of associations in selling goods and was constantly seeking fresh patterns to copy. [19] From the perspective of consumption, Wedgwood was a master at manipulation of the market. As he suggested, 'Fashion is infinitely superior to merit in many respects; and it is plain from a thousand instances that if you have a favourite child you wish the public to fondle and take notice of, you have only to make choice of proper sponsors.'[20] With linen too, there is evidence that as early as the 1730s the promoters of Irish linen were seeking the approval of the highest in the land which would provide the basis of recommendation to others. The Linen Board trustees recorded the presentation in 1734 of a piece of 40 hundred cloth, woven in Larne, to Anne, eldest daughter of George II, on the occasion of her marriage to the prince of Orange.[21] A ceremonial damask table cloth, depicting a map of the streets of the city of London and the coronation procession of George I, which was woven some time after 1727 in Waringstown, the County Down village developed by the Waring family, was undoubtedly intended to promote the skills of Irish damask weavers.[22] Key members of the Linen Board and the

Dublin Society used their influential political office in England to further Irish linen consumption. The duke of Dorset, who was president of the Dublin Society while he was lord lieutenant of Ireland in the 1730s and the 1750s, was steward of the royal household in 1736. He established a policy for the royal household of buying Irish woven diaper and damask in preference to French or Dutch products and this policy lasted from 1736 until the end of the reign of George II in 1760.[23] The friendship of Lord Conway and his wife, Isabella, with the prince of Wales may have provided the basis for the royal warrant awarded to William Coulson, a Lisburn damask manufacturer, by the prince upon his appointment as regent in 1811.[24] A damask napkin with the cypher of the prince of Wales was produced for him in 1818 with the name of Coulson woven in the border of the cloth. The practice of weaving the manufacturer's name into damask linen provided an attribution of authenticity, similar to china and pottery, as well as promotion for the manufacturer.

The extent of the highest patronage was not confined to the English monarchy. Coulson's Lisburn manufactory was visited in 1818 by Grand Duke Michael of Russia, in 1819 by Archduke Maximilian of Austria and also by Hassan Khan, the Persian ambassador to England, and in 1820 by the ex-crown prince of Sweden, the son of Gustavus VII.[25] Russia, Austria and Sweden all had embryonic home damask linen manufactures for which the Irish firm may have set the standard. Other damask firms too, such as Michael Andrews's Royal Damask Manufactory at Ardoyne outside Belfast, cultivated British and foreign royalty.[26]

While royal connections and noble patronage provided the cream of the sales, there is also evidence that Irish linen manufacturers worked hard at extending and maintaining the London market for their sales. In 1816 the damask manufacturer John Blizard of Waringstown, County Down, wrote to John Foster, former speaker of the Irish house of commons, asking for a position in managing Foster's damask manufactory in Louth. As part of his credentials Blizard referred to his recent visit to London where he was 'forming new connections and learning new patterns' and that he executed 'arms, crests, cyphers etc. in a style that pleases equal to Mr Coulson'.[27] In 1825 John Andrews of Comber, County Down, indicated how the connections, in other words the sales, determined the character of his business operations. His firm had to supply 'such an assortment as would enable us to hold our connections and go on with our business, for we can only hold our connections in this country [England] now, by supplying them with articles of all varieties'.[28] Indeed, in 1818 Coulson explained to the Linen Board that the reason for his reluctance to take up its grant following his successful application for funds to increase his number of damask looms was as a 'consequence of the falling off in the consumption of the article, their stock of Damask accumulating so heavily . . . the produce of [new looms] must inevitably remain on their hands'.[29] Thus did the market drive the production whether in the form of unique products undertaken for the cultivation of patronage or in the form of finding new patterns and making new business connections to promote them.

If the best designers had a common background of exposure to neo-classical influences during their training this was demonstrated in the overlap between linen products and other aspects of material consumption. The outcome of a common background and harmonisation of design influences among manufacturers of china, cutlery, glassware and table linen enabled the creation of 'room sets', in keeping with interior architecture in the typically later Georgian 'Adam' style, providing an integrated approach to a domestic lifestyle in the manner of modern 'Shaker' or 'Laura Ashley' interior design. Examples from eighteenth-century Ireland as well as England provide evidence of the vitality of both the Irish and English markets for linen goods. Not only the neo-classical plasterwork motifs but also wallpaper printing design had strong connections with linen and cotton, all of which would have contributed to the fashion for lightness and brightness. Mary Delany wrote to her sister in 1750 that she had replaced her old stuff beds at Mount Panther 'and in their stead am putting up blue and white linen and blue and white paper hangings'.[30] Advertisements and trade cards in London and Dublin suggest that the use of the same pattern on fabric and wallpaper was quite common from early in the century. A trade card of Abraham Price, wallpaper seller, London, *c.* 1715 advertised 'Figur'd paper hangings, Wholesale and Retale, in Pieces of Twelve Yards Long, in Imitation of Irish Stitch, Flower'd Sprigs and Branches'. In 1753, Thomas Ashworth of Donnybrook was advertising his 'Donnybrook patterns for hanging Rooms' as printed to match his 'Chintz Patterns for Furniture in the Cotton and Linen Way'.[31] Copyright of patterns, even when introduced in 1787, did not include designs for wallpapers and, indeed, the fact that initially copyright protected fabric patterns for only a matter of months may indicate the extent to which pattern emulation was seen as both appropriate and inevitable. While design patterns have always been derivative, the growth of middle-class incomes and the spread of ideas about fashion meant that the scale of the market for such ideas was larger in the late eighteenth and early nineteenth century than possibly any earlier period. Moreover while modern 'room sets' are commonly the outcome of integrated manufacturing processes, either vertical or horizontal, the eighteenth-century 'lifestyle' was the product of integrated consumer choice.[32] Perhaps the strongest evidence of a desire to display an ordered and tastefully integrated interior is demonstrated by its application in institutional settings. When the state apartments in Dublin Castle were redecorated it was instructed that 'the wallpaper or paint colour should match the new carpet and that the new oilcloth on the staircase should dictate the colour of the walls'.[33]

Another example of the fashionable use of linen in domestic interiors was for household upholstery. Chequered linens – blue and white or red and white, made either of linen warp and weft or of linen warp and cotton weft – were in the peak of household fashions and clothing by the second half of the eighteenth century. The effects of such ephemeral demand were seen even in small country businesses where, for one generation or barely more, domestic hand loom weavers were drawn into production for faraway markets. The place name of Chequer Hall, near Ballymoney, County Antrim, remains today to enable location of such an intensive trade undertaken by John Adams in the late eighteenth century where yarn was bleached, dyed and woven up on the premises.[34] Like the imitation Indian calicoes produced in England, of which they themselves were copies, chequered cloth found a wide sale within Ireland for upholstery for seating and curtaining for windows and beds and, in a lighter weight, for shirtings. At mid-century, Thomas Newenham's Dublin house was furnished such that 'every piece of seat furniture had its chequered linen cover'.[35] The Drumcondra copper-plate printing factory, newly opened when it was visited by Mrs Delany in 1752, had a Dublin wholesale warehouse advertising 'linens, cottons, lawns and cambrics . . . fit for Women's Gowns, Men's Waistcoats, Covers of Chairs, Screens and Hangings'.[36] The acceptance of such light fabrics for household furnishings as well as dress was a substantial shift from the lustred silks, moreens and poplins of previous generations.[37] Indeed, given Ireland's technological advances in textile printing – paralleling the adoption of copper-plate printing in Jouey in France in the second half of the century – and the prohibition on exporting printed linens until 1779 so as to protect the English industry, the buoyancy of Irish home consumption of 'chequered, striped, printed, stained and dyed linens' for household use seems not in doubt.

The growing American colonial market from the second half of the eighteenth century took Irish linen exports as part of a range of European consumer products – linens, woollens, metalware, pottery – all of which as purchased items, not home-made, were deemed necessary to a colonial lifestyle.[38] Estimates of exports are blurred by the 'invisible' proportions of Irish linens exported to England which were re-exported across the Atlantic and by the effects of the American wars but in 1784 direct linen exports to America and the West Indies were over three million yards when exports to England were twenty-four million yards. It may be said that insofar as exports increased to Britain, a share of the increase was attributable to resales to America.[39] English exports as a whole to America increased spectacularly after 1750 as family economics increasingly meant eschewing self-sufficiency in favour of engagement with the market in the purchase of goods as a means of freedom as valid as personal independence and civil rights.[40] The possession of consumer goods, in home furnishings and in dress, provided boundary markers for the socially mobile in a society such as North America without traditional identities. The acquisition of imported British goods, such as textiles, provided the possibility of a common framework of experience and a shared language of consumption but the impact of possession was dependent upon appropriate use. The development of tea-drinking, for example, required a knowledge of tea etiquette in the use of pots, bowls, strainers, sugar tongs, cups and slop-dishes. The correctness extended beyond the utensils for, as Benjamin Franklin wrote from London to his wife Deborah in 1758, regarding his dispatch of six coarse diaper breakfast cloths, 'they are to be spread on the Tea Table, for nobody breakfasts here on the naked Table, but on the Cloth set a large Tea Board with the Cups'.[41] Social boundary markers also enabled the conscious movement across boundaries as in the case of a rough clad traveller in Maryland who claimed gentlemanly status by virtue of the 'good linnen [sic] in his bags, a pair of silver buckles, silver clasps, and gold sleeve buttons, two Holland shirts and some neat night caps'.[42] Possession of material goods displayed in the home or on the person provided a means of passage through American society which acknowledged custom but was not restricted by it.

The example of the colonial emphasis on acquisition of material consumer goods indicates that the development of consumption patterns in the late eighteenth century was grounded in social attitudes as much as in elite emulation encouraged by patronage or manipulation of taste by merchant producers. Evidence of social attitudes in Ireland which influenced the uses of linen can be indicated by its new association with customary social occasions. Linen's identification with cleanliness and purity has always linked it with human rites of passage from the christening gowns of infants to shrouds for the laying out of the dead. Wider distribution of wealth led to greater expenditure in these areas such as more decorative christening robes embellished with lace while the decency of burial led to acquisition and treasuring of linen shrouds. All the panoply associated with dress and accessories suitable for that most custom-bound event, mourning, could become the subject of change when Mrs Conolly, widow of the speaker of the Irish house of commons requested that 800 scarves distributed to mourners at his funeral in 1729 be made of linen.[43] A social custom thus became a medium for political statement and was an early example of eighteenth-century Irish economic nationalism.

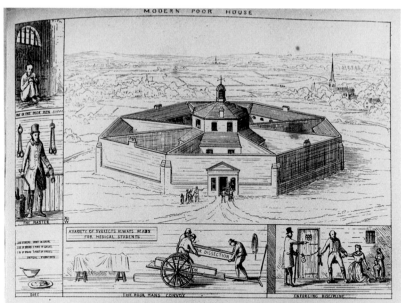

CONTRASTED RESIDENCES FOR THE POOR

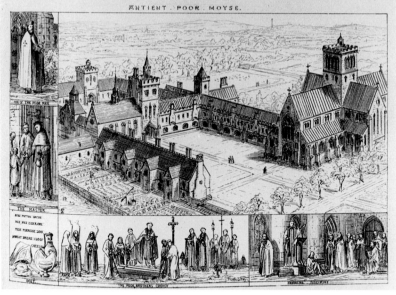

Plate 1 'Contrasted residences for the poor', in A.W.N. Pugin, *Contrasts; or, a parallel between the noble edifices of the middle ages and corresponding buildings of the present day, shewing the present decay of taste* (London, 1841). The uplifting grandeur of the medieval almshouse is set against its stark and punitive modern counterpart.

Plate 2 Two women from the English part of Ireland, with a Gaelic kern and old man, Lucas de Heere, *c.* 1575. The women, from the gentry and mercantile elites, are dressed in contemporary English style. While the kern's clothing is vividly coloured and detailed, the old man's faded green mantle displays the austerity of Gaelic civilian attire.

By permission of the British Library, Additional Manuscript 28330

Plate 3 'The Ladies Catherine and Charlotte Talbot', John Michael Wright, 1679.
The elder girl wears a fine linen smock trimmed with needle-point lace.
Courtesy of the National Gallery of Ireland

Plate 4 'An interior with members of a family', Philip Hussey, 1750s. Wealth is shown in the distinctive wallpaper, carpet, furniture and the quality of the fabrics worn – broadcloth, heavy satin, lace and fine linen.
Courtesy of the National Gallery of Ireland

Plate 5 'Mullins's hut at Scull, County Cork, 1847', *Illustrated London News* (20 Feb. 1847), p. 116. The class dimension of the famine: a well-dressed gentleman bears witness to the sufferings of a family whose staple food has failed. Courtesy of the National Library of Ireland, N.L.I. LB 05 L1

Plate 6 'Contrasts, St Patrick's Day, 1847', *Illustrated London News* (13 Mar. 1847), p. 169. Here austerity, in the moralised vocabulary of self-restraint (in this case, temperance), leads to comfort and respectability: the 'luxury' of self-indulgence leads only to poverty and violence.

Plate 7 View of the interior of Kilcornan convent chapel, Clarinbridge, County Galway, with the sculptural group, 'The Ascenscion', by John Hogan surmounting the tabernacle and altar. Behind the altar the painting of 'The Transfiguration' may be seen.
Photograph *c.* 1870 courtesy of the Irish Sisters of Charity

Plate 8 Martin Cregan (1788–1870): Portrait of Mrs Frances Xaviera Elizabeth
Redington, *née* Dowell, mother of Sir Thomas Redington, and patron of Kilcornan
convent, Clarinbridge, Co. Galway, 1848. Oil on canvas 71 x 57 cm.
Courtesy of the proprietors, The Oyster Manor Hotel, Clarinbridge, County Galway

Plate 9 Martin Cregan (1788–1870): Sir Thomas Redington (*c.* 1849) whose appointment as under-secretary in 1846 smoothed the way for A.W.N. Pugin to be given commissions in Ireland, including the design for the new buildings at St Patrick's College, Maynooth. Oil on canvas 88.4 x 68.6 cm.
Private collection

Plate 10 'Depressed dukes', *Punch*, vol. cvi (30 June 1894), p. 302. The dukes of Devonshire and Westminster deplore the introduction of graduated death duties in the 1894 budget.
Courtesy of the National Library of Ireland

Letters to a Farmer's Wife

DEAR MARY:

The bad season with so much cold in the early months and the more unpleasant and unhealthy wet months following have been very discouraging to all classes, but particularly to those engaged in farm work. And if the men look grumpy and depressed, who can blame them?

However, we womenfolk must keep our courage up. and do our best to fight against long odds in all that concerns the home.

A cheery smile and the lilt of a song will do much to dispel depression and gloom whatever the vagaries of the weather and however heart-breaking the outlook.

PROPER SHELTER FOR POULTRY.

One difficulty to be faced during wet weather is the provision of shelter for the poultry as they too feel the want of freedom and exercise and soon loose their vitality if some means are not provided during long spells of wet weather.

Where there are sheds and out-houses there is no difficulty of this kind as they have ample shelter as well as scratching and dusting places to keep them happy and healthy.

But where housing space is limited to a small henhouse with no other shelter available the birds either mope together in miserable inactivity or stand outside in the rain and mud. Therefore if at all possible some kind of shelter should be erected in which some clean litter is scattered so the fowl can exercise and dust themselves.

EXERCISE IS IMPORTANT.

Exercise is necessary to keep up healthy circulations. And the dusting is necessary to dislodge insects. People may sometimes wonder why a hen or chicken seems to enjoy rolling in dry mould dust or cinder ashes if no other dusting material is available. Her enjoyment lies in the fact that she is having a dry shampoo!

Ducks, geese, and other water fowl take their daily bath to keep their skin and feathers in order but the hen prefers dry shampoo so she rolls, twists and turns and ruffles her feathers to get the dust right through to the skin, after which she shakes herself thoroughly. In this ruffling and shaking all insects are dislodged and shaken out with the dust. After which she gives her skin a thorough searching with her beak to clean away any insects or particles of dirt that may be too firmly lodged to be dispelled with a mere shaking.

Granny's Green Soup

This is a vegetarian soup, very nourishing and so easy to make.

Take 1 small head of cabbage, 1 pint of milk, 1 tablespoonful of butter and 1 level tablespoonful of flour, pepper and salt to taste.

Boil cabbage till tender and strain and chop very fine or rub through sieve if possible. Bring milk to boiling point, add cabbage and butter, pepper and salt to taste. Thicken with flour. Simmer slowly, stirring while simmering. Serve very hot.

A DUSTING SHED.

Few people realise the necessity for a proper dusting shed for fowl. It is an absolute necessity because the health of the fowl depends largely on the facilities allowed them for their daily bath, so the dusting shed must be included in the poultry range, small or large as the case may be, according to the number of fowl kept, if they are to maintain a healthy condition.

Have you ever noticed the routine which the broodie hen follows on being taken off her nest. She runs to a drinking vessel, takes a few beak-fuls of water, then off to the nearest dust heap where she rolls and tosses and flings up the dust. After shaking herself well she goes in search of food. Rarely does she vary this routine. A drink—a bath —food. And I can safely say she would forego the food for her "physical jerks" in the dust heap— a fact which proves the necessity for the inclusion of a dusting place for your poultry especially during inclement weather.

SUITABLE PERCHES.

Some people keep fowl in a haphazard kind of way allowing them to roost anyhow, and anywhere, and feel more or less disgruntled if they don't show the same margin of profit as those of her neighbour whose fowl are kept under proper conditions. Suitable perches should be arranged of proper shape and size so that the hens can rest in comfort.

Most foot-trouble in fowl is caused by ill-fitted badly arranged perches. The perches should be smooth no lumps or roughness on the surface to irritate the feet. They should not be flat or wide just sufficient for a good grip for the hens claw, and no sharp edges. Those should be smoothened down with emery or glasspaper.

DROPPING BOARDS.

Rarely one sees dropping boards arranged in hen houses except where the owner is a professional or at least enthusiastic about the business of poultry rearing. Dropping boards make a great difference in keeping the house in good order, as they prevent the floor from getting soiled and they can be slipped out so easily, cleaned and returned, thus saving much trouble and labour as well as keeping the floor from getting badly soiled.

❖   ❖   ❖

LATE TURKEYS.

Nell—Don't worry about your late turkeys being small. The weather has been against them. They have plenty of time to pull up. A small plump turkey will sell at any time.

GIVE THEM BUTTERMILK.

Bridget—Give your hens some buttermilk to drink occasionally and they will not require any other medicine.

Slán agaibh anois,
MARGARET.

Plate 11 'Letter to a farmer's wife', *Woman's Life* (15 Aug. 1936). The 'austere' side of rural women's lives in the 1930s.
Courtesy of the National Library of Ireland, N.L.I. IR 05 W3

Plate 12 Front cover, *Woman's Life* (25 Oct. 1947). Women's magazines contributed to the growing cult of appearance in the 1940s.
Courtesy of the National Library of Ireland, N.L.I. IR 05 W3

Changing attitudes to cleanliness were also closely associated with the increased use of linen fabrics. The single benefit of linen fabric compared with woollen cloth was its laundering. The replacement of heavy woollen hangings and upholstery by lighter weight linens (and cottons) with a consequent reduction in vermin and bugs may be seen as a practical part of the enlightenment's association of cleanliness with civilised society. In an age with limited urban domestic water supplies, frequent changes of laundered clothing gave the appearance of freshness to the visible areas of the body and this required the ownership of sufficient articles to provide the changes – during the 1740s twenty-six shirts were owned by Nicholas Peacock, a middling member of the Limerick gentry.[44] While bathing was by no means universally accepted as beneficial to health, the association of linen and diaper cloth with the toilette was taken for granted. In the 1730s, Queen Caroline had a wooden bath tub lined with linen and used 'ell-wide holland' sewn into bathsheets of 'two breadths and three ells long'.[45] The practice of lining bath tubs with linen fabric for comfort continued to be apparent nearly one hundred years later in an inventory of the household furniture of Mount Stewart, County Down, home of the marquis of Londonderry, which identified '3 chamber baths, white lyned'.[46]

An explanation of consumption also calls into discussion the role of women as decision-makers in dress as well as in household purchases. Expenditure on women's dress at the end of the eighteenth century was probably fifty per cent greater than on men's attire. Paradoxically, linen's durability contributed to this because, if incomes permitted, new costumes could be purchased without apparent extravagance when older gowns were reused and reworked into children's wear or household items before ending up as rags.[47] The fashions in ladies' costume and dress which followed the prevailing neoclassical tastes of lightness and brightness were easily identifiable with linen fabrics. While woollen stuffs continued to have a place for day wear, lighter dress was *de rigueur* for evening outings to public places, assemblies and the theatre, and socialising in private houses. Fine Irish cambrics and lawns imitated the Indian-style muslins, the output of the cotton spinning-mills of Belfast, Glasgow and Manchester, as well as the far east. Where added warmth was required, more layers were added, such as neckerchiefs or shawls. The relative cheapness of the thinner fabrics allowed the less wealthy to appear in vogue. Those in a position to spend more ordered dress lengths which were heavily embroidered – the sewed muslin or cambric whitework or 'Ayrshire needlework' which became the height of fashion at the end of the eighteenth and beginning of the nineteenth centuries.[48] Thus the number and variety of garments in a fashionable lady's wardrobe increased as ladies spent more on their appearances, and also as the rich sought to widen the social distance between themselves and their inferiors.[49]

Such changes in the popular use of fabrics were made possible by a widening and deepening of the market which disseminated information on fashionable styles. One mechanism was the French fashion doll displayed in London, Dublin and North American shops which was dressed in the latest costume fashions of the Paris season. The arrival of the French doll underlined the supremacy of Parisian ladies' fashion above those of London for the customers in the English provinces and in Dublin.[50] As with fine table linens, royalty set the tone. In 1727 Queen Caroline requested Lady Lansdowne to obtain from Paris, for royal inspection, a fashion doll dressed by the milliner to the French princesses.[51] By the end of the century the dolls, which ranged from one metre high to lifesize, had become widely available models for hairstyles, headgear and accessories, as well as clothing. They were capable of being undressed and dressed so that dressmakers could replicate the garments' construction. Not only did they provide models of fashion for the forthcoming season on first arrival, they also had a much longer existence, being passed from one dressmaker to another for discussion and commission before touring the provinces to bring delayed images to those eager to keep up with the centre of society.[52] In this way the passage of the fashion dolls through the land both intensified the possibility of social emulation in dress while reinforcing the social distance between Paris and London or Dublin, and between city and province. Dorothea Herbert's recollection of her feelings of humiliation on arrival in Dublin wearing dresses of 'her mother's fine home made linen' conveys the strength of the desire to conform to tastes established beyond the household circle.[53]

A second mechanism of spreading ideas of fashion in dress was through print, in periodical illustrations and newspaper advertisements. Besides articles of a literary and intellectual interest, specialist London journals such as *Le Beau Monde, Ackermann's Repository* and *The Lady's Magazine* carried fashion plates intended to stimulate demand, encourage conformity and develop a regular appetite for novelty.[54] In Ireland, the short-lived periodical *Magazin à La Môde*, published in Dublin between 1777 and 1778, may have provided a similar function. Written entirely in French, its message not only conveyed local and foreign news, but also reinforced the prestige associated with the ability to participate in French culture. It was available at booksellers in sixteen towns throughout Ireland.[55] Newspapers, too, carried details of seasonal fashions, and, most importantly, shopkeepers' advertisements of their changing stock. These emphasised the newly arrived 'English and Irish Calicoes, Cottons and Linens of the latest and most fashionable prints',[56] while the advertisement of Margaret Clements, Milliner, Mantua, Fancy Dress Maker and Haberdasher, 23 Dawson Street, Dublin, drew attention to her July 1795 stock of 'Linens, Lawns and Cambricks, India, British and Irish muslins'.[57] English merchants and retailers in Bristol and Chester, the two major eighteenth-century ports for Ireland, and also major ports for transatlantic trade, were equally specific in their descriptions of stock. John Peach of Bristol indicated in 1756 that he dealt not only in Irish linens, but also 'in Irish Sheeting Brown and White and Dyapers of all Breadths, Brown Hempen and Flaxen Sprigg Linen and Hessen and Holles. Likewise printed Linen, Cotton and Printed Hats'.[58] The Peach family supplied the colonies with ready-made clothing manufactured under a putting-out system from Irish linen imports. In the north-west, Brown's of Chester was one of the earliest shops to provide provincial England with high fashion accessories and haberdashery directly from London. The shop had been supplied with linens by Andrews of Comber since 1760, initially directly on a consignment basis and later through wholesalers in Liverpool and London.[59]

While conventional wisdom has, until recently, associated 'modern' consumer shopping patterns with the marketing techniques of the nineteenth-century department stores, recent research on the shops of the eighteenth and early nineteenth-century linen drapers and merchants has identified their techniques of providing deliberately enticing environments for the promotion of their goods. Glass was used extensively for internal walls as well as shop-fronts which encouraged the activity of purchasing to take on a prolonged form of discourse beyond the mere decision to buy. The shop, the sales process and the goods all contributed to the venture. Cloths were displayed hanging from unrolled bales on tiered shelving to give an air of profusion. Smaller items were kept in wrappers or parcels which kept them clean, enabled organisation of storage and also created an atmosphere of promise and mystery which the astute shopkeeper could exploit in salesmanship.[60]

Eighteenth and early nineteenth-century retail drapery shops played a leading role in stimulating demand. It was commonplace for such merchants to keep a stock of pattern books to advise purchasers on styles for their cloth and to procure dressmakers and tailors to make up the garments. The relationship between customer, cloth merchant and manufacturer was thus completely the reverse of what it was to become later in the nineteenth century when dominated by mass market production.[61] This meant that the distinction between wholesale and retail trading was necessarily blurred and it also reinforced both the gradation in fashion according to the distance from the capital cities and the attempts to attract custom by overcoming the geographical distance. In the 1790s, the prestige of selling London fashions at the beginning of the season was seen by Brown's of Chester as worth a six-day journey by stagecoach for their forewoman. Shops in Dublin constantly referred to their stocks from London while goods ordered from Dublin shops by customers living in the provinces carried a higher social cachet than stock available in the local towns.[62] Material goods thus carried a variety of social meanings.

Studies of the growth of the Irish linen industry have, in general, viewed the eighteenth century developments as shadows of the nineteenth century changes driven by industrialisation. Once the mechanically powered innovations are taken out of the analysis, the influence of the consumer revolution on the extension of the domestic industry in Ireland is apparent. The significance of the social shape of the eighteenth-century market for linen goods was that it encouraged the variety and novelty of product diversity. This feature was abandoned during the nineteenth century by the subsequent standardised production techniques which reduced choice by replacing it with mass consumption. The late twentieth-century applications of computer technology in design have enabled repossession of variety in production which has meshed with the prevailing economic orthodoxy of consumer supremacy.[63] Plus ça change.

NOTES

1 Eric L. Jones, 'The fashion manipulators: consumer tastes and British industries, 1660–1900' in Louis P. Cain and Paul J. Uselding (ed.), *Business enterprise and economic change* (Ohio, 1973), p. 198.

2 Emily Boyle, 'Vertical integration and deintegration in the Irish linen industry, 1830–1914' in Marilyn Cohen (ed.), *The warp of Ulster's past* (London, 1997), pp 211–28.

3 Jones, 'Fashion manipulators', p. 198.

4 Neil McKendrick, John Brewer and J. H. Plumb (ed.), *The birth of a consumer society* (London, 1982); see also Cary Carson 'The consumer revolution in colonial British America: why demand?' in Cary Carson, Ronald Hoffman and Peter J. Albert (ed.), *Consuming interests: the style of life in the eighteenth century* (Virginia, 1994), pp 483–700.

5 T. Veblen, *The theory of the leisure class: an economic study of institutions* (London, 1925).

6 C. Gill, *The rise of the Irish linen industry* (Oxford, 1925), appendix ii; John Horner, *The linen trade of Europe* (Belfast, 1920), pp 201–4.

7 N. B. Harte, 'The rise of protection and the English linen trade 1690–1790' in N. B. Harte and K. Ponting (ed.), *Textile history and economic history: essays in honour of Julia de Lacy Mann* (Manchester, 1973), pp 74–112.

8 Toby Barnard, 'Integration or separation? Hospitality and display in Protestant Ireland, 1660–1800' in L. Brockliss and D. Eastwood (ed.), *A union of multiple identities* (Manchester, 1997), pp 185–6; Toby Barnard, 'Art, architecture, artefacts and ascendancy' in *Bullán*, i, no. 2 (autumn 1994), pp 17–34.

9 David Dickson, 'The place of Dublin in the eighteenth century Irish economy' in T. M. Devine and David Dickson (ed.), *Ireland and Scotland, 1600–1850* (Edinburgh, 1983), pp 185–6.

10 H. D. Gribbon, 'The Irish Linen Board, 1711–1828' in *Belfast Natural History and Philosophical Society: Proceedings and reports*, 2nd series, vol. ix (1970/1–1976/7), p. 33.

11 R. Gillespie (ed.), *Settlement and survival on an Ulster estate: the Brownlow leasebook: 1667–1711* (Belfast, 1988), p. xxxvi.

12 *Precedents and abstracts: proceedings of the Irish Linen Board, 1711–37* (Dublin, 1784). Minutes of Thursday 27 August, 1724.

13 P.R.O.N.I., Waring papers, D695/205. Premiums totalling £100 were offered by the Linen Board in 1750–1 for cloths of certain specifications 'after the manner of the Hambro Damask'.

14 James Meenan and Desmond Clarke (ed.), *The Royal Dublin Society, 1731–1981* (Dublin, 1981), chapter 1.

15 'Drawing is the mistress of all manuel [*sic*] Arts and Masonry, Carving, Stucco-forming, jewellry, Furniture and Damask Weaving etc . . .' wrote John Esdall in the *Dublin Daily Advertiser*, 24 August 1736, quoted by Anne Crookshank and the Knight of Glin, in *The watercolours of Ireland* (London, 1994), p. 47.

16 John Turpin, 'The school of ornament of the Dublin society in the 18th century' in *R.S.A.I. Jn*, cxvi (1986), pp 38–50.

17 Crookshank and the Knight of Glin, *Watercolours*, p. 49.

18 Hilary Young (ed.) *The genius of Wedgwood: exhibition catalogue* (Victoria and Albert Museum, London, 1995), p. 14.

19 Wedgwood opened shops in provincial towns where he felt the custom would be right. These included Dublin and Bath. Mairéad Reynolds, 'Wedgwood's man' in *Heart of Breifne*, i (1982), pp 8–14.

20 *Wedgwood catalogue*, p. 14.

21 W.H. Crawford, 'Ulster landowners and the linen industry' in J. T. Ward and R. Wilson (ed.), *Land and industry* (Newton Abbot, 1971), pp 117–44.

22 E. Lewis, 'An 18th century linen damask tablecloth from Ireland' in *Textile History*, xv, no. 2 (1984), pp 235–44.

23 David Mitchell, 'Look to the keeping of the naperie: table linen in the courts of Europe in the seventeenth and eighteenth centuries' in *Rencontre de l'école du Louvre*, forthcoming.

24 'Coulson's of Lisburn' in *Belfast Municipal Museum and Art Gallery Quarterly Notes*, lvii, June 1938, p. 3.

25 L.A. Clarkson and Brenda Collins, 'Photo-industrialisation in an Irish town: Lisburn, 1820–21' in *VIII International Congress of Economic History. Section A2* (1982).

26 John Burls (ed.), *Nine generations* (Comber, 1958), p. 127 referring to Andrews's Ardoyne damask manufactory supplying table linen to William IV as a continuing contract.

27 P.R.O.N.I., Massereene papers, D 207/28/180, 26 October 1816.

28 1825 linen trade report, quoted by W.H. Crawford, 'The evolution of the linen trade on the eve of industrialisation' in *Irish Economic and Social History*, xv (1988), p. 39.

29 *Report of the trustees of the Irish Linen Board for 1818*, p. 269.

30 Angelique Day (ed.), *Letters from Georgian Ireland: the correspondence of Mary Delany, 1731–68* (Belfast, 1991), p. 162.

31 David Skinner, 'Irish period wallpapers' in *Irish Arts Review*, xiii, 1997, pp 53–61; Ada K. Longfield, 'History of the Irish linen and cotton printing industry in the 18th century' in *R.S.A.I.Jn*, vii (1937), p. 38; Claire Walsh, 'Shop design and the display of goods in eighteenth century London' in *Journal of Design History*, viii, no. 3 (1995), p. 162.

32 John Styles, 'Manufacturing, consumption and design' in John Brewer and Roy Porter (ed.), *Consumption and the world of goods* (London, 1993), pp 527–54.

33 Mairéad Dunlevy, 'Dublin in the early nineteenth century' in Brian P. Kennedy and R. Gillespie (ed.), *Art into History* (Dublin 1994), pp 185–206.

34 Personal communication, S. Speers.

35 The Knight of Glin, 'Early Irish trade cards and other eighteenth century ephemera' in *Eighteenth Century Ireland*, ii (1987), p. 119.

36 Longfield, 'Linen and cotton printing', p. 31.

37 Mairéad Dunlevy, *Dress in Ireland* (London, 1989), p. 127.
38 Adrienne Hood, 'The material world of cloth; production and use in eighteenth century rural Pennsylvania' in *William and Mary Quarterly*, 3rd series, iii, no. 1 (Jan. 1996), pp 43–66.
39 Gill, *Rise of Irish linen industry*, pp 177–80.
40 T. H. Breen, 'An empire of goods: the anglicisation of colonial America, 1690–1776' in *Journal of British Studies*, xxv (Oct. 1986), pp 467–99; Carol Shammas, *The preindustrial consumer in England and America* (Oxford, 1990).
41 Florence M. Montgomery, *Textiles in America 1650–1870* (New York, 1984), p. 218, quoting the Franklin papers 7:381.
42 T. H. Breen, '"Baubles of Britain": the American and consumer revolutions of the eighteenth century' in *Past and Present*, no. 119 (May, 1988), p. 81.
43 Barnard, 'Hospitality', p. 134.
44 Daniel Roche, *The culture of clothing* (Cambridge, 1989), p. 178; Barnard, 'Hospitality', p. 132.
45 Joanna Marschner, 'Queen Caroline of Ansbach: attitudes to clothes and cleanliness 1727–37' in *Costume*, 31 (1977), p. 35
46 P.R.O.N.I., Londonderry Papers, D654/51/1.
47 Amanda Vickery, *The gentleman's daughter: women's lives in Georgian England* (London, 1998), pp 151, 184.
48 Mairéad Dunlevy, *Dress in Ireland*, pp 129–31; Brenda Collins, 'Sewing and social structure: the flowerers of Scotland and Ireland' in R. Mitchinson and P. Roebuck (ed.), *Economy and society in Scotland and Ireland, 1500–1939* (Edinburgh, 1988), pp 122–254.
49 Roche, *Culture of clothing*, p. 116; Ben Fine and Ellen Leopold, in 'Consumerism and the industrial revolution' in Social *History*, xv (1990), pp 151–79, discuss the role of domestic servants in social emulation.
50 Sarah Foster, 'Going shopping in eighteenth-century Dublin' in *Things*, iv (1996), p. 43.
51 Marschner, 'Queen Caroline', p. 29.
52 Neil McKendrick, 'The commercialisation of fashion' in McKendrick, Brewer and Plumb (ed.), *The birth of a consumer society*, p. 44.
53 Foster, 'Going shopping', p. 39.
54 McKendrick, 'Commercialisation of fashion', p. 48.
55 Máire Kennedy, 'The distribution of a locally-produced French periodical in provincial Ireland: the *Magazin à La Môde*, 1777–1778' in *Eighteenth Century Ireland*, ix (1994), pp 83–98.
56 *Belfast Newsletter*, 24 November 1791.
57 P.R.O.N.I., Granard papers, T3765/1/3/3/1.
58 Beverley Lemire, 'Developing consumerism and the ready-made clothing trade in Britain, 1750–1800' in *Textile History*, xv (1984), p. 35.
59 J. Burls (ed.), *Nine generations*, pp 115, 130; McKendrick, 'Commercialisation of fashion', p. 90.
60 Walsh, 'Shop design' p. 164; Roche, *Culture of clothing*, p. 320.
61 Roche, *Culture of clothing*, p. 281.
62 A. Adburgham, *Shops and shopping 1800–1914* (London, 1967), pp 8–9; Foster, 'Going shopping', pp 45, 60; Toby Barnard, 'The world of goods and County Offaly in the early eighteenth century', in T. O'Neill (ed.), *Offaly, history and society* (Dublin, 1998).
63 A similar view is expressed by Maxine Berg, 'Luxury and labour: luxury markets and global labour from the 1790s to the 1990s' paper presented to Women's History Association of Ireland, Limerick, 1998.

8 'The whole country was in motion':[1] mendicancy and vagrancy in pre-famine Ireland

Laurence M. Geary

'What has the beggar to care about in this world? He has no taxes, no tithes, and sure he has no outgoings at all'
(William McDonnell, labourer, Kilkee, County Clare)[2]

Mendicancy is a survival strategy in a world deficient in or devoid of public assistance. The pre-famine Irish poor, unlike their English counterparts, had no legal entitlement to poor relief, a situation that was not changed by the passing of the poor law act of 1838. This measure was circumscribed by the political philosophies of the day and was flawed both in its thinking and its execution. The act was grudging and demeaning, intended to degrade and deter, and was unreservedly hated by those it was supposed to relieve. It was also hopelessly inadequate, designed to accommodate no more than 100,000 individuals in a society where some 2.5 million were regularly at risk. To adapt John Mitchel's famous dictum: Ireland may not have died of political economy but numbers of the Irish poor certainly did.

The absence of a statutory provision for the relief of poverty compelled the disadvantaged to rely on their own resources and the charity of their neighbours. The inquiry into the condition of the Irish poor, which sat for a number of years in the 1830s under the chairmanship of Richard Whately, archbishop of Dublin, reported that virtually every part of Ireland was overrun with beggars. Denis Charles O'Connor, a medical doctor from Cork, recalled 'the hordes of beggars, professional and casual, that filled the country roads and towns' in the years before the famine. Cork city was 'inundated with them', he said. 'They blocked up the doors of the principal shops, or attended the public conveyances at their arrival and departure, cursing or praying with equal fervour, as their application was granted or refused.'[3] An earlier report referred to Dublin beggars 'soliciting, teasing, praying and cursing alternately', as they received or were denied relief.[4] O'Connor depicted a mendicancy network, a cast of itinerants forced to live on their wits, among them 'the sturdy cripple, who negotiated marriages and brought news about the intended rebellion, and the pilgrim who had seen all the holy places, who never wore a hat or cut his beard, and never changed his clothes. For his prayers and his piety the latter was a welcome guest at every farmer's house.'[5] A report from Naas, County Kildare, stated that 'the go-between, "bouthy", or match-maker' generally received twice as much as ordinary beggars. Their business was 'to carry messages from the farmers' daughters to their bachelors and look out for husbands for them'.[6]

The suggestion that begging and alms-giving were not always prompted by necessity was given substance by other commentators, among them the Church of Ireland archbishop of Tuam, the Hon. Power Le Poer Trench, who informed the Poor inquiry that begging was a trade and charity a duty.[7] Nassau Senior, Whately's friend and fellow political economist, noted a pronounced difference between English and Irish attitudes to beggars and begging. In England, he said, mendicants were outcasts, whereas in Ireland they were an essential part of 'the society of the family'. Senior observed that beggars had their regular seat before the potato bowl, a place by the fire, and a space on which to sleep. He added that mendicants brought 'news, flattery, conversation, prayers, the blessing of God, and the good-will of men'.[8] The beggar was a social lubricant and the peasantry would be 'lonesome' without him, John O'Leary, an innkeeper at Inishannon, County Cork, informed the Poor inquiry.[9]

This was a philosophical, rather romantic, response to mendicancy, an acceptance of beggars and begging as part of the pre-famine social fabric. However, there was a darker side to the equation, one that was associated with imposition and petty theft, the public exposure of disease and deformity, the demoralisation of the individual and society. Commentators were disgusted by the graphic nature of what was on display. In the mid-1770s, Richard Woodward, dean of Clogher, referred to the 'loathsome, infectious and frightful objects' on public view.[10] In Dublin, thirty years later, individuals, 'exhibiting all the horrors of decay and death', were laid on beds in the streets, while a companion harangued passers-by to contribute to their relief.[11] In Cork, William Makepeace Thackeray was pestered by beggars 'howling supplications to the Lord'.[12] Dr O'Connor observed that 'when you escaped a diseased leg, you came right on a scrofulous arm, in turning from which you were confronted by a deformed face. If you did not look sharp, you trampled on a cripple.'[13]

Some of this was genuine, much of it deliberately contrived. The young and impecunious William Carleton, after leaving his native Tyrone, possibly in 1818, spent his first night in Dublin in a cellar, where two pence procured a straw bed, known as a 'shakedown'. Here, and in a number of similar shelters, 'the lame, the blind, the dumb, and all who suffered from actual and natural infirmity' sought nightly refuge. There were also impostors of every kind, most of them stripped of what Carleton called 'their mechanical accessories of deceit', their crutches, wooden legs, artificial cancers, scrofulous necks, artificial wens, and similar devices. These amounted to 'a mighty mass of imposture', reflecting what Carleton called 'perverted talent and ingenuity'.[14]

There were two main classes of beggars, professional and occasional, and society drew a sharp distinction between them. Casual or occasional beggars were generally forced into the practice by short-term distress. Professional or habitual beggars were variously known as 'fair beggars', 'trading beggars' or 'boccoughs'. By the mid-1830s, the latter term had lost its original meaning of lameness and had become associated with imposture. It was applied to sturdy, wandering beggars who feigned disease or deformity or who mutilated or impregnated their children in order to excite compassion.[15] These professional beggars attended markets, fairs and religious festivals or patterns and were commonly regarded as importunate, dissolute and drunken. The rector of Miltown Malbay, County Clare, depicted them as card-sharps and tricksters, who separated 'unwary countrymen' from their savings by means of 'thimble-rigging and other low games'.[16] The local dispensary doctor observed that the 'boccoughs' were 'a serious annoyance on market days to pregnant women' and on occasion were 'even malicious enough to frighten horses by suddenly protruding their crippled limbs in a crowd'.[17] James Brasil, a small farmer from Newmarket-on-Fergus, concluded that they were 'a shocking bad set'. They drank, cursed and fought and set a bad example to the rest of the population.[18] Professional or habitual beggars provoked a particularly negative response in Ulster, especially in the more Protestant areas, where they were widely regarded as anti-social, drunken, mendacious and promiscuous.[19]

Perceptions of mendicancy were coloured by class, religion, gender and domicile. Begging was endemic in town and country but there is insufficient evidence to indicate whether it was more prevalent in urban or rural areas. It seems likely that imposture would have featured more in the larger centres of population, with consequent implications for tolerance levels. We are on firmer statistical ground with gender. There were more destitute women than men in pre-famine Ireland. In general, women's employment opportunities were more restricted. Widows, single mothers and deserted wives, especially those with young, dependent children, were in a particularly difficult position. Another factor was the tradition of seasonal migration in Ireland. Large numbers of men tramped from the poorer to the richer counties, from west to east, or to England and Scotland, for harvest work. The spalpeen or migrant labourer

> Cut his stick and oil'd his brogues the latter end of May,
> And off for England he set sail to cut the corn and hay.[20]

In their absence, the families of these migrant labourers generally supported themselves by begging. The wives of unemployed or under-employed men were invariably driven to similar shifts. Furthermore, men and women had different attitudes to begging. Able-bodied men regarded the practice as particularly shameful and rarely begged. They seemed more concerned with the social niceties, with respectability. Women were no less aware of the social taint attached to mendicancy, but the responsibility for putting food in their children's bellies devolved ultimately on them.[21] There was also the practical consideration that women and children were treated more compassionately than able-bodied men and the latter generally separated from their families for the duration of the day's begging. James Rattigan, an able-bodied beggar from County Roscommon, observed: 'It is better for me to keep out of sight; and I stay a mile generally behind my wife and children on the road. They beg, and the people are good to them; God reward them for the same. I never ask; I'd get nothing.'[22]

While gender and the urban-rural divide influenced attitudes to beggars and mendicancy, the greatest determinant was class, and class was closely linked with religion. The response of the lower classes to the quotidian reality of poverty, mendicancy, and vagrancy differed markedly from that of their social superiors. It was generally more tolerant, generous and accommodating. According to the Catholic archbishop of Tuam, John MacHale, 'The relief of beggars falls especially on the humbler classes . . . Not only does the support of the poor fall upon the poor but a more unfeeling class than the higher order of gentry, who are generally absentees, never existed in any country.'[23] The pre-famine experience was that Irish property did not relieve Irish poverty. Virtually the whole burden of supporting the poor devolved on shopkeepers, tradesmen, small and middling farmers and labourers, many of whom were on the verge of beggary themselves.[24] Gates, high walls, guard dogs and other physical barriers, buttressed by those of a psychological nature, excluded mendicants from the homes of the wealthier classes.[25] 'The gentleman has his gatekeeper and he keeps his gates closed', noted a County Clare labourer, 'but the poor man's door is always open'.[26]

According to William Wilde, the potato was 'the circulating medium for the mendicant'.[27] It was customary, almost a social obligation, for householders to give at least a handful of potatoes to every beggar who called. A report from County Donegal noted, 'It frequently occurs that not a word passes between the beggar and donor. The bag is laid down on the floor, and filled with potatoes as a matter of course.'[28] Considerable quantities could be accumulated in the course of a day's begging. The general practice was to dispose of the surplus to huxters in exchange for tobacco, snuff, soap, salt, herrings, and cheap clothing. Milk and meal were occasionally dispensed by the charitable. Money was rarely given and then only in urban areas. A labourer from Newmarket-on-Fergus, County Clare, observed that a beggar about the town would give 'ten times more blessings for a half-penny than he would for potatoes or a sup of milk'.[29] Thomas Healy, a beggar from the same county, preferred to receive money because, he said, it was easier to carry than a bag of potatoes. Money was also essential to buy tobacco 'and how can we do without tobacco?' he asked rhetorically.[30]

Religion, compassion and custom were the main impulses that encouraged marginal men and women to share their meagre food resources with the less privileged. John Hickson, Lord Lansdowne's land agent in County Kerry, informed the Poor inquiry that 'they give from downright Christian charity. There is no kind of fear in it. Even in times of scarcity it is the custom to relieve, and they would be ashamed to send a beggar away empty.'[31] William King, from Headford, County Galway, stated: 'When I give, I do so for the good of my soul, the honour of God, and for their benefit.'[32] In County Donegal, it was considered unlucky 'to refuse the beggar'.[33] Some contributed because they feared the beggars' curse, others because they sought their benediction.[34] For many, alms-giving was a form of insurance, a foundation for their own provision should their personal circumstances deteriorate. Dr O'Connor of Cork observed that since 'all lived on the verge of poverty, each thought it might be his own turn next to want the charity he so freely bestowed'.[35] The concerns of some were directed towards the next world rather than this. John Griffin, a weaver from County Galway, stated, 'I give, recollecting that I have another place to go to, where, if I give alms, I will receive four-fold reward.'[36] A freeholder from the same county put it even more succinctly when he stated that charity was 'the best way to heaven'.[37]

The evidence contained in the Poor inquiry report suggests a homogeneous, almost reckless generosity among the Irish peasantry. While there is an element of truth in this, it is an oversimplification of lower class attitudes to mendicancy. The texture of the peasant response was moulded by the relationship between the individual and society, as well as the tension between sympathy and shame, tolerance and repulsion. This emotional conflict reflects one of the social subtleties of pre-famine Ireland, the distinction between poverty and destitution. Independence and self-sufficiency, however marginal, were treasured. Mendicancy was personally and socially degrading, a public confession of failure. The practice of begging at a distance from the normal place of residence, the desire to preserve

anonymity and dignity, was evidence of this. The Poor inquiry provides
many examples of this yearning for respectability. The dispensary medical
officer at Killaloe, County Clare, claimed that pride made the poor 'scorn
the reproach of being a beggar'.[38] A witness from County Roscommon
stated that his family would not beg in public. 'Shame is not lost', he said,
'and the shame is the grand thing'.[39] It was reported from Clonmel, County
Tipperary, that 'an honest labourer would rather eat dry potatoes by his
industry than if he got beef by begging and it is a common feeling among
tradesmen and labourers that they would rather die than beg for relief.'[40]
William Carleton's fiction also suggests that some chose death before the
social disgrace of begging. In Carleton's famine novel, *The black prophet,*
Condy Dalton is infuriated by his daughter's suggestion that she should
beg rather than see the family starve:

'Beg!' shouted the old man with a look of rage – 'beg!' he repeated, starting to his
feet and seizing his staff – 'beg! you shameless and disgraceful strap. Do you talk of
a Dalton goin' out to beg?– Take that.' And as he spoke, he struck her over the
arm with a stick which he always carried. 'Now, that will teach you to talk of
beggin'. No! – die – die first, die at wanst; but no beggin' for any one wid the
blood of a Dalton in their veins. Death – death a thousand times sooner!'[41]

Lower class generosity was also conditional. It was severely, sometimes
callously, constricted in times of crisis, during outbreaks of disease, for
instance. During the 1817–19 fever epidemic, when as many as 1,500,000
Irish people may have been stricken, beggars and vagrants were blamed for
spreading the infection. They were publicly denounced by the Catholic
clergy, the medical profession and government officials. Beggars were
badged in some areas and forcibly excluded from others by constables and
armed guards. They were unwelcome everywhere. It was reported that the
poor 'drove all beggars from their doors, charging them with being the
authors of their greatest misfortunes, by spreading the disease through the
country'.[42] These communal fears and concerns were given legislative
recognition in an act of 1819 which specifically targeted 'strolling beggars,
vagabonds and idle poor persons seeking relief'. On the recommendation
of a magistrate, churchwarden or health officer, such individuals could be
detained in any place of public confinement for twenty-four hours, in the
course of which they could be forcibly stripped and have their persons and
clothing washed and disinfected. They were then deported from the parish.[43]
    While the response of the lower classes to beggars and begging was
qualified and far from simple, the burden of poor relief fell disproportionately on their shoulders. The reaction of the middle and upper classes
was altogether less sympathetic. Much of it was highly intemperate, indeed
hostile.[44] The higher social classes regarded mendicancy as morally tainted,

demoralising to the individual and society, a barrier to social progress.[45] They were repelled by the visibility and importunity of begging. Mendicancy was a public nuisance. It impinged on the citizen's freedom of movement, interfered with trade and commerce and threatened the security of the wealthier classes. Like their social inferiors, the better-off were empirically aware of the relationship between mendicancy, vagrancy and the spread of disease.[46]

Some regarded mendicancy as subversive, a threat to the established social order. When Lord John Russell introduced the Irish poor law bill in the house of commons on 13 February 1837, he referred to the country being overrun by marauders and mendicants.[47] The implied association between mendicancy and lawlessness was touched on by other commentators. The Cork doctor, D. C. O'Connor, referred to the theft of fowl from farmyards and clothing from washing lines by a wily class who were half beggars, half pedlars.[48] O'Connor's jocular style could not entirely mask his middle-class concerns. While some linked pilfering and similar petty annoyances with beggars and their trade, others took an altogether more serious view of their activities. In mid-1823, the secretary of the Bannow parochial committee in County Wexford blamed itinerant beggars for 'a complication of evils', including idleness, filth, disease and profligacy of every description. Another grievance resulting from the influx of strangers was 'the dissemination of false and inflammatory reports', which, he said, fomented great excitement in 'the constitutionally mercurial temperament' of his countrymen and undermined 'habits of order and peace'.[49] A decade earlier, a Cork pamphleteer phrased it more bluntly. In his view, itinerant beggars were 'the most active and efficient agents of rebellion and sedition'.[50]

Quantification

It is easier to qualify than quantify begging in pre-famine Ireland. By its very nature, mendicancy was a fluctuating phenomenon, one that was influenced by a number of economic and social variables. Need was greatest during the so-called meal months or hungry months of summer, that interregnum between the exhaustion of one year's potato crop and the harvesting of the next. During this period, it was customary for substantial numbers to close up their cabins and take to the roads. While the males sought employment in the more prosperous parts of the country, or in England or Scotland, the distaff side and the children roamed the countryside, begging their subsistence. It is impossible to distinguish the propelling force behind this annual migration, to differentiate between compulsion and custom.

An account from the early 1730s suggests that seasonal begging was common and was a profitable avocation. On completion of the necessary farm work – the sowing and planting of corn and potatoes, and the harvesting of turf for cooking and firing – many of those who lived in mountainous areas either hired out their cows or sent them to summer grazing in higher pastures. They arrayed themselves and their families in their most tattered clothing and traversed 'the richest parts of the kingdom', begging the whole summer long until harvest time. Seasonal begging proved so lucrative that servants and day labourers abandoned their regular employment, claiming that they could earn more by begging than by working. Many 'strollers' paid their rent out of the proceeds and with the help 'of their cattle, corn and potatoes live idle the whole winter'.[51]

During the later eighteenth century and the first half of the nineteenth, begging appears to have been driven by necessity rather than choice, by deteriorating economic and social circumstances. This was a period of rapid population growth, sub-division of land holdings and contracting food supplies. Subsistence crises, minor famines and recurring outbreaks of disease created a large pool of genuine want. The thirty years between the ending of the Napoleonic wars and the commencement of the great famine were ones of dearth and deprivation, during which there was a marked increase in the numbers of beggars and vagrants. William Carleton described the upsurge as 'incredible',[52] a contention for which there is plenty of statistical support. The most telling was the finding of the Poor inquiry in the mid-1830s that some 2,385,000 individuals were in need of assistance for thirty weeks of each year.[53] Only a fraction of this number would have resorted to begging but the figures indicate the poverty crisis in pre-famine Ireland.

The response

The government's response was reactive rather than remedial – essentially one of containment – and was fundamentally inadequate. Legislation, dating from the reign of Henry VIII, empowered the authorities to licence, punish or institutionalise beggars and vagrants. In extreme cases, vagrants could be transported for a term not exceeding seven years. The concept of removing an intrusive under-class from public view and of putting them to work for their own and society's good was pragmatic rather than philanthropic and owed much to the precepts of political economy, of individual and communal responsibility.

The distinction between the deserving and undeserving poor, between necessity and imposture, was acknowledged in a 1772 act of the Irish parliament which provided for the establishment of workhouses or houses of industry in every county and county of a city or town.[54] Under the terms of the act, the helpless poor could be licensed to beg or supported in these institutions, while the able-bodied or sturdy beggars could be removed from the streets and assigned menial and repetitive tasks. However, as only eleven houses of industry were established, the act was largely ineffective. The Dublin institution could cater for 110 able-bodied beggars but in 1816 the government ordered that the building be used to accommodate lunatics instead. Thus, at a time of grave economic and social crisis, there was no institution in Dublin for the reception of beggars and vagrants. In 1820, twenty-four cells were reserved in the house of industry for this purpose and this number was subsequently increased to forty. This was a hopelessly inadequate response and a revolving-door situation prevailed. The lack of accommodation rendered the laws against vagrancy and mendicancy ineffectual.[55]

The inadequacy of the official effort to check mendicancy and vagrancy resulted in the formation of voluntary associations for this purpose, in Dublin, Limerick, Ennis, Roscrea, Clonmel and several centres in the north of Ireland. The Association for the Suppression of Street Begging in Dublin, usually called the Mendicity Association, was established in January 1818. According to its manifesto, the number of street beggars had greatly increased as a result of the post-Napoleonic trade and agricultural depression, the return to civilian life of many soldiers and sailors, 'two years of dreadful scarcity', and the fever epidemic that was raging throughout the country. The situation in Dublin was 'at once afflicting and disgusting to its inhabitants', the manifesto continued. Mendicancy was such that the benevolent were 'imposed upon, the modest shocked, the reflecting grieved, the timid alarmed'. A refusal of alms was often followed by the 'threats and imprecations of crowds of mendicants'.[56]

A guiding principle of the Association was to discourage indiscriminate alms-giving. The members believed that the only effective way to check imposture and deceit was to channel relief to the deserving poor through organisations such as theirs. This view was widely shared. The suggestion by the Church of Ireland archbishop of Tuam in the mid-1830s that begging was a trade and charity a duty was challenged by his colleague in Dublin, Archbishop Whately, who claimed that indiscriminate charity exacerbated the social problems of mendicancy and vagrancy. In his view such a practice reduced 'multitudes to beggary'. Whately argued that 'if no one relieved beggars, there would be no such class of persons as beggars . . . He who gives to a beggar does not even think to rescue him from beggary but encourages him to continue in beggary.' Impulsive alms-giving did not bestow a moral benefit on either the donor or the recipient. There was no amelioration in the beggar's condition. His degradation continued.[57]

The Dublin Mendicity Association and similar voluntary organisations could never redress the interrelated problems of poverty, mendicancy and vagrancy. These organisations' lack of resources and their dependence on public subscriptions limited them to alleviating but not eliminating poverty and beggary. They provided a grudging subsistence of work and food within their institutions. The government shared a similar social philosophy. It, too, attempted to institutionalise Irish poverty. In the late 1830s, Lord Melbourne's government rejected the Whately commission's radical proposals for the social and economic regeneration of Ireland in favour of a system of indoor poor relief based in workhouses. The Whately commission had recommended extensive state involvement in promoting public works and assisting emigration to the colonies. The government was singularly unenthusiastic about these proposals, regarding them as inappropriate, expensive and contrary to the prevailing precepts of political economy. The government's decision to introduce the English poor law system to Ireland was a politically bankrupt response to the question of Irish poverty.

A fundamental principle of the poor law proposals of the late 1830s, one enunciated by Lord John Russell in the house of commons on 5 February 1838, was the suppression of mendicancy and vagrancy in tandem with the public relief of destitution.[58] However, the vagrancy clauses of the poor law bill were struck out at the committee stage and the government's promise to introduce a separate measure for the suppression of mendicancy was never implemented. After the enactment of the poor law legislation, Ireland was effectively without a law restraining mendicancy. There were such laws on the statute books but there was a reluctance to enforce them because of their harsh penalties – imprisonment, corporal punishment, transportation – and the absence of a legal entitlement to poor relief.[59] As a result, begging was necessarily tolerated as the only protection against starvation.[60]

Ratepayers and poor law guardians were unhappy with the situation whereby poor relief and mendicancy were tacitly allowed to coexist after 1838. In the following year, forty boards of guardians demanded that this anomaly be tackled. The traditional concerns of the propertied classes concerning mendicancy surfaced in their demands. The Limerick guardians referred to 'the evils' that resulted from public begging. These evils were fleshed out by their colleagues in Ennistymon, who depicted mendicancy as 'a nursery of idleness and larceny'. The Sligo guardians had a similar perception. They regarded mendicancy as 'a nursery for idleness and vice', a 'great and lamentable evil', one that perpetuated the worst features of the national character. There was a consensus among the various boards of guardians that the poor law could not be effective as long as strolling beggars were allowed to pursue their avocation and impose themselves on small farmers and the industrious poor, whose circumstances were little better than their own. The guardians were convinced that as long as there was a vestige of charity in Ireland, vagrants and mendicants would refuse to enter the workhouses.[61]

The poor law commissioners, too, demanded an effective legal measure for the suppression of mendicancy, arguing that there was a moral as well as a practical imperative for such a measure. According to the commissioners, mendicancy and vagrancy fostered 'desultory and demoralising habits' and created a state of dependency that inhibited any general or permanent improvement in Irish economic and social conditions. 'Whilst mendicancy is allowed to range unrestrained over the country, its moral taint will mingle with and deteriorate the entire mass of the population', they argued. Furthermore, mendicancy should be suppressed as a 'sanitary measure of police for checking contagion, bad habits, and the growth of crime, as well as for the protection of the rate-payers against mendicants belonging to their own union, and against the incursion of strangers'.[62]

Some people believed that mendicancy and vagrancy would disappear of their own accord once the poor law system was fully operational. This view was based on the assumption that ratepayers would not shoulder the double burden of paying taxes to support the poor institutionally while relieving mendicants and vagrants who called to their homes. The reality was otherwise. The establishment of the workhouses did not impede the flow of charity to those who appeared to be in genuine need. It was also found that those who entered these institutions were not mendicants but the poor who had never begged.[63] Beggars, especially the able-bodied, displayed the greatest antipathy to the workhouses. Thackeray reported from Cork in mid-1842 that 'the people like their freedom, such as it is, and prefer to starve and be ragged as they list. They will not go to the poor-houses, except at the greatest extremity, and leave them on the slightest chance of existence elsewhere.'[64] The Poor inquiry discovered that the able-bodied and their families would 'endure any misery rather than make a workhouse their domicile'.[65] In general, those who availed of these institutions did so because they were desperate or because they were old and infirm and no longer had the stamina for the mendicant life. For most individuals, pride and personal liberty were the overriding considerations. They preferred the freedom of itinerancy, 'the run of the country', as a County Longford cottier phrased it, to the regimentation, debasement, and virtual incarceration of the workhouse.[66] The prevailing attitude was reflected in the response of John Foster, an old beggarman from Connaught, who informed the Poor inquiry that he would rather have 'the free range outside', where he could supple his 'joints by a walk through the country'.[67]

The poor law act of 1838 failed to repress mendicancy and vagrancy and may have exacerbated the problem. That was certainly the case in Dublin. The laws regulating the house of industry and the foundling hospital were repealed under the 45th section of the act, thereby negating the powers of the magistracy to coerce able-bodied beggars. The result was a significant increase in mendicancy. Public meetings were held, deputations met the lord lieutenant, and demands were made by concerned citizens for effective legislation to deal with 'the disgusting and demoralising exhibitions of mendicancy' that were encountered on the streets of Dublin.[68]

The poor law commissioners supported this and similar demands. In their earliest annual reports relating to Ireland, they referred to the necessity for a measure to repress mendicancy in order to ensure the effectiveness of the poor law act. However, by mid-1842, a change of attitude was detectable. The commissioners sought to 'diminish' rather than 'repress' mendicancy. This appears to be an acknowledgement that the related problems of poverty, mendicancy and vagrancy were more intractable than previously thought and suggests an official doubt as to the adequacy of the poor law system to deal with the realities of Irish life.[69]

If this represented a retreat from absolutes on the part of those at the top, the practical operation of the poor law act encouraged even greater administrative flexibility at local level. The experience of many unions was that the void left by the removal of local beggars to the workhouse was filled by an influx of strangers, a situation that imposed additional financial demands on the ratepayers. As a result, many sought a return to the situation that prevailed before the poor law system came into operation. The Hon. Charles Clements, assistant poor law commissioner, reported from Omagh on 8 December 1841 that there was a growing desire among the people in various parts of the country 'to encourage mendicancy rather than incur the expense of maintaining the paupers in the workhouse'.[70] The poor law commissioners recounted the case of one electoral division in the Kilmallock union, where the ratepayers 'came in a body to the workhouse and demanded to have their poor delivered up to them', believing that the presence of local beggars would discourage strangers from attempting to ply their trade in the area. The commissioners granted the ratepayers' wish and the paupers 'were carried back with great demonstrations of rejoicing, to be supported by almsgiving in the accustomed mode'.[71]

These reports reflect the extent and complexity of mendicancy in pre-famine Ireland. They also suggest that the idea of addressing the problem through the medium of the poor law was inherently flawed. There was not enough workhouse accommodation to cater for those in need. A significant expansion of workhouse space would not have solved the problem because the whole philosophy that underpinned the system ran counter to the prejudices and mores of the pre-famine peasant population. The able-bodied were loath to enter these institutions but even when they did their place on the local begging circuit was filled by strangers. There was thus no reduction in the overall number of beggars. Furthermore, as we have seen, pre-famine mendicancy was not entirely premised on want – although need was pressing – but on a compound of religious, psychological and sociological considerations. Intimations of this complexity began to impinge on the poor law commissioners after a number of years. In their annual report dated 2 May 1842, the commissioners observed: 'Whenever a measure for the repression of mendicancy shall receive the sanction of parliament, it ought undoubtedly to be carried into effect with caution and moderation, and with a due regard for the feelings and opinions which necessarily accompany a practice so deeply rooted in the habits of the Irish people.'[72]

Mendicancy had a Malthusian dimension, which made a legislative solution difficult. The condition was a manifestation of Irish poverty and could only have been addressed by dealing with the social conditions that gave rise to the problem. The government's response to the findings of the Whately commission showed that it was unwilling to do so. The poor law was merely tinkering with the problem of poverty in Ireland. But to go beyond this would have required a fundamental change in the prevailing political philosophy.

In its absence, Irish social problems continued to increase. This was most clearly seen in Dublin. A police return showed that there were 2,641 beggars on the streets of Dublin on 2 May 1846, despite the existence of the north and south Dublin union workhouses and the Mendicity Association.[73] In February 1847, the latter deplored what it termed 'the extensive and pernicious prevalence of mendicancy in this metropolis'.[74] In the following month, Dublin was described in one newspaper editorial as 'the beggared capital of a starving nation'. The distress was so great that more and more individuals were reduced to mendicancy, many of them driven to the most demeaning shifts in an attempt to survive, including singing for alms. 'On every side of us', the editorial continued, 'despairing and broken tones are chanting "Where is the land like the land of the west", "Home sweet home", and "Erin is my home" . . . Hundreds, thousands, bred to industry, have now to make fellowship with the hardened vagrants, the makers of their own sores, with the broken bully, and the outworn prostitute.'[75]

By that time, of course, the country was in the throes of the great famine, a cataclysmic natural disaster that accomplished what the law, voluntary organisations, and successive governments had singularly failed to do. The famine cut a swathe through that class from which beggars and vagrants were drawn. The mortality and emigration returns of the mid- and late 1840s corresponded with the numbers who were found in the previous decade to be in need of some form of poor relief for more than half of each year. This is not to suggest that mendicancy and vagrancy were not a feature of post-famine Ireland, but the spectacle of the whole country in motion did not survive the middle of the nineteenth century.

NOTES

1   Francis Barker and John Cheyne, *An account of the rise, progress, and decline of the fever lately epidemical in Ireland, together with communications from physicians in the provinces, and various official documents* (Dublin, 1821), ii, 36.

2   *Poor inquiry (Ireland). First report from his majesty's commissioners for inquiring into the condition of the poorer classes in Ireland, with appendix (A) and supplement*, H. C. 1835 (369), xxxii, *Appendix (A): vagrancy*, p. 626.

3   Denis Charles O'Connor, *Seventeen years' experience of workhouse life: with suggestions for reforming the poor law and its administration* (Dublin, 1861), pp 9–10.

4   Samuel Rosborough, *Observations on the state of the poor of the metropolis: humbly suggesting a general system of practical charity; for the alleviation of misery, encouragement of industry, and the repression of mendicancy* (Dublin, 1801), p. 4.

5   O'Connor, *Seventeen years' experience of workhouse life*, p. 11.

6   *Poor inquiry (Ireland). First report, with appendix (A): vagrancy*, p. 556.

7   Ibid., p. 488.

8   Anon [N. W. Senior], 'Sixth, seventh and eighth reports of the poor law commissioners', *Edinburgh Review*, lxxvii (April 1843), pp 400–1.

9   *Poor inquiry (Ireland). First report, with appendix (A): vagrancy*, p. 650.

10 Richard Woodward, *An address to the publick, on the expediency of a regular plan for the maintenance and government of the poor* (Dublin, 1775), p. 12.

11 Rosborough, *Observations on the state of the poor of the metropolis*, p. 6.

12 W. M. Thackeray, *The Irish sketchbook 1842* [1843], (Gloucester, 1990), p. 83.

13 O'Connor, *Seventeen years' experience of workhouse life*, p. 10.

14 William Carleton, *The autobiography of William Carleton* (London, 1968), pp 164–5.

15 Arthur Dobbs, *An essay on the trade of Ireland, part 2* (Dublin, 1731), pp 45–7; Woodward, *An address to the publick*, pp 7–12; *Fifth report of the general committee of the Association for the Suppression of Mendicity in Dublin, for the year 1822* (Dublin, 1823), p. 24.

16 *Poor inquiry (Ireland). First report, with appendix (A): vagrancy*, p. 621.

17 Ibid., p. 620.

18 Ibid., p. 645.

19 Ibid., pp 709, 718, 720, 726, 730, 763, 764, 786.

20 Quoted in [W. R. Wilde], 'The food of the Irish', *Dublin University Magazine*, 43 (February 1854), pp 127–46, at p. 129.

21 Mary Cullen, 'Breadwinners and providers: women in the household economy of labouring families, 1835–6', in Maria Luddy and Cliona Murphy (ed.), *Women surviving* (Dublin, 1990), pp 85–116, at pp 106–115; *Poor inquiry (Ireland). First report, with appendix (A): vagrancy*, pp 513, 524, 549, 556, 573, 634.

22 *Poor inquiry (Ireland). First report, with appendix (A): vagrancy*, p. 516.

23 Ibid., p. 490.

24 Ibid., pp 476, 477, 490, 506, 622, 627, 632, 646, 736, 755; Ignatius Murphy, *A people starved: life and death in west Clare, 1845–1851* (Dublin, 1996), p. 49.

25 *Poor inquiry (Ireland). First report, with appendix (A): vagrancy,* pp 564, 622.
26 Ibid., p. 646.
27 [Wilde], 'The food of the Irish', p. 133.
28 *Poor inquiry (Ireland). First report, with appendix (A): vagrancy,* p. 755.
29 Ibid., p. 646.
30 Ibid., p. 627.
31 Ibid., p. 683.
32 Ibid., p. 477.
33 Ibid., p. 735.
34 Ibid., pp 477, 679, 687.
35 O'Connor, *Seventeen years' experience of workhouse life,* p. 11; Ignatius Murphy, *Before the famine struck. Life in west Clare, 1834–1845* (Dublin, 1996), pp 28–9.
36 *Poor inquiry (Ireland). First report, with appendix (A): vagrancy,* p. 479.
37 Ibid., p. 487.
38 *Poor inquiry (Ireland). First report, with appendix (A): the sick poor,* p. 317.
39 Ibid., p. 295.
40 *Poor inquiry (Ireland). First report, with appendix (A): vagrancy,* p. 700.
41 William Carleton, *The black prophet. A tale of Irish famine* (1847) (Shannon, 1972), p. 127. For an instance of individuals opting to starve rather than beg, see *Distress in Ireland. Extracts from correspondence published by the central relief committee of the Society of Friends, no. 1* (Dublin, 1847), p. 15.
42 Barker and Cheyne, *An account of the rise, progress, and decline of the fever,* i, 325–6, 371, 469, ii, 83, 142, 149–150.
43 58 Geo. III, c. 47, 'An act to establish fever hospitals, and to make other regulations for relief of the suffering poor, and for preventing the increase of infectious fevers in Ireland' (30 May 1818); 59 Geo. III, c. 41, 'An act to establish regulations for preventing contagious diseases in Ireland' (14 June 1819).
44 *Dublin Correspondent* (?1816), quoted in William Parker, *A plan for the general improvement of the state of the poor of Ireland* (Cork, 1816), pp 104–5.
45 *The act for the more effectual relief of the destitute poor in Ireland. Sixth annual report of the poor law commissioners* (London, 1840), pp 27–8.
46 *Poor inquiry (Ireland). First report, with appendix (A): vagrancy,* pp 477, 479, 484.
47 *Hansard's parliamentary debates* (hereafter *Hansard*), 3rd ser., xxxvi, col. 454 (13 Feb. 1837). The bill became the poor relief (Ireland) act (1 & 2 Vict., c. 56) (31 July 1838).
48 O'Connor, *Seventeen years' experience of workhouse life,* pp 10–11; W. Steuart Trench, *Realities of Irish life* (1868), (London, 1966), p. 56. Trench referred to seasonal migration as 'piratical' expeditions.
49 *Society for improving the condition of the Irish peasantry. Report transmitted to the committee from the parish of Bannow, in the county of Wexford, through Thomas Boyse, Esq.* (London, n.d.), pp 4–5.
50 Parker, *A plan for the general improvement of the state of the poor of Ireland,* p. 17; *Poor inquiry (Ireland). First report, with appendix (A): vagrancy,* p. 476.
51 Dobbs, *An essay on the trade of Ireland,* pp 45–8. For another account of summer begging, see Thomas Reid, *Travels in Ireland* (1823), quoted in Andrew Hadfield and John McVeagh (ed.), *Strangers to that land. British perceptions of Ireland from the reformation to the famine* (Gerrards Cross, 1994), pp 256–7.
52 Carleton, *The black prophet,* pp 186–7.
53 *Third report of the commissioners for inquiring into the condition of the poorer classes in Ireland* [43], H.C. 1836, xxx, 5; P. M. A. Bourke, 'The use of the potato crop in pre-famine Ireland' in *Journal of the Statistical and Social Inquiry Society of Ireland,* xxi, pt. 6 (1967–8), pp 72–96.

54 11 & 12 Geo. III, c. 30, 'An act for badging such poor as shall be found unable to support themselves by labour, and otherwise providing for them, and for restraining such as shall be found able to support themselves by labour or industry from begging.'

55 *Sixteenth report of the managing committee of the Association for the Suppression of Mendicancy in Dublin, for the year 1833* (Dublin, 1834), pp 60–5; Francis White, *Report and observations on the state of the poor of Dublin* (Dublin, 1833), pp 22–3.

56 *Fifteenth report of the managing committee of the Association for the Suppression of Mendicancy in Dublin, for the year 1832* (Dublin, 1833), appendix, poor law commission.

57 Richard Whately, *Christ's example. An instruction as to the best modes of dispensing charity. A sermon delivered for the benefit of the relief and clothing fund, in Doctor Steevens' Hospital* (Dublin, 1835), pp 12–13, 22–5.

58 *Hansard*, 3rd ser., xl, cols. 787–9 (5 Feb. 1838).

59 [Senior], 'Sixth, seventh and eighth reports of the poor law commissioners', pp 395–9.

60 *The act for the more effectual relief of the destitute poor in Ireland. Sixth annual report of the poor law commissioners* (London, 1840), p. 28.

61 Ibid., pp 28–9, 257–62.

62 Ibid., pp 26–9, 257–62; *The act for the more effectual relief of the destitute poor in Ireland. Eighth annual report of the poor law commissioners* (London, 1842), p. 370.

63 *The act for the more effectual relief of the destitute poor in Ireland. Eighth annual report of the poor law commissioners*, pp 371–2.

64 Thackeray, *Irish sketchbook*, p. 83.

65 *Third report of the commissioners for inquiring into the condition of the poorer classes in Ireland*, p. 5.

66 *Poor inquiry (Ireland). First report, with appendix (A): vagrancy*, p. 565.

67 Ibid., p. 496.

68 *The act for the more effectual relief of the destitute poor in Ireland. Eighth annual report of the poor law commissioners*, pp 368–9.

69 Ibid., p. 21.

70 Ibid., pp 369–70.

71 Ibid., pp 21–2.

72 Ibid., p. 22.

73 *Twenty-ninth annual report of the managing committee of the Association for the Suppression of Mendicancy in Dublin, for the year 1846* (Dublin, 1847), p. 15.

74 Ibid., p. 13.

75 *Nation*, 27 March 1847.

9 The charities and famine in mid-nineteenth century Ireland

Tim P. O'Neill

The charities and the state in the early nineteenth century shared a view that poverty and famines were caused by providence and a belief that human affairs were regulated by a divine agency, generally for human good. This ultimately led to a general passivity and unquestioning approach to the question of poverty and relief and one of the great changes to come in the nineteenth century was a rejection of providentialism.

There were generally two types of poor in Ireland – the permanent poor and the temporary poor who emerged in crisis years caused by crop failures. The attitudes to the relief of both were different. There was no statutory poor law in Ireland until 1838 though some institutions for the relief of poverty did get some government support. There was a vast array of charitable institutions established for the relief of the permanent deserving poor in particular categories.[1] So orphan societies, societies for distressed gentlefolk, denominational charities, prison gate societies, the mendicity institutions and charities for Magdalens were common especially in the towns and cities. There was a general acceptance that the habitually poor were deserving of relief. Social custom dictated that the wandering beggars should be treated hospitably. In normal seasons, farmers were estimated to have given one million pounds' worth of food annually as charity to the poor. As a general proposition the state saw the relief of poverty as a duty for those with wealth and property and saw its role as that of encouraging such philanthropy. Only in extreme cases would it intervene when the poor were in life-threatening situations. So from the early nineteenth century there were interventions by the state to aid the sick poor, lunatics and fever victims. The problems of poor in isolated regions where there were no resident gentry were also monitored by the state with a view to its intervention should the need arise.[2] For the victims of minor famines the state generally stayed in the background, monitored the crises, gave strategic secret charity and only finally assisted when all other charities were exhausted.[3]

The nineteenth century began with a forgotten famine which lasted for twenty months in 1799 and 1800. An estimated 40,000 died due to starvation and famine diseases during this crisis. Private charity was officially encouraged and soup kitchens were opened in many towns. Government funds were held back until the autumn of 1800 when they were used clandestinely to buttress flagging charities. Only in the following spring did the government openly intervene. No large-scale national charitable committee was established to relieve this distress and charity was local, even estate-based, rather than national.[4] The minor famines of the post-Napoleonic wars period saw the flowering of a remarkable period of philanthropy for the temporarily distressed. In 1822 emergency relief committees in both Britain and Ireland responded without question to reports of food shortages in Ireland and accepted that it was the appropriate moral responsibility of the rich to provide for the distressed in Ireland.[5] Peel, who during this year was the architect of the state response to the crisis which saw a million people distressed after the potato failed, deliberately delayed state intervention while there was private relief arriving in the distressed areas, and encouraged the establishment of charities at a local level to force local men of wealth to give and administer relief in their localities.[6] Peel had originally drawn up these plans in 1817 having studied the relief plans used in 1801.[7] His 1822 plan was the blueprint he followed twenty-three years later when the great famine began. He established a central relief commission in Dublin to handle applications, he imported some food for sale at cost and he encouraged local dignitaries to fulfil their moral duty. In 1822 in both Ireland and the United Kingdom every large town had a temporary relief committee for the relief of Irish distress. The response was remarkable as the records of the London Tavern Committee in the Guild Hall Library show. Over £0.3m was collected in various parts of Ireland and England. Charity sermons were preached in most churches for the starving of the west of Ireland. The motivation was Christian charity and a sense of moral obligation. Economic recovery in England and the absence of any serious hostility to Irish poverty assisted this surge of charity for Ireland. In contrast in 1817 during the post-Napoleonic depression in England there was a poor response to appeals for Irish distress. So large was the London fund in 1822 that the committee in its report could comment on the large surplus that would enable the committee 'to devote [it] to the permanent improvement of those districts'. The surplus proved in the committee's words that the leading object for which the subscription had been raised had been accomplished and that the funds had not been wasted in extravagant objects.[8] This surplus became the basis of the Irish Reproductive Loan Society which gave low interest loans in the distressed districts and also funded a number of other activities such as a clothing society.[9] By 1845 this loan fund capital still stood at £67,586.[10]

In 1822 the demand that the state should bear a greater burden of poor relief was mainly voiced in parliament to the embarrassment of the government which felt it was wrongly blamed for all the calamities in society.[11] While in the political arena perceptions were changing, the reports of the charities in 1822 were uncritical of government and accepted their role willingly.[12] Yet new ideas were being articulated. Dr James Henry in a letter to the secretaries of the Mendicity Institute in Dublin argued that

When in any society the number of cases of extreme want so much exceeds its ordinary amount, that voluntary assistance of the benevolent is no longer sufficient for their relief, when such cases crowd the public streets and become a public nuisance, there is a reasonable presumption that this undue quantity of pauperism does not arise from accidental causes, but from something wrong in the constitution or government of the society. And it becomes the duty of those who have the good of society at heart, not to establish an Institute to suppress the nuisance of mendicity, but to institute an inquiry into the causes which have produced it, with a view to applying to them their appropriate remedy.[13]

This view fitted well with that of the Utilitarians for whom the remedy for poverty lay in preaching the principles of political economy and in promoting both self-help and self-denial. W. J. Fox, writing in 1834, complained that English moral sensibility 'is so irregularly and partially excited, that it penetrates so little below the surface, and that it so very often diverts attention and exertion from the root and trunk of national immorality to some petty branch or quivering twig'.[14] In the twentieth century Henry would have been very comfortable with those who argue that the roots of poverty are to be found in economy-wide problems rather than individual characteristics.[15] The argument against short-term solutions was questioned and the issue of the wider structural reform was raised. Henry was also conscious of the residential isolation of the rich from the poor and was aware of the difficulties of sensitising the wealthy to the plight of the poor.

In the next major crisis in 1831 the consensus approach to charity was fragmented. Anglesey, the lord lieutenant, was highly critical of Irish landlords and he reflected a growing view that many of Ireland's woes were properly laid at their door.[16] He followed Peel's plans for relief and had the same basic attitude to the role of the state, which he saw as secondary to the obligations of the rich in society to support the poor. He clashed with William Smith O'Brien, a spokesman for Clare landlords, on this issue.[17] But in 1831 an even more radical change had taken place in the charities, and while they were again organised as they had been in 1822, they quickly divided on sectarian grounds. The Cornhill Committee of 1831, the successor to the London Tavern Committee, was abandoned by those who would contribute only to charities organised by Protestants, and so the Exeter Hall Relief Committee was set up.[18] Even some of the correspondents

to the Cornhill Committee queried whether any partiality was being shown
to either Protestants or Catholics.[19] In Dublin this split was replicated and
here the Sackville Street Committee canvassed Protestant aid while the
Dublin Mansion House Committee attempted to continue the tradition of
non-sectarian aid.[20] The Sackville Street Committee reported that it had
proceeded under a sense of responsibility to God, while those who gave
were moved by a sense of Christian benevolence. The committee also
hoped that the starving people could be cured of their spiritual destitution
of the word of God.[21] A deep-seated suspicion of the Catholic clergy and
Catholics in general had arisen in the intervening years. Philanthropic
sectarianism was to become a feature of the Victorian age in England.[22]
This was caused by the combined impact of the struggle for Catholic
emancipation, millenarianism, the bitterness that the efforts of the Second
Reformation Protestant evangelical movement had generated in the poverty-
stricken west, and the growing political power and influence of the Catholic
hierarchy. The tithes controversy added to this sectarian divide right
through the 1830s. Edward Nangle's first missionaries arrived in Achill on
a ship bearing relief, and John MacHale had begun his career in Killala as
the Catholic church's banner-carrier to oppose the Protestant evangelicals
by attempting to bring missions to the same areas.[23]

The immediate and obvious result of these controversies was that all
charities lost out. While the numbers distressed in 1831 were just over half
the number distressed in 1822, the charitable response from the principal
charities that published reports was approximately a third of the 1822
response. In 1822 approximately one million were distressed. While in
1831 over half a million were in receipt of aid in Mayo and Galway, the
numbers elsewhere were lower than in 1822.[24] Attitudes to Irish poverty
were hardening. The English public, who had been so generous in 1822,
were less moved by reported distress in 1831, and the squabbles between
the charities led to all getting fewer contributions. The English public were
also preoccupied with the impending arrival of cholera then advancing
through Europe. In the house of commons the clamour for reform meant
that Irish poverty gained little attention. Yet the relief of temporary distress
in 1831 was primarily dealt with by the private charities. The reports of the
charities did not criticise the state's role in relief. The Cornhill Committee
simply commented that it hoped that the landed proprietors and the legislative authorities would turn their attention to the permanent improvement
of the condition of the west. This charity was anxious that such a crisis
would not recur as appeals were 'humiliating to those with whom they are
locally connected and derogatory to the national character of the United
Kingdom'.[25] It did not call for a poor law though some who had written to
the committee had said that a reformed poor law on the lines of the

English poor law was essential for Ireland.[26] The state could and did still hold to the view that relief was the primary duty of the rich and especially property owners.[27]

Throughout the 1830s a period of reform in Ireland saw the state accept the need for a poor law for the relief of the ordinary objects of charity, which was introduced to satisfy a growing demand that Irish property should support Irish poverty. This caused outrage among those who had voluntarily given aid in the past and an inevitable feeling that the state was exceeding its role. If property was now to be taxed, then the moral imperative was removed and the state could follow the logic of that position and assume greater and greater responsibility in that arena. The outrage at this mandatory tax – the poor rate – was felt by those who had a clear view of their moral obligations and also by those who complained that it failed to take into account the many bankrupt landowners in Ireland. Ironically the introduction of the poor law was viewed with suspicion by Daniel O'Connell who believed that such a law 'would plunge you (i.e. the poor) into deeper misery . . .'. For others private charity could no longer prevent starvation in Ireland and the introduction of a poor law was essential. George J. D. Poulett Scrope wrote in 1834:

You may contrive to prolong a precarious existence on the charity of your poor neighbours (you may ask in vain of the rich); or your despair may drive you to take by stealth and force, what is necessary to keep you alive. But the law does not recognise these means of prolonging your existence. The law says, if you cannot rent land, or obtain employment, *you shall starve.*[28]

The poor rate was not designed to deal with temporary food shortages. When there was a food shortage in 1839, potato prices rose sharply. Appeals from William Roache, an R.M. in Tralee, Pierce Mahony, a Kerry landowner, and J. Redmond Barry, a west Cork landowner, convinced government that unusual crop failure had occurred. The government sent a Captain H. D. Chads, a naval officer, to tour the west. He looked at rentals and relief and his report was published in a remarkable parliamentary paper showing the contributions of named landlords to the relief of their tenants. Chads travelled the western counties between 21 June and 13 August 1839.[29] Inspection had long been a part of the government response.[30] Chads's task was to examine the state of the food supply, to see whether local relief had been given and to offer roughly matching funds to stimulate such local efforts if the situation appeared to him to demand it. From Kilrush in County Clare which was to command so much attention during the great famine he sent a number of reports. In Moyarta, which had a distressed population of 13,000, there were no public subscriptions but Mr Westby, a local landowner, had contributed £100, Lady Burton had given £10 and £30 had come from smaller subscriptions. But Chads's report then went on to list Dr FitzGerald, John McDonald, Rev. Joley, Charles Wilmot Smith, Hugh Hickman and Randall Borrough, all landowners in the area as non-contributors after application was made to them or their agents.[31] The list of non-contributors is a clear indication that many were refusing to contribute voluntarily, either because of inability or more likely because there was now a poor rate and they objected to the continuation of the old system of voluntary aid at the prompting of government. While these lists were published in 1839 in the parliamentary papers, no comparable lists were produced during the great famine and certainly the non-contributors were never given this prominence. Here, on the eve of the great famine, the government's attitude to landed property is clearly to be seen. These individuals were named publicly for their failure to act.

When the great famine began in 1845, it was again Peel, now prime minister, who was at the centre of relief administration. The story of his effort is well documented but he must have felt that this was another of the periodic famines, that its extent would be limited and manageable and that, as in the past, the state could play an ancillary role to the private charities. As he had done in 1822 he established a central relief committee which encouraged local contributions. It was acknowledged that a local committee was the best proof of distress and its existence ensured that there would be in every area a committee of local gentry. But Peel went further; the lord lieutenants of the counties were ordered by Dublin castle to organise committees and this they did through their deputy lieutenants.[32] The incentive for all relief committees was the promise of some matching government funds. The west by 1845 had over a quarter of a century of experience of such committees, and in spite of the number of absentees, personnel were easy to find. The committees were quickly formed and the requirements of the Castle could be anticipated by secretaries who knew the formulae that yielded results. In the areas not traditionally distressed the role of the lieutenants and their deputies was crucial to the success of these committees. In counties such as Offaly, which had rarely experienced distress before, the local committees initially were confined to the friends of Lord Rosse, the lord lieutenant of the county. It was the autumn of 1846 before the local committees there expanded and the clergy became active. As famine continued in 1846, the numbers of committees also grew every-where and this was greatly encouraged by the matching funds policy of the whig government which succeeded the tories in 1846. Great pressure was put on landowners – resident and non resident – to assist through the local committees so that the benefit of their contributions could be max-imised. There were even some who disliked having their charity scrutinised and only reluctantly consented to join neighbours to qualify for the additional state aid. Once the matching funds disappeared in August 1847, the local committees, in general, also disappeared.[33] The motivation for retaining local committees was gone and it becomes more difficult to trace private local charity from that point, as it became an unrecorded matter known only to donors and recipients. The local contributions in 1846 were recorded as £104,689 18s 1d and in 1847 as £199,569 4s 5d.[34]

The approach here followed the pattern of the previous thirty years. As in earlier times, when the state put pressure on individuals there was a limited response, and when the pressure was removed the committees tended to disappear. The response to appeals for local charity encountered similar problems in each crisis. Many landowners were absentees, some were bankrupt and many were unwilling to contribute. There were also outstanding examples of local charity such as the Gore Booths of Lissadell. Sir Robert Gore Booth personally imported 2,584 tonnes of food, which he sold at low prices and even at a loss in 1847. He organised an emigration scheme for his tenants and was a major supporter of local relief committees both in contributing funds and in administering relief. Rent arrears in Lissadell exceeded annual rental on that estate before the famine but Gore Booth had both the wealth and the will to assist.[35] Richard Gamble, an Offaly landowner of more modest means, was also a tireless relief worker but was a poor contributor in cash terms and worked diligently to preserve his income, his lifestyle and his estate from ruin, during the famine years.[36] Many landowners initially failed to comprehend the scale of the problem in 1845 and 1846. The initial reaction to reports of distress was one of scepticism. For the gentry in many of the counties it was incomprehensible that the famine was happening or could happen, in their area. They also knew that the west was probably in a worse state. Lord Rosse had written in 1822 that 'We have foreborne to apply for relief to government in consequence of the superior distress existing in other parts of the Kingdom.'[37] That attitude persisted in 1845 and 1846. As late as 1847, the third earl of Rosse still believed in the relative wealth of his area.[38] For others, in areas where food shortages had occurred every few years since 1800, there was a full and comprehensive realisation of the implications of food shortages. Lord Monteagle recognised the seriousness of the crisis and commented that this was no repetition of common distress and asked administrators to rouse themselves above their miserable, and in many cases vindictive, thoughts, while reminding them that 'England owes us a debt for the wrongs of centuries.'[39] In Donegal, landlords like Sir James Dombrain were amongst the first to signal the approach of famine and he was to be a central figure in both government and private relief schemes.[40] He had organised relief during distress in Donegal in the 1830s. He was supported by many of the Protestant charities and was to remain active as an organiser of relief into the 1860s.[41] By 1845 personnel on relief committees in the west had had twenty-eight years experience of drafting letters seeking relief. The well-known letter of Patrick McKye from Donegal was originally written in the 1830s but was recycled during the great famine as it contained the correct blend of statistics and analysis of poverty to be effective.[42] The bulk of private relief was channelled to the west and other areas that were unaccustomed to distress were slow in applying for aid, were apologetic in their approach and received less aid even when it was urgently needed. This goes some way towards explaining the excess mortality in wealthier areas.[43]

When the whigs stopped matching local subscriptions in the summer of 1847, there were many attempts made to continue local efforts but these drew mixed responses. Many took the view that if the government aid was ending then the local committees should also attempt to return to normality, regardless of the situation on the ground. One scheme that was attempted in the autumn of 1847 was to get local landowners to employ a number of distressed labourers in proportion to the poor law valuation of their holding. This drew many favourable responses but many objected vehemently to it. In County Offaly, the Rev. Ralph Coote wrote to the organisers and stated bluntly that: 'he had already done as much as he could for his tenants.' His neighbour, W. J. Briscoe, while willing to help, hoped that not only the landlords but also the tenant farmers would come forward and give employment. Henry Kemmis agreed to spend as much as the voluntary levy though few of his tenants required relief. However, he would not be obliged to contribute to a local fund and he demanded that the tenant farmers should also contribute.[44] The larger landowners generally contributed to this scheme but the tensions in rural society militated against any spirit of co-operation between the tenant farmers and landlords. Seizure of crops by tenants and distraining by landlords led to an increase in agrarianism, lawlessness and even threats of rebellion. This persuaded many landlords to become absentees during the famine years, in some cases never to return as permanent residents in their areas. From 1848, many gave only privately and where they controlled the distribution. It is impossible to get any accurate estimate of the final contribution of the local charities in the last years of the famine. The growing class war was aggravated by widespread evictions[45] and from 1847 there was little co-operation between the classes. It is difficult to believe that in 1848 and 1849 the amounts for aid from local charities exceeded those collected in 1846 and 1847; certainly no more than £300,000 would have been raised. Many commentators noted the collapse of private relief and the abandonment of relief work by people who had previously been active. By 1849 the Quakers saw the second failure as having pauperised the farming community. The poor rates, which were heaviest in districts that could least afford them, prevented many landlords from providing either employment or aid. The Quakers saw clearly the widening circle of poverty. 'Many families are now [May 1849] suffering extreme distress, who three years since enjoyed the comforts and refinements of life, and administered to the necessities of those around them.'[46] Christine Kinealy has estimated that relief raised privately in Ireland amounted to £1,000,000 but that large portions of it were subscribed 'by people who had no connection with the country'.[47] Certainly many landlords used their network of friends and relations abroad to attract funds for their own tenants and for their own areas. Yet in many counties the worst years of the famine arrived after official aid to local charities ended in 1847. A second crisis followed the collapse of the potato crop in 1848 when yields dropped to a quarter of the 1847 harvest.[48] This led to great suffering in 1848 and 1849 when both the resources of the poor and the enthusiasm of the rich for charity ran out. The full extent of landlords' contributions can never be quantified. Landlords on the eve of the famine were estimated to have been in receipt of twelve million pounds in rent annually.[49] A contribution of approximately £600,000 in the period 1845 to 1850 did not constitute an enthusiastic response by Irish property to Irish poverty. In 1822 a local contribution of £41,177 was collected to meet local distress in the ten poorest western counties.[50] In the great famine landlords were less willing to support charities than they had been a quarter of a century earlier. The growing political hostility, the religious controversies, the spread of ribbonism and the general breakdown of the relationships between landlord and tenant had all contributed to this decline in charity.

The farmers, mentioned above, had always been the great supporters of the wandering vagrants and poor neighbours in Ireland. De Tocqueville was told that a farmer who had only thirty acres in Ireland reserved a fifth of his harvest annually for alms even to his own detriment. It has been estimated that in pre-famine Ireland farmers gave one million pounds worth of potatoes annually to the poor.[51] It was obvious that with the collapse of this crop, the easiest form of food aid was removed. Furthermore the high level of emigration and evictions led to social dislocation which meant that many farmers, while in no danger of starvation, became cautious. Many were demoralised in an abandoned, depopulated landscape, many feared the next year, others were saving the fare to emigrate and the old spirit of charity died in the face of the ruin of the farmers' world.[52]

The major relief committee established in London during the great famine was the British Relief Association, which raised almost £400,000 for Irish relief.[53] Economic difficulties in England did not militate against a more substantial and more sustained private relief effort there. But what was important was the disenchantment of the English public with the Irish poor. The *Illustrated London News* on 6 February 1847 wrote that 'we have spent money and done no good'. The press had mixed reactions and while the *Tablet* could write that 'no society and no government was ever ruined or injured by a prudent and frugal attempt to provide food and labour for those who have no other recourse',[54] *The Times*, the most influential paper of the time, blamed the Irish for not helping themselves: 'One feature of the famine in Ireland, that has forcibly impressed itself on the English public, is the astounding apathy of the Irish themselves to the most terrible scenes under their eyes, and [which are] capable of relief by small exertion. [This] is without parallel in the history of civilised nations.'[55] Here the frustration, donor fatigue and incomprehension are all expressed. The result was that by summer of 1847, there was a withdrawal by most charities from Ireland at a time when they were still needed and the field of aid was left to government and Irish property. The political impact of the 1848 rebellion confirmed the English public's view of the Irish as a disloyal, untrustworthy and undeserving race. Crucially politicians and administrators agreed with public opinion and did nothing to inspire a new charitable drive in England. Even the authors of charity pamphlets accepted racial theories that gave the Irish simian features. *Punch* in 1851 described the poor Irish as 'the missing link between the gorilla and the Negro', ten years before Charles Kingsley described the Sligo poor as 'white chimpanzees'.[56] Lord John Russell, various lords lieutenant, Charles Wood and Charles Trevelyan, instead of leading public opinion, accepted that both providence and Malthus were good authorities for minimal intervention. The very people who in the earlier minor famines would have orchestrated private relief, during the great famine were standing idly by. This critical view of the Irish militated against the English public having sympathy for the Irish poor. It is also clear that whatever sympathy existed favoured the Scottish poor. Referring to Ireland, Trevelyan commented that 'to provide for us in our necessities is not in the power of government'. But referring to Scotland he said, 'The people cannot, under any circumstances be allowed to starve, and if they are not employed by the proprietors in reproducing works on their estates, they must be employed on comparatively unproductive works at the expense of the proprietors.'[57] Trevelyan ensured that Scotland received a sixth of the funds of the nominally independent British Relief Association whereas it had a mere one-twentieth of Ireland's destitute population. This then became a further reason for deploring the state of Ireland as it could be argued that the Scots had triumphed through greater self help in contrast to the indolent Irish.[58] In English eyes the Irish poor were undeserving and that justified minimal intervention by both public and non-governmental relief agencies.

In Dublin there were two relief committees established as in 1831. The old Sackville Street Committee was reactivated and its secretaries were Lord George Hill, Sir Edward Waller and John Porter. The patrons included the archbishop of Dublin and well known supporters of evangelical Protestantism such as Lord Lorton. This committee raised £42,346 5s 0d prior to 1848.[59] The larger Dublin committee was the General Central Relief Committee in College Green which was the successor to the 1831 Mansion House Committee, raising £63,744 and acting as an agent for distribution for some of the British Association funds. This committee was mixed religiously and its secretaries were Digges La Touche, Thomas Hatton and Sir Edward McDonald. Like other large charities it attempted to end its work in 1847, but in the spring of 1849 it was asked by many of its supporters to resume its duties as 'Notwithstanding the conviction that the utter destitution of 1849 far surpasses anything the country has yet endured, they hitherto abstained from soliciting further subscriptions being but too well aware how much the resources of Ireland are exhausted by the continuance of three years of famine, and by those whose means at all enabled them to assist their perishing neighbours.'[60] In 1849, the Rev. Dr Spratt, a Carmelite priest, called a meeting at the Royal Exchange. By then he argued 'many had steeled their hearts against the cry of the starving and thousands who felt for their terrible distress, on account of their own pressure, were unable to relieve them'. His committee gathered a further £5,326 in 1849 in spite of donor fatigue and lack of resources.[61] Another non-denominational fund was that established to distribute relief sent from India. It distributed almost £14,000 collected in India and before the end of 1846 it had received over 2,000 requests for aid. The trustees of the Indian relief fund included the two archbishops of Dublin, and the duke of Leinster and Lord Cloncurry. Significantly its secretary was Thomas L. Synott, the Dublin publican who was mainly responsible for the distribution of aid sent to the Catholic archbishop, Dr Murray.[62] The large committees, organised during the great famine, reflected the sectarian divide in the charities, which had first become obvious during the 1831 crisis. The intervening political clashes over the queen's colleges, the poor law and the controversy over the charities bill had kept the sectarian divide open.

The famine period also saw a new period of evangelical activity especially in the west where Alexander Dallas was beginning his mission. Irene Whelan's work on souperism has shown persuasively that there was extensive use of food to assist missionary efforts by evangelical Protestants and the colonies in Achill and Dingle were seen as refuges for Catholic converts where food was liberally dispensed.[63] Some missionaries in the west even saw the famine in millenarian terms as the precursor of distress among all nations before the second coming of Christ.[64] The west was targeted by the proselytisers from the 1820s and the obvious poverty of those areas has been read as a reason for those areas being so selected. Yet there were other reasons. The Protestant archbishop of Tuam was a keen supporter of this movement and his Catholic counterpart of slightly later years, MacHale, was an uncompromising opponent. The suggestion has validity that prior to this period the remote west was very poorly served by any clergy and this made it an obvious area for such attention.[65] The connection between relief and religious fervour is a complex one. Almost all charity workers in the great famine were motivated by the imperative of Christian charity and many felt that the recipients should respond accordingly. Some expected the recipients to conform to particular denominational practices but many, like Mrs Beecher in Schull, were simply anxious that the poor should be practising. 'I have provided some clothing for them [the poor], on condition that they will attend their place of worship every Sunday.' She wrote in May 1849, 'I do not ask them whether they are Protestants or not, I want them to be Christians'.[66] For others religious conformity to Protestantism carried with it other political and social implications and many were as evangelical in their belief in the necessity to introduce those changes as they were in their attempts to introduce doctrinal and liturgical change. English public opinion, concerning the racial characteristics of all the Irish, was reflected in the attitudes of some evangelical Protestants to their poorer Catholic neighbours. Women's charities were also organised. In December a ladies relief committee was established in Dublin. Mrs Whately, Miss Warren, Miss Digges LaTouche and Miss Pim were the secretaries and the Quaker influence is obvious. It raised £12,855 9s 0d. It began by giving donations of food and later in response to appeals from the clergy it changed its relief to providing employment for females and supplying clothing for the destitute.[67] The London Tavern Committee of 1822 had also set up ladies clothing societies and a number of local female charities were set up in various counties.[68] A feature of women's role in charity was that many began to concentrate on providing female employment in knitting or other cottage crafts. Some women did work on ordinary relief committees,[69] but these were in the minority and, as in 1822, women had a separate role and sphere in philanthropic activities. For better-off women, philanthropic work was seen as almost a part of their social duty.[70] Polite society in the early nineteenth century professed its horror at the nakedness of the Irish poor. As a means of granting relief and at the same time covering the naked bodies for moral reasons, clothing societies became popular. Work on such charities was essentially regarded as women's work by contemporaries.

The sectarian clashes have been emphasised, but the reality of the famine experience was that in many areas there was little tension between the churches. Much depended on the individuals. In the west MacHale was still opposing the evangelical Protestant movement. Fr Spain, parish priest of Birr, was very critical of the local relief efforts and his opposition reflected older local antagonisms.[71] The Protestant charities generally favoured particular areas like Donegal. But as Donal Kerr has shown, in many areas the clergy of all denominations co-operated and indeed some of the charities insisted on this as a prerequisite to giving assistance. In Dublin, the Carmelite, Fr Spratt, worked for all charities. Kerr has also given a good account of the role of the Catholic church in raising funds and in distribution, especially by individual priests and members of religious orders. The pope's appeal in his encyclical early in 1847 led to large if unquantifiable amounts being sent to the Irish bishops and they in turn made their individual appeals.[72] Archbishop Murray of Dublin, it has been estimated, raised £150,000, though recent research cuts that figure by half. MacHale would have been another major magnet for aid as he had built up a network of contacts over the previous half century but his papers do not survive. The aid that the bishops continued to attract from abroad was a significant aspect of relief, especially after the summer of 1847. But while MacHale became a public and vocal critic of government action, the other bishops were generally very restrained in their public comments and the failure to take any collective action reflected their own political disunity. All the hierarchy, including MacHale, believed in the ranking of society in separate social strata. The clergy had no difficulty in collecting the pennies of the poor for the building of new post-emancipation churches on a grand scale and MacHale regretted his inability to purchase appropriate statues for his churches. Bishops and clergy were very conscious of their own position in the social hierarchy.[73] The differences between the individual members of the hierarchy were reflected among the clergy at a local level. Where some preached rebellion, most subscribed to the prevalent view respecting private property as a sacred right which could not be interfered with even in the face of famine, and accepted the wider United Kingdom ideologies of class. It was not till the synod of Thurles in 1850 that the bishops protested jointly on behalf of the poor while exhorting them to respect the rights of private property. By then, they were responding to the twin accusations that they were silent on famine and that they were 'accomplices of assassins' for not denouncing outrages.[74]

The role of emigrants as donors through their remittances to family and friends also comes within the broad scope of this paper. It is impossible to assess the value of remittances as, like all charity, much of it went unrecorded. The Quakers in their report gave figures for remittances from 1848 to 1851 amounting to £2,948,697.[75] Emigrants were not necessarily the poorest and the evidence of a massive wave of emigration beginning after the second crop failure in 1846 shows that many were fleeing the threat of famine while they still had the resources to go. These were often major supporters of those who remained on family farms and the evidence of their letters shows that in some areas every family had emigrants who were supporting them. Even the emigrants who were sent out on assisted passage were reported as contributing. The Gore Booth ships had also taken starving tenants from the Sligo estate of Lord Palmerston. Those emigrants were widely reported as being among the most impoverished and miserable, but within twelve months they had remitted £2,000 to relatives in Sligo.[76] There seems little doubt but that the scale of remittances from 1847 onwards was a major factor in the survival of many potential famine victims. While there are some estimates as to the value of remittances from North America there were other popular emigrant destinations about which relatively little is still known. South Africa and Australia were regularly referred to as possible destinations in these years and those who went there conformed to the pattern of their peers in North America. The *Freeman's Journal* reported that in the decade 1851 to 1861, £11 million had been remitted from North America alone.[77] Any account of charity has to acknowledge this extraordinary generosity.

The response to the appeals from Ireland and from the pope also drew responses from the wider world community. Concern, the Irish charity, has elevated the Choctaw Indians to a prominent place for their contribution and made them an icon for the 'widow's mite' type of contributors in its battle for aid for modern famine victims. In a letter from New York to the Quakers dated 19 March 1847, M. Van Schaick stated that 144,450 dollars had been collected. He then noted that, 'among the contributions last received is a sum of 170 dollars, of which the greatest part was contributed by the children of the forest, our red brethren of the Choctaw nation. Even those distant men have felt the force of Christian sympathy and benevolence, and have given their cheerful aid in this good cause, though they are separated from you by miles of land and an ocean's breadth.'[78] They were among the many abroad who contributed, and who had no knowledge of, or contacts in, Ireland. It is impossible not to notice the bemusement with the idea of 'the people of the forest' contributing. The Choctaws' involvement with the Irish famine has become a symbol for present day charities of the poor helping the poor.[79]

No account of private charity could overlook the relief work of the Quakers.[80] Following Joseph Bewley's letter in November 1846 they established the Central Committee, and its importance has been universally recognised. Quaker relief was of exceptional importance for three reasons. They were amongst the first in the field, the scale of their activities relative to the size of their numbers made their operation remarkable and their innovative approach made them acknowledged experts. The ability of their members to see the Irish poor as deserving in the face of much hostility to that view, shows them to have been a group capable of independent thought and deep Christian commitment to the poor. They distributed almost £200,000 in total, they pioneered soup kitchens and as Helen Hatton has shown, their relief continued right through the famine period. This money was raised from friends around the world. Their members who visited the distressed areas, Tuke, Webb, Forster, Bewley and Goodbody, were influential voices that acted as a counterbalance to many prevailing views. Their criticisms of government were mild but Hatton argues that contemporaries would have readily understood the import of those challenges to accepted views on aspects of Irish poverty.[81] The influence of Quakers as commentators on matters of poor relief can be seen in Arthur Balfour's dependence on James Hack Tuke when planning the Congested Districts Board in the 1890s. Tuke had by then almost fifty years experience in poor relief in Ireland.[82] The Quakers have found their historians but there is still little written about the Methodist, Baptist, Presbyterian and other religious charities listed in the appendix to this paper.[83]

After the great famine the charities became more assertive, more critical of governments and less influenced by the notion of God's providence. The Quakers in 1849 complained about the problems associated with encumbered estates but generally they believed it was not for them to 'penetrate the secret designs of the Most High'.[84] But the changed attitudes can be seen in 1862 in the report of the Mansion House Committee. Established as usual in Dublin with the lord mayor's approval and support, its report mentions distress in the manufacturing districts in the north of England and commends the charitable response to the suffering poor and the legislative amendment to the English poor law to assist them. In contrast the report notes the failure to introduce either legislative or administrative measures 'to enforce the provisions for relief which exist in the Irish Poor Law'.[85] The critical note is a new development in charity reports and the contrast between the treatment of the Irish and the English poor was a new note for the charities also as they generally confined their public comments to ritualistic and sometimes sycophantic words of gratitude and appreciation. In the 1860s, there was no revival of the large English charities to deal with emergency distress in Ireland. Part of the reason for this was again the failure of the government to orchestrate such a development and the persistence of the view of the Irish poor as undeserving.[86]

By the 1860s emigrants were still prepared to support the distressed Irish, but their support was different in two aspects from that offered during the famine. By the 1860s many emigrants had broken their immediate family bonds with Ireland and were sending aid to well known public figures like William Smith O'Brien or Archbishop MacHale.[87] Secondly the emigrants were more publicly critical of the failure of the government not just to relieve distress but also to take steps to eliminate the causes of that distress. The emigrants were no longer looking at Ireland as when they had first reached the emigrant shores as economic refugees but were now viewing Ireland against the standards they had come to expect in their adopted homes. Meanwhile back in Ireland, in 1862 the landlords in Mayo and Galway gave £5,000 to the Dublin Mansion House Committee and they at least were behaving in a traditional manner.[88]

The government in 1862 also behaved in a traditional manner, denying distress, keeping relief to a minimum until private charity was exhausted, and blaming the Irish as the authors of their own woes. Sir Robert Peel the younger had little of his father's understanding of Irish poverty and was much more of an ideologue. He was opposed to intervention and saw most reports of distress in Ireland as ritual requests for public works or undeserved relief.[89] Distress in the early 1860s was serious – more serious in its economic impact than the distress of 1879–80 – but was still handled by the workhouses and by private charities. One estimate put private donations at £100,000 in that crisis. Why was there not a stronger response in Ireland? In parliament the Irish members condemned the government's inaction but Irish politics at that period, before the establishment of Cardinal Cullen's National Association in late 1864, was preoccupied with the rise of the fenians.

By the time of the crop failures of 1879 the political climate had changed. Governments faced with that crisis were confronted by a united political front in Ireland after the New Departure. In the aftermath of that crisis the charities were very critical of the role they were expected to play. The Mansion House Committee report condemned the poor law as ineffective and claimed that this 1879–80 crisis would have swept away thousands but was prevented by private charity almost alone. It claimed that it took £1,270,000 to satisfy the immediate cravings of want for seven months and then asked the question whether the crisis would close the history of Irish famines. It then called for the reform of the poor law and for the redistribution of the western population to prevent it oscillating between poverty and starvation. The necessity of international appeals for aid it described as a scandal. Adopting a recommendation of the Quakers, the report then turned to the question of land tenure in Ireland. It said that 'the possession of land should be so far considered as a trust for the benefit of society at large, that no private arrangements should be permitted to interfere with the public good'.[90] While the Quakers, in the aftermath of the great famine, had suggested land reform, they had done so with the proviso that land legislation should be 'permissive and enabling and not compulsory'. Now in the 1880s the charities were joining in the call for land legislation and rejecting their traditional role. Gladstone's government in 1880 had orchestrated private relief through the duchess of Marlborough's Relief Committee. The government's outlay in 1879–80 was over £2 million but much of that was advanced as loans and the charities claimed that only their efforts had prevented widespread deaths. After this the government began the search for longer-term solutions as is reflected in the extent of the loan schemes initiated. One commentator reported 3,789 deaths from famine or starvation in that crisis and a series of parliamentary commissions began the search for long-term solutions to the problem of what was by then structural western poverty and distress. The suggestions ranged far and wide from emigration, to 'transplanting', to cottage industry. In 1879–80, it was estimated that £200,000 was sent to the Irish bishops from America. Remittances to relatives and friends were put at £150,000 and the Mansion House Relief Committee and the duchess of Marlborough's Committee raised £271,000.[91]

By the 1890s it was widely believed that if the money spent on relief of emergency distress in the west had been advanced for economic development before the crises arose, it could have effected a radical cure of the chronic poverty in those regions.[92] Wellington had contended that between 1806 and 1838 not a year passed in which the government was not called upon to give assistance to relieve poverty and distress in Ireland.[93] Frustration with unending relief expenditure was a feature of pre- and post-famine Ireland. Arthur Balfour, frustrated by the failure to achieve long term relief turned finally, when distress again threatened in the west in 1889, to the veteran Quaker philanthropist, Tuke, who had been active in the west since the famine. For most of a year they worked on plans and the Congested Districts Board was established to rid the west of the spectre of starvation. At the same time the government assumed the major responsibility for the relief of emergency distress in the crises of the 1890s. This time, unlike its stand during the great famine, it did so with an open acknowledgement of its primary responsibility. A long ideological debate was at an end, at least as far as the western poor in Ireland were concerned.[94]

Finally, was the famine of 1845–51 a 'no-fault' famine?[95] Long before the famine, English politicians, by their own standards, had accepted that they had a responsibility to prevent deaths from starvation regardless of any political philosophy.[96] It was well proved in 1822 that a combination of private charity and state aid could be organised to overcome famine. This was forgotten in the years 1846–49 and the state response was both inept and totally inadequate. English charity was discouraged by the press's view of the Irish and the response of Irish property was parsimonious. The reactions of landowners generally showed that they were prepared to dabble in relief almost as a social obligation without committing themselves to any massive charitable payments. Irish landlords preserved their financial status during the famine. Cormac Ó Gráda has shown that only those landlords who were already deeply indebted were the ones to be forced into the encumbered estates courts. Traditionally it was thought that many had been bankrupted because of problems arising from the famine. The fact that so few were ruined financially by the famine can be read also as evidence that they preserved their economic status by modest charitable contributions, widespread evictions and prudent management of their estates. The rate of evictions exacerbated the problems of tenant farmers and spread the impact of famine to all segments of Irish society.[97] Lord Rosse had no doubt in 1849 'but that a combination against rents exists upon the estates of the smaller proprietors, – who are embarrassed by the serious depreciation in their incomes during the last season, that they will be constrained to press their rights more strongly than they would otherwise would do'.[98] Even the Catholic church had to be shaken out of its acceptance of the inevit-ability of the events that happened. By 1850, at the synod of Thurles, it condemned evictions as 'ruthless oppression'.[99] Relatively few landlords earned reputations as generous.[100] The lesson for famine survivors was that relief was as important for the rich as for the poor. The failure to give more created a new political climate in Ireland, which saw many of the rich being forced to become absentees and the eventual emergence of a new political elite.[101]

To the question whether the great famine could have been averted, the current view of economists is that the scale of the problem was too great for any relief scheme to have prevented widespread excess mortality. It is difficult to see how the food deficit of £50 million could have been bridged but strategic aid distributed more efficiently in 1846 and 1847 could have prevented the cumulative effect of the famine. The incomprehension of the famine victims has to be looked at with some sympathy when the relatively vast wealth of many Irish estates is considered. Even if all could not have been saved, a greater effort by the wealthy in Ireland and the United Kingdom could have both reduced the appalling level of excess mortality and prevented the shattering of the sometimes brittle social cohesion in Ireland. Government aid is estimated at £10 million for the great famine but Mokyr has drawn attention to the £69 million spent on the Crimean war and Kinealy has mentioned the £20 million spent by the British government to compensate slave owners in the 1830s. The wealthy in both England and Ireland did not contribute aid as their wealth would have allowed them to do and as they had done in 1822. Furthermore the clearance policy of landowners as a reaction to famine exacerbated the problem. Potato failure was the ultimate cause of the famine, the government of the day failed its people, but the failure of the entitlement of the poor to domestic charity in Britain and Ireland was a subsidiary and man-made cause. As with North Korea or Sudan in 1998, there is no such thing as a 'no-fault' famine.

NOTES

1   G. D.W. (compiler), *Dublin charities, being a handbook of Dublin philanthropic organisations and charities* (Dublin, 1902). This lists the charities and indicates their origins. See also James David LaTouche, William Disney and George Renny, *Report on certain charitable institutions in the city of Dublin which receive aid from parliament* (Dublin, 1809).

2   R. Peel to H. Goulburn, 20 June 1822 (B.L., Add. MS 40328, f. 100).

3   Cf. Tim P. O'Neill, 'The state, poverty and distress in Ireland, 1815–45' (Unpublished PhD thesis, NUI, 1971).

4   Roger Wells, 'The Irish famine of 1799–1801: market culture, moral economies and social protest' in A. Randall and A. Charlesworth (ed.), *Markets, market culture and popular protest in eighteenth century Britain and Ireland* (Liverpool, 1996), pp 163–93; D. Dickson, 'The gap in famines: a useful myth?' in E. M. Crawford (ed.), *Famine: the Irish experience 900–1900* (Edinburgh, 1989), pp 96–111.

5   *Report of the committee for the relief of the distressed districts in Ireland appointed at the City of London Tavern on the 7 May, 1822* (London, 1823), pp 4–31. (Hereafter cited as *Report of the London Tavern Committee, 1822*.)

6   Gregory to Peel, 17 June 1822 (B.L., Add. MS 40264, f. 259).

7   Peel to Whitworth, 13 June 1817 (B.L., Add. MS 40293, ff 109, 115–6 also 40204, f. 239).

8   *Report of the London Tavern Committee, 1822*, pp 4–31 and 190–4.

9   See manuscript records in the Guild Hall Library. As in all periods of distress there were those who regarded the poor as unworthy. William Kertland in 1822 wrote that 'mendicants are, generally speaking, lusty drones, and their habitual begging no better than a species of robbery of the public hive', *Patrick and Katleen: a domestic tale in verse on mendicity* (Dublin, 1822), p. 30.

10   *Second annual report of the corporation of the Irish reproductive loan fund institution, 1846*, p. 3 (P.R.O., London, Treasury papers, T. 91/213).

11   Cf. Sir Edward O'Brien's speech, *Hansard*, 2nd ser. vii (29 Apr. 1822), cols. 146–9.

12   Cf. *Report of the proceedings of the committee of management for the relief of the distressed districts in Ireland, appointed at a general meeting at the Mansion House Dublin.* (Dublin, 1823), pp iv–xv. (Hereafter cited as *Mansion House report, 1822*). An interesting attempt at permanent improvement was the establishment of the Irish Reproductive Loan Society which began loan funds in the distressed districts with the surplus from the London funds of 1822. See for example *Report of the Irish reproductive loan fund, 1836*, Treasury papers (P.R.O., T. 91/213); or County Mayo committee and trustee minute book, 1822–41, Treasury papers (T. 91/181). See also manuscript records of these committees in the Guild Hall Library, London.

13   James Henry, MD, *A letter to the secretaries of the Mendicity Institution* (Dublin, 1840), p. 9.

14   W.J. Fox, 'Improvement of the working class' in *The Monthly repository*, n.s., 1834, viii, p. 628. Fox's article was a response to F. Place's pamphlet on the issues of drunkenness and education.

15 A. Dale Tussing, 'Poverty research and political analysis in the United States: implications for Ireland' in *Economic and Social Research Review*, v, no. 1 (1973), pp 75–98.

16 Anglesey to Grey, 15 January 1831, 5 March 1831, 15 April 1831 and 5 June 1831 (Durham University Archives, Grey of Howick papers).

17 Tim P. O'Neill, 'Clare and Irish poverty, 1815–1851' in *Studia Hibernica*, no. 14 (1974), pp 7–27; *Considerations addressed to the landed proprietors of the county of Clare* (Limerick, 1831), passim.

18 *A statement of the proceedings of the western committee for the relief of the Irish poor, 1831* (London, 1832), passim. Hereafter cited as *The report of the Exeter Hall Committee, 1831*).

19 *Report of the committee appointed at a public meeting at the Mansion House in the city of London for the purpose of adopting measures for the temporary relief of the distress that unhappily prevailed in certain parts of the west of Ireland, together with an appendix.* (London 1831), p. 34. Hereafter *Cornhill committee report, 1831*.

20 *Report of the Mansion House Relief Committee appointed at a public meeting held on the 25 September 1829* (Dublin, 1830). For 1831 Mansion House Relief Committee see *F.J.*, 21 March, 6 April, 7 June, 19 April, 6 and 8 June and 12 August 1831.

21 *Report of the proceedings of the committee of the relief association for the suffering peasantry of the west of Ireland* (Dublin, 1833), pp 7–8. All monetary aid sent by this committee was sent to Protestant clergymen. Cf. appendix 1 (hereafter cited as *Report of the Sackville Street Committee, 1831*).

22 Brian Harrison, 'Philanthropy and the Victorians' in *Victorian Studies*, ix, no. 4 (June 1966), pp 364–7.

23 Tim P. O 'Neill, 'Seán MacHéil agus bochtaineacht an iarthair', in A. Ní Cheannain, (eag.), *Leon an Iarthair* (Baile Átha Cliath, 1983), pp 25–37.

24 Final report of the commissioners for the employment of the poor in Ireland, 31 August 1822, N.A., CSO, registered papers, 1822, carton 1960; *Cornhill Committee report, 1831*, pp 27–9. See appendix 1.

25 *Cornhill Committee report, 1831*, pp 9–10.

26 Ibid., p. 32.

27 Anglesey to Grey, 15 January 1831 (Durham University Archives, Grey of Howick papers).

28 G. Poulett Scrope, *Friendly advice to the peasantry of Ireland* (Dublin, 1834), pp 1–6.

29 Chads reports (N.A., CSO, official papers 1839, no. 108).

30 Singer and Henderson, two government agents, toured Donegal in 1817 and the police reported during all food crises. Captain Haines inspected in 1831 and Sir John Hill was knighted for his inspection and famine relief services in Ireland and Scotland in the 1830s. All their reports were unpublished and compiled to inform government and to help in the organisation of relief. O'Neill, 'The state, poverty and distress in Ireland, 1815–45'.

31 This was the area of the Kilrush poor law union where in the great famine wholesale clearances took place. Cf. Capt. Kennedy's reports in *Reports and returns relating to evictions in the Kilrush union*, H. C. 1849 (1089), xlix, p. 12; *Hansard*, 3rd ser., cv (1849), cols. 1286–95. In 1822 the barony of Moyarta had 2,519 heads of families or 12,000 persons dependent on voluntary relief. In 1822 a mere £3,382 0s 10d was raised by local contributions in Clare. *Report of the London Tavern Committee, 1822*, pp 115 and 150. See also letters and reports on distress in Clare 1822, London Tavern Committee MS 7471, Guild Hall Library, London.

32 See Tim P. O 'Neill, 'The famine in Offaly' in Tim P. O'Neill and Willie Nolan (ed.), *Offaly: history and society* (Dublin, 1998), passim.

33 Ibid.

34 *Transactions of the Central Relief Committee of the Society of Friends during the famine in Ireland in 1846 and 1847* (Dublin, 1852), p. 46. Hereafter cited as *Transactions*.

35 Deirdre Ryan, 'The Lissadell estate of Sir Robert Gore Booth; famine and emigration, 1845–47' (Unpublished MA thesis, UCD, 1996).

36 Gamble Papers (N.A., MS 3493, 3521 and 3486).

37 *Report of the London Tavern Committee*, 1822, p. 143.

38 Rosse to Sir W. Somerville, 23 October 1849 (N.A., Outrage papers, Offaly, 1847, no. 15/558).

39 Cited in Helen E. Hatton, *The largest amount of good: Quaker relief in Ireland, 1654–1921* (Kingston, 1993), p. 180.

40 Dombrain was a member of Peel's 1845–6 relief committee.

41 Tim P. O'Neill, 'Minor famines and relief in Galway 1815–1925' in G. Moran and R. Gillespie (ed.), *Galway, history and society* (Dublin, 1996), passim.

42 Tim P. O'Neill, 'Poverty in Ireland, 1815–45' in *Folk Life*, xi (1973), p. 26.

43 See J. Mokyr, *Why Ireland starved: a quantitative and analytical history of the Irish economy, 1800–1850* (London, 1983), pp 263–8; Noel Kissane, *The Irish famine, a documentary history* (Dublin, 1995), pp 172–3.

44 Tim P. O'Neill, 'The famine in Offaly', op. cit.

45 *Transactions of the Central Relief Committee of the Society of Friends during the famine in Ireland in 1846 and 1847* (Dublin, 1852), p. 447, compiled by Jonathan Pim.

46 Ibid., p. 447; Tim P. O'Neill, 'The famine in Offaly', forthcoming.

47 C. Kinealy, *A death-dealing famine; the great hunger in Ireland* (London, 1997), p. 148.

48 J. Donnelly, *Land and people in nineteenth century Cork* (Boston, 1975), pp 73–132; O'Neill, 'The famine in Offaly'. In Cork and Offaly the potato yield fell from 8 tonnes in 1847 to 2 tonnes per acre in 1848.

49 Cormac Ó Gráda, 'Poverty, population, and agriculture, 1801–45' in W. E. Vaughan (ed.), *A new history of Ireland, v, Ireland under the union, 1801–70* (Oxford, 1989), vol. v, p. 113.

50 *Report of the London Tavern Committee, 1822*, p. 150.

51 O'Neill, 'Poverty in Ireland, 1815–45', p. 23.

52 John Keegan, *A young Irishman's diary* (Cambridge, 1928), p. 104.

53 *Report of the British Relief Association* (London, 1849), passim.

54 *Tablet*, 23 March 1847.

55 *The Times*, 8 March 1847.

56 Margaret Preston, 'Discourse and hegemony: the language of charity in nineteenth century Dublin', forthcoming.

57 Eneas McDonnell, *Irish sufferers and anti-Irish philosophers; their pledges and performances* (London, 1848), pp v–vii.

58 Peter Gray, 'Famine relief policy in comparative perspective: Ireland, Scotland and north-western Europe, 1845–49' in *Eire-Ireland*, xxxii (1997), p. 106.

59 *Report of the proceedings of the Irish Relief Association for the destitute peasantry formed during the period of famine in the west of Ireland in 1831 at 16 Sackville Street, Dublin* (Dublin, 1848), passim. Also known as the *Irish Relief Association*.

60 *Report of the General Central Relief Committee for all Ireland from 1 July 1848 to 1 September 1849* (Dublin, 1849), p. 6; *Report of the general relief committee of the Royal Exchange, 3 May to 3 September 1849* (Dublin, 1849), p. 33.

61 *Report of the general relief committee of the Royal Exchange, 3 May to 3 September 1849* (Dublin, 1849), p. 33.

62 *Report of the trustees of the Indian relief fund* (Dublin, n.d.), passim; Charles Trevelyan, *Irish crisis* (London, 1880), pp 84–5;C. Kinealy, 'Potatoes, providence and philanthropy: the role of private charity during the Irish famine' in Patrick O'Sullivan, *The meaning of the famine: the Irish world wide, history, heritage, identity* (London, 1997), p. 158.

63 Irene Whelan, 'The stigma of souperism' in C. Poirtéir (ed.), *The great Irish famine* (Cork, 1995), pp 135–54; D. Bowen, *The Protestant crusade in Ireland 1800–70*

(Dublin, 1978), *passim*; Pascal A. E. Majerus, 'The Second Reformation in west Galway: A. R. Dallas and the Society for Irish Church Missions to the Roman Catholics, 1849–59' (Unpublished MA thesis, UCD, 1991).

64 A. Dallas, *Point of hope in Ireland's present crisis* (London, 1849), instruction number 11.

65 David Miller, 'Irish Catholicism and the great famine' in *Journal of Social History*, ix, no.1 (Sept. 1975), p. 85.

66 Letter to trustees of Dickenson fund, May 1849, Society of Friends papers (N.A., 2/507/3).

67 *Report of the Ladies Relief Association for Ireland, 1846 to 1850* (Dublin, 1850), passim.

68 *Report of the London Tavern Committee, 1822*, pp 321–41; in Offaly a number of clothing societies were established by ladies.

69 See for example the work of Lady Gore Booth in Sligo during the famine. Deirdre Ryan, 'The Lissadell estate', p. 30; Evidence of Sir R. Gore Booth, *Second report from the house of lords select committee on colonisation from Ireland*, H.L., 1847–48 (593), xvii, p. 268.

70 Gertrude Himmelfarb, *The idea of poverty: England in the early modern age* (London, 1984), pp 1–5; Margaret H. Preston, 'Lay women and philanthropy in Dublin, 1860–80' (unpublished MA thesis, NUI, 1991).

71 Michael Crotty, *A narrative of the reformation at Birr in the King's County, Ireland* (London, 1847), passim.

72 Kinealy, 'Potatoes, providence and philanthropy' in P. O'Sullivan, op. cit., p. 149.

73 Tim P. O 'Neill, 'The catholic church and the relief of the poor, 1815–45' in *Archivium Hibernicum*, xxxi (1974), pp 132–45; J. Canon Guinan, an Offaly priest, claimed that the grandeur of Catholic churches built by and large by the pennies of the poor were justified by the words of Solomon, 2: 11. J. Guinan, *Scenes and sketches of an Irish parish; or priest and people in Doon*, 6th ed. (Dublin, 1925) p. 5.

74 Donal Kerr, *The Catholic church and the famine* (Dublin, 1996); Bob Cullen, *Thomas L. Synott: the career of a Dublin Catholic 1830–70* (Maynooth, 1997), *passim*.

75 *Transactions*, pp 47 and 358. Parliament estimated emigrants' remittances as follows:

    1848   £460,180
    1849   £540,619
    1850   £957,087
    1851   £990,811

The Quakers believed that many remittances never came to the attention of the government investigation, *Transactions*, p. 47.

76 K.A. Miller, *Emigrants and exiles* (Oxford, 1985), p. 303.

77 *F.J.*, 28 March 1862.

78 *Transactions*, p. 247.

79 C. Kinealy, *This great calamity: the Irish famine, 1845–52* (Dublin, 1994), p. 163; C. Kinealy, *A death-dealing famine*, p. 102; Mary Daly, 'Historians and the famine: a beleaguered species?' in *I.H.S.*, xxx, p. 592.

80 Journal of the Central Relief Committee of the Society of Friends, 31/12/1846 to 6/3/1852, Daily memoranda of W. Todhunter, 22/10/1845 to 15/2/1849 and reports (N.A., Society of Friends papers, 2/207/3,4,and 5; 2/506/40 and 2/507/45).

81 Hatton, *The largest amount of good*, pp 79–246; Richard S. Harrison, *Richard Davis Webb; Dublin Quaker printer, 1805–72* (Dublin, 1993), pp 54–72.

82 Tim P. O'Neill, 'The 1890s; new beginnings for the west and the baseline reports of the Congested Districts Board', forthcoming. See also J. H. Tuke, *The condition of Donegal* (London, 1889), passim.

83 David W. Miller, 'Irish Presbyterians and the great famine', pp 165–81 below puts Presbyterian relief in context.

84 *Transactions* (1849 circular).

85   *Report of the Mansion House Relief Committee, 1862* (Dublin, 1862), p. 13.
86   Tim P. O'Neill, 'Minor famines and relief in County Galway, 1815–1925', passim; James S. Donnelly, 'The agricultural depression of 1859–64' in *Irish Economic and Social History*, iii (1976), pp 33–55.
87   *Nation*, 26 April 1862.
88   *Report of the Mansion House Relief Committee, 1862,* passim.
89   *Hansard parliamentary debates*, 3rd ser., clxvii (1862), pp 413, 423.
90   *The Irish crisis of 1879–80; proceedings of the Dublin Mansion House Relief Committee, 1880* (Dublin, 1881), pp 73–7.
91   Ibid.
92   Walter Callan, 'Memorandum on the financial aspect of the relief of distress in Ireland' (N.A., Royal commission on congestion papers, box 5).
93   William P. O'Brien, *Poor law and poor law guardian inspectors; the great famine in Ireland and a retrospect of the fifty years 1845–95 with a sketch of the present condition of the congested districts* (Dublin, 1896), p. 62.
94   Tim P. O'Neill, 'The food crisis of the 1890s' in E. M. Crawford (ed.), *Famine: the Irish experience, 900–1900* (Edinburgh, 1989), pp 176–97.
95   C. Ó Gráda, 'Making Irish famine history today' in *Ireland's famine: commemoration and awareness* (Dublin, 1997), pp 51–2.
96   As early as 1822 Sir Robert Peel had accepted that, 'I feel most strongly the particular embarrassment of the situation in which the government is placed by applications of this nature for the means of subsistence for a large portion of the population from public funds. Within a comparatively short period it has been necessary on two occasions for the government to adopt measures for the maintenance of the distressed in Ireland, which nothing but absolute necessity could warrant but which that necessity has rendered unavoidable.' Peel to Wellesley, 19 June 1822 (B.L., Add. MS 37299, ff 234–7).
97   See Tim P. O'Neill, 'Famine evictions' in Carla King (ed.), *Parnell summer school papers, 1997*, forthcoming.
98   Lord Rosse to Sir W. Somerville, 23 October 1849 (N.A., Outrage papers, Offaly, 1849, no. 15/558).
99   Donal Kerr, *The Catholic church and the famine* (Dublin, 1996), p. 77.
100 Even those who were generous tended to be tarred with the same brush as others of their class. Gamble in Offaly had a reputation of great cruelty to his tenants and Gore Booth lost the trust of his tenants and political support by 1852. Rev A. L. Shaw, *Parish of Killoughy* (Killoughy, n.d.), p. 45; Rev. T. O'Rourke, *History of Sligo – town and county* (Dublin, 1889), p. 18: cited in Ryan, 'The Lissadell estate', p. 78.
101 Mr William Lucas of Brusna, County Offaly, was shot dead on 18 October 1847 while escorted by a police guard. The police report stated that 'the cause, of this murder, is deemed in consequence of Mr Lucas having evicted some refractory tenants and levelled their houses'. (N.A., Outrage papers, Offaly, 1847, nos 15/546–7). John Julian, county solicitor, had warned Lucas of the 'insanity of residing in the county'. Julian to Rosse, October 1847 (N.A., Outrage papers, Offaly, 1847, no. 15/558).

Appendix 1

*Principal British and Irish non-governmental
relief committees and funds, 1815–45*[1]

Year		Totals
1816	Dublin Mansion House Committee[2] £18,586	
	Total 1816	£18,586
1817	Estimate of various charities[3] £300,000	
	Total 1817	£300,000
1822	London Tavern Committee[4] £304,181	
	Dublin Mansion House Committee[5] £18,340	
	Various local subscriptions in distressed districts[6] £44,585	
	Total 1822	£367,106
1826	Royal Exchange Fund, Dublin[7] £13,000	
	Total 1826	£13,000
1829	Dublin Mansion House Committee[8] £6,094	
	Total 1829	£6,094
1831	Cornhill Relief Committee, London[9] £50,939	
	Exeter Hall Relief Committee, London[10] £30,000	
	Dublin Mansion House Committee[11] £3,570*	
	*This committee also distributed £5,000 of government aid[12]	
	Sackville Street Committee[13] £20,675	
	Total 1831	£110,184
1839	Estimate of various charities[14] £4,879	
	Total 1839	£4,879
1842	Estimate of various charities[15] £3,516	
	Total 1842	£3,516

NOTES

1 All amounts to the nearest pound.
2 *Dublin directory, 1842* (Dublin, n.d.), annals 1816. Report of the Mansion House Relief Committee quoted in *F. J.*, 26 December 1816.
3 *Report of the proceedings of the committee of management for the relief of the distressed districts in Ireland, appointed at the Mansion House* (Dublin, 1823), appendix 11, p. vii; Peel to Sidmouth, 21 July 1817 (B.L., Add. MS 40293, f. 157).

4 Sir C. E. Trevelyan, 1849 in *Transactions of the Central Relief Committee of the Society of Friends during the great famine in Ireland in 1846 and 1847* (London, 1852), pp 26–8, Hereafter cited as *Transactions, 1848*; also C. E. Trevelyan, *Irish crisis* (London, 1848), pp 7–9.

5 *Report of the proceedings of the committee of management for the relief of the distressed districts in Ireland, appointed at the Mansion House* (Dublin, 1823), passim; *Report of the committee for the relief of the distressed districts in Ireland, appointed at a general meeting held at the City of London Tavern on the 7 May 1822* (London, 1823), pp 347–'9.

6 *Report of the London Tavern Committee, 1822*, p. 150.

7 *Dublin directory, 1842*, op. cit., annals 1826; see also *F.J.*, 5, 25 and 26 August, 17 October and 2 December 1826.

8 *Report of the Mansion House Relief Committee appointed at a public meeting held on 25 September 1829, at a meeting at the Royal Exchange, for the relief of the distressed manufacturers of the city of Dublin and its vicinity* (Dublin, 1830), appendix 1.

9 *Report of the Cornhill relief committee* (London, 1831), pp 12–14; see also *Final report of the Irish distress committee* (London, 1835), *passim*.

10 *A statement of the proceedings of the western committee for the relief of the Irish poor* (London, 1832), p. 6 and appendices 8 and 10.

11 *F.J.*, 7 June and 12 August 1831; *Morning Chronicle*, 23 November 1847 and *Transactions, 1848*, p. 29.

12 Captain Haines to Captain J. Dombrain, 8 June 1831. N.A., Transferred papers, 1A/50/31.

13 *Report of the proceedings of the committee of the relief association for the suffering peasantry in the west of Ireland* (Dublin, 1833), passim, abstract of cash account.

14 Relief granted by government for employment 21 June–13 Aug. 1839 (N.A., Official papers, 1839, no. 108).

15 A list of districts to which relief has been sent for the distressed poor from 17 June to the 10 August 1842 (N.A., Registered papers 1842, carton 1097, Z11170).

Appendix 2

Principal British and Irish non-governmental
relief committees and funds 1845–1851[1]

Local contributions to attract matching governmental funds, 1846	£104,690[2]
Local contributions to attract matching governmental funds, 1847	£199,569
British Relief Association, total received:£470,041, five sixths	
for Ireland [One sixth for Scotland]	£391,701
Central Relief Committee, College Green, Dublin: £83,935,	
less £20,190 from British Relief Association	£63,745
Irish Relief Association, Sackville Street, Dublin[3]	£42,446
Relief Committee of the Society of Friends, Dublin, £198,314 less	
amount received from the Committee of Friends in London and	
interest £39,250[4]	£159,064
Society of Friends, London	£42,906
Indian Relief Fund	£13,920
National Club, London	£19,930
Wesleyan Methodist Relief Fund	£20,057
Irish Evangelical Society, London	£9,264
Baptists' Relief Fund, London	£6,142
Ladies' Irish Clothing Society, London:£9,533 less amount received	
from the British Association £5,325	£4,208
Ladies' Relief Association for Ireland:£19,584 less amount received	
from the British Association £7,659	£11,925
Ladies' Industrial Society for the Encouragement of Labour among	
the Peasantry[5]	£25,752
Belfast Ladies' Association for the Relief of Irish Distress	£2,617
Belfast Ladies' Industrial Association for Connaught[6]	£4,616
Two Belfast collections	£10,000
Estimates of emigrants' remittances[7]	
1848	£460,180
1849	£540,619
1850	£957,087
1851	£990,811
Estimate of funds distributed by	
Archbishop Daniel Murray:	£70,000 to £150,000[8]

NOTES

1   Unless otherwise stated all amounts are taken from *Transactions, 1848*, pp 45–8, 358 and 474–8 and reconciled where possible with the charities' reports mentioned in the text.
2   Amounts in all cases to the nearest pound.
3   *Report of the Irish Relief Association for the destitute peasantry (being a reorganisation of the association formed during the period of famine in the west of Ireland in 1831), 16 Sackville Street, Dublin* (Dublin, 1848), passim. This report gives a slightly lower amount. Lord George Hill was one of the secretaries of this committee and its moving light.
4   Helen Hatton, *The largest amount of good*, pp 9–11. Hatton points out that Quaker relief was wider than that recorded in the *Transactions, 1848* and that there were many subscriptions for specific purposes not recorded in that report.
5   *Report of the Ladies Relief Association, founded December 1846* (Dublin, n.d.), passim. This gives a total amount of £25,752 for the full period up to 1851 as follows: 1845, £469; 1846, £12,855; 1847, £7,747; 1848–9, £3,904; 1850, £777.
6   Many of the reports by the non-governmental charities are to be found in the Society of Friends papers in N.A., 1A/42/37, 2/507/3.
7   *Transactions, 1848*, p. 358.
8   Bob Cullen, *T. L. Synnott*, passim; Donal Kerr, *The Catholic church and the famine*, passim.

Appendix 3

Principal non-governmental relief committees and funds, 1858–1898[1]

1858–60	Gweedore and Cloughaneely, County Donegal appeal [2]	£5,725
1860–62	Dublin Mansion House Relief Committee	
	and *Society of Friends* [3]	£41,000
	Estimate of smaller subscriptions	£100,000
1863	J. Pim	£4,332
1879–80	Duchess of Marlborough's fund, the *New York Herald*	
	fund, the National Land League fund, the Canadian	
	Fund committee and the Philadelphia Fund Committee	£300,000
	Dublin Mansion House Relief Committee	£180,000
	Parliament of Canada	$100,000
	American aid to Irish bishops	£200,000
	Estimate of total for 1879–80 [4]	£830,000
1886	J. H. Tuke's appeal	£1,326
	The Times, *Spectator* and *Pall Mall Gazette* appeals	£2,723
	Society of Friends	£1,157
1890–92	Balfour and *Times* appeal [5]	£50,287
1897–98	Mansion House Relief Committee, Dublin	£11,155
	Manchester Town Hall appeal	£20,000
	Catholic bishop of Liverpool	£1,395
	Catholic bishop of Salford	£704
	Glasgow Observer appeal	£100
	A.. D. H. Texas	£40

NOTES

1 Amounts in all cases to the nearest pound.
2 See *Report from the select committee on destitution (Gweedore and Cloughaneely) together with the proceedings of the committee of evidence, appendix and index*, H.C. 1857–58 (412), xii, 89, passim; Breandan MacSuibhne, 'Agrarian improvement and social unrest: Lord George Hill and the Gaoth Dobhair sheep war' in W. Nolan, L. Ronayne and M. Dunlevy (ed.), *Donegal, history and society* (Dublin, 1995), p. 571.
3 *Report of the Mansion House Relief Committee, 1862* (Dublin, 1862), *passim; Report of the Mansion House committee for the relief of distress, 1858–1865* (Dublin, 1865), passim; Letters and reports on distress in Ireland 1862–65 (N.A., Society of Friends papers, 2/507/3).
4 *The Irish crisis of 1879–80: proceedings of the Mansion House Relief Committee, 1880* (Dublin, 1881), pp 72–86; the Land League divided its American funds collected for both political purposes and relief 17% to 83% respectively. T. W. Moody, *Davitt and Irish revolution 1846–82* (Oxford, 1981), p. 356.
5 For charities in the 1890s see Tim P. O'Neill, 'The food crisis of the 1890s'.

10 Irish Presbyterians and the great famine

David W. Miller

Around the beginning of March in 1847 a certain John Dilworth, who was administering in Ireland 'the benevolence of Christian friends in England', visited a house which he found to be 'like a pig-sty'. The family, he learned, had left the local workhouse to escape fever and dysentery. The man of the house had already been sent to bed by 'want', and despite Dilworth's efforts he, his wife and a daughter died a few days later. On his next visit after the burial of the first three victims, 'just within the door of the wretched habitation', Dilworth saw

a young man, about twenty years old, sitting before a live coal, about the size of an egg, entirely naked; and another lad, about thirteen, leaning against a post. On turning to the right, I saw a quantity of straw, which had become litter; the rest of the family, reclining on this wretched bed, also naked, with an old rug for a covering. The boy who stood against the post, as I stood looking at the head of a human being which appeared above the rug, directed my attention to an object at my feet, which I had not seen before, and over which I had nearly stumbled, the place being so dark – and, oh! what a spectacle! a young man about fourteen or fifteen, on the cold damp floor – off the rubbish – dead! – without a single vestige of clothing – the eyes sunk – the mouth wide open – the flesh shrivelled up – the bones all visible – so small round the waist, that I could span him with my hand. The corpse had been in that situation for five successive days.

The shocked Dilworth obtained a coffin and some food and clothing for the survivors, but when he called a week later he found yet another corpse and the three remaining children unable to choke down the food which had been provided. A physician who for a time visited the three children advised Dilworth not to expect any of them to survive.[1]

Readers familiar with the historical literature on the famine will not be surprised by the content of Dilworth's account. Literally hundreds of equally chilling reports must have appeared in contemporary newspapers. What makes this account especially interesting is the fact that John M'Clean (or McLane), the father, was not a Catholic cottier in some western or southern locality such as Skibbereen, but a Presbyterian weaver living just outside Lurgan, about fifteen miles from Belfast.[2]

How Presbyterians experienced the famine

The answer to the question 'Did Presbyterians starve?' as we have just learned, is 'Yes', but how common was the experience of the M'Cleans among their co-religionists? As it happens, a few days after Dilworth's letter appeared in the *Belfast News Letter*, the official in Dublin Castle who was responsible for relationships with the Presbyterian church, George Mathews, sent out a circular letter to the ministers of the General Assembly asking each of them to state 'the number of persons in your Congregation, who have died since last July; and should the severity of the late Winter have increased the mortality beyond the average amount of preceding Seasons, be good enough to note any explanation upon this point which you think necessary'.[3] Despite considerable weaknesses in Mathews's survey instrument,[4] and the fact that few Presbyterian congregations maintained burial registers, it is possible to glean some insights from the returns.

Returns were received from ministers of 154 out of the 470 congregations throughout Ireland. Most of the respondents did not believe that their flocks had suffered unusually high mortality. However, some fifty-one of the returns seem to imply that mortality had increased among congregation members and/or that there was some mortality because of inadequate nutrition. Figure 1 depicts the geographic distribution of responses in the northern part of the country; respondents from the

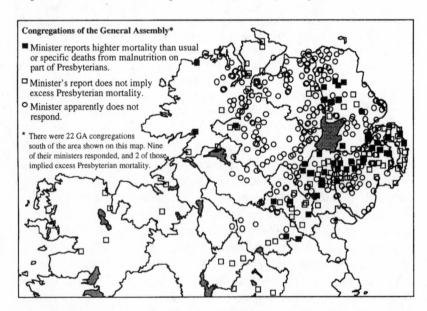

Figure 1 Ministers' responses to inquiry about Presbyterian mortality, July 1846–April 1847
Source: see n. 3.

Presbyterian heartland of Down and Antrim (including Belfast) were significantly more likely than those from the rest of Ireland to report excess mortality.[5] No doubt the farther a congregation was from the Presbyterian heartland the likelier it was to conform to the description of the Tralee congregation by its minister: 'small and its members generally in comfortable circumstances'.[6] Where Presbyterians were thicker on the ground they tended to include a wider range of social classes.

The importance of this geographic distinction emerges in responses from a handful of ministers who ignored Mathews's literal instructions and drew distinctions between the official members of their congregations and other local Presbyterians whom they described with terms such as 'the poor not regularly connected with the congregation', 'not immediately connected', or 'not strictly under pastoral care'.[7] The Rev. Frederick Buick of Ahoghill put his finger on the problem when he lamented, 'I am afraid the returns will not be accurate as there are many families who belong to no congregation. And of the deaths in these there will be no return made.'[8] Clearly there were poor, nominal Presbyterians who were suffering from the food shortage to a degree that was rare among those better-off Presbyterians who tended to be regular church members.

So while the responses to Mathews's query are consistent with the received view that Presbyterians suffered less than Catholics in the famine – certainly there were no Presbyterian Skibbereens – they almost certainly understate excess Presbyterian mortality simply because most respondents took their instructions literally and ignored deaths among poor Presbyterians who were not congregation members in good standing. Furthermore, some Presbyterian spokesmen were simply in a state of denial that their community was truly suffering. In their official reply to a letter concerning slavery from the Presbyterian Church, U.S.A. (Old School) they inserted a paragraph on the famine which concluded with the following language:

We are grateful to Almighty God, while we humbly regard it as a practical illustration of the industry and general comfort promoted by our beloved Church, that in Ulster, where our principles are most widely disseminated, the visitation has appeared in a much less aggravated form than in those provinces in which the Romish system still, unhappily, maintains its degrading and paralyzing ascendency.[9]

While it was certainly true that the impact of famine was less severe in Ulster than in Connacht or Munster (though more severe than in Leinster where the 'Romish system' also maintained its 'ascendency'),[10] 'general comfort' had been a good deal less evident to the M'Cleans than it seems to have been to their spiritual leaders.

For Presbyterians as well as Catholics the famine did more than suddenly inflict suffering on individuals; it was a catalyst of long-term change in class structure. In the case of Catholics, a huge agrarian underclass of cottiers and labourers subsisting on potatoes raised on tiny holdings was decimated by the famine and virtually eliminated over the remainder of the century. In east Ulster technological change had created a comparable class of poor Presbyterians by forcing down the earnings of the numerous handloom weavers to subsistence levels before the potato failure dramatically raised the cost of subsistence. Though Presbyterian weavers who actually starved, like John M'Clean, were exceptional, emigration of many weavers hastened the transition to factory-based power-loom production, which virtually eliminated handloom weaving by the end of the century.[11] Even where weaving was not central to the local economy, Presbyterian population decline seems to have occurred mainly among those not 'regularly connected' with congregations. The Maghera congregation, for example, seems to have weathered a decline of about 30 per cent in the local Presbyterian population between 1845 and the early 1860s while experiencing only an 11 per cent decline in the number of families in connection with it and no decline at all in the number of families affluent enough to contribute to the minister's support.[12]

The famine hastened a process which had been going on for some time: the transformation of Ulster Presbyterianism from a communal religion whose constituency was the whole community of Scottish settlers to a class-based religion which, like Presbyterianism elsewhere in the English-speaking world, mainly served a middle-class constituency. This transition was ritually manifest in the replacement of annual 'holy fairs' with more frequent and decorous indoor celebrations of communion. Schmidt has argued that the earlier reformed form of the Lord's Supper – which brought together worshippers from a large geographic area and included the less devout in its penumbra of drink, conviviality and courtship – had a festal character which reaffirmed traditional community in Scotland and frontier America.[13] Westerkamp has demonstrated the role of Ulster Presbyterians in transmitting this cultural form from Scotland to colonial America before 1760, and Killen attests to the role played by the Seceders – the growth sector in Irish Presbyterianism between the 1750s and the 1820s – in sustaining the holy fair.[14] The week-long interruptions of work by these 'fairs', which Schmidt contrasts with the demands of modern capitalist industry, would have been altogether congenial to the handloom weavers in the Ulster countryside, whose preference for leisure over increased income was notorious.[15]

It was, however, in Belfast that the consequences for the poor of the increasingly middle-class character of Presbyterianism were most obvious to contemporaries. Since 1843 a Belfast town mission in connection with the General Assembly had been systematically addressing the problem of the unchurched by employing seminary students and licentiates as missionaries responsible for specific districts of the city.[16] In 1846, the Rev. James Morgan, moderator of the General Assembly and minister of the fashionable Fisherwick Place church, was urging a plan loosely based upon the celebrated and controversial efforts of Thomas Chalmers over the preceding generation to address the same problem in Scottish cities. Working from the missionaries' estimate of 1,200 nominally Presbyterian families in Belfast, Morgan proposed to mobilise a substantial fraction of the 4,000 communicants in the eleven city congregations as 'visiters' to 'take charge of' the unchurched families.[17] Like the efforts of Chalmers himself,[18] it was a visionary scheme that ignored the way in which religion increasingly functioned for the middle class as a way of demarcating class boundaries.

What Presbyterians did about the famine

The appearance of disease in the 1845 potato crop seems to have been greeted by Presbyterians, at least in Belfast, as a troubling development that called for familiar solutions. At a meeting on 3 November of the city's 'principal inhabitants' which called for suspension of duties on food, the Rev. John Edgar, a well-known temperance advocate, proposed and won unanimous consent for a resolution calling for an end to distillation from grain for one year, in order to conserve the food supply.[19] In an editorial entitled 'The year 1845' in its final number for the year, the Belfast Presbyterian paper, the *Banner of Ulster*, alluded to the potato failure only obliquely, as a conjuncture that had brought justly deserved ruin to avaricious speculators in railway stock.[20] In general the state of the crop ranked behind American slavery as a subject of public discourse in Belfast. By the spring of 1846 there was some destitution among the handloom weavers, and a relief committee was set up so that Ballymacarrett, a working-class suburb across the Lagan from Belfast, could take advantage of government provisions for distressed localities.[21] Ulster Presbyterians, however, no doubt expected normal conditions to return with the next harvest and seem to have contemplated no need for extraordinary measures as summer approached.

The situation changed dramatically with the failure of the 1846 harvest. In a special General Assembly meeting in late August primarily concerned with negotiations with the government over higher education, 'many brethren' referred to the 'alarming indications of God's judgments . . . especially in the almost total failure of the potato crop'. The Assembly called for services of 'special humiliation and prayer' but recommended no direct steps to relieve the suffering.[22] Two weeks later, however, John Edgar would take an initiative that would mobilise a section of the Belfast elite for such steps. An indefatigable activist in a number of charitable and reform causes, Edgar had, by sheer dint of energy and eloquence, overcome the disadvantage of a pulpit in a poor and obscure Belfast congregation of Seceders, as well as quite possibly the ugliest face of any public man in Irish history save Napper Tandy, to become one of the two or three most prominent ministers in Belfast. At harvest time in 1846 he was on an inspection tour of the Assembly's network of Irish language schools in Connacht. So moved was he by the devastation of the potato crop near Killala, County Mayo, and the dignity of the local people in their suffering that he dashed off an eloquent letter to the editor of the *Banner of Ulster* appealing for immediate assistance. 'Relief must come at once', he wrote, 'or they will all be dead'.[23] Edgar made the early proceeds of his efforts available for distribution by sixteen different individuals in Connacht, of whom eight were Roman Catholics – one of them the bishop of Killala. In October, to raise further resources Edgar organised a 'Belfast Ladies' Relief Association for Connaught', which immediately began to organise a bazaar of needlework.[24]

Of course, a ladies' bazaar was not the most direct way to tap into the substantial wealth of the Belfast elite, but on 24 December Edgar took advantage of another town meeting, which had just endorsed his year-old remedy for starvation by calling upon the government to stop distillation from grain, to force his more recent project upon the male elite's agenda. Those present could not, he argued, ask the government to grant their request to halt grain distillation 'without giving evidence that they themselves felt deeply about the matter' of distress in the country. Accordingly it was agreed to have another meeting to initiate a plan to receive subscriptions for the relief of such distress. At that meeting, on 19 January, there was a brief exchange that foreshadowed difficulties to come. Morgan made the somewhat specious but strategic objection that the wording of the resolution seemed to imply 'that no relief could be given to the poor of Belfast out of the funds raised. He did not think sufficient had been done for the poor of Belfast.' He thus forced Edgar to concede that the committee of subscribers which would manage the fund would have the power to grant relief to Belfast 'should that be necessary'.[25]

During the first half of 1847 Belfast became increasingly aware of the encroaching problems of the rest of Ireland. Refugees from the countryside flocked to Belfast, and Edgar found himself reminding a meeting in February that the purpose ought not to be 'merely driving the beggars off our streets', but assisting the poor who were crowding the town.[26] By mid-March grants of £2,805 had been made from subscriptions of £6,747. Some 39 per cent of the grants had gone to Belfast and vicinity and only 33 per cent to localities outside Ulster. Facing pressure to direct even more of the funds to Belfast in the light of government decisions that seemed to be tackling some of the urgent rural needs, Edgar argued that the original intention of applying the money 'without reference to locality' had been 'for the purpose of setting a noble example'. He had found it difficult in committee 'to obtain for distressed Connaught trifling grants', compared to which the grants to the Belfast area were 'most liberal'. [27] During the next few weeks additional significant grants were made to Belfast.[28] Meanwhile, an epidemic of typhus fever began in Belfast in late April; on 15 June it was reported to be 'rapidly extending itself among the middle classes'.[29] About a week later the committee of the relief fund decided to retain the remainder of the fund as a reserve for 'cases of emergency connected with Belfast which may hereafter arise'. 'It may save trouble to parties at a distance to be aware', the *News Letter* reported, 'that no further grants are henceforth available for them from this fund.'[30]

With this announcement the concerted effort of the male industrial and mercantile elite of Presbyterian Belfast to relieve distress in the country-side came to an end. However, two weeks after the termination of grants from the relief fund to localities outside Belfast, the American evangelical Asenath Nicholson visited the city and found it a beehive of *female* philanthropic activity:

Here was a work going on, which was paramount to all I had seen. *Women* were at work; and no one could justly say that they were dilatory or inefficient. Never in Ireland, since the famine, was such a happy combination of all parties, operating so harmoniously together, as was here manifested.[31]

And although what immediately impressed Nicholson was the greater willingness of Belfast ladies than their Dublin counterparts to visit the *local* poor in their homes, she went on to describe with enthusiasm the Ladies' Association's new initiative: the formation of female industrial schools in Connacht.[32] This new initiative resulted in part from those changes in government policy which seemed to render private efforts for the simple provision of food redundant.[33] Early in his famine relief campaign Edgar had expressed a special interest in the plight of the women of Connacht; he spoke of meeting a girl carrying gleanings of barley in 'a rough, heavy creel' and expressed the hope that the image of this 'genuine Irish Ruth' might awake 'some gallant and generous spirit on behalf of their poor starving countrywomen, forced to serve as beasts of burden, and eke out, in hunger and nakedness, a wretched existence'.[34] This concern over the special indignities and burdens which the famine imposed upon women was echoed by correspondents of the Ladies' Association.[35] The solution that seems to have occurred simultaneously to urban and rural philanthropists was to train women in skills to enable them to engage in some branch of textile manu-facture in their homes.[36] It was not easy to find a viable economic niche within which to pursue this strategy, but sewed muslin was identified as a product in which hand work still added sufficient value to make it a feasible proposition.[37] Accordingly, a number of schools, each superintended and supported by a local Protestant lady and staffed by a needlework mistress from the north, were established for young women in Connacht.[38]

The concept of a woman's 'sphere' emerges in the Association's publications. Initially it is described somewhat vaguely as a divinely assigned 'noble and unlimited sphere'.[39] By the end of 1847, however, the ladies had developed a rather more explicit understanding that the Almighty had assigned them 'the sphere of industry, education, and religion'. Although bible teaching was officially part of the curriculum in all the Association's industrial schools, there are reasons to suspect that it enjoyed a lower priority than instruction in vocational skills. Asenath Nicholson saw instruction only in knitting and sewing when she visited an industrial school near Belmullet.[40] The Rev. Michael Brannigan, a missionary who had also established some industrial schools in Connacht during the famine, appealed to the 1848 General Assembly for support for his schools, identifying 'knitting and flowering' as the glory of the ladies' schools, 'whilst the Bible, the Shorter Catechism and the Confession of Faith are the glory and the object' of his.[41] The Rev. William Johnston of Belfast had sought to resolve the controversy by calling for the Assembly to support 'the intellectual and evangelical training' in Brannigan's schools, which he implied was 'the sphere of the Church' leaving 'the industrial department to be taken up by the ladies of Ulster, or those kind and Christian friends whom Providence may dispose and enable to carry on the work', among whom the most likely were 'the ladies of Scotland and Dublin' who were already financing Brannigan's initiative.[42]

The emergence of a well-understood separate sphere for women was, of course, characteristic of other European and North American societies in the mid-nineteenth century. The articulation of that concept at this juncture in Ulster was a gender-specific indicator of the ongoing transformation of Presbyterianism from a communal to a class-based religion. The creation of a large mercantile and industrial middle class in Belfast over the preceding half-century had placed many women in a situation in which remunerative work outside the home after marriage was strongly discouraged. An important latent function of Presbyterianism was to reconcile these women to such constraints by sanctifying a set of philanthropic extensions of the domestic sphere, including bazaars, which drew upon domestic textile skills passed on to these women from their foremothers in east Ulster's proto-industrial phase, and organising the training of Connacht peasant women in similar skills along with such middle-class virtues as cleanliness. The opportunity for a few unmarried women to have the well-monitored adventure of teaching these skills and dispositions in the wild west of Ireland was consistent with the function of the overall enterprise. And as was the case in the response of the male sector of the Belfast middle class to the crisis, an overriding consideration was to enable the poor to survive somewhere other than Belfast.

How Presbyterians thought about the famine

In recent scholarship 'providentialism' has been identified as a major factor in the responses of the British public and policymakers to the famine.[43] Ultra-Protestants saw the famine as punishment for the prevalence of popery and for such 'national sins' as the recent increase in the Maynooth endowment. A more popular providential interpretation represented the famine as a warning against national extravagance, which ought to be redressed by acts of charity toward the starving. However, as Peter Gray has shown, what made providentialism an important component of policy formation was the 'Christian economics' of a number of contemporary British evangelicals. These thinkers envisaged the political economists' arguments for free markets as God's 'natural economic laws' to impose moral discipline. A 'special' or 'direct' providence like the famine, therefore, could be understood as the almighty's way of prompting the state to cease obstructing the operation of his laws. Policymakers and elite British opinion fostered such thinking by placing 'the blame for the state of Irish society squarely on the moral failings of Irishmen of all classes'.[44]

Many Victorians had to reconcile a scientific world view committed to the explicability of phenomena through natural causes with a residual Calvinism committed to the singularity and omnipotence of supernatural agency. Most educated Englishmen would have recoiled with embarrassment at the tendency of their forebears two centuries earlier to attribute even routine curiosities to supernatural causes, but the possibility of supernatural intervention in the natural world did force itself upon their attention when events posed the central conundrum of theodicy: if God is good he is not God – or at any rate not the absolutely sovereign God of Calvin's *Institutes*. We should think of Irish society as existing on the margins of this intellectual world. Members of its own elites were capable of thinking in the same terms as the British elite, but they were also the leaders of a broader Irish public, Catholic as well as Protestant, which tended to see the famine as some sort of divine judgment and felt little need to reconcile that perception with the laws of either natural or economic science. Indeed, in the Ireland of the famine era we can cross the boundaries of the intellectual world in which supernatural agency must be unitary. According to Brannigan, who was fluent in Irish, after the 1846 harvest failure it was believed in the Killala district 'that, in a pitched battle at

Downpatrick Head, the Connacht fairies had been vanquished, and that the northern fairies had blighted, or rather carried off, the potato crop'.[45]

When addressing policy-makers Presbyterian spokesmen were quite capable of blending political economy with providential thinking.[46] In discourse within the Presbyterian community, however, the subtleties of the Christian economists tended to be eclipsed by straightforward speculation about whom God was punishing and for what sins. The *Banner* probably articulated the dominant lay viewpoint when it attributed the almighty's wrath to the boasts of sabbath-breaking repealers.[47] Clerical leaders were more disposed to identify sins of the Presbyterians themselves as objects of divine judgment. An October address by the Assembly's committee, over Moderator Morgan's signature, listed five such sins, ranging from sabbath breaking to 'not having honoured the Lord with our substance as we ought'.[48] Interestingly, there were also Presbyterian clergy who hesitated to speculate over exactly which sins and sinners were being punished. An anonymous clerical correspondent of the *Banner* ridiculed speculation on 'this awfully mysterious subject' by quoting an alleged remark of a 'a very ingenious neighbour' of his 'that challenges given and accepted at farming dinners, respecting the produce of the land, have *caused* the failure of the potato'.[49]

It is impossible to say how widespread among Presbyterian clergy was this correspondent's willingness to forego speculation about the precise causes of divine wrath, but his use of the word 'mysterious' echoes the usage of John Edgar, who frequently distanced himself from Christian economics by referring to the famine as a 'mysterious Providence'.[50] Denouncing that 'species of heartless philosophy current which says this calamity will, in the end, be good for Ireland, because it will cure the Irish of their laziness, and force them to seek a better food than potatoes', he declared that he did not believe the Irish were lazy and asked, 'is a man called on to work himself to death for eightpence a-day?' Cold and learned talk 'about the necessity of teaching the Irish, in present circumstances, a taste for luxuries, for the comforts of life, and so forth', he continued, 'evidences melancholy apathy, and ignorance too, of the real state of the case' in the parts of Connacht which he had visited.[51]

Although he continued to characterise God's afflictive visitations as 'mysterious', before the end of 1846 Edgar himself had assigned a reason for the almighty's actions. In his celebrated pamphlet *A cry from Connaught*, he argued that through the potato failure providence had opened up a field for missionary endeavour. 'I advocate no proselytism in a bad sense, and no bribery', Edgar wrote, but he urged that the misery of the west enabled Protestant missionaries to win the hearts of Catholics by kindness.[52] In the succeeding months this interpretation of providence's design gained such favour among Presbyterian clergy that in his moderatorial sermon in July, 1847, Morgan, ever alert to new opportunities to torment the consciences of his co-religionists, asked rhetorically 'Have we not reason to fear that God is visiting us with this as a punishment for our neglect; we did not send the gospel to them.'[53] Edgar took up the theme less penitentially, stressing the opportunities presented by a 'mysterious Providence' in a situation in which 'thousands' of Catholics were 'disgusted with their priests', grateful 'for Protestant benevolence' and 'anxious to learn the faith from which such generous practice flows'.[54] The extent to which this interpretation of providence's intent by leaders of the Assembly was accepted throughout Ulster Presbyterianism is certainly open to question. Giving to the home mission cause lagged far behind what its advocates thought was demanded by the times,[55] a circumstance which no doubt reflected in part the economic hardship prevailing in many congregations.[56] Nevertheless, the Assembly leaders clearly had resolved the great problem of theodicy posed by the famine in terms of their community's evangelistic duty towards Irish Catholics.

What the famine tells us about Ulster Presbyterianism

So by harvest time, 1847, Edgar's conception of the famine as a providential act not of punishment, but of deliverance, governed the Assembly's response to the calamity. The last previous mighty act of God to which Ulster Presbyterianism had had to respond was the French revolution. As I have argued elsewhere, the willingness of ordinary Presbyterians to contemplate political cooperation with Catholics in the 1790s presumed that the external world of politics and society was a suitable arena in which to expect providential action, and therefore, of course, the liberation of the elect among the adherents of false churches to embrace true reformed religion. A major feature of the 'evangelicalism', which began to change Ulster Presbyterianism between the 1790s and the 1840s, was the shift of that arena from the external world to the internal world of the individual's mind and affections,[57] and that was certainly the way in which Presbyterians, by the time of the famine, expected Catholics to be converted, if at all.

To understand the failure of those expectations in the famine years let me propose two models for thinking about it. The first model is the Republic of Ireland in the 1950s. In that stable society the vast majority of the population were secure in their Catholic identity, and the church was not widely perceived by its adherents to be dysfunctional. Any Protestant efforts to seek mass conversions in such a society would have been a waste of resources, but I believe it has implicitly tended to be our model for thinking about Protestant missionary efforts in the nineteenth century.

The second model is the Hispanic community in the United States (and indeed in many parts of Latin America) during the 1980s and 1990s. In that society certain evangelical, especially pentecostal, Protestant churches have been making extraordinary gains.

Ireland in the mid-nineteenth century lay somewhere between the two models. The Rev. Henry M'Manus, an Irish-speaking Presbyterian missionary, argued in 1841 that, unlike English-speaking Catholics, many of 'the Gael' had 'strictly speaking, scarcely any religion at all. Being too poor to repay the trouble of instruction, and too secluded to learn much by intercourse with their neighbours, they are compelled to live and die in the most awful ignorance.'[58] M'Manus's claim that a large share of the Irish-speaking population was virtually unchurched, and Edgar's belief that many were alienated from priests who were seldom seen except to exploit their parishioners financially,[59] though exaggerated, were not preposterous. M'Manus's observations turn out to be remarkably consistent with results of analysis of the mass attendance data from the 1834 public instruction commission report (see figure 2).[60] When the directors of the home mission declared in their 1849 report, 'Our Mission field for reclaiming captives from the Man of Sin lies in the counties of Tyrone, Donegal, Sligo, Mayo, Roscommon, Galway, and Kerry',[61] they were articulating a very rational strategy. What they lacked were tactics.

To understand why their tactics were such a dismal failure we can look to the work of Allan Figueroa Deck, S.J. He finds that many contemporary Hispanic Americans have been converted to evangelical Protestant sects because of alienation from an American Catholic church that is increasingly focused on retaining the allegiance of relatively well-educated, middle-class Catholics. As a marginalised group, such Hispanics are responsive to the promise of personal conversion and the charismatic, emotion-laden, tactics of certain evangelical sects, though they are not especially attracted to mainstream Protestantism.[62] So what was the religious style of the Presbyterianism being promoted in the west of Ireland in the 1840s? Although the mission enterprise itself was a component of the new evangelicalism, it is simply not clear that, prior to the 1859 revival, evangelicalism had brought very much change in the religious style of Irish Presbyterianism as experienced by its typical adherent.[63] It remained a system whose hallmark was having the 'right' answers to theological questions (which of course would lead to 'correct' ethical and religious standards of conduct).

This fundamentally cognitive understanding of believerhood was reflected in the main mechanism by which Presbyterians sought to reach the Catholics on the eve of the famine: the Irish school. In several hundred Gaeltacht locations literate Irish-speakers – almost invariably Roman Catholics – were employed to teach students to read and write the Irish

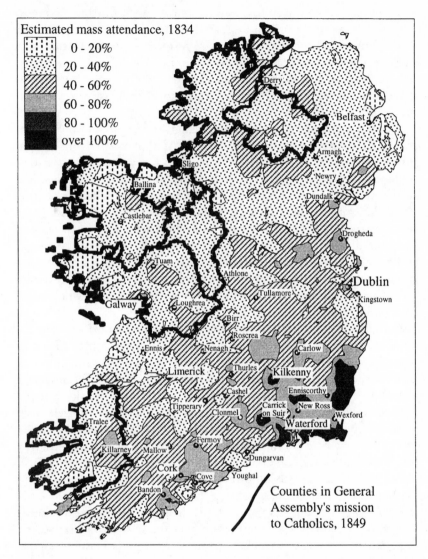

Figure 2 Contour map of estimated attendance as percentage of Catholic population, 1834
Source: see n. 60.

language and to progress to reading (and, if bilingual, translating) the scriptures.[64] The apparent confidence in rationality which underlay this enterprise – that intellectual engagement with the inspired text could, unaided by any intermediary, effect religious transformation – should be evaluated in light of stories which were frequently repeated by advocates of the programme. The Irish schools over a large area in Ulster had originated in a beggar's discovery of an Irish new testament 'by the wayside', and those of Connacht resulted from 'an English sportsman' having presented a bible to a peasant.[65] Whatever their claims to historicity, the fascination with such stories reflects a very incomplete transition to an understanding of believerhood which might generate the rich armoury of conversionist tactics already being employed by American evangelicals in the mid-nineteenth century.

Given the prevailing Presbyterian religious style, it should not be surprising that obstacles to conversion of the Catholics were conceived as primarily cognitive. J. W. Yule, a missionary in Kerry, feared that the souls of those dying around him were 'going down to hell' after he learned that many men could not give satisfactory answers to his religious queries. 'Preaching will not do', he concluded sadly, 'for the vast majority could not understand it.'[66] The Rev. James Carlile proposed a corps of lay teachers who would carry out 'a more minute sifting of the minds of the people' and bring down 'the doctrines of salvation more to the level of their capacities than ministers can accomplish'.[67] Rigorous cognitive preparation was regarded as a necessary prerequisite for any affective role which might be played by eloquent preachers.

Catholics in some parts of the west of Ireland did indeed resemble the nominal Catholics among Hispanic immigrants in the American southwest today, in that the Catholic church may well not have been meeting their spiritual needs effectively. However, what the Irish Presbyterian church had to offer in the 1840s and early 1850s was a cold, rational religious system very different indeed from the Pentecostal evangelicalism which has proved so attractive to American Hispanics. It is true that in 1859 Ulster Presbyterianism was for a time convulsed by an extraordinarily emotional and enthusiastic revival, but by that time the Catholic church, owing both to the leadership of Paul Cardinal Cullen and to the fall in population that had alleviated some of the strain on pastoral resources, was increasingly able to address the needs of adherents. We should remember the painful admissions of a few clergy that the famine was hardest on Presbyterians 'not regularly connected' with their congregations. In targeting the poorest of the poor in Catholic Ireland for conversion in the famine years, the Presbyterians were seeking to win from the Catholic community the very stratum that they had already lost within their own community.

NOTES

1 *Belfast News Letter*, 2 Apr. 1847.

2 Lurgan Workhouse Register, (P.R.O.N.I., BG.1R–1, 1841–47, pp 269–70, entries 5396–98).

3 'Presbyterian clergy[:] Papers found in Mr Mathews's press' (N.A., Official papers 1849/95) hereafter Mathews papers. The author thanks the National Archives for permission to quote from this collection. For a copy of the circular itself see Alexander G. Ross to Mathews, n.d.

4 Mathews's request seemed to imply that workhouse deaths should be omitted from the return and did not define whether the 'severity of the late winter' referred only to the weather or included also the food shortages and disease.

5 A chi-square test on the following table yields significance of .005.

	Antrim & Down	Rest of Ireland	Total
Excess mortality reported	33 44%	18 23%	51 33%
No excess mortality reported	42 56%	61 77%	103 67%
Total	75 100%	79 100%	154 100%

6 William W. Chestnut to Mathews, 12 Apr. 1847 (Mathews papers).

7 Ibid., Henry William Carson [1st Keady] to Mathews, 12 Apr. 1847; Alexander G. Ross [Markethill] to M., n.d.; Alexander McIlwaine [Ballyblack] to M., 20 Apr. 1847; John Weir [Townsend Street, Belfast] to M., 12 Apr. 1847.

8 Frederick Buick to Mathews, 20 Apr. 1847 (Mathews papers).

9 *Gen. Ass. Presb. Ch. Ire. min. 1847*, p. 624.

10 Joel Mokyr, *Why Ireland starved: a quantitative and analytical history of the Irish economy, 1800–1850* (London, 1983), p. 266.

11 Philip Ollerenshaw, 'Industry, 1820–1914' in Liam Kennedy and Philip Ollerenshaw (ed.), *An economic history of Ulster, 1820–1940* (Manchester, 1985), pp 62–108, at pp 66–86.

12 Thomas Witherow, *The autobiography of Thomas Witherow, 1824–1890* (Draperstown, 1990), p. 63; S. Sidlow McFarland, *Presbyterianism in Maghera: a social and congregational history* (Mahgera, 1985), p. 95; *Gen. Ass. Presb. Ch. Ire. min. 1864*, 'Statistics of the Presbyterian Church in Ireland', bound after p. 448. *First report of the commissioners of public instruction, Ireland*, H.C. 1835, xxxiii, p. 308.

13 Leigh Eric Schmidt, *Holy fairs: Scottish communions and American revivals in the early modern period* (Princeton, 1989).

14 Marilyn J. Westerkamp, *Triumph of the laity: Scots-Irish piety and the great awakening, 1625–1760* (New York, 1988); James Seaton Reid, *The history of the Presbyterian church in Ireland*, new edition with additional notes by W. D. Killen, 3 vols (Belfast, 1867), iii, p. 376.

15 Schmidt, *Holy fairs*, pp 193–4; Charles Coote, *Statistical survey of the county of Armagh* (Dublin, 1804), pp 264–5; J. Byrne, *An impartial account of the late disturbances in the county of Armagh* in David W. Miller, *Peep O'Day boys and Defenders: selected documents on the disturbances in County Armagh, 1784–1796* (Belfast, 1990), p. 46. Ollerenshaw, 'Industry', p. 74.

16 An older town mission representing all evangelical denominations continued to exist, but the union in 1840 of the seceding and general synods, the two largest such denominations, invited this more systematic initiative under General Assembly auspices. W. D. Killen, *Memoir of John Edgar* (Belfast, 1867), pp 163–5.

17 *Banner of Ulster* (Belfast), 19, 26 May, 15 Sept., 20 Oct. 1846. For a rural counterpart to the proposed Belfast effort, see letter from Rev. John Johnston, Tullylish, headed 'A mission to the heathens of the County Down', ibid., 26 June 1846.

18 See Stewart J. Brown, *Thomas Chalmers and the godly commonwealth in Scotland* (Oxford, 1982).

19 *Banner*, 4 Nov. 1845.

20 Ibid., 30 Dec. 1845.

21 Ibid., 10 Apr. 1846.

22 *Gen. Ass. Presb. Ch. Ire. min. 1846*, p. 558; *Banner*, 1 Sept. 1846.

23 Killen, *Edgar*, 200–8; *Banner*, 18 Sept. 1846.

24 Killen, *Edgar*, 209–25; *Banner*, 25 Sept., 3 Nov. 1846.

25 *B.N.L.*, 19 Jan. 1847.

26 Ibid., 23 Feb. 1847.

27 Ibid., 23 Mar. 1847. *Banner*, 23 Mar. 1847.

28 *B.N.L.*, 2, 30 Apr. 1847.

29 Ibid., 23 Apr., 4, 21 May, 8, 15 Jun. 1847.

30 Ibid., 25 Jun. 1847.

31 Asenath Nicholson, *Lights and shades of Ireland* (London, 1850), p. 249.

32 Ibid., pp 250–52.

33 John Edgar, *The women of the west. Ireland helped to help herself* (Belfast, 1849), p. 42.

34 Killen, *Edgar*, p. 216.

35 *Report of the Belfast Ladies' Relief Association for Connaught: extension and permanent operation. Third edition, containing extracts from recent correspondence* (Belfast, 1847), pp 13–15, 22.

36 Ibid., pp 25–6. William Bennett, *Narrative of a recent journey of six weeks in Ireland in connexion with the subject of supplying small seed to some of the remoter districts: with current observations on the depressed circumstances of the people* (London, 1847), pp 93–4; Killen, *Edgar*, pp 235–7.

37 Edgar, *Women of the west*, p. 45.

38 Killen, *Edgar*, pp 235–8.

39 'Report and appeal of the Belfast Ladies' Relief Association for Connaught' in Edgar, *Women of the west*, p. 32. For application of the concept to the female *recipients* of philanthropy, see 'Female industry in Connaught', ibid., p. 35. For a useful survey of philanthropy in Belfast see Alison Jordan, *Who cared? Charity in Victorian and Edwardian Belfast* (Belfast, 1993).

40 Nicholson, *Lights and shades*, p. 304.

41 *Banner*, 7 July 1848.

42 *Missionary Herald*, no. 67 (July, 1848), p. 563.

43 Boyd Hilton, *The age of atonement: the influence of evangelicalism on social and economic thought, 1795–1865* (Oxford, 1988), pp 73–114. Peter Gray, '"Potatoes and Providence": British government responses to the great famine' in *Bullán: An Irish Studies Journal*, i, no. 1 (spring, 1994), pp 75–90.

44 Peter Gray, 'Ideology and the famine', in Cathal Póirtéir (ed.), *The great Irish famine* (Cork, 1995), pp 86–103, at pp 91–2.

45 Killen, *Edgar*, p. 202. As late as 1933, according to a Connacht informant of the Irish Folklore Commission, 'Bhi sé ráite gur ar shon na mbarranna bhíodh sídheóga Cúige Chonnacht agus Cúige Uladh a' troid, agus creidtear má bhíonn droch-bharranna i

gConnachta gurb shin bliain a gcailleann sídheóga Chonnacht an cogadh'; Seán Mac Giollarnáth, 'Seanchas Beag Thuama' in *Béaloideas*, xvi (1946), p. 87.

46 See 1847 General Assembly address to the lord lieutenant, *Banner*, 5 Oct., 1847.

47 *Banner*, 26 Feb. 1847.

48 Ibid., 13 Oct.1846. For other examples of Morgan's thinking on this issue see ibid., 23 Feb. 1847, and James Morgan, *Recollections of my life and times: an autobiography* (Belfast, 1874), pp 275–6.

49 Ibid., 23 Mar. 1847. The correspondent signed himself 'a country bishop', although the *Banner* surmised, probably correctly, that he was an orthodox Presbyterian clergyman.

50 Killen, *Edgar*, pp 208, 212; *Northern Whig*, 19 Nov. 1846 (resolution moved by Edgar at meeting to establish soup kitchens in Belfast); *Banner*, 15 Jan. 1847 (letter from Edgar concerning home mission collections). 'Home mission: annual collections', *Missionary Herald*, no. 64 (Apr. 1848), p. 540. In the wake of the appearance of potato disease in 1845, it was probably Edgar who introduced the expression 'mysterious providence' into an appeal by Belfast clergy for abstinence from distilled spirits to conserve the supply of food: *Banner*, 11 Nov. 1845.

51 Killen, *Edgar*, pp 209–22.

52 [John Edgar], *Select works of John Edgar* (Belfast, 1868), pp 481–92.

53 *B.N.L.*, 9 July, 1847.

54 *Missionary Herald*, no. 56 (Aug., 1847), pp 458–9; *Banner*, 9 July, 1847.

55 'Ninth annual report of the Assembly's home mission, presented to the Assembly at its meeting in Belfast, July, 1849', *Missionary Herald*, no. 80 (Aug.1849), pp 683–7, esp. p. 687.

56 See J. W. Kernoghan, *The parishes of Kilrea and Tamlaght O'Crilly: a sketch of their history with an account of the Boveedy congregation* (Coleraine, 1912), p. 65; James C. Rutherford, *The life and times of the Reverend John Orr, M.A. of Portaferry* (Belfast, 1912), pp 31–3; C. W. P. MacArthur, *Dunfanaghy's Presbyterian congregation and its times* (Dunfanaghy, 1978), p. 17. On the other hand, the First Kilraughts congregation actually had a higher balance in hand in August 1847 than in September 1845; S. Alexander Blair, *Kilraughts: a kirk and its people* (n.p. [1973]), p. 83.

57 David W. Miller, 'Presbyterianism and "modernisation" in Ulster', in *Past and Present*, no. 80 (Aug. 1978), pp 66–90.

58 *First report of home and foreign missions*, 1841, p. 21.

59 Edgar, *Select works*, pp 490–1.

60 The methods by which this map was created are described in David W. Miller, 'Mass attendance in Ireland in 1834' in S. J. Brown and D. W. Miller (ed.), *Piety and power in Ireland, 1760–1960: essays in honour of Emmet Larkin* (Belfast and South Bend Ind., 1999).

61 *Missionary Herald*, no. 80 (Aug. 1849), p. 684.

62 Allan Figueroa Deck, S. J., 'The challenge of evangelical/pentecostal Christianity to Hispanic Catholicism', in Jay P. Dolan and Allan Figueroa Deck, S. J., *Hispanic Catholic culture in the US: issues and concerns* (Notre Dame, 1994), pp 409–39.

63 Alfred Russell Scott finds various exhortations by individual clergy and judicatories to the practice of more vital godliness in the 1830s and 1840s. He fails however, to find evidence that such appeals made much difference in the religious lives of Presbyterians before the 1850s. Alfred Russell Scott, *The Ulster revival of 1859* (Belfast, [1994]), pp 36–48.

64 For an account of the methods, see *First report of the home and foreign missions, 1841*, pp 13–19.

65 Edgar, *Select works*, p. 485. See also, Thomas Armstrong, *My life in Connaught, with sketches of mission work in the west* (London, 1906), p. 29.

66 *Missionary Herald*, no. 53 (May 1847), p. 431.

67 Ibid., no. 63 (Mar. 1848), p. 536.

11 Luxury and austerity, patronage and charity: landlords and a Galway convent

John Maiben Gilmartin

The Redingtons were considerable landlords in County Galway. Their great house, with a private chapel, was at Kilcornan in the neighbourhood of Oranmore near Clarinbridge, about eight miles from the city of Galway. The origins of the Kilcornan Redingtons are not entirely clear. In Burke's *Landed gentry* they are said to have been 'settled in Ireland at the time of Cromwell's invasion'.[1] Were they Cromwellian settlers? When subsequently did they become Roman Catholic? In a memoir of 1854 by Sir Thomas Redington (1815–62) about the Redington family, it is related that a Redington was a Cromwellian soldier turned farmer.[2] His grandson married either in 1719 or 1729 a Margaret Lynch of Galway city (a member of one of the Galway 'tribes'); in turn, their son married the daughter of a de Burgo, a landowner in the Clarinbridge district. This brought them to that locality, and shortly afterwards they became Roman Catholic. The Redingtons were at one stage tenants of the Monivea branch of the Galway Blakes.[3]

Christopher Redington (1780–1825), the father of Thomas Redington, the patron and landlord who concerns us, married in 1812 a Miss Francis Xaviera Elizabeth Dowell of Mantua House, in County Roscommon. The Dowells were rich and like other similar Connacht families they had prospered through trade, in their case through extensive business interests in the wine trade of Cadiz. Consequently Miss Dowell, who became Mrs Redington, the foundress and patron of Kilcornan convent, had interesting continental connections. These connections partly explain the remarkable works of art that she presented to the Sisters of Charity for their convent chapel at Kilcornan which in 1844 she founded and endowed as the convent, or as it was quaintly called, the priory of St Mary.[4] The term 'priory' is not a term normally used to describe the convents of nineteenth-century active sisterhoods and its use at Kilcornan suggests the influence of the cult of medieval romanticism.

This same romantic historicism compelled the vital new religious congregations of Irish women which had recently sprung up, including the Sisters of Charity (1815), to attire themselves like medieval enclosed nuns – which they were not – and to observe an increasingly medieval way of life as the century wore on. This was reflected in the gothic design of both the private chapel in the great house and the convent chapel of Kilcornan. On the other hand, the furnishing of the convent chapel with a neo-classical high altar surmounted by an important sculptural group by John Hogan, a large oil painting, which hung above it, as well as the plate, textiles and reliquaries, all attested to the 'new' Catholicism that was now in the ascendant. The discreet Catholicism of the penal era was being replaced by a confident counter-reformation revival mentality. It was intended that worshippers in the convent chapel at Kilcornan would, figuratively speaking, be transported by the elaborate liturgy and décor to Rome. Nineteenth-century Rome was the wellspring of revived triumphant Counter-Reformation values, which had largely been shaped and given their original external forms in the sixteenth and seventeenth centuries. A desire for a revival of such values is evident in the Roman Catholic church from the early nineteenth century. It could be said to date from the restoration of Louis XVIII in 1814. Many new or restored religious orders appeared at that time. The restored Jesuits and newly founded sisterhoods such as that of the Sacred Heart are cases in point, and both were particularly keen to restore the world of the French 'ancien régime'. After the upheavals and experiments of the revolutionary era, throne and altar once again became synonymous in much of Catholic Christendom.

In the world of art and design a similar nostalgia for the seemingly secure and privileged pre-French-revolutionary world showed itself. The 'rococo revival', first seen in the décor and furnishings of Benjamin Dean Wyatt's dining room at Apsley House, London, in the late 1820s is evidence of this. Revived baroque and rococo designs often overlay severe neo-classicism to produce a rich, curious and charming style very prevalent in the 1830s, and which can be found in the décor of the many new church buildings and furnishings commissioned by the Catholic church in Ireland at this time. St Andrew's, Westland Row, Dublin (1830s) is a good example,[5] and several features, including the high altar, showed affinity with counterparts in Kilcornan convent chapel. Sadly, St Andrew's interior has been severely marred by ill-advised re-ordering in the 1970s, though it at least partly survives unlike Kilcornan convent.

It is significant that Mrs Redington's given names were Francis Xaviera, indicating on the part of her Dowell parents an interest in the revived Jesuit order and its saints. The Irish Sisters of Charity too, for whom Kilcornan convent was founded in 1844, were deeply influenced by the Ignatian ethos. Mrs Francis Xaviera Elizabeth Redington had one son, Thomas Nicholas Redington, born in 1815. He was born at the old

Kilcornan House and was sent to school at Oscott College near Birmingham. Afterwards he went to Cambridge University but did not take his degree. Returning to Ireland, he went into public life. He became M.P. for Dundalk in 1837. In 1846 he was appointed under-secretary of state for Ireland, a major achievement for a Roman Catholic at the time. This position effectively made him head of the Irish civil service. In 1847 he became a commissioner of national education and a poor law commissioner. The great famine soon followed, and Redington busied himself with organising famine relief. His was a difficult role. When serious food riots took place in Ireland he was ordered to London to explain matters and was reprimanded. However, in 1849 at the end of her first visit to Ireland, Queen Victoria awarded Thomas Redington a knighthood (K.C.B.), in recognition of his services to charitable work, especially famine relief. Redington married in 1842 a Miss Anne Talbot, daughter of John Hyacinth Talbot, M.P., of Talbot Hall, County Wexford and his wife Anne, the only daughter of Walter Redmond of Ballytrent House, County Wexford. This marriage represented a considerable leg up socially for the Redingtons, as Miss Talbot's cousin was the countess of Shrewsbury and Lord Shrewsbury was lord high steward and high seneschal of Ireland and a prominent courtier at Dublin Castle. The Shrewsburys also spent much of their time in Rome.

The family name of the earls of Shrewsbury was also Talbot, so two distant branches of the Norman Talbots were united by this marriage. John Talbot, sixteenth earl of Shrewsbury and Waterford (1791–1852), was a Roman Catholic peer. He married in 1814 Maria Theresa, daughter of William Talbot of Castle Talbot, County Wexford and had two daughters and a son who died in infancy. The first daughter, Lady Mary Alathea, married in 1839 Philip Andrew, Prince Doria Pamphili-Landi, a leading Roman nobleman. He died in 1876 and there was issue. The second daughter, Lady Gwendoline Catherine, married in 1835, becoming the first wife of Mark Anthony, eldest son of Prince Borghese, another leading member of the Roman nobility. The pair had an only daughter.[6] When Thomas Redington married Anne Talbot the marriage was celebrated with memorable splendour at Alton Towers the English seat of the Shrewsburys. Amongst the guests were Prince and Princess Doria Pamphili-Landi: the *Tuam Herald* expended much purple prose on the event.[7]

Lord Shrewsbury knew 'the father of the gothic revival', Augustus Welby Northmore Pugin, and it was through him that the great gothic revival architect was introduced into Ireland. Pugin visited Lady Shrewsbury's family the Wexford Talbots, who became his clients, and consequently it is no coincidence that most of Pugin's work in Ireland is to be found in the south-east. Close links already bound the Wexford Catholic gentry families such as the Talbots and Redmonds, and, as noted above, a Redmond was married to John Hyacinth Talbot, father-in-law of Thomas Redington. Consequently there were ties between these Wexford families and Kilcornan House, despite its remote situation. When in 1846 Thomas Redington became under-secretary of state for Ireland, Pugin gained a friend in high places. Redington was instrumental in securing the commission for Pugin to design the new buildings at St Patrick's College, Maynooth, made possible by the increase in the grant to Maynooth by Sir Robert Peel's government.[8] In 1838 (before Pugin's appearance in Ireland) Mr Thomas Redington, as he then was, had old Kilcornan House enlarged and rebuilt in the Tudor revival style by the English regency architect George Papworth.[9] There is a theatrical, insincere appearance about the house with its cream stuccoed mock medieval battlements, typical of late regency design and which must have been repugnant to Pugin. Pugin, it should be remembered, was of great importance as a designer at this time and his views on design were immensely powerful. He gave to buildings a moral character, so that we can say that they look 'insincere'. However he was too fanatical and died too young (at the age of forty in 1852) to succeed fully in his aims, which were nevertheless taken up and implemented by the Ecclesiological Society and others.

George Papworth, the architect responsible for rebuilding Kilcornan in an unconvincing and uncharacteristic Tudor style (his only Irish essay in Tudor design), had already worked on the Carmelite church, Whitefriar Street, Dublin, and a yacht club at Kingstown (Dun Laoghaire), as well as on other Irish projects. While Papworth was undoubtedly the architect of Kilcornan House, he is unlikely to have designed the family chapel. The interior of the chapel, a simple rectangular room rising two storeys over an under croft to a height of about fifty feet, is, in the view of the present writer, so Puginian in its gothic design (especially the scissors beam roof and three light window) that it must have been designed by Pugin himself. However, documentary proof of this has yet to be found. Besides his work on the house, Papworth probably also had some part in designing Kilcornan convent. As previously mentioned, the convent was founded in 1844 in an existing small house before the gates that mark the start of the mile-long drive to the great house. Two gabled extensions were added to each end of the facade of the existing house. One became the chapel, a simple rectangular room which rose the full two storeys; here too, I suggest, Pugin's influence on the design can be detected, as it was similar in scale and was a perfunctory version of the chapel in Kilcornan House. The convent chapel was in fact a microcosm of the battle of styles being waged in the 1840s, 1850s and 1860s between the classicists and gothicists: the modest architecture being gothic notably in the lancet windows and the scissors beam roof, while the furnishings were neo-classical. At the other end of the convent facade the corresponding addition became the refectory. Some charming gothic detail was present in the convent interiors; especially noteworthy was the hall with gothic doors dividing it from the well-lit inner hall. Today the facade survives, as a front to what is now a hotel, but the original interiors were totally destroyed in 1995.

Before the coming of the Sisters of Charity Mrs Redington senior had already attempted to encourage religious orders to set up in the district. She had brought in the Patrician Brothers, who almost certainly lived in the future convent house. However, disputes arose with local residents and the brothers had to leave Clarinbridge. Evidence about the coming of the Sisters of Charity is to be found in the correspondence of Mother Mary Aikenhead, founder of the Institute of the Irish Sisters of Charity. An extract from a letter reads:

25 June 1844. Last night, under the patronage of the holy precursor [St John the Baptist] we forwarded mother rectress [this was Mother Baptist Griffin, a sister of the noted poet Gerald Griffin; she was to rule Kilcornan convent for about thirty years], Sisters M. Regis, and M. Christina to prepare our new foundation of St Mary's priory, Kilcornan, for the community. They are to sleep, until beds can be got up in the little convent, at the great house, where only Mrs Redington, senior, and Miss Anglim are. Doctor French [bishop of Kilmacduagh and Kilfenora (1825–52) and the last warden of Galway],[10] the bishop of the diocese in which St Mary's priory stands, is at the great house to meet them.[11]

Later four more sisters and two lay sisters arrived to augment the community.

16 July 1844 was the day of foundation and dedication of the convent to 'Our Lady of Mercy' as it was officially called. Formal possession took place and in a letter of 13 July Mary Aikenhead notes that 'the beautiful marble altar of the chapel of St Mary's priory is to be consecrated and the little church dedicated'.[12] Mother Aikenhead also tells us that Mr Troy (a nephew of Archbishop John Troy of Dublin) and Mrs MacSweeney have provided help: 'the purse affairs are a constant source of little and great difficulties, but so is our holy vow of poverty to be observed'.[13] The bell of the priory 'Auxilium Christianorum' was christened on 25 August 1852. So the décor was being assembled for several years after the priory opened. Hogan's sculptural group (see plate 7) was not placed above the altar until 1850. Before the end of July 1844 two schools had been opened, as well as a mission four miles away. The people's spiritual and corporal necessities were deemed so much in need of attention that the sisters soon extended their area of responsibility to encompass an area of seven miles around the convent.

Mrs Redington senior, the founder of the priory, endowed it for five sisters and presented the fine works of art for the chapel, while her son Thomas Redington gave twelve acres of land. This was a very generous gift, for twenty acres in those days was considered a substantial farm.

Mrs Anne Redington helped the sisters to start a lace-making school. Anne Redington was of a practical bent and helped the school by using her friendship with Mrs Errington of Kingstown (Dun Laoghaire), County Dublin, to find outlets in London and even Paris for the products. At first these products were woollen socks and the like, but soon the girls acquired skills in making fine lace work which was much admired at a time when lace was found on so many domestic accessories as well as on lay and clerical dress. 3s. 6d. a week was the wage in 1845 and it relieved only a little the grinding poverty that was the lot of most of the people around Clarinbridge. This school continued for many years and continues today as the local industrial school. A photograph of the community of Kilcornan convent, probably taken in the centenary year 1944, shows the sisters' costume and those of the clerics unchanged since the early years of the foundation. A hundred years of Tridentine Catholicism and charitable endeavour is documented in this photograph of the Sisters of Charity gathered about the redoubtable Bishop Michael Browne of Galway.

In the chapel of Kilcornan convent Hogan's white marble group 'The ascension' was the principal treasure.[14] The creator of this masterpiece was John Hogan (1800–58), who, together with John Henry Foley (1818–74), has a claim to be called Ireland's greatest sculptor.[15] Hogan was of Waterford and Cork origins, being the product of a notable mésalliance between a Catholic artisan and a Church of Ireland descendant of Lord Chancellor Sir Richard Cox.[16] For many years Hogan lived and studied in Rome. About 1840 his career reached a peak when his statue of Bishop James Doyle (J.K.L.) was erected in Carlow cathedral. During the 1840s Hogan longed to return to Ireland permanently, and despite the disastrous famine years he did come back several times, finally settling in Ireland in 1849. He brought with him his Italian wife and six children; five more children were to be born in Dublin. Hogan's art reflected the resurgent Irish Catholic church, as well as the rising tide of Irish nationalism associated with Daniel O'Connell and Young Ireland.[17]

John Turpin points out that Hogan was a sculptor of ideas and that his art was powerful, controlled and religious: 'his style was nourished by a study of antique, Roman, renaissance, baroque and neo-classical sculpture, begun in Cork and completed in Rome'.[18] He was much influenced by the great Italian sculptor, Canova (d. 1822), a piece of whose work was already to be seen in Galway. He was also influenced by the Danish sculptor Thorwaldsen. Hogan brought international neo-classicism in sculpture to Ireland. He was a devout Roman Catholic; his sister Margaret (also a sculptor) became a Sister of Mercy, while two of his children became Loreto Sisters at Rathfarnham Abbey, Dublin. This account of Hogan is a necessary prelude to a consideration of the major work of art at

Kilcornan convent, which was the high altar in the chapel, consecrated in 1844. The prevailing religious ethos in the Catholic church allowed for much expensive and lavish display, despite the destitution of the poorer classes. This was believed to be justified by the passage in John's gospel, xii (3–8) in which Christ was anointed by Mary Magdalen with expensive ointments and Judas asked why the ointments were not sold and the proceeds given to the poor. Christ replied that the poor were always present, whereas he, Christ, was not. There were, however, those, even then, who took a different view.[19] The artistic ensemble in Kilcornan chapel must have seemed impressive to the congregation, especially when the altar was decorated with candles and silver ornaments, and the choir sang during a newly introduced 'Roman devotion' such as the '*Quarant' ore*' or 'Forty hours' (plate 7).

The high altar of Kilcornan convent chapel is composed of many different rare marbles and inlaid with semi-precious stones, making it one of the most valuable and elegant altars in Ireland. The renaissance-style white marble altar has a frontal which in the centre has a carving depicting in relief the lamb of God standing in a roundel against a blue background made of lapis lazuli. A white marble tabernacle stands on the altar in the form of a classical Roman triumphal arch with sienna yellow Corinthian pillars; above a band of lapis supports the cornice. Delicately sculpted in white marble and in low relief two angels ornament the tabernacle doors, above which is the niche for exposition. Surmounting and crowning the whole ensemble was the white marble sculptural group by Hogan 'The ascension', which was placed on top of the tabernacle in about 1850.

Hogan had already been patronised by the Loreto Sisters and by the Irish Sisters of Charity, whose founder Mother Mary Aikenhead, Turpin suggests, may have commissioned the group for Kilcornan.[20] In fact this was probably not the case. Mother Aikenhead would not at the time have had the money for such an enterprise, though she often sent whatever she could for the nuns and their work. An account in the order's archives implies that Mrs Redington senior gave the sculptural group to Kilcornan.[21] It is a small and charming group. The subject has erroneously been thought to be 'The transfiguration', notably by John Turpin. Sarah Atkinson and Thomas McGreevy have held the correct view:[22] the wounds in Christ's hands confirm that it must be 'The ascension'. Christ is shown elevated in a swirl of drapery, while at his feet SS Peter and John are struck by amazement. It is indeed a largely baroque piece, influenced by the seventeenth-century Italian sculptor Bernini. Yet the controlled design indicates that the group belongs to the neo-classical era. Consideration of the high altar poses the question as yet unanswered: while Hogan certainly made the sculpture group, who actually made the rest of the altar with its angel-decorated tabernacle? I suggest that Hogan, aided by Roman assistants (some of whom were highly accomplished, for instance Restaldi)[23] designed the whole ensemble, which we know from the convent annals was made in Rome. Certainly, this is an important cultural treasure, something most unexpected to find in the Galway countryside and one that would not look out of place in a Roman church. As with other such works of art made in Rome and brought to Ireland, the altar was probably brought by oxen and cart to Leghorn and from there shipped in a dismantled state to Galway. Brought to Kilcornan it would have been reassembled 'in situ'. Unhappily, it has now been separated into two parts and moved to two separate locations. In 1995 the convent closed and was demolished, to be replaced by a new building, the Oyster Manor Hotel, built on the site behind the convent and incorporating the old facade. The facade, now painted oyster pink, has an incongruous modern portico and before it a curious little fountain and pond. Local people demanded that the high altar stay in the locality, so it is now to be found in an unhappily cramped situation in a small much 'restored' nineteenth century chapel-of-ease at Rooveagh, two miles distant. This chapel, by the gothic revival architect George Ashlin (1837–1921) and C. T. Redington, was erected through the patronage of Sir Thomas Redington's only son Christopher Talbot Redington (d. 1899), who actively assisted Ashlin in the design. A commissioner for education, C. T. Redington was an authority on church architecture, and he brought over Italian artists to decorate Rooveagh.

The high altar from Kilcornan is difficult to see properly in its new position, as a smaller altar stands before it, but it is at least safe, hopefully, and preserved to await a better future. 'The ascension' was removed, about 1995, from the top of the tabernacle to the prayer room of the modest bungalow that is the new home of the Sisters of Charity. More recently still (about 1998) it was brought to Dublin and may now be seen in St Mary's, Merrion Road, where it is displayed in the chapel. This is not a happy solution either, as the altar at Rooveagh now looks incomplete, while the sculpture group is lost to Clarinbridge. It is very regrettable, but at least both pieces are still in the possession of the Sisters of Charity and reasonably accessible. Later replicas by Hogan of 'The ascension' may be seen in St Andrew's, Westland Row, Dublin and Glanmire church, Cork.

In addition to the high altar and sculpture group, the convent chapel was endowed by Mrs Redington with a large painting, about twelve feet high, oil on canvas of 'The transfiguration' in a black and gilt frame. This hung above and behind the altar. Further research needs to be done to ascertain the identity and provenance of this work, which sadly is apparently no longer extant. It may have been a contemporary copy of Raphael's great picture now in the Vatican museums, or more probably an eighteenth- or nineteenth-century version such as the one in the National Gallery of Ireland, once thought to be by Mengs, now reattributed to James Durno (1750?–95) which was discussed at a recent symposium.[24] We now have little to work on regarding the Kilcornan painting except for a unique early photograph which shows it 'in situ'. My own enquiries about the painting produced the information that it started to sag and fall apart in about 1965, and when several years later reordering took place in the chapel in line with the recommendations of the second Vatican council, the picture was taken down and apparently broken up and destroyed. On a happier note, most of the other art treasures from Kilcornan convent chapel survive in responsible ownership. What, it may be asked, was the doctrinal reason for the picture of 'The transfiguration' in Kilcornan convent chapel? The answer is that the transfiguration is a metaphor for healing, and healing and transforming were two attributes of the mission of the Sisters of Charity.

Among the textiles in the sacristy at Kilcornan were two fine nineteenth-century chasubles probably of Irish manufacture: one made of white satin ornamented with gold arabesques, the other a violet vestment, also richly decorated. Both are superb examples of nineteenth-century craftsmanship and attest again to Mrs Redington senior's generosity; both are happily still extant in a private collection. Mrs Redington senior also gave fine plate for use at the altar. A neo-classical chalice is companion to an especially interesting monstrance. The monstrance is made of silver gilt and has a pyramidal base on which four seated figures hold instruments of the passion and support a figure of religion bearing a wreath and holding up the gloria with both arms. Both pieces have Roman assay marks and the monstrance is inscribed 'Francisca Xaviera Elizabeth Redington' and 'Dona Dedit A 1836' and 'Gregory XVI PM Benedixit'. It is 26 inches (66 cm.) high. The chalice, with a cup made of pure gold, is of the same date.

In addition to these notable pieces, Mrs Redington gave a large wooden box reliquary 36 inches (92 cm.) high in the form of a classical temple, and three smaller silver reliquaries, two 16 inches (41 cm.) high, resembling monstrances, and one 22 inches (56 cm.) high, in the form of a cross. All are surmounted by crowns of victory and ornamented with the symbols of the passion. Very elegantly designed and wrought in silver, they are of Roman manufacture and convey well the 'Roman' atmosphere that Mrs Redington tried to create at Kilcornan. A gothic brass censer of Puginesque design also in the plate collection recalls the opposing Puginian view in the battle of styles current at the time. The reliquaries remind us in particular of Mrs Redington senior, and her family's continental ties with Spain and Italy, especially with the Roman noble family of Doria Pamphili. In her memoirs Lady Gregory recalls Mrs Wilson-Lynch, a daughter of Sir Thomas and Lady Redington, visiting Coole Park as an old lady and reminiscing about the better days in County Galway before the famine when the Roman cousins used to visit Kilcornan House and no doubt Kilcornan convent chapel with its splendid Roman décor.[25]

Surviving letters in the order's archives make it possible to build up a picture of life in Kilcornan in the early years. There is a reference to the disturbing effect caused to the convent regime by Mrs Redington's frequent visits to see the nuns at their recreation, bringing visitors who perhaps introduced worldly levity into the monastic regime. 'Try to discourage Mrs Redington' was the refrain! Also the curate Fr Mullins seemed pleased by whatever discomfited the gentry. One account explains that the superioress did not wish old clothes for the poor to be given to a certain man, as it would, she thought, be unseemly for him to go about Clarinbridge in recognisable cast-offs of Sir Thomas Redington! Sir Thomas was widely considered to be a good landlord, but he was always anxious that monies sent to the sisters for the poor should be distributed first to his own tenants.[26]

Another letter tells us 'that balls and any lavishness in party giving' were to be given up as the full extent of the famine disaster dawned on the Redingtons. Then Mrs Redington senior cancelled her £1 a week donation to the convent because of a '£2,000 debt inherited from her father'.[27] Later Sir Thomas too withdrew financial help and Mother Aikenhead made her telling comment in a letter in which she wrote 'let us help and pray for the miserable poor, but even more let us pray for the miserable rich'.[28] Meanwhile the sisters, even though they were badly provided with food for themselves, went out in all weathers to visit and to help the poor and the dying. Going to houses and visiting in this way was a novel activity for nuns at this time; as a result they were called 'the walking nuns'. Heretofore, such external activities had never been permitted, or seen in Ireland.

In 1849 Sir Thomas considered that the famine was over, but in fact there were hard times in the district for many years, and during the next seventy years poverty and misery abounded around Clarinbridge. The sisters continued their work of running schools, overseeing the lace factory, and keeping a library. Rare photographs record them on their charitable rounds in the 1930s.[29] By then they made their rounds by horse and car; earlier they had usually gone about on foot, except when Mrs Redington was in residence and lent them a horse and car.

By 1930 the Kilcornan Redingtons had faded into history. When Sir Thomas died young in London in 1862, he left a son, Christopher Talbot, and four daughters. Christopher was in public life as a commissioner for education; and as already noted, he was an 'amateur' of art and architecture. He never married and died in 1899, but his sisters married into various landed families. They participated in the responsibilities of the local gentry and the social round. One sister, Mrs Wilson-Lynch, took over the Kilcornan estate for a short time. Surviving letters show the family to have been interested in artistic matters. In 1911 one cousin, Lady Dillon-Mahon, made charming sketches and watercolours showing Kilcornan in the last years as a family house.[30] Subsequently, Kilcornan House was sold off and there was an auction in the early 1920s. Many of the archives were destroyed and the contents dispersed. Kilcornan House then became a residential home for the handicapped, run to this day by the brothers of charity. Sadly shorn of its correct roofing it still stands today, well-maintained as a remedial centre, and with the chapel intact, but for how long?

The old convent is no more, but important works of sculpture and art remain at Kilcornan to attest to the artistic discernment and continental links of those who lived there in the nineteenth century. The reliquaries and some of the vestments from Kilcornan have found new and caring owners. Until now the only known surviving family portrait was that of Mrs Redington senior (plate 8) which had been in the possession of the Sisters at Kilcornan until 1995. Today, incorrectly labelled and identified as 'Annie Redington' (Lady Redington), it incongruously graces a hospitality room called 'The Annie Redington Room' in the new Oyster Manor Hotel on the site of the convent. However, in the summer of 1997, I was fortunate to discover four further surviving family portraits from Kilcornan, which were sold at auction in the 1920s. These are of Sir Thomas and Lady Redington and a splendid life-size group portrait of John Hyacinth Talbot M.P., his wife and two daughters, as well as a portrait of the countess of Shrewsbury (*née* Talbot), by an Italian artist. The first three portraits are by Martin Cregan P.R.H.A. (1788–1870). (During a long career Cregan became the foremost portrait painter in Ireland in the mid-nineteenth century.) The portrait of Lady Redington is recorded as having been painted in 1848 and that of her husband probably at the time of his knighthood in 1849 (plate 9).

The large group portrait of John Hyacinth Talbot and his wife (*née* Redmond) and two daughters was exhibited in the R.A. in 1847.[31] This splendid portrait group, painted about 1826, may be securely attributed to Joseph Haverty, R.H.A. (1794–1864): a contemporary document in the possession of the present owners relates that John Hyacinth Talbot was at pains to tell Haverty how to depict his wife when he was painting the picture. J. H. Talbot is shown seated with his wife Anne Redmond while their daughters Anne (the future Lady Redington) and her sister Jane disport themselves in the foreground. These portraits are of major historic and artistic importance and are striking evidence of the confident and established position that the Roman Catholic upper classes had achieved by 1850.

A black marble fireplace in the hotel hall is the only relic from the interior of the old convent. In a leafy copse a decent distance away from the hotel the Sisters of Charity of the past have been reburied in a circle around the stone cross erected by Christopher Talbot Redington which marks the last resting place of their great friend and patron, Mrs Francis Xaviera Elizabeth Redington. She died at Boulogne in 1872, ten years after the death of her son Sir Thomas.

In conclusion, it may be said that for many reasons Kilcornan revisited is a thought-provoking experience. It might be possible for some to say 'et in Arcadia ego', but others would say that those were the days when everyone was rich except the poor. The Redingtons are an interesting example of a Roman Catholic landed family who were at one stage very successful. Their peak of achievement came in 1849 when, after over a hundred and fifty years of progress up the social ladder, Thomas Redington achieved his knighthood. The interconnections too with the Wexford gentry and with some very prominent families in England and on the continent are notable, and greatly assisted Thomas Redington's rise to modest fame. Their world was an 'old English' or 'Norman' one. Gaelic Ireland was still all around them at Kilcornan, especially in the everyday language of the people, but it seemed to mean nothing to them. The act of union could never be threatened while the Redingtons and their peers held sway. It must be remembered too that this story belongs mostly to a period before the high tide of nineteenth-century nationalism. Were the Redingtons really Cromwellian in origin, as Thomas Redington suggested? In the present state of knowledge this cannot be proved conclusively. Their benevolent patronage of the Sisters of Charity had a feudal air about it, which recalled life in contemporary Poland or Hungary. Certainly all contemporary accounts spoke well of the Redingtons and particularly of Sir Thomas as a landlord, although during the famine years he apparently became hard with his tenants and was criticised by the sisters. The Redingtons tried, nonetheless, according to their lights in very difficult circumstances to do their Christian and public duty.

The story of Kilcornan also illustrates the serious loss being sustained at present by the Irish heritage of religious art and architecture. This is occurring in every denomination, but it is especially serious in the case of Irish religious houses. In the 1960s and 1970s the Irish eighteenth-century patrimony was the cultural area most at risk: in the 1990s it is the religious heritage, especially that of religious houses, which is gravely threatened.

NOTES

1 [John] Bernard Burke, *A genealogical and heraldic dictionary of the landed gentry of Great Britain and Ireland* (London, 1868), ii, 1260. For Sir Thomas Redington see also *D.N.B.*

2 Memoir of Sir Thomas Redington, N.U.I., Galway, James Hardiman Library, Wilson Lynch papers, L.S.B. 93–125.

3 I am grateful to local historian Mr Joseph Murphy of Clarinbridge for this information, and to Rev. F. Finnegan S.J. and Mr Patrick Melvin for valuable information about the origins and connections of the Redington family.

4. Sarah Atkinson, *Mary Aikenhead: her life, her work, and her friends* (Dublin, 1879), p. 30

5 Samuel Lewis, *A history and topography of Dublin city and county*, first published 1837 as part of *A topographical dictionary of Ireland* (Dublin and Cork, 1980), p. 140.

6 See Edmund Lodge, *The peerage of the British empire*, 8th ed. (London, 1839), pp 448–9.

7 For two relevant newspaper notices, see appendix (*Tuam Herald*, 3, 10 Sept. 1842).

8 Frederick O'Dwyer, 'A.W.N. Pugin and St Patrick's College Maynooth', *Irish Arts Review Yearbook*, xii (1996), pp 102–9, at p. 107.

9 Jeremy Williams, *A companion guide to architecture in Ireland, 1837–1921* (Dublin, 1994), p. 206. Williams suggests that Crace may have been responsible for the interiors of the house. In view of the close relationship of the Talbots and Redingtons, I suggest that A.W.N. Pugin must have been responsible for much of the interiors at Kilcornan. The firm of Beardwood also worked on the convent there. For Papworth, who settled in Dublin *c.* 1812, see *D.N.B.*

10 See Martin Coen, *The wardenship of Galway* (Galway, 1984), especially ch. 5.

11 Mary Aikenhead, *Letters of Mary Aikenhead* (Dublin, 1914), p. 162

12 Ibid., p. 434.

13 Ibid., p. 162.

14 John Turpin, *John Hogan: Irish neoclassical sculptor in Rome, 1800–1858* (Dublin, 1982), pp 88–9.

15 Jeanne Sheehy, *The rediscovery of Ireland's past: the Celtic revival 1830–1930* (London, 1980), pp 50–6.

16 Turpin, *John Hogan*, pp 19–23.

17 Ibid., pp 69–97; Sheehy, *The rediscovery of Ireland's past*, p. 54.

18 Turpin, *John Hogan*, p. 12.

19 A Loreto Sister, *Joyful mother of children: Mother Mary Frances Teresa Ball* (Dublin, 1961), p. 172.

20 Turpin, *John Hogan*, pp 171–2.

21 Annals of Clarinbridge, Religious Sisters of Charity Generalate (R.S.C.G.), Gilford Road, Sandymount, Dublin. For permission to publish photographs and quote extracts from letters I am grateful to Sr M. Bernadette O'Leary, archivist, Irish Sisters of Charity.

22 Thomas McGreevy, 'Some statues by John Hogan' in *Father Mathew Record* (August 1943); Sarah Atkinson, 'John Hogan' in *Irish Quarterly Review*, viii, no. 30 (July 1858), pp 493–588.

23 Restaldi is known to have been at work on the piece in 1849 (Turpin, *John Hogan*, pp 94, 172).

24 See Nicola Figgis, 'Raphael's "Transfiguration": some Irish grand tour associations' in *Irish Arts Review Yearbook*, xiv (1998), pp 52–6, in which the author discusses various representations of the subject, though without making mention of the Kilcornan example. For the Mengs/Durno painting, see National Gallery of Ireland, *Illustrated summary catalogue of paintings* (Dublin, 1981), no. 120 (p. 108).

25 *Lady Gregory's journals, vol. ii: Books thirty to forty-four: 21 February 1925–9 May 1932,* ed. Daniel J. Murphy (Gerrard's Cross, 1987), pp 313–14. I am grateful to Mr Joseph Murphy for drawing my attention to this entry.

26 R.S.C.G., H8/1(1), letters 13, 17.

27 R.S.C.G., H8/1(4), letter 262.

28 R.S.C.G., H8/1(5), letter 298.

29 Photofile, R.S.C.G.

30 Boxfile County Galway (Kilcornan), Irish Architectural Archive, Merrion Square, Dublin.

31 Private collection. See W. G. Strickland, *A dictionary of Irish artists* (1st ed., Dublin and London, 1913) reprint (Shannon, 1968), i, 230–1.

Appendix

Marriage of Miss Anne Talbot and Mr Thomas Redington

Alton Towers, Staffordshire – the Earl and Countess of Shrewsbury are receiving a select circle at their splendid seat, among whom are the Prince and Princess Doria Pamphilias [*sic*], who arrived from Italy on Monday, Mr John Henry Talbot, and Miss Talbot, Mr Thomas Nicholas Redington, M.P. The Towers are very gay this week in consequence of the festivities attendant on the marriage of Miss Talbot, cousin to the noble earl, to Mr. Redington M.P.
(*Tuam Herald*, 3 Sept. 1842)

The magnificent residence of the Earl of Shrewsbury offered to the visiting parties, that crowd to see it in the fine weather, more than even its usual display of all that is gorgeous and beautiful on Tuesday last, on the occasion of the marriage of a cousin of the countess, the interesting daughter of John Talbot, Esq., late member for [New] Ross, with T. N. Redington, Esq., M.P., for Dundalk. The rich chapel, unique certainly among the private chapels, royal and noble, in England, was tastefully decorated with the spoils of the vast gardens of the Towers and the many-coloured shadows of the stained windows added greatly to the effect of the procession of the noble and gentle as they preceded the blooming bride to the altar. Wonderfully does the imposing ritual of the Catholic church add to the solemnity of its edifices and the awfulness of its ceremonies! The bride in her jewels, rich and rare, her maids in attendance, Miss Margaret Talbot (a true queen beauty), and Miss Amherst, the lovely kinswoman of the noble earl – the array of birth and elegance – wreaths and favours of beautiful flowers – all were forgotten at the moment, when, accompanied by subdued tones from the great organ in the high loft, cross-bearer, priests and acolytes ushered in the mitred bishop with the ancient-looking crozier in his hand and arrayed in cope of cloth, gold and jewels. All eyes centered on the holy man. The ceremony began after the manner of the olden times, previously to the celebration of a solemn high mass by the Right Rev. Dr Walsh, as high-priest, assisted by the Rev. Drs Rook and Winter, as deacon and sub-deacon and with a little stretch of the imagination we might have fancied the venerable prelate a William of Wyckam and ourselves people some hundreds of years antedated, when religion still reigned in the hearts and even the senses of high born and low, lay folk and ecclesiastics. The bride was given away by her father. The touching and parental exhortation of the venerable prelate from his throne had already cast a sober hue over the bright faces and me-thought more than one tear was dropped. At this taking of vows Protestants at least are not always sufficiently religious or even serious in making or witnessing. After all was over, the party left the chapel two by two, the bride last, accompanied by the groom and the attendants. The display presented from the gallery of the dining-room was only less imposing than that of the chapel. The large gold service was of most extraordinary richness and beauty – epergnes of choicest fruits, various rare exotics, interspersed with nameless delicacies and wonderful achievements in the way of culinary art, amongst which, of course, the broad bride-cake was not forgotten. In fine, the whole fete was every way worthy of the premier earl of England and the hereditary high steward of Ireland and Catholics may well be proud of their ancient religion in such houses as Alton Towers and with such representatives as Lord and Lady Shrewsbury.

(*Tuam Herald*, 10 Sept. 1842: I am grateful to Mr Patrick Melvin for drawing my attention to these notices).

12 Poverty and plenty: the Victorian contrast

Asa Briggs

The sense of contrast is as strong in nineteenth-century Britain as the sense of change. It was self-conscious and ubiquitous. It influenced both interpretations of British history and the identification of topical issues. It also coloured historical writing, scholarly and popular. Past and present; ancient and modern; city and countryside; labour and capital; work and idleness; rich and poor; England and Ireland.

In this paper, which is short, exploratory, and in no sense definitive – but directly related, I hope, to other papers at the conference – I want to focus on one particular (and favourite) Victorian contrast: that between poverty and plenty, encapsulated in the socialist complaint, a descriptive indictment of an 'unjust society', 'poverty in the midst of plenty'. It was because I have been interested for many years in this contrast that I gladly accepted the invitation to take part in what I know will be an interesting and important conference in a historic place that has long figured on my mental map and I have long wished to visit.

How words are paired is at least as interesting as how politicians are paired. 'Luxury', Professor Berry's theme, was usually paired – and is – with necessity (not with 'austerity') in the period with which I am concerned. The pairing was already set when the period began. For twentieth-century historians pairs now seem as worthy of study as contrasts, and more manageable. We have stripped away the imagery that Thomas Carlyle used when he called language 'the garment of thought'. Yet when we in our turn contrast or pair 'poverty' and 'plenty' we no more get rid of clothes than we do of food. Nor can we get rid of the concept of comfort and the related idea of levels of comfort familiar to the Victorians. And to the older pair 'deprivation' and 'ostentation' we would now add 'exclusion' and, hopefully, 'inclusion'.

When in the 1830s – an important decade for statisticians – the statistician of progress, G. R. Porter, moved beyond statistics to his optimistic interpretation of the future of society, he announced that 'the working classes' (with exceptions, such as the handloom weavers) had already shared in 'the greatest advances in civilisation that can be found recorded in the annals of mankind', and in later editions in 1847 and 1851 he provided ample detail of further 'improvement'. He brought in a very different word, too – 'indulgence' – applied not to the aristocracy but to 'labourers':

if by reason of the cheapness of provisions the wages of the labourer afford means for indulgence, sugar, tea and coffee are the articles to which he earliest has recourse. The consumption of this class of articles affords a very useful test of the comparative conditions at different periods of the labouring classes.[1]

Porter's test had become irrelevant by the last decades of the nineteenth century, when 'plenty' was associated with a far wider range of things, new and old, but it was within Porter's historical frame that Samuel Smiles talked of the 'labouring classes' enjoying sprees at the peaks of trade cycles. He quoted not an aristocrat but a 'captain of industry', who complained that he could not afford lamb, salmon, young ducks, green peas, new potatoes and such like 'until after his "hands" [not mouths] had been consuming these delicacies of the season for two or three weeks'.[2]

Aristocratic sprees, which did not need to follow the trade cycles, were outside Smiles's line of vision. They were, however, within eighteenth-century lines of vision, not least in Ireland where 'high living' was a feature of society and extravagant 'entertaining' a prized social value. As late as 1847, when famine was on the point of transforming Irish society, the whig Lord Bessborough, installed in power, was as conscious of the sprees as of the horrors. They were more visible to him. A 'good landlord', and a friend of Daniel O'Connell, he told Lord John Russell that it was 'balls and drawing rooms' that were 'knocking him up', his own expression, not the responsibilities of his position. One of his guests, Richard Monckton Milnes, later Lord Houghton, described vividly the parties, the *tableaux vivants* and the charades of that year which goes down in the history books as the year of the temporary relief act,[3] setting up soup kitchens, when after bitter arguments about what food should be provided – and at what cost – no fewer than three million persons were being fed by 'government' on a July day.

There was certainly contrast here. A few months earlier, Russell had explained that 'we cannot feed the people' – this message had to be 'thoroughly understood' – and in the summer of 1847 the Irish poor law extension act[4] constituted an attempt to deal with Ireland in the same way as England. Passed nine years after the first Irish poor law act of 1838[5] which allowed solely for indoor relief, it was no more capable of controlling the situation than the abundant charity that had always been held up as a virtue. Recently built workhouses provided what an observer called 'a picture of demi-savage life' that reinforced old prejudices. Charity itself had been given a somewhat new twist when the famine was seen as 'providential', or a 'visitation of God'.

Neither the much-studied history of the nineteenth-century poor law nor the centuries-old history of charity can be left out of this address which, although it deals mainly with words and verbal distinctions, recognises that what mattered were human experiences even when they were not capable of articulation in speech. A young poet, James Clarence Mangan, quoted in *The hungry voice: the poetry of the Irish famine*, movingly caught the sense of 'endless Funerals', and of 'one groanful grave':

> It was as though my Life were gone
> With what I saw!
> Here were the FUNERALS of my thoughts as well!
> The Dead and I at last were One.[6]

These four lines capture the immediacies of the famine more permanently than the mass of official papers offering endless suggestions concerning how to deal with famine, almost all deemed too expensive to implement. And it seems more than symbolic that Mangan was himself to die of cholera in 1849, the year when his poem was written.

In very different social, economic – and political – circumstances almost half a century later, in England, not in Ireland, the duke of Devonshire, whose brother had been killed while walking in the Phoenix Park, restated older aristocratic attitudes to luxury, necessity, and charity, when confronted in 1894 with Sir William Harcourt's death duties:[7]

I do not contend that it is a necessity that I or my family should be in a position to keep up great places like Chatsworth or Hardwick, or Bolton Abbey, or Lismore in Ireland. I do not contend that it is a necessity that we should be placed in a position where we can enjoy the luxury of striving to be surrounded by a contented and prosperous tenantry and people. I do not contend that it is a necessity for us that we should have the privilege of aiding in every good and charitable work in every part of the counties with which we are connected. These things have been a pride and pleasure to my predecessors and to myself, but they are not necessities.

Nevertheless, the duke, who like his assassinated brother (married to Mrs Gladstone's niece) was a liberal, albeit now a liberal unionist, conceived of the 'luxuries' he enjoyed as conferring public benefits. He was defending a form of society that had changed in the nineteenth century without disappearing. The poor law was outside *his* vision: it was administered by thoroughly non-aristocratic boards of guardians.

Not surprisingly, Devonshire's sentiments were challenged, as, indeed, they would have been half a century before. *Punch*, which had dealt irreverently with the ostentatious display of city dinners in the London of the 1840s – and throughout its life had presented the Irish in vicious stereotypes – could handle dukes as toughly as lord mayors or boards of guardians:

The duke of Devonshire, one of the wealthiest landgrabbers in the world, is suffering from a fit of melancholia because Sir William Harcourt's budget provides that landlords shall in future pay taxes like other people. Was ever such a thing heard of? How on earth is the fabulously rich duke of Devonshire to find money for his race-course orgies, and his country house parties, and the other resources of idling luxury if he pays his taxes?

The *Punch* cartoon on the subject was called 'Depressed dukes'. Devonshire was not alone.

How often was it possible – and with what justification – to speak, in terms, as the duke did, of a 'contented and prosperous tenantry and people'? Much had happened to agriculture since the repeal of the corn laws. How plausible – and relevant – was it to proclaim – and list – 'every good and charitable work in any part of the counties with which we are connected'? How different had private and public attitudes to poverty become since the development of urbanisation, a process to which the duke had contributed and from which he benefited, not to speak of industrialisation? The duke did not doubt that a tenantry could be 'contented'. Nor did he doubt that charity was a social as well as a moral necessity. Who were the doubters?

Such are the questions that I want to pose in this paper, giving some of the answers that were given at the time, answers that must always take account of changes in legislation, particularly in the poor law, and in politics and administration, all of which lead back to the contrast – not to a pairing – that between poverty and property. In long-term perspective the Victorian period stands out as distinctive. Why? It has to be related both to the period before it began – that ending, although it was not a climax, with the new poor law of 1834 – and to the period after it ended – with the emergence of what was a climax, 'the welfare state', though there was no finality to it. Ironically, it was only when the values that lay behind the welfare state began to be challenged – and when its costs began to be assessed, and above all, projected – that the Victorian period itself began to be reopened for more searching and critical study.

In Ireland, most of which fell outside the scope and range of industrialisation in the Victorian period, there were other features of the story that made it different from that of England. In his memoirs, written in 1883, the Protestant William Allingham recalled his childhood, as did most writers of autobiographies, including those of the poor as well as the rich. Born in Ballyshannon, County Donegal in 1824, it seemed natural to him that he was being brought up in 'a discontented and disloyal country' – in other words, one in sharp contrast with any over which the duke of Devonshire felt that he was presiding. It seemed natural to him, he wrote, that 'the humbler class' – he did not speak of 'the labouring class', or 'the poor' – 'should hate those above them in the world'. And he introduced religion directly into his picture: the 'humbler class' was 'almost synonymous with Roman Catholic'. Allingham remembered arguing about this point as a boy with his nurse, who lived on to the age of ninety-three, long surviving famine. He had praised Protestants on the grounds that 'the Catholics, you see, are poor people', to which she replied simply, 'it may be different in the next world'. There was no need to conjure up the word 'providential' in this context, which drew the sharpest of all contrasts, that between this world and the next. 'A good answer', Allingham recorded in his memoirs, adding that at no time in his life had he been addicted to arguing for argument's sake or for 'triumph'.[8]

Argument might be stilled or suspended in the nineteenth century for a variety of reasons, ranging from tact to insecurity of conviction, but it could not be stifled, and it was encouraged, sometimes in triumphant language, by extended modes of communication – travel, newspapers, above all periodicals. It was one of the greatest and most sensitive of travellers, Alexis de Tocqueville, who visited both England and Ireland just before the Victorian period began,[9] who noted the paradox, far-reaching in its implications, that industrial workers could find themselves in the trough of trade cycles – to which they were always vulnerable – without the bare subsistence – another key word, not only in political economy – which was available to peasants. Moreover, they had become accustomed to thinking of items – outside peasants' possible range of spending, even of knowing about – which were not available to them at such times as 'necessities'. It was already true in the mid-1830s that for industrial workers it was 'the lack of a multitude of things' that represented poverty.

This recognition of de Tocqueville was one of the thoughts that lay behind my deciding to write the third volume of my trilogy on the Victorians, *Victorian things* (1988), when I set out to examine the multitude. It was the recognition too that lay at the heart of the late Victorian sense of 'poverty in the midst of plenty'. England when de Tocqueville visited it was the richest country in the world, yet one-sixth of its inhabitants were living at the expense of 'public charity'. The situation was quite different in peasant Portugal or peasant Ireland where there was no poor law in operation:

When one crosses the various countries of Europe, one is struck by a very extraordinary and apparently inexplicable sight. The countries appearing to be the most impoverished are those which in reality account for the fewest indigents, and among the people most admired for their opulence, one part of the population is obliged to rely on the gifts of the other in order to live.

There were various ways of explaining what de Tocqueville saw, but there was one corollary of profound importance that he thought he saw clearly:

In a country where the majority is ill-clothed, ill-housed, ill-fed, who thinks of giving clean clothes, healthy food, comfortable quarters to the poor? The majority of the English, having all these things [de Tocqueville had not yet been to America] regard their absence as a frightful misfortune; society believes itself bound to come to the aid of those who lack them, and cures evils which are not even recognised elsewhere. In England the average standard of living man can hope for in the course of his life is higher than in any other country in the world. This greatly facilitates the extension of pauperism in the kingdom.

The idea of 'curing evils' gives a modern ring to the passage which seems to anticipate twentieth-century notions of 'relative deprivation' and 'a revolution of rising expectations'. Yet it was social compassion, not incipient 'consumerism', that de Tocqueville had in mind when he wrote of 'society believ[ing] itself bound to come to the aid' of those in need. He was picking up a point to be made by Lord Althorp, representative of a great ruling whig aristocratic family, the Spencers, when he introduced the new poor law bill in the house of commons in 1834. Admitting that it violated the economic law that required everyone to provide his or her own subsistence by his or her own labour, he defended it on the grounds that it fulfilled a higher law, the religious and human duty to support those who were 'really helpless and really unable to provide for themselves'.[10]

Althorp's language was persuasive in what was still a largely land-based parliament. For posterity – or at least academic posterity – de Tocqueville's language was less convincing. What was society? At its base, among industrial workers, still a minority of the 'labour force', there was to be a militant popular anti-poor law reaction after the passing of the 1834 act and the attempt to implement it not in villages but in towns, a reaction that drew its dynamic from the belief that an 'old society' had maintained the rights of the poor while a new industrialising society was destroying them. Richard Oastler now came into the picture as well as Thomas Carlyle. There was a long-term question which Carlyle asked. How would the poor themselves respond to the tensions of the changing society in which they were living? Would hunger and lack of employment foment revolution?

Carlyle believed (wrongly) that they would. Later in the century, however, in a new social context when despite economic and social advance the maxim still held that 'the poor are always with us', George Bernard Shaw, who did not believe in revolution, put trust in the mobilisation of popular discontent to change society. With England and Ireland in mind he maintained that 'the virtues of the poor may be readily admitted and are much to be regretted. The best among the poor are never grateful. They are ungrateful, discontented and rebellious. They are quite right to be so.'

Shaw was flatly contradicting what Walter Bagehot had written in *The English constitution* (not 'the *British* constitution'). 'A country of respectful poor, though far less happy than when there are no poor to be respectful, is nevertheless far more fitted for the best government.' In the twenty years between the two contrasting versions of politics, Bagehot's and Shaw's, the franchise had been extended to include some, though not all, of the poor, and new or more sharply defined distinctions had been drawn largely by the providers of charity, between the 'deserving' and 'undeserving' poor and by politicians, including radical politicians, between the 'independent poor' and the 'residuum'. There had also been a significant improvement in the material conditions of most of the poor which had its origins not in legislation but in market economics. It was manifest in shops and shopping lists as well as in business order books. There was a demand as well as a supply side to it which can be examined in part in the pages of John Burnett's *Plenty and want: a social history of diet in England from 1815 to the present day* (1966: revised ed., 1979). Burnett also edited a number of working-class autobiographies.[11]

De Tocqueville depended a generation before Bagehot on older distinctions drawn by a number of writers who straddle the eighteenth and nineteenth centuries, taking part in a debate about the poor and the poor laws which was wide-ranging and covered population, wages, and attitudes towards the future. Thomas Malthus has given his name to the debate[12] and provided it with some of its enduring images, like that of the feast which he subsequently deleted from the next edition of his *magnum opus*; but it was Patrick Colquhoun in his pamphlet *The state of indigence, and the situation of the casual poor in the metropolis explained* (1799) – a group much to be studied in mid-Victorian England – followed seven years later by a larger *Treatise on indigence* (1806), who most clearly drew what came to be a basic distinction:

In contemplating the affairs of the poor, it is necessary in the first instance to have a clear conception of the distinction between *Indigence* and *Poverty*. Poverty is that state and condition in society where the individual has no surplus labour in store, and consequently, no property but what is derived from the constant exercise of industry . . . *Indigence* . . . and not *poverty* is the evil. It is that condition in society which implies *want*, *misery*, and *distress*. It is the state of any one who is destitute of the means of subsistence and is unable to labour to procure it to the extent that nature requires. [Thereby Colquhoun included able-bodied workers, unable to find work as well as those always unable to work.] The natural source of subsistence is the labour of the individual; while that remains with him he is denominated *poor*: when it fails in whole or in part he becomes *indigent*.

Colquhoun's distinction was treated as fundamental by the royal commission on the poor laws, appointed in 1832 and reporting in 1834, which prepared the way for the new poor law of the same year, a measure that went through parliament quickly in relatively good times, years of good harvests and favourable trade. (One of the few matters of real parliamentary debate was whether or not its scope should be restricted to rural areas.) The act, which faced popular opposition from the start, changed the poor laws but did not abolish them. It sought above all else to draw an even sharper (though not new) distinction than that between 'indigent' and 'poor' – that between 'paupers' and 'poor', a distinction that outlasted Bagehot and Shaw. A stigma was to be attached to all who accepted relief which, it was laid down, should be offered in the workhouse (again, not a new institution, but one that was hardened by the application of 'principle'). Paupers should be worse off than the lowest paid wage workers outside. This sharpest of distinctions was best expressed by the novelist Harriet Martineau, 'Except the distinction between sovereign and subject, there is no social difference in England so wide as that between the independent labourer and the pauper; and it is equally ignorant, immoral, and impolitic to confound the two.'

The most important and influential of the political economists concerned with the poor law commission, Nassau Senior, had not accepted Malthus's theory of population, nor his gloomy conclusions: indeed, he pointed towards 'consumerism' more obviously than de Tocqueville:

As wealth increases what were the luxuries of one generation become the decencies of their successors. Not only a taste for additional comfort and convenience, but a feeling of degradation in their absence becomes more and more widely defused. The increase, in many respects, of the productive powers of labour must enable increased comforts to be enjoyed by increased numbers, and as it is the more beneficial, so it appears to me to be the more natural course of events . . .

It is interesting to note that Senior had written a pamphlet on Ireland in 1831 (*Letter to Lord Howick on a legal provision for the Irish poor*), where he had concluded that poverty in Ireland was so chronic and ubiquitous that no poor law could alleviate it. While some measures of public compassion were advisable (for the orphan, the sick, the maimed and the blind), no relief should 'diminish industry or providence'. He favoured public works and efforts to raise agricultural productivity.

Another Englishman directly concerned with the evolution of the new poor law in England was drawn into dealing with Ireland when, despite Senior's advice, a poor law was introduced in 1838 dividing Ireland into 130 unions with workhouses run by boards of guardians consisting of representative taxpayers, administering indoor relief only. George Nicholls (Sir George he was to become) not only participated in the story as a poor law commissioner and as secretary to the poor law board in London, but

wrote both *A history of the English poor law*, published first in 1854 and
then, with a supplement, as a three-volume edition in 1898–9, and *A history
of the Irish poor law* (1856). He represented the commission in Ireland
from 1838 to 1841. His volumes were dedicated to boards of guardians in
'the hope' that they and 'their successors' (his word) would find them
'useful'. The motto chosen to introduce the three volumes came from
Charles Babbage, who usually figures in a different historical context – the
history of computing – and it had more of a Malthusian ring to it than
Senior's passage of hope about society:

wherever for the purpose of government, we arrive in any state of society at a class
so miserable as to be in want of the common necessities of life, a new principle
comes into action. The usual restraints [a Malthusian term] which are sufficient on
the well-fed are often useless in checking the demands of hungry stomachs . . .
Under such circumstances [and there was no glimpse of future plenty here] it may
be considerably cheaper to fill empty stomachs to the point of holy obedience
than to compel starving wretches to respect the roast beef of their more industrious
neighbours [the roast beef that figured prominently in anti-poor law and chartist
propaganda]; and it may be expedient, in a mere economical point of view [the
poor law commissioners claimed to be arguing not in the name of expediency but
of principle] to supply gratuitously the wants even of able-bodied persons, if it
can be done without creating crowds of additional applicants.

There was an echo in this last thought of Malthus's terrible feast, 'nature's
mighty feast', where 'plenty' is changed into scarcity because too many
'intruders' break into the banqueting hall. Malthus had been unequivocal:

A man who is born into a world already possessed, if he cannot get subsistence
from his parents on whom he has a just demand, and if the society [back – or on –
to de Tocqueville's term] do not want his labour, has no claim of *right* [Oastler's claim]
to the smallest portion of food, and, in fact, has no business to be where he is.

There is no evidence that Nicholls, who died in 1865, himself pictured
or shared Malthus's picture of 'nature's mighty feast'. He does not figure in
the *Dictionary of National Biography*. Nor does Thomas Mackay, author
of *The English poor* (1889), published in the same year as Shaw's *Fabian
essays*, who wrote the third of the three Nicholls volumes dealing with the
English poor law after 1834. But Nicholls's life was dealt with in seventy-
eight pages at the beginning of volume one by H.G. Willink (an ancestor
of Churchill's second world war minister of health?) who was chairman of
the board of guardians in a union that followed a tough policy. Willink's
most interesting, if revealingly naif, passages deal not with England but
with Ireland. 'It might have been better', he concluded,

for [Nicholls] to have kept clear of Ireland . . . to have avoided mixing himself up
with the matter at all. There was plenty to do in England. . . . The framing and
introduction of the Irish law [of 1838] was a good experiment, enough to tax the

ability of a greater man than he to the very utmost [he did not touch on the greatest test, that of the famine, not very far away]. It was forced through, by no wish of his own, in an unreasonably short space of time.

Ireland was a 'distressful country' with 'grievances'; and its 'unhappy state' before the introduction of the 1838 poor law was 'due to a vast multiplicity of causes which no one species of measure could be expected to remove'. Willink, writing in the 1890s, doubtless had in mind the variety of measures introduced in post-famine Ireland, where the poverty of rural Ireland remained if, because of emigration, in attenuated form, many of them concentrating in a farmer society on questions of land tenure. The conditions anticipated by Senior still did not operate.

In dealing with England Mackay, strongly influenced by Herbert Spencer and popular 'evolutionism', believed that the one species of measure that would be disastrous would be 'socialist' in character. Too indiscriminate often in the pre-1834 past both poor law policy and charity had sapped the 'independence' of labourers and their families, creating 'dependence' and discouraging individual effort. The best way of helping the poor was teaching them to help themselves. When boards of guardians offered outdoor relief, as some of them did when Mackay was writing,

the whole atmosphere of the family and of the neighbourhood becomes tainted with the dull dependent spirit of pauperism. Early marriages and large families appear rather an advantage than otherwise, and the doctrine is widely advertised that the State can or will be responsible for the maintenance of all comers into this over-stretched world.[13]

Outdoor relief, moreover,

had a tendency to lower wages. For a woman [an interesting choice of reference] who gets a few shillings a week from the parish can undersell the labour of those who are entirely dependent on their wages, or of those who having husbands or fathers to support them, are not obliged to accept starvation wages, but are able to compete 'intelligently' with their employers.[14]

I should add that for all this prudent talk Mackay had one passage where he admitted, as many of his contemporaries (following Henry Mayhew) did, that there was an appealing element of independence in the ways of the 'casual poor':

The ragged clothes and slouching air of the casual makes his employment impossible, and he is bound to the life of a tramp all his days. Such a life has its enjoyments; he begs and steals a bit, he sleeps in the open in summer, and shares in the fortuitous charity of London and large towns during the winter.[15]

In another passage, Mackay describes 'the life' of 'irregular labourers' as 'though very degraded . . . not altogether without its pastime and pleasure'.[16]

I need hardly add that in Ireland, against a different rural and urban background, such a life was also felt to have its attractions.

In the same year (1889) as Mackay's book was published, the first volume of Charles Booth's *Life and labour of the people* appeared, dealing exclusively with the east end of London, where, as Pat Ryan has shown,[17] different boards of guardians were following different policies. Booth felt the attractions there too and described them vividly. It was in his 'industry' series rather than in his 'poverty' series, however, that he recreated 'the sights, sounds, and almost the smell of Londoners at work', and indeed, in the streets.[18]

I have had no time in this paper to deal with the statistics either of poverty or plenty (Leone Levi's and Robert Giffen's[19] as well as Booth's), although this is a subject which involves the examination of wage rates, poor rates and family size which has often preoccupied me. It was at the core of my work on Seebohm Rowntree,[20] whose book *Poverty*, a study of York, which appeared in 1901, was described by a liberal journalist as a 'thunder clap'.[21] Both he and Rowntree were concerned, as later surveys were to be, with differences in incomes and in spending patterns between different sections of 'the poor' and with the effects on both of the 'pauper class', later to be called an 'under-class', below them. In Rowntree's case, he drew attention too not to the trade cycle, in which the harvest now figured less prominently, but to the life cycle of individuals and families.

Relating statistical evidence to economic or moral generalisation is a necessary task for the historian of poverty and plenty, and in concentrating in this paper on primary written sources I have done no more than touch on the mass of recent writing, local and national, on the implementation of the 1834 poor law. This was given a great stimulus in 1978 when Anthony Brundage produced his *The making of the new poor law: the politics of inquiry, enactment and implementation, 1832–39* (London, 1978).

With my own interest in cities as well as in things, I was greatly impressed by the volume edited by Michael Rose in which Pat Ryan's conclusions were set out.[22] *The poor and the city: the English poor law in its urban context, 1836–1914* (Leicester, 1985) deals *inter alia* with the Irish poor in England not in Ireland, often living in ghetto conditions. In Bradford in 1848 Stephen Power, an Irishman who had lived there for eighteen years, was told by the board of guardians that 'the notion of a five years residence in the parish entitling a person to claim relief was a delusion' and in 1852 – one year after the Great Exhibition had expressed thanks for 'Plenty', on visible display – James McKinley, a 65-year old woolcomber, who had lived in Bradford for over twenty years, was told that if he accepted relief he would be sent back to Ireland. (The cases are quoted in an excellent contribution by David Ashforth[23] on the area where

I myself was born.) The acts of settlement, the legacy of which was continued in the new poor law, and how the legacy was handled in different places is a subject worthy of study.

The book which has influenced me most in preparing this address as much for its commentary as for its basic quotations, many of which have long figured in my own anthology, is Gertrude Himmelfarb's *The idea of poverty* (1984) which demonstrates in every chapter how in the nineteenth century – and this was its main distinguishing feature – '"the annals of the poor" ceased to be "short and simple" and became long and complicated'. Himmelfarb found one very pertinent quotation too about the self-identification of the distinctiveness of the century, which I had never seen. It came from a review of Mrs Gaskell's novel *Mary Barton* (1848):

It embodies that dominant feeling of our times – that the ignorance, destitution and vice which pervade and corrupt our society must be got rid of. The ability to point out how they can be got rid of, is not the characteristic of this age. That will be the characteristic of the age that is coming.[24]

Booth and Rowntree turned to that issue by the beginning of the new century. So, too, of course, did William Morris, who in his socialist 'chants', published in 1885, four years before Booth, promised the effective action on the part of the poor (and not just the paupers) that Shaw advocated:

O ye rich men hear and tremble! for with words the sound is rife,
Once for you and death we laboured; changed henceforward is the strife
We are men, and we shall battle for the world of men and life
And the host is marching on.[25]

This was not the only dynamic of the future. De Tocqueville and Senior were not relegated to past history. Yet it was of historic importance that the poor were not to be 'regulated'. They were to be part of history making.

Before I conclude with two quotations that appear in Himmelfarb's book I would like to turn briefly to one important but little used source for all studies relating to words – Roget's *Thesaurus* (1852), which went through twenty-eight editions before the author died in 1869, aged 91. In his system of word classification, to which he devoted most of his labours, Roget, a Protestant, placed his section on 'wealth' before his section on 'poverty', and placed a section on 'money', which was to figure (negatively) in a colourful 'poverty' cluster, before 'wealth'. Dickens would have concurred. I should add that 'acquisition' is the first word-heading in the relevant sub-group, called 'possessive relations', placed under the major heading 'volition', and 'possession' the second, and, more important, that 'property' comes before 'money'. More strikingly, 'taking', 'stealing' and 'thief' come before 'selling', 'merchant', 'mart' and 'market'. The poverty cluster (no careful distinctions here) includes 'Lady Poverty, asceticism, poorness, meagreness, . . . impecuniosity, hardupness . . . mendicancy, penury, pennilessness, pauperism, destitution, indigence, neediness'. There are internal references to 'shreds and tatters' but not to 'the ragged poor', or 'fustian jackets'. Under the adjective 'poor' we encounter 'not well-off' 'not blest with this world's goods', 'hard-up', 'impecunious', 'insolvent', 'penurious', 'poverty-stricken', 'moneyless', 'destitute', 'down to one's last penny', 'without a bean'.

The word 'plenty' appears where one would expect it to be, given Roget's approach to classification – in a group called 'prospective volition', within the 'volition' group. It is not a word-heading on its own, however, and is listed under 'store', and is linked with 'cornucopia', 'abundance', 'outpouring' and 'plenitude'. The last of those is linked in its turn with 'affluence' – in the twentieth century to provide through its adjective 'affluent' a label for J. K. Galbraith's 'society' – 'riches', 'wealth', 'ample', 'enough', and (it might under a different system have been a pair with 'subsistence') 'superfluity'. 'Plenteous' is linked with 'plentiful'.

'Poverty' figures solely in Roget as a misfortune not as a blessing. 'Luck' is not mentioned with it, as writers of fiction would have mentioned it in industrial and pre-industrial society. Nor is religion. There is no 'holy poverty'. One pairing of 'poverty' is with 'drudgery', and the two words were paired also in Morris's essay of 1885 *Useful work versus useful toil*. In anthologies of epitaphs 'the poor' do not feature directly, but the anony- mous writer of the one epitaph that does take up the subject made the most of the drudgery and the only way out of it. The drudgery was associated there (as in many places elsewhere) with domestic service:

> Here lies a poor woman who always was tired,
> For she lived in a house where help wasn't hired.
> Her last words on earth were 'Dear friends I am going,
> Where washing ain't wanted, nor cooking, nor sewing.
> There all things is done just exact to my wishes,
> For where folks don't eat there's no washing of dishes.
> In Heaven loud anthems for ever are ringing,
> But having no voice, I'll keep clear of the singing.
> Don't mourn for me now, don't mourn for me never;
> For I'm going to do nothing for ever and ever.'[26]

The poor woman had 'friends', but her hope lay beyond this world.

Roget ended his relevent section on poverty, however, with a memorable final group of this-worldly words associated with impoverishment. There is dynamic of a kind here – to 'reduce to poverty', to 'leave destitute', to 'beggar', to 'pauperise', to 'ruin', to 'cripple', to 'fleece', to 'dispossess', to 'disinherit', to 'disendow', to 'cut off with a shilling', ending, most simply, with the verb to 'deprive'.

We can play games that Roget never intended with such word clusters, which cover condition and action, individual and collective, and both attributes and values. For example, 'pauperise', 'dispossess', 'disinherit', and 'disendow' are associated outside the *Thesaurus* in life with a legal framework that was changing in Victorian England. I would like to end, however, with the two quotations, both very familiar, that Himmelfarb placed at the head of the introduction to her book (subtitled 'England in the early industrial age'). Neither of them came from that age. Both claim a wider framework of reference than any century. They are very different from the motto Nicholls chose for his *History*. In 1770 Samuel Johnson, who knew something at first hand both about poverty and plenty, wrote that 'a decent provision for the poor is the true test of civilisation . . . The condition of the lower orders, the poor especially, [note that for him, as for others, they were not, in his view, the same thing] was the true mark of national discrimination.' In 1926 the socialist R.H. Tawney, living in an industrial age but choosing scarcely ever to write about its history, proclaimed that there was no touchstone, 'except the treatment of childhood, which reveals the true character of a social philosophy more clearly than the spirit in which it regards the misfortunes of those of its members who fall by the way'. Tawney did not use the term 'the poor', and not all of those 'who fell by the way' were poor by some of the contemporary criteria noted in this paper. Himmelfarb goes on:

it is surely significant that on the eve of the [industrial] transformation, from the heart of that 'old society' there should have issued sentiments which could so readily have been endorsed by one of the most progressive thinkers of our own time. Whatever else changed during this period, in this respect at least the end was in the beginning.[27]

NOTES

1 G. R. Porter, *The progress of the nation in its various social and economical relations from the beginning of the nineteenth century to the present time*, new ed. (London, 1851), p. 562.
2 Samuel Smiles, *Thrift* (London, 1875), ch. 4.
3 10 Vict., c. 7 (26 Feb. 1847).
4 10 Vict., c. 31 (8 June 1847).
5 1 & 2 Vict., c. 56 (31 July 1838).
6 Chris Morash (ed.), *The hungry voice: the poetry of the Irish famine* (Blackrock, 1989), p. 133.
7 For the introduction of death duties in the 1894 budget see R. K. Webb, *Modern England* (London, 1969), pp 423–4.
8 *William Allingham: a diary* (London, 1907), pp 19, 25.

9 Alexis de Tocqueville, *Journeys to England and Ireland*, ed. J. P. Mayer (London, 1958).

10 *Hansard*, 3rd ser., xxii (17 Apr. 1834), cols 877–8.

11 John Burnett (ed.), *Useful toil: autobiographies of working people from the 1820s to the 1920s* (London, 1974).

12 Thomas Malthus, *Essay on the principle of population* (London, 1798).

13 Thomas Mackay, *The English poor* (London, 1889), p. 214.

14 Ibid., p. 215.

15 Ibid., p. 198.

16 Ibid., p. 144.

17 Below, n. 22.

18 Rosemary O'Day and David Englander, *Mr Charles Booth's inquiry* (London, 1993), p. 122.

19 Leone Levi, *Wages and earnings of the working classes*, 1st ed. 1885 (Shannon, 1971); Robert Giffen, *Economic inquiries and studies*, 1st ed. 1904 (Shannon, 1971).

20 Asa Briggs, *Social thought and social action: a study of the work of Seebohm Rowntree, 1871–1954* (London, 1961).

21 Masterman preferred Rowntree's account of York to Booth's account of London (C. F. G. Masterman, 'The social abyss', *Contemporary Review*, lxxxi (1902)). See Kevin Bales, Martin Bulmer and Kathryn Sklar, *The social survey in historical perspective 1880–1940* (Cambridge, 1991).

22 Pat Ryan, 'Politics and relief: east London unions in the late nineteenth and early twentieth centuries' in Michael Rose (ed.), *The poor and the city*, pp 134–72.

23 David Ashforth, 'Settlement and removal in urban areas: Bradford, 1834–71' in *The poor and the city*, pp 58–91 at p. 82.

24 Himmelfarb, *The idea of poverty*, p. 520.

25 'The march of the workers', from William Morris, *Socialist chants* (London, 1885).

26 A slightly amended version of this epitaph appears in Nigel Rees, *Epitaphs* (London, 1993), p. 234. The origin of the epitaph, often called 'The maid-of-all-work', has been disputed.

27 Himmelfarb, *The idea of poverty*, p. 3.

13 'A living saint if ever there was one': work, austerity and authority in the lives of Irish women of the house, 1921–1961

Caitriona Clear

When I first solicited personal testimony about the working lives of women doing household work in their own homes ('women of the house' is my preferred term) in independent Ireland between 1921 and 1961, I was struck immediately by the written replies that referred to luxury and comfort mainly in terms of its absence. My newspaper appeal (which went into national and provincial newspapers in April 1995) was very generally worded and simply asked for information about the work of the house, but in the responses people sat down and wrote, the questionnaires they filled in, the tapes they made and in their conversations with me, the extraordinarily hard work and austerity of these workers – particularly rural women before the coming of electricity and piped water – was emphasised. Women remembering their own working lives exhibited, in about equal measure, great pride at the range and application of their skills, and resentment at the deprivations they had experienced. People, male and female, remembering their mothers' lives in the 1920s, 1930s, and 1940s, saw these lives as having been very hard and narrow and, whether on or off farms, characterised by ceaseless hard work. 'She died in 1966 a saint if ever there was one', wrote a bachelor from a medium-sized farm in south Tipperary, and such evaluations were not confined to unmarried sons of permanently co-resident mothers. Similar, if not identical, sentiments were expressed by many other contributors to the project:

My recollections of Mother were she was always at home cooking . . . Mother's life revolved around her home. . . . She never went to a hairdresser despite living in town. . .

I can't remember my mother ever going out at night as there was always a baby around.

At night she'd sit knitting or sewing, darning socks. . . She worked all her life. . .

My mother was never a night out of the house until she had to go to hospital. She never had a holiday, and very few days at the seaside. I never knew her to go to a hairdresser and she never used make-up.

Well the main thing about it . . . was the wife and mother, she stayed at home all the time, except now she'd go to town to sell fowl, or turkeys at Christmastime. Or if there was material wanted for clothes for the family, she'd take off and go down shopping.

Entertainment by modern standards, nil.

And really her life revolved – we discussed here, my wife and myself – mostly around her own family; her total horizon ended once she went outside the family group . . . she WAS the house really.[1]

These sentiments could be dismissed as retrospective idealisation of the Irish mother, already familiar to us in songs such as 'A mother's love is a blessing' ('You will never miss your mother's love/Till she's buried beneath the clay'). Feminist theory since 1945 has insisted that such idealisation virtually enslaves women.[2] In the Irish context, Catherine Rose, Jenny Beale and Ailbhe Smyth, among others, have interpreted the idealisation of the mother in Ireland as a cosmetic exercise, masking what was a relatively powerless, subordinate, social and constitutional role. Article 41.2 of Eamon de Valera's 1937 constitution is usually cited as an example of such hollow rhetoric, as are the 'comely maidens' of de Valera's 1943 St Patrick's day speech.[3] Marriage bars against women in national school teaching and the civil service, sex-specific labour legislation in the 1930s, and the controversy over the mother and child scheme of 1950–51, are all taken as further evidence of the simultaneous idealisation and repression of the woman of the house, on a par with what was happening to Italian, Spanish, Portuguese and 'Aryan' German women under fascist regimes.[4] However, it is argued here that while there was certainly profound unease about women's citizenship in the first decades of the new state, and repeated attempts to limit women's public activity and to curtail their private freedom, these were *not* accompanied by a parallel idealisation or glorification of women of the house in official discourse, political debate, government commissions, the transactions of social/statistical societies, or indeed in legislation. The reference in the 1937 constitution to the contribution of women/mothers to 'the common good' is remarkable precisely because it did not originate in any official policy of idealisation of women of the house, nor did it give rise to such idealisation. Rarely indeed were such sentiments to be encountered even in Catholic publications. It will also be argued that any praise heaped on these women was and is constructed in popular discourse, in what James Fentress and Chris Wickham call 'social memory' – a people's own agreed-upon memories of the past.[5]

The arguments presented in favour of excluding women from the civil service and from juries in the 1920s, and married women from national school teaching in 1932, were 'practical' ones; women's household work would be neglected if women were engaged outside the house in professional work or citizenship duties; there would be local resentment at two-income families (in the case of married teachers). There was no invocation of the sacred vocation of home-making.[6] Arguments against female participation in some kinds of industrial work in the mid-1930s were rooted in a determination to create men's, and, by definition, bread-winners' jobs rather than the inevitably lower-paid women's jobs. In many western countries at this time, feminists who argued for women's unqualified right to work found themselves up against the objections not only of many men and many male trade unionists, but of single women who objected to married women taking the bread out of their mouths, or married women who feared that their husbands would be made redundant by single or married women. The Irish Women Workers' Union considered a motion in 1932 to bar from membership women whose husbands were employed.[7] Elsewhere I have discussed how the commissioners inquiring into vocational organisation in 1940 were uncomfortable with the attempts by women's organisations to claim recognition of, and representation for, women's household work in the proposed National Vocational Assembly. The fact that in the report of 1943 'home-makers' were in the end granted only one seat in the proposed assembly – and that a co-optive one – caused two of the commissioners to issue addenda in protest.[8] The comments on 'home-makers' in the report recognised the importance of household work, but firmly refused to idealise it, remarking that it was work like any other. The report also expressed fears that too much representation on a vocational assembly would give 'home-makers' excessive power – they could, after all, already vote, and in any case exercised considerable power over their menfolk. (Members of other vocational groups that were given generous representation also exercised the parliamentary franchise so this part of the argument is a little hard to understand; the 'influence over the menfolk' point seems to take for granted that men's agreement was necessary for anything that women wished to do.[9])

1943 also saw the eventual government decision to act upon an interdepartmental report on children's allowances which had been some years in preparation. These allowances were introduced in 1944, for every third and subsequent child.[10] The demand for children's allowances or mothers' pensions as they were also called had originated in the 1890s, promoted by women's organisations (which conceived of such a benefit as 'payment in respect of motherhood') and proponents of Catholic social teaching, who saw it mainly as a supplement to breadwinner wages.[11] The (all-male) Irish interdepartmental committee that looked very thoroughly into the worldwide history of the campaign for children's allowances noted that in Britain its supporters had insisted on its importance as a direct payment to mothers. However, the committee argued that in Ireland it would be more appropriate to pay fathers. Women's organisations in Ireland, at any rate, took little or no interest in claiming this allowance for women: they had failed to press for it in submissions to the commission on vocational organisation, and it was not on the programme of either the Irish Countrywomen's Association or the Irish Housewives Association. (Lucy Kingston attended a meeting in 1944 to argue that the payment should be made to mothers, but the decision to pay the fathers had already been taken, so it is not clear what the purpose of the meeting was.)[12] Senator Helena Concannon was the only public figure to argue that the children's allowance should be seen as a fulfilment of the promise implicit in Article 41.2 of the constitution, and she objected that the benefit was too small to serve this purpose. Concannon has had a bad press from feminist historians who judge her either as a 'silent sister' or an unthinking echo of Eamon de Valera; this issue shows her in a different light.[13] Hers was a lone voice, however, linking the constitution and the proposed allowances.

During the dáil debate on the subject in November 1943, Liam Cosgrave came out in favour of making the allowances payable in the first instance to mothers rather than to fathers. Seán Lemass, who was introducing the measure, did not agree: 'There may be some social theory behind that suggestion. If there is, I disagree with it.'[14] Lemass and the interdepartmental committee envisaged the allowance first and foremost as a subsidy to breadwinner wages. Liam Cosgrave, however, had the backing of most of his party colleagues in Fine Gael for paying the mothers, including that of his father, W. T. Cosgrave, who argued that the tradition of the *bean a' tí* as manager of the household should not be interfered with. Brigid Redmond, another Fine Gael T.D., took the maternalist line that having money in their possession would develop women's sense of civic and economic responsibility.[15] Other T.D.s feared that men might only spend the allowance in the pub. Clann na Talmhan deputies, mainly from the west, stood up one after another to contend that because the woman was the budgetary head of the household, she should have this money paid to her. They also argued, in common with some Fine Gael deputies, that mothers naturally had a better-developed sense of familial responsibility than fathers. This was too much for William Norton of the Labour party, who made an impassioned plea for the fathers of Ireland and their fidelity and service to their families. James Larkin, senior, who came around in the end to paying the mothers, expressed his discomfort at any idealisation of either mothers or fathers, many of whom, he opined, did not deserve it. In the end, the fathers won the day, but uneasiness with idealisation of the woman of the house was notable in the debate in the dáil and in the seanad. Senator Michael Tierney deplored the 'sentimentality' of those who wanted to pay the mothers. The only sentimentality the present writer could discern was Clann na Talmhan T.D. William F. O'Donnell's brief, pious contribution: 'Each of us is the son of a "mother machree". . . Let us thank our mothers'.[16]

There are many other indications of uneasiness with investigations or explorations of women's household work. The interdepartmental committee charged with investigating the possibility of setting up dower-houses on farms in 1943 had to be reminded more than once by their chairman that their terms of reference were to investigate the practicability of this proposal to give young married couples a chance to start out on their own, not to comment on the validity of the committee's terms of reference. (It was decided in the end that if the government subsidised a second dwelling-house the risks of subdivision of land would be too great.)[17] The fact that this committee was set up in the first place shows that Eamon de Valera was aware of the very real problems people, especially women, experienced in the multi-generational household; living with in-laws or parents was believed by most of those who replied to my request for information to be at best a regrettable necessity, at worst, a dreadful mistake. When the question of the marriage bar for women national schoolteachers resurfaced, from 1953, the constitutional recommendation about women/mothers was certainly invoked to support the continuation of such a bar, but invoked unsuccessfully, for the bar was lifted in 1958.[18] The report of the commission on emigration (1954), and the *Limerick rural survey* (1958–64), both acknowledged that employment for married women might be a key incentive for couples to stay and set up families in Ireland.[19] Women's apparent reluctance to marry in Ireland was noted throughout the 1950s; the blame for this was placed firmly on Irish men.[20] However, it followed that if men who chose not to marry were shirking their duty, then men who married were heroic and unselfish, and the standing and self-sacrifice of the father of the family was all the more enhanced.

The commission on emigration did not even acknowledge the hard work and health risks involved in continuous child-bearing for women – risks already well documented by Dublin obstetricians who developed an internationally acclaimed expertise in this field[21] – noting simply that because the childrearing period lasted only twenty years in a 'man's earning life' it did not impose an undue burden on families.[22] This twenty-year childrearing period was ridiculously conservative when it is considered that actual child*bearing* could, and frequently did, span twenty years. Those who expressed reservations to the emigration commission about the continued policy of encouraging large families did so (with one distastefully eugenic contribution) mainly on the grounds of child health and family economy, but rarely addressed the poor health of mothers.[23] Yet the national nutrition survey, which was carried out between 1946 and 1948, had drawn attention to the poor health of mothers of large families.[24] It is remarkable how often concern about women's health and welfare surfaced in inquiries and surveys on all matters from housing to youth unemployment to nutrition to emigration, only to be submerged again by what seems to have been a deliberate refusal to engage with the effects of the day-to-day maintenance and reproductive work of the woman of the house. The emigration commission, for example, noted in the mid-1950s that domestic servants had become hard to find and very expensive, and therefore suggested that middle-class families be subsidised to employ servants. This caused Ruaidhri Roberts to point out (in a strongly worded reservation to the survey's report) that if anybody needed subsidised household help, it was the over-burdened, hardworking working-class mother.[25] Meanwhile, an organisation that tried to put forward a public image for women of the house – the Irish Housewives Association, whose demands fell well within the acceptable parameters of 'women's interests' of the period – children's welfare, consumer issues, housing – was mistrusted and treated with hostility by vehicles for Catholic social teaching.[26]

In his minority report to the emigration commission, Bishop Cornelius Lucey of Cork also deplored the trend towards smaller families. He suggested that urban women were a bad bet in the reproductive stakes, not only because urban stock died out after three generations (!), but also because urban women were currently choosing to limit their families so that they could avail of the recreational and cultural amenities of towns.[27] Leaving aside the curious degeneracy theory, how true was Dr Lucey's perception of the rising importance of pleasure and recreation in women's – particularly urban women's – lives? There is little doubt that lower-middle and working-class townswomen worked almost as hard as their farming sisters, even in serviced dwellings. The *Household budget inquiry, 1951–52* tells us that in all social classes, urban and rural, more money was spent on men's than on women's clothes, which suggests much work knitting and sewing to produce clothing for women. The *Inquiry* also noted that the smaller the town, the more likely the woman of the house was to bake her own bread, and several contributors mentioned that in families with growing children five or six cakes of bread were baked each day, in the town as well as the country.[28] The hard work of the farm woman in the days before electrification and piped water is proverbial and will not be disputed by anybody. In 1946 48 per cent of all Irish households had no piped water, and not only did water have to be hauled into the house for every purpose and disposed of after use (this was true of many non-farming dwellings up to the end of the period), but a big fire had to be kept going summer and winter, for cooking food not only for the family, but for the livestock. Food had to be prepared for poultry and calves and other animals. In addition, butter was often made two or three times a week, and scrupulous cleanliness had to be observed in this task: moreover, there was the thorough scrubbing and scalding of the utensils, the washing of the butter itself with spring water, and the sheer effort and elbow grease involved in operating the churn.[29]

It would take an entire paper to detail all the work performed by the farm woman of the house. However, even in houses with running water and electricity, the woman without paid help or labour-saving devices also worked very hard under difficult conditions. Washing machines and vacuum cleaners were by and large confined to the two upper income levels.[30] If there was water on tap, it was unlikely to be hot water. Granted, cooking could be done at the flick of a match or a switch, which meant no continuous bending, or keeping toddlers and children away from the fire and the pots on it, but the absence of such fires meant that houses were more likely to be cold and the working environment of the woman of the house often damp and draughty. There was lino on the floors which had to be polished; those of my informants from non-farming backgrounds invariably mentioned the labour involved in keeping lino shiny.[31] Electric light mercilessly exposed dust and grime, necessitating more regular cleaning and redecoration. Family size might have fallen slightly in the 1950s, but there is some evidence that spaces between births became shorter in this period.[32] This meant two or three children in nappies at one time – nappies that had to be washed by hand. The urban woman of the house literally 'got out' of her domestic environment and workplace more often than the rural woman, but this often meant no more than the daily trip to the shops with a baby in the pram, an ex-baby sitting on the toddler seat fixed to the front of the pram, and a pre-school child by the hand. The farm woman got out, it was often pointed out to me, only to sell fowl or eggs or butter at the market, and rarely at any other time. This, however, was a trip she could take unencumbered by children, unless she needed them to help her, and it was recognised that the money she earned was hers to dispose of.

Rural and urban women had regular contact with neighbours, usually other women. In his research into Dublin families in the late 1940s, Alexander Humphreys noted that the better-off artisans in housing estates and in old neighbourhoods did not depend upon their neighbours to the same extent as unskilled or semi-skilled labourer families in tenements or cottages.[33] The almoner in Dublin's Rotunda hospital noted this in 1955 when she commented ruefully that the mothers whose houses were most suitable for home deliveries – those settled on the new housing estates on the perimeter of the city – were the very ones who came into hospital to have their babies, because, unlike the mothers in the tenements, they had 'no-one to help them out there'.[34] Yet the passing of 'rambling' and neighbourly interdependence, in town and in country, was not mourned by any of my informants, all of whom, regardless of social class and occupational status, stressed that such neighbourliness had its disadvantages as well as its advantages. In this respect it is significant that although one of Kevin Kearns's contributors to his oral history of the Dublin tenements stated that when the tenements were demolished 'it tore me apart';[35] most of the other contributors were able to lament the passing of the warmth while revelling in the comforts and the improved privacy of the modern way of life.

There are, in the 'complaints' about the lives of women of the house in the past, two recurring themes – never 'getting out' and never having 'a bit of style'. Continuous childbearing was not complained about as such; Mary Healy's attitude is typical: 'Six children I had in the space of eight years: I never considered the rearing of my family a burden, and I think a large family is a great blessing if only one has the money to look after them.'[36] Childbearing and child rearing were complained about mainly because of the way they hampered women's freedom to get out of the house, or to spend time and money on themselves and their appearance. As a Cork woman, married in the early 1950s to a man with a small business, said to me, 'As you know yourself, when you've small children, you haven't time to put a bit of cream on your face.' A Mayo woman who came back with her Irish husband from England in the mid-1950s to work her aged mother's small farm, said she resented no longer going out to work because she couldn't even buy 'a bit of cream for my face' or any of what she called 'those little bits of perks'.[37] It is striking that two women in widely different regional/occupational/ socio-economic settings would have defined 'time for themselves', as we would call it today, in such similar terms. The sociologist Lorelei Harris noted that in west Mayo married women in the 1970s valued the money they earned outside the home for the freedom it gave them to buy things for themselves and for the house.[38]

Several of my informants gave what they considered to be proof positive of the low status of women in so-called 'traditional' marriages – the made match with separate spheres of labour, in a rural setting – when they noted that the woman could never have 'nice things' for herself or for the house, that *he* would spend any disposable cash on new stock or equipment for the farm. The farmer in question was not necessarily portrayed as brutally authoritarian, just insensitive to the woman's needs. The most convincing evidence of the importance of 'nice things' – for women themselves, their children, and their houses – came from the number of women who answered my very generally worded questions about recreation and relaxation by reference to knitting, sewing and crafts. For my part this was totally unexpected and completely unprompted: I would never have conceived of such activities as anything other than work. Work it certainly was, but it seems to have also been viewed by many as 'time for themselves'. Women detailed the clothes they made for themselves, for their small children or older daughters, the elaborate knitting patterns, the drawn-thread-work on flour-bag pillowcases or blouses, the jumpers they knitted; 'I wouldn't be satisfied with plain knitting, it would have to be Fair Isle', as one Mayo farmer's wife who married in 1949 said. An artisan's wife in Limerick and mother of nine children was in heaven when she inherited a sewing machine from her mother-in-law in 1936 and a pile of dressmaking magazines to boot – previously she had done all her sewing and embroidery by hand. A Sligo woman described in detail how to make window-blinds from flour-bags and sally rods, another woman, from Mayo, how to do drawn-threadwork embroidery on flour-bag blouses. These crafts had to be done in the evening, by farm women certainly, and by most townswomen. The only woman I came across who had time during the day for sewing was the Dublin wife of an insurance official, who had part-time paid help in the 1930s; she spent her afternoons sewing and knitting, once bringing thirty home-made dresses for her daughter on their annual month's holiday, so that she would not have to be washing. 'My mother made all my clothes', several women reared in the 1930s and 1940s told me proudly, and went on to describe in detail coat-dresses and skirts made for work or for dances.[39]

All this indicates the importance of the aesthetic in women's lives. The meteoric rise in the number of female hairdressers between 1921 and 1961 (by a factor of 20, with the major growth occurring between 1946 and 1961) is another such indication of the growing importance of appearance.[40] However, on suggesting this in private conversations and public presentations, I often come across women, usually those born in the 1950s, who say indignantly that their mothers never had time to think or worry about appearance, that they knew nothing of style, and that they never read a woman's page or a woman's magazine in their lives. This apparent lack in their mothers' lives is represented as both a deprivation and a virtue. Maura Laverty's writings about rural and small town Kildare in the 1920s tell of farmers' wives and townswomen who were interested in 'the latest styles', whether worn to mass on Sunday by returned emigrants, sent home in a parcel from England or America, or displayed in the drapery shop window of the local town.[41] Photographs from the entire period show, alongside the black shawls and the big skirts, the modern hairstyles and fashions of town and country girl alike.[42] *Woman's Life*, the Irish woman's magazine in circulation from the 1930s to the 1950s, regularly carried letters and problems from girls and women from small farming backgrounds as well as from working- and middle-class urban girls and women. A film-star lookalike competition in 1938 yielded entries from all over Ireland. Women from all over the country, urban and rural, sent in pictures of 'Happy Irish babies' in the 1930s. Representatives from *Woman's Life* attended an advertising conference in Galway in 1954, which indicates that their readership made it worth their while to do so.[43] Reading magazines was obviously not unheard of. Yet none of my contributors admitted to having read magazines or women's pages. One woman vociferously denied ever having seen a magazine when she was working in a small town in the west in the 1940s: 'not at all, no, no, never', but then went on to say that one person would buy a magazine and it would be read by half the country. Other women said that they read or bought magazines only for knitting patterns, though this itself signifies the importance of innovation in clothes – for themselves or their families – in their lives.[44]

Reluctance to admit to having been tuned in to this kind of culture can come only from defensiveness and a fear that any such admission will take from the overall impression of 'sainthood' and austerity which it seems necessary to convey. Such defensiveness can be read as a reaction against the constant and indiscriminate criticism of 'the modern woman' in the 1930s and 1940s. Denigration of women's household skills and use of resources, their abilities and their judgment, often came from those who defended women's rights. Brigid Redmond (who, as noted above, in 1943 wanted to pay children's allowances to the mothers) wrote an article in 1938 promoting the Irish Countrywomen's Association in which she deplored the constant waste and ignorance of the average farm household.[45] Máire MacGeehin, who objected to the abysmal representation for 'home-makers' on the proposed national vocational assembly in 1943, believed that education of women of the house was vital to offset harmful alien influences.[46] Mary Hayden, a long-time feminist and champion of women's citizenship, commented that working-class women could hardly cook and were wasteful of the resources they had.[47] Other organisations, like the Joint Committee of Women's Societies and Social Workers, which described itself as feminist, suggested that working-class women needed help and supervision in managing their babies, cooking, and keeping house.[48] The widely read *Irish Messenger of the Sacred Heart* constantly drew attention in the 1920s, 1930s and early 1940s to women's 'neglect' of the home, lamenting at one stage that the home had become a place 'to keep clothes in and for sleeping'. Criticism of women's apparent obsession with their appearance also appeared regularly. The *Messenger* 'question box' replied somewhat wearily to a correspondent in the late 1940s that it was not a sin to wear make-up, though it was a regrettable sign of the vanity of the times.[49] The fact that the question was posed in the first place was significant. One of the reasons why women liked Fr John Hayes, founder of Muintir na Tíre, was, according to one female member, because he liked to see women dressed nicely and wearing make-up, in contrast to the censure and disapproval they had come to expect from priests.[50]

Were lower-middle class/working-class/medium- to small-farming women of the house in Ireland, 1921–61, 'saints'? This might seem to be an unhistorical question, but what drives me to attempt to answer it is that the term is not confined to retrospective accounts of Irish women in these years. Alice Walker refers to African-American women of the same period as women of very deep spirituality and powers to endure all kinds of unhappiness and hardship:

They forced their minds to desert their bodies and their striving spirits sought to rise, like frail whirlwinds from the hard red clay . . . Our mothers and grandmothers, some of them: moving to music not yet written. And they waited.

Walker suggests that many of these women were frustrated artists, and that it was in their gardens and other everyday fields of endeavour that they expressed their creativity.[51] While it would be unwise to draw too close an analogy between African-American southern women and working-class/ lower-middle class/small farming Irish women in the period in question, Walker's perspective on these women's lives is close enough to that of my Irish informants who are also one generation removed from the 'saints' they describe, for us to refer to her vision. She, like many of my informants, is trying to wrest 'meaning' out of human lives which she sees as having been unbearably hard, and to link her own vastly different life with that of women only one generation earlier.

There can be no doubt that these women lived lives that were 'hard' in the sense of hard-working, and that their well-being, if they were married, was dependent upon the character of their spouses. William Norton, as already mentioned, pointed this out in 1943, implying in effect that since it was men's sense of fairness and generosity that allowed women to be budgetary heads of households, then men should be given recognition for this by being paid the allowance, which they could then sign over to the women to collect. This seems to have been in effect what happened in most households, even in those where the man had firm control of the financial reins. As one Cavan farmer's wife, who married in 1929 and whose husband always held the purse, put it: 'I made sure I lifted it!'[52] Handing over an unopened pay-packet to the woman of the house – 'that was more or less automatic', as one Cork man, an industrial worker who married in the early 1950s, put it – was quite common, particularly in working-class marriages, and the *Limerick rural survey* noted, as if this were a well-known fact that needed no explanation, that the smaller the farm, the more likely the woman was to hold the purse.[53] Humphreys also found this in Dublin in the later 1940s, and Kevin Kearns's oral history of the Dublin tenements notes that the man who did not hand over his paypacket was seen as selfish. In Frank McCourt's memoirs of his childhood in Limerick in the 1940s an alcoholic father left his family in the most appalling want; what compounded the misery was the shame at being the only family in the lane where the paypacket was not handed over.[54]

Farmers and self-employed artisans, however, did not have pay-packets to hand over, so how can power be evaluated in such a setting? Tessie Liu offers some ground-breaking ways of understanding how power might have been exercised by women in the 'traditional', family business house-hold. Liu confirms for farm households in nineteenth-century France what we also suspect about households in twentieth-century Ireland, urban and rural: that women's level of access to material comfort and recreation was a lot lower than that of men, and that women were more or less tied to one place by continuous childbearing and child rearing and ceaseless life-maintenance work. However, she suggests that women could and did exercise considerable emotional power by playing on these realities and representing themselves as more altruistic than their menfolk, more hard-working and ready to forgo luxuries and recreation, more dedicated to the survival of the household and its members.[55] This sort of manipulative martyrdom would be abhorred by modern relationship counsellors or even by nineteenth-century advocates of the companionate marriage, but in the absence of any other kind of power it served its purpose. The evidence presented in this paper is compatible with a similar phenomenon in Ireland. Such passive power – not always in its extreme form of patient endurance of physical abuse or financial deprivation, but sometimes simply in the form of inescapable and visible hard work and self-denial – may have lasted longer in Ireland than in other western countries (though the austerity engendered by wartime conditions and their legacy in Europe well into the 1950s should not be forgotten). Nowhere in my research or among my informants did I come across the pathetic, emotionally depen-dent middle-class wives described by Betty Friedan, even among women who embarked upon modern (i.e., where spouses were freely chosen) breadwinner-housewife marriages in the late 1950s.[56] Here is where the authority conveyed by austerity can be seen. The persistence of large families by western standards right up to the 1960s, the low level of material comfort, the importance of knitting, sewing and baking for everyday necessity as well as aesthetic pleasure, meant that total immersion in the minutiae of every child's emotional and personal development and devotion to shopping for things for the house was simply not possible. The woman of the house might have been living for others in the sense of working to maintain life in others, but the actual work was so demanding of energy and imagination, and so time-consuming, that she was not living vicariously, any more than someone in a service profession – a nurse, a teacher, a doctor – lives vicariously.

Moreover, there is some evidence that women began, from the late 1940s, to insist upon what comforts they could, even if these were picked from a fixed menu – long lying-in periods after childbirth, a growing preference for hospital or nursing home births rather than home births (despite the medical authorities' efforts to encourage the continuation of domiciliary births for uncomplicated cases) and, bottle feeding, which could be shared by a spouse or performed by an older child, rather than the physical tie of breast-feeding (despite the encouragement of breast-feeding by health care professionals).[57] There was also the growing interest in 'style', nods in the direction of the cult of appearance, or an impression of extraordinary virtue and deprivation if such comforts – cream for the face, even an annual visit to a hairdresser, a new winter coat once a decade – could not be had. In Irish women's magazines and women's pages in Irish newspapers in the 1950s, the emphasis was almost entirely on appearance, either of the self or the house, knitting and craft patterns, sometimes recipes. The sort of exhortatory articles described by Betty Friedan for 1950s America, on childcare, and children's and husbands' emotional needs, rarely if ever featured in Irish-produced magazines. The comforts and luxuries partly gained or, at least, aspired to by women of the house in the 1950s might not sit very well with current feminist or 'green' ideas of what, in the long term, is good or useful for individual and public health and welfare. However, all of these seem to have served as worthwhile escapes from endless hard work, necessary self-denial and the expenditure of self.

Can we charge Irish women of the house with 'false consciousness' for not having protested, sufficiently loudly or in large enough numbers, against the quite serious and severe attacks upon their citizenship and economic freedom in the decades in question? Organised groups of women are known to have objected to the 1937 constitution, yet a trawl through the newspapers – the two most widely read, the *Irish Independent* and the *Irish Press* – for 1937 reveals no letters or opinions from individual female citizens about the constitution. It might be argued that many women did not have time to read newspapers, so it is not in letters columns that 'real' or 'ordinary' women's opinions are to be found. However, a letter from a Galway clergyman in the *Irish Independent* in the spring of 1938, which mildly questioned Irish females' cooking abilities, unleashed a flood of correspondence on this subject, which showed no signs of abating after six weeks and included letters not only from domestic economy instructresses, but from 'ordinary' women from around the country. One indignant mother of two apprentices, for example, sent in her weekly menus to prove that she was a good and imaginative cook.[58] This suggests two things: first of all, that Irish women of the house took pride in their household skills and resented attacks on these skills more strongly than they resented attacks on their citizenship, and secondly, that if they took such offence at a relatively inoffensive letter, they must have really bristled at the constant denigration in those years of their skills and suggestions of their need to be educated, not only in household work, but in motherhood and childcare.

For most of this forty-year period official discourse was either indifferent to, or negative about, Irish women's household and life-maintenance work. Yet these women managed to pass on and to lodge in the social memory of late twentieth-century Ireland an impression both of superlative ability and ceaseless drudgery and devotion to duty. This in itself is an indication of the considerable informal and emotional power attached to austerity.

NOTES

1 Personal testimony. I placed a notice seeking information about women's house-hold work 1921–61 in the *Irish Independent*, the *Cork Examiner* and provincial papers all over the country, in April 1995. Many responses were received, some in the form of detailed letters, others included invitations to meet. Letters, answered questionnaires, tapes and transcripts of all responses are in my possession. For further information see Caitriona Clear, 'Women of the house: women's household work in Ireland 1921–1961, discourses, experiences, memories' (PhD thesis, N.U.I. [U.C.D.] 1997).

2 Simone de Beauvoir, *The second sex* (London, 1953); Betty Friedan, *The feminine mystique* (London, 1963); Germaine Greer, *The female eunuch* (London, 1970); Shulamith Firestone, *The dialectic of sex* (London, 1972), all take up this theme. Adrienne Rich, *Of woman born: motherhood as experience and institution* (New York, 1976) is usually cited as one of the most influential feminist texts on motherhood. 'A mother's love is a blessing' is a ballad that was very popular at house dances and sing-songs in the 1940s, according to personal testimony.

3 J. J. Lee, *Ireland 1912–1985* (Cambridge, 1989), p. 241.

4 Catherine Rose, *The female experience: the story of the woman movement in Ireland* (Galway, 1975); Jenny Beale, *Women in Ireland: voices of change* (Dublin, 1986); Ailbhe Smyth, (ed.) *Irish women's studies reader* (Dublin, 1993); Frances Gardiner, 'The unfinished revolution' in *Canadian Journal of Irish Studies*, xviii, no.1 (1992), pp 15–39; Maryann Valiulis, 'Power, gender and identity in the Irish Free State' in *Journal of Women's History*, vi–vii (winter/spring 1995), pp 117–36.

5 James Fentress and Chris Wickham, *Social memory: the construction of the past* (Oxford, 1992).

6 Mary Clancy, 'Aspects of women's contribution to the oireachtas debate in the Irish Free State 1922–37' in Maria Luddy and Cliona Murphy (ed.) *Women surviving: studies in Irish women's history in the 19th and 20th centuries* (Dublin, 1990); Eoin O'Leary, 'The I.N.T.O. and the marriage bar for women national teachers' in *Saothar: Journal of the Irish Labour History Society*, xii (1987), pp 47–52; see also correspondence between

department of education and Irish National Teachers' Organisation 14/3/32–15/11/32 (N.A., S7985 A, B, C, D).

7 Mary E. Daly, *Industrial development and Irish national identity 1922–39* (Dublin, 1992); Mary Jones, *These obstreperous lassies: a history of the Irish Women Workers Union* (Dublin, 1988); Gisela Bock and Pat Thane (ed.), *Maternity and gender policies: women and the rise of European welfare states 1880–1950s* (London, 1991); Alice Kessler-Harris, 'Gender ideology in historical reconstruction: a case from the 1930s' in *Gender and History*, i (spring 1989), pp 31–49, discusses hostility to married women working in the U.S. in this period.

8 Caitriona Clear, '"The women cannot be blamed": the commission on vocational organisation, feminism and 'home-makers' in independent Ireland in the 1930s and 40s' in Mary O'Dowd and Sabine Wichert (ed.), *Chattel, servant or citizen: women's status in church, state and society* (Belfast, 1995), pp 179–86.

9 *Report of the commission on vocational organisation* (Dublin, 1944), P 6743, pp 414–15.

10 Children's allowances act, 1944/2 [Éire] (23 Feb. 1944); Lee, *Ireland 1912–1985*, pp 277–85.

11 On the European historical background to 'mothers' pensions' and children's allowances, see Bock and Thane, *Maternity and gender*; Seth Koven and Sonya Michel, 'Womanly duties: maternalist politics and the origins of welfare states in France, Germany, Great Britain and the United States 1880–1920' in *American Historical Review*, xcv (1990) pp 1076–1108. Patrick King, C.C., 'Family allowances' in *Catholic Bulletin*, xxviii (Jan.–June 1938), pp 310–12, sums up the Catholic position.

12 Correspondence on family allowances, 13/11/39 – 16/3/43, and report of interdepartmental committee on family allowances 1943 (N.A., S12117, A, B). On Lucy Kingston, see Daisy Lawrenson Swanton, *Emerging from the shadow: the lives of Sarah Anne Lawrenson and Lucy Olive Kingston, based on personal diaries, 1883–1969* (Dublin, 1994), p.109.

13 *Seanad Éireann debates*, xxviii, 442–6 (13 Jan. 1944). On Concannon as 'silent sister', see Margaret Ward, *Unmanageable revolutionaries* (Dingle, 1983), p. 241.

14 'Children's allowance bill: payments to mothers proposal lost' in *Irish Press*, 3 Dec. 1943; *Dáil Éireann debates*, xcii, 223–4 (23 Nov. 1943).

15 See Koven and Michel, 'Womanly duties'.

16 *Dáil deb.*, xcii, 593 (23 Nov. 1943, 2 Dec. 1943); *Seanad deb.*, xxviii, 418–33, 676–9 (13, 27 Jan. 1944).

17 Report of the interdepartmental committee on the question of making available a second dwelling-house on farms (1943) (N.A., S13413/1).

18 O'Leary, 'The I.N.T.O.'; also N.A., S7985, A–D.

19 *Commission on emigration and other population problems, 1948–1954, reports* (Dublin, 1956), Pr 2541, p. 81; Jeremiah Newman, 'Social provision and rural centrality' in Jeremiah Newman (ed.), *The Limerick rural survey 1958–64* (Tipperary, 1964), pp 248–306, particularly p. 260.

20 See, e.g. Kevin Devlin, 'Single and selfish' in *Christus Rex*, vi (1952), pp 223–31, and the various contributions, particularly those by John A. O'Brien, Paul Vincent Carroll, Edmund J. Murray, Shane Leslie, Mary Frances Keating, John D. Sheridan, in John A. O'Brien (ed.), *The vanishing Irish* (London, 1954).

21 Derek Llewellyn-Jones, *Everywoman: a woman's health guide for life* (London, 1982 ed.), p. 290, mentions that the term 'grande multigravida' (to describe women who have had at least four previous pregnancies) originated in Dublin. For the dangers of multiparity, as apprehended by his father Dr Bethel Solomons in the 1920s, see Michael Solomons, *Pro-life? The Irish question* (Dublin, 1992), pp 6, 14. For one of the many contemporary references to this phenomenon, see J. K. Feeney (Master, Coombe hospital), 'Complications associated with high multiparity: a clinical survey of 518 cases' in *Journal of the Irish Medical Association*, xxxii (1953), pp 36–55.

22 *Emigration commission*, pp 97–101.

23 *Emigration commission*, reservation no.1 (Dr W. R. F. Collis and Arnold Marsh), pp 220–1; reservation no. 6 (Rev. A. A. Luce), pp 230–1; reservation no. 8 (Arnold Marsh), pp 234–7.

24 Department of health, *National nutrition survey parts i–vii* (Dublin [1953]), Pr 804, especially part vii, summary, p. 23.

25 *Emigration commission*, pp 172–3, and Ruaidhri Roberts, reservation no. 11, pp 253–4. Government never acted on the commission's extraordinary suggestion, but neither did it act on Roberts's eminently sensible one.

26 Hilda Tweedy, *A link in the chain: the story of the Irish Housewives Association 1942–1992* (Dublin 1992), passim; see also Vigilans, 'As I see it' in *Christus Rex*, ii (1948), p. 75, and iii (1950), pp 74–5.

27 Most Rev. Cornelius Lucey, minority report, *Emigration commission*, pp 335–63, especially pp 340, 357.

28 Central Statistics Office, *Household budget inquiry 1951–52* (Dublin, 1954), Pr 2520, pp xxxix–xli; xlvii-li.

29 Michael J. Shiel, *The quiet revolution: the electrification of rural Ireland* (Dublin, 1984), chap. 17, and pp 206–7.

30 *Household budget inquiry*, passim; also personal testimony.

31 Personal testimony. Ann Hathaway's *Homecraft book* (Dublin, 1944) which addresses itself to the lino-floored, small, serviced house, gives an indication of the amount of work required to keep such houses clean and warm, and their inhabitants fed and clothed on small incomes.

32 Brendan Walsh, *Some Irish population problems reconsidered* (Dublin, 1968), Economic and Social Research Institute paper no. 42; Cormac Ó Gráda, in *Ireland: a new economic history* (Oxford, 1994), suggests that family size began falling from the 1930s. A. J. Humphreys, *New Dubliners: urbanisation and the Irish family* (London, 1966) suggests that middle-class families were beginning to practise 'family limitation' in the 1950s. My own research, comparing numbers of children per length of marriage in the 1930s and the 1950s, suggests that birth intervals were shorter in the later decade: 'Women of the house', chs 6 and 7.

33 Humphreys, *New Dubliners*, pp 92, 184–5.

34 Eleanor Holmes, 'The social service department' in 'Clinical report of the Rotunda hospital 1954–5', *Irish Journal of Medical Science*, no. 371 (Nov. 1956), pp 3–8.

35 Kevin C. Kearns, *Dublin tenement life: an oral history* (Dublin, 1994), p. 92.

36 Mary Healy, *For the poor and for the gentry: Mary Healy remembers her life* (Dublin, 1989), pp 84–7.

37 Personal testimony.

38 Lorelei Harris, 'Class, community and sexual divisions in north Mayo' in Chris Curtin, Mary Kelly, Liam O'Dowd (ed.), *Culture and ideology in Ireland* (Galway, 1984), pp 154–71.

39 Personal testimony.

40 In 1926 there were only 170 female hairdressers in Ireland, in 1936, 1,295; 1946, 1,840; and 1961, 3409. *Census of Ireland*, I.F.S.,1926, x (Dublin, 1934) P 1242; 1936, ix (Dublin, 1942), Pr 5260; 1946 and 1951 (Dublin, 1958), Pr 4511; 1961, iii (Dublin, 1963), Pr 7415.

41 Maura Laverty, *Never no more* (London, [1942]) passim.

42 See e.g., E. E. O'Donnell, *Father Browne's Ireland* (Dublin, 1989), pp 15, 28, 47, 99; Dorothea Lange and Gerry Mullins, *Dorothea Lange's Ireland* (London, [1996]), pp 42, 77.

43 *Woman's Life* was published in Dublin from 1936 and continued until the mid-1950s (files in National Library of Ireland); Hugh Oram, *The advertising book: a history of advertising in Ireland* (Dublin, 1986), p.176.

44 Personal testimony.

45 Brigid Redmond, 'Rural home-makers' in *Irish Monthly*, lxv (Sept. 1937), pp 602–10.

46 Máire MacGeehin, 'A scheme for the rural guilds' in *Irish Monthly*, lxv (Dec. 1937), pp 799–813.

47 Mary Hayden, 'Woman's role in the modern world' in *Irish Monthly*, lxviii (Aug. 1940), pp 397–402.

48 Clear, '"The women cannot be blamed"'.

49 *Irish Messenger of the Sacred Heart* (1921–61), passim. See, e.g., xliii, no.2 (Feb. 1930), 'General intention for February: recognition of the sanctity of marriage', pp 95–6; on make-up, 'Question box' in *Irish Messenger,* lxi (Jan. 1948), p. 23

50 Stephen Rynne, *Father John Hayes: founder of Muintir na Tíre, people of the land* (Dublin, 1960), p. 178.

51 'In search of our mothers' gardens', pp 231–43 (particularly p. 232) in Alice Walker, *In search of our mothers' gardens: womanist prose* (London, 1984).

52 *Dáil deb.*, xcii, 583–6 (2 Dec. 1943).

53 Patrick McNabb, 'Family roles', *Limerick rural survey*, pp 228–9.

54 Humphreys, *New Dubliners*, p. 203; Kevin Kearns, *Dublin tenement life*, p.118; Frank McCourt, *Angela's ashes* (London, 1996), passim; personal testimony.

55 Tessie Liu, 'Le patrimoine magique: reassessing the power of women in peasant households in 19th-century France' in *Gender and History*, vi, no.1 (Apr. 1994), pp 13–36.

56 Betty Friedan, *The feminine mystique*.

57 See Clear, ' Women of the house', chaps 6, 7, and conclusion.

58 For a sample of the correspondence, see 'They all say the same: Irish girls can't cook'; 'Can Irish girls cook? Our readers reply to the critics'; 'More opinions from readers'; 'Cooking in Ireland: more views from readers' in *Irish Independent*, 30 Mar., 4, 6, 8 Apr. 1938.

Contributors to this volume

TOBY BARNARD is a fellow of Hertford College, Oxford, and holder of a British Academy research readership, 1997–99. He has published voluminously on seventeenth- and eighteenth-century Ireland and Britain, most recently *The abduction of a Limerick heiress: social and political relations in mid-eighteenth-century Ireland* (Maynooth, 1998). He is currently co-editing essays on the dukes of Ormonde and completing a study of the Irish Protestant ascendancy.

CHRISTOPHER J. BERRY is professor of political theory, department of politics, University of Glasgow. His most recent book is *Social theory of the Scottish Enlightenment* (Edinburgh, 1997).

ASA BRIGGS has held chairs of history at the Universities of Leeds and Sussex. He was vice-chancellor of the University of Sussex from 1967 to 1976 and provost of Worcester College, Oxford, from 1976 to 1991. His books include a trilogy *Victorian cities, Victorian people* and *Victorian things* (1954–88) and five volumes of a history of British broadcasting (Oxford, 1961–95). A former president of the Workers' Educational Association, he was chancellor of the Open University from 1976 to 1991.

L.A. CLARKSON is professor emeritus of social history at the Queen's University of Belfast. His books include *The pre-industrial economy in England, 1500–1750* (London, 1971), *Proto-industrialization: the first phase of industrialization?* (London, 1985), and (with E.M. Crawford) *Food in Ireland 1500–1920: a social history* (Oxford, forthcoming).

CAITRIONA CLEAR is a lecturer in the department of history, NUI, Galway, author of *Nuns in nineteenth-century Ireland* (Dublin, 1987) and of several articles on homelessness in post-famine Ireland and women's work in twentieth-century Ireland.

BRENDA COLLINS is research and publications officer at the Irish Linen Centre and Lisburn Museum, Lisburn, County Antrim and has published widely on the themes of the linen industry, Irish emigration and local history. She is currently co-editing (with Philip Ollerenshaw) *Historical perspectives on the linen industry in Europe* (Oxford, forthcoming).

COLMÁN ETCHINGHAM is a lecturer in the departments of modern history and old and middle Irish at NUI, Maynooth, and author of, among other works, *Viking raids on Irish church settlements in the ninth century: a reconsideration of the annals* (Maynooth, 1986).

LAURENCE M. GEARY is a member of the department of history, University College Cork, and the author of the *Plan of campaign, 1886–1891* (Cork, 1986).

JOHN MAIBEN GILMARTIN is a lecturer in the history of art and design in the Dublin Institute of Technology and formerly deputy keeper, City Museums and Art Gallery, Birmingham. He has published on a wide range of subjects in scholarly journals, including, most recently, on Casimir Markiewicz and the knights of St Patrick in *The Irish Arts Review*, 1995.

FELICITY HEAL is a fellow of Jesus College, Oxford and the author of, inter alia, *Hospitality in early modern England* (Oxford, 1990).

JACQUELINE HILL is a senior lecturer in the department of modern history, NUI, Maynooth, and the author of *From patriots to unionists: Dublin civic politics and Irish Protestant patriotism, 1660–1840* (Oxford, 1997).

COLM LENNON is a senior lecturer in the department of modern history, NUI, Maynooth, and the author of, among other works, *Sixteenth-century Ireland: the incomplete conquest* (Dublin, 1994).

DAVID W. MILLER is a professor of history at Carnegie Mellon University. His works include *Queen's rebels: Ulster loyalism in historical perspective* (Dublin, 1978).

TIM P. O'NEILL is a barrister and lecturer in the department of modern Irish history in University College Dublin.

Index